The Biblical Outlook

Topics in Jewish Philosophy

THE BIBLICAL OUTLOOK
Topics in Jewish Philosophy

by Rabbi Shlomo Polachek

Translation by Rabbi Shmuel Himelstein

PENINA PRESS

The Biblical Outlook

Topics in Jewish Philosophy

Published by PENINA PRESS

Translated from Hebrew by Rabbi Shmuel Himelstein

COVER DESIGN: Shanie Cooper
EDITORIAL AND PRODUCTION DIRECTOR: Daniella Barak
EDITOR: Batsheva Pomerantz

Soft Cover ISBN: 978-1-936068-27-2

First edition. Printed in Israel

Distributed by:

Urim Publications
POB 52287
Jerusalem 91521, Israel
Tel: 02.679.7633
Fax: 02.679.7634
urim_pub@netvision.net.il

Lambda Publishers, Inc.
527 Empire Blvd.
Brooklyn, NY 11225, USA
Tel: 718.972.5449
Fax: 718.972.6307
mh@ejudaica.com

www.UrimPublications.com

Contents

In Appreciation

AS I PRESENT THIS book to the reader, I would like to express my thanks and appreciation to those who helped me in writing and publishing it.

First and foremost my thanks to Rabbi Levi Meier of Los Angeles, U.S.A. The selection of the verses of the Bible for the topics brought in the book, which took a number of years, was done jointly with Rabbi Meier. It would have been impossible to write this book without the work carried out at that stage.

My thanks to Mrs. Nehama Stern who worked meticulously on the manuscript, for her enlightenment and comments.

My thanks to my wife Zipora and my daughter Lea, who read sections of the manuscript and made useful comments.

Special thanks to my son Hillel (Ben Shlomo) and to Mrs. Adina Sternberg who reviewed the manuscript in its entirety and made many useful comments.

Special thanks to my son Shmuel who reviewed portions of the manuscript, made useful comments, and helped greatly with suggestions for making progress towards the publication of the book.

My thanks to Rabbi Naftali Bar Ilan, Prof. Shalom Rosenberg, and Mr. Meir Hovav, who saw the manuscript, made useful comments, and helped in enabling progress to be made in the preparation of the book.

I would like to mention with gratitude Prof. Aharon Mirsky, of blessed memory, who saw the manuscript, made important comments, and gave me useful advice which enabled progress to be made on the book.

Needless to say, the responsibility for the content of the book lies solely with me.

My thanks to Mrs. Orit Berger and Mrs. Madeleine Ravenna who contributed greatly to the technical aspects of typing the book and to my daughter Ruti who contributed to its progress. My thanks to Mr. Chaim Shachak who advised me regarding publishing the book. Thanks to the staff of Hemed Press for their help in the publication.

I would like to express my thanks to all those who were not directly involved in preparing the book but were involved in the religious intellectual ferment in the Yavneh Religious Students Organization in the United States and in similar circles, in the years 1964-1970, which was the background for the writing of the book. Special thanks to Rabbi Shlomo Riskin.

I also owe thanks to the rabbis who taught me at the Rabbi Isaac Elchanan Yeshiva in New York, and especially to the Gaon, Rabbi Yosef Dov Soloveichik, of blessed memory, and Rabbi Avigdor Cyperstein, of blessed memory.

My thanks to my father, Dr. Abraham A. Polachek, and my mother, Mrs. Rhoda Polachek, for the support and help they gave me throughout the years of work on this book.

My thanks and appreciation to my wife Zipora, who supported me with understanding and love throughout, in spite of the great amount of time which was devoted to the various stages of the writing.

I am appreciative of the inspiration from an individual, whose image has accompanied me ever since my childhood, even though I was not privileged to know him personally: my grandfather, the Gaon Rabbi Shlomo Polachek, of blessed memory, the Meitcheter Ilui.

My thanks to the Holy One, Blessed Be He, who was good to me and enabled me to start and complete this work.

Shlomo Polachek
Shevat 5764 (February 2004)

In Appreciation for the English Version

PUBLICATION OF THE translation of *The Biblical Outlook* into English gives me an opportunity to express appreciation to those who enabled it to appear.

Firstly, I want to express appreciation for the encouragement I received with the publication of the original Hebrew version of the book from Rabbi Levi Meier, of blessed memory. He expressed his enthusiasm at the time of the publication and indicated that an English translation would expose the book to a wider audience. Unfortunately, he was not able to see its publication. May his memory be for a blessing.

Thanks to Rabbi Shmuel Himelstein for his efforts in translating the book to English.

Thanks to the people at Urim Publications who helped to enable the publishing of the book: Yaacov Peterseil for his encouragement, Batsheva Pomerantz for her assistance and cooperative spirit as editor, and Daniella Barak for her overseeing the entire operation.

I regret that since the publication of the original Hebrew version, my father passed away. May his memory be for a blessing.

I was privileged to have the support, encouragement and assistance of my dear wife Zipora throughout the process. I'm duly thankful.

My thanks again to the Holy One, Blessed Be He, who was good to me and made it possible for this version of the book to appear.

Shlomo Polachek
Shevat 5771 (January 2011)

Chapter 1 – Introduction

THE AIM OF THIS book is to present the philosophy of Judaism. The reason for writing it is the search for a philosophy based on clear and unequivocal Jewish sources. These sources are the Biblical books along with the *halachic midrashim* – the exegesis of the text relating to Jewish practice as set by the Sages. The reasons for using these sources as a basis follow.

The Torah

Moses wanted God to erase his name from the book which He had written, should God not forgive the People of Israel. God answered him, saying that He would only erase from His book those who had sinned against Him – this being the confirmation that He, indeed had written it.[1] Furthermore, God made a covenant with the People of Israel.[2] The text of the covenant – God's commandments[3] and the punishments for those who violate it[4] – appears in the Torah scroll which Moses wrote as given by God, and which he in turn transmitted to the priests and the elders of Israel.[5] The

1 Exodus 32:32–33.
2 Deuteronomy 28:69.
3 Ibid., 30:10.
4 Ibid., 29:20.
5 Ibid., 31:9. See also *Bava Batra* 15a.

Torah scroll was placed inside the Ark of the Covenant for preservation[6] and at the end of each seventh year it was read before all of Israel.[7]

The Prophets and the Scriptures

The words of the Prophets were also placed in their mouths by God: "I will raise them up a prophet from among their brothers, like you, and will put My words in his mouth; and he will speak to them all that I will command him."[8]

In Tractate *Yadayim*, the Mishnah brings the law that if one touched the scrolls of the Holy Scriptures, they render one's hands *tameh* – ritually impure.[9] The Talmud in Tractate *Megillah* brings the view of Shmuel that the scroll of Esther does not render one's hands *tameh*, i.e., that this scroll is not part of the Holy Scriptures. The Talmud there asks whether, according to Shmuel, the scroll of Esther was not written with Divine Inspiration.[10]

The conclusion in Tractate *Megillah* is that, according to all views, the scroll of Esther was written with Divine Inspiration. The above-mentioned Mishnah brings a dispute regarding the Song of Songs and Ecclesiastes, and here, too, the consensus is that they are also part of the Holy Scriptures.

The conclusion to be drawn from this is that for a book to be included in the Holy Scriptures, it must have been written with Divine Inspiration. One must regard all books written with Divine Inspiration as binding.

The list of the books of the Prophets and the other books which are included in the Holy Scriptures is brought in Tractate *Bava Batra*. The books of the Prophets are Joshua, Judges, Samuel, Kings, Jeremiah, Ezekiel, Isaiah, and the Twelve Minor Prophets. The books included in the Scriptures are Ruth, Psalms, Job, Proverbs, Ecclesiastes, Song of Songs, Lamentations, Daniel, Esther, Ezra (including Nehemiah), and Chronicles.[11]

---

6 Ibid., 31:25–26.
7 Ibid., 31:10–11.
8 Ibid., 18:18.
9 *Yadayim* 3:5.
10 *Megillah* 7a.
11 *Bava Batra* 14b.

The Oral Law

By Jewish tradition, the Written Law (the Torah) was transmitted along with a commentary – the Oral Law. This tradition has been substantiated in various ways. For example, Maimonides in the introduction to his work, the *Mishneh Torah*, presents such proof. Not all commentators agree on the extent of the Oral Law handed down along with the Written Law.

Midrashei Halachah – Exegesis of Text Relating to *Halachah*, as Presented by the Sages

In Deuteronomy it states that if one needs to clarify *practical questions*, they are to be brought to the priests and judges for clarification.[12] The right to make practical decisions was transferred over the generations to the Sages,[13] and in questions of *halachah* (practice) the rulings of the Sages are binding.

(In order to avoid misunderstandings, various regulations and restrictions of the Sages and common customs are included in some places.)

The Aggadah

As far as *Aggadah* (homiletical passages) is concerned, we find that the *Geonim* and other Sages believe that these are not binding as *halachah* is.[14] Disputes among the Sages regarding *Aggadah* topics are not settled.[15]

---

12 Deuteronomy 17:8–11.

13 See Maimonides, *Introduction to the Mishneh Torah.*

14 In the *Mavo HaTalmud* (Introduction to the Talmud) attributed to R. Shmuel HaNagid, which has appeared in all editions of the Talmud since 5474 (1714), the following is stated: "*Haggadah* is an interpretation which is brought in the Talmud on any topic which is not a commandment. That is *Haggadah* and you are not to deduce anything from it except what seems reasonable. Know that whatever our Sages brought as the *halachah* regarding any commandment is from our teacher Moses, who received it from God Himself, and one may not add to or subtract from it. However, whatever interpretations are given to the verses, according to what occurred to individuals or what they thought, and whatever seems reasonable based on these interpretations, may be studied; one need not rely upon others." There are those who disagree as to whether the author of *Mavo HaTalmud* was indeed R. Shmuel HaNagid. In any event, it appears clearly from the formulation of this text that it is a direct translation from Arabic to Hebrew from *Mavo HaTalmud* by R. Shmuel Bar Hofni Gaon, sections of which are

While it is true that Maharal and other Sages disagree about the binding nature of *Aggadah*,[16] even according to Maharal, proper understanding of *Aggadah* is not unequivocal.[17] Therefore, according to all opinions, one cannot set *Aggadah*, as it exists today, on the same level as the words of God in the books of the Bible. That is the reason why they are not included in this work.[18]

Binding Principles

As not every action described in the Bible is a source for emulation, and the commentators do not have a unanimous view about the justness of various actions depicted in it,[19] the search in the sources and the choice of messages to be included in this book was based on the following basic principles:

---

quoted in a number of other works. See, for example, *Hilchot HaNagid* by Mordechai Margoliyot, (Jerusalem: Yehudah Leib and Minnie Epstein Foundation of the Academy for Jewish Sciences in the United States, 5722, 1962), as well as a quote from *Mavo HaTalmud* of R. Shmuel Hofni Gaon brought by A. Kavili in *Sefer HaYovel Le'A. A. Harkavy*, (St. Petersburg: 5669, 1909). The quote is also brought in *Toratan shel Geonim – Kitvei R. Shmuel bar Hofni Gaon* in the context of the subject of "*Mavo HaTalmud*," (Jerusalem: A. Wagshal, 5752, 1992).

This is also the view of Rav Sherira Gaon and Rav Hai Gaon. They are quoted in the *Encyclopedia Talmudit*, under "*Aggadah*." HaRan Gaon is quoted by the Maharal of Prague in his *Be'er HaGolah*, Sixth Section.

15 R. Shmuel HaNagid, *Mavo HaTalmud*: "In the case of any dispute where the dispute does not have any practical consequence but is merely a matter of opinion, it is not determined that the *halachah* is in accordance with any specific rabbi."

16 Maharal of Prague, *Be'er HaGolah*, Sixth Section, quotes HaRan Gaon who writes that one does not rely on *Aggadah*, and interprets this that one does not rely on the words of *the Aggadah* to explain the *Aggadah* according to its simple meaning.

17 Maharal, ibid.: "One does not deduce matters from the *Aggadah* because it was not elucidated by means of questions and answers, for had it been so it would have been appropriate to deduce the *halachah* from the *Aggadah*. However, since it was not clarified that way, one does not deduce the *halachah* from the *Aggadah*."

18 Of course, there is importance also in the *Aggadah* of the Sages, as well as Torah viewpoints as penned by our greatest Sages throughout the ages, especially in regard to important issues which this book does not deal with.

19 For example, in *Bereshit Rabbah* 67, in dealing with the way Jacob pretended to be Esau in order to receive the blessing from Isaac, there are those who justify this action while others criticize it: "'When Esau heard the words of his father.' R. Chanina said, 'Whoever

a) God's statements about what is considered just and what is considered unjust are binding.
b) Statements made by the author of one of the books of the Bible about what is considered just and what is considered unjust are binding.

Notes on the Basic Principles

The only source about which there is a question about applying these principles is Deuteronomy. Moses's speech to the Children of Israel is described in a number of places as having been said by God's command, but the speech is interrupted a number of times. However, the logical sequence of the speech and the way to which our Sages related to it afterwards indicate that it should be treated as a single unit – and all of it was said according to God's word.

We have related to the Song of Songs and Ecclesiastes as works which were written under Divine Inspiration. In the Song of Songs, we have a description of Israel's love for God, and in Ecclesiastes, we find contemplations about life's various purposes, leading to a final conclusion. Likewise, we relate to the suggestions of conduct in Proverbs as binding, and to the descriptions of events in Psalms as words of truth.

The messages in the Bible are from God, and are therefore consistent and compatible with one another.

The *halachic midrashim* of the Sages are evident in this book in the chapter describing God's commandments.

Organization of this Book by Topic

The topics chosen were among the most important ones in Jewish philosophy: understanding God and His ways, and His expectations of human beings. The first chapters focus on God, the way He relates to the

---

says that the Holy One, Blessed Be He is lax [in dispensing justice] may his bowels be lax, but He is long-suffering and ultimately collects that which is due Him. Jacob caused Esau to cry out once, as it states, "When Esau heard the words of his father he cried out." And when was he punished? In the capital, Shushan, where it states, "He cried out with a loud and bitter cry." Immediately after that we are told, "Your brother came with guile."' R. Yochanan said, 'He came with the wisdom of his Torah.'"

world and the way He is revealed to people. Afterwards we describe God's demands of people. The last chapters discuss various aspects of the way God relates to people. These chapters include topics such as reward and punishment, repentance and forgiveness, prayer, God's intervention in history, God's deeds, and a description of the End of Days.

Each chapter and sub-chapter in the general table of contents has an opening statement. After reading it, one can study any topic in the detailed table of contents of that chapter or sub-chapter. At the end of each chapter is a short summary.

One can, of course, read the volume sequentially, but it is also useful to read chapters based on the reader's preferences.

Each topic is brought, as much as possible, in its entirety. However, not all verses related to a given topic are brought as references, where some are identical or similar.

The reader will find that the messages are brought on occasion as a continuum and on occasion as isolated statements. This stems from the nature of the messages themselves and the desire to cover each topic as it appears in the Bible.

The references are as found in the Koren Bible.

In an endeavor that is so comprehensive, a number of errors may have crept in during the course of the work. I apologize for this.

It is my hope that this volume will help in understanding God's word and will encourage all of us to observe His commandments, and that as a reward, God will be good to us.

Chapter 2 – God's Attributes

The Bible has numerous descriptions of the attributes of God, as they are revealed in the world.[1] *These are divided into the following:*

- *His eternal existence*
- *His omnipotence*
- *His knowledge and wisdom*
- *His relationship to the world and mankind*
- *Other attributes*
- *His manifestations*

Each topic is presented separately.

• His Eternity and His Existence

His Eternal Existence

God told the prophet Isaiah that no god existed before Him and none will come after Him.[2] He is the first and the last.[3]

God told the prophet Malachi that He does not change.[4]

---

1 The question whether these are attributes or just adjectives describing God's actions, as Maimonides states in his *Guide for the Perplexed*, is a metaphysical one by nature. It does not belong within the framework of this book. The Bible uses the terminology of attributes, and that is how they are presented in the present work.

2 Isaiah 43:10.

3 Ibid., 44:6.

The heavens and the earth may disappear, but God exists eternally.[5]

God has always existed.[6] He existed even before the world was created and, from the time it was created until the end of time, He is God.[7]

His Eternity and Recognition of This Eternity

Recognition of the decisive importance of God's eternity was shown in the event which expressed it for the first time. At the Burning Bush, Moses asked God what he was to say to the Children of Israel when they wanted to know His name. God's reply was "I shall be as I shall be... sent me to you... the God of your fathers, the God of Abraham, the God of Isaac, and the God of Jacob sent me to you. That is My name and that is My remembrance from generation to generation."[8] The Name based upon the theme of existence represents the eternal existence of God.

God's eternity is the primary attribute whereby mankind recognizes Him. All the stages of the Divine plan of the Exodus from Egypt were aimed at having people recognize this.

God told Moses that He would harden Pharaoh's heart and would bring about many miracles in Egypt, so that the inhabitants of Egypt would know that "I am the Lord [the Tetragrammaton or *Shem Havaya* – God's four-letter name – *yod, heh, vav, heh:* Y-H-V-H, representing His existence]."[9]

He will redeem the Children of Israel so that they might tell their children and children's children about God's deeds in Egypt and then they will know "that I am the Lord [*Shem Havaya*]."[10]

Many of God's miracles were performed with that aim. The manna in the desert fell so that the Children of Israel would know "that I am the Lord [*Shem Havaya*] your God."[11] Ezekiel's prophecies indicate that destruction

---

4 Malachi 3:6.
5 Psalms 102:26–28.
6 Ibid., 93:2.
7 Ibid., 90:2.
8 Exodus 3:14–15. See Rashbam.
9 Ibid., 7:1–5.
10 Ibid., 10:1–2
11 Ibid., 16:11–12.

and the subsequent redemption would come upon Israel so that they might know "that I am the Lord [*Shem Havaya*]."[12]

God's revelation to the Children of Israel on Mount Sinai begins with the words, "I am the Lord [*Shem Havaya*] your God who took you out of the Land of Egypt from the house of bondage."[13] When God first revealed His attributes to Moses, He twice used the Tetragrammaton.[14]

A Pledge to Fulfill Promises

Abram heard from God about the enslavement of his descendants in the future, when God began to address him with the words, "I am the Lord [*Shem Havaya*] who took you out of Ur of the Chaldees to give you this land to inherit it."[15] The Lord who took Abram out of Ur of the Chaldees would be present in the future and would enable Abram's descendants to inherit the Land of Israel. So too do we find the words "I am the Lord [*Shem Havaya*]" when God spoke to Moses, with the meaning being that He would fulfill His promise to the forefathers to take the Children of Israel out of Egypt.[16]

The words "I am the Lord [*Shem Havaya*] who has spoken" emphasized His intention to bring about the deaths of the generation which had left Egypt in the desert because of their complaints after hearing the spies.[17]

Reason for Observing the Commandments

The eternal existence of God is the reason for the demand to observe His commandments. God said to Moses: "Speak to the Children of Israel and say to them: 'I am the Lord [*Shem Havaya*] your God.... You shall do My ordinances and observe My statutes, to walk in them. I am the Lord [*Shem Havaya*] your God. You shall observe My statutes and ordinances which a person should do and will live by them. I am God.'"[18] Even though a

12 Ezekiel 5:13.
13 Exodus 20:2.
14 Ibid., 34:6.
15 Genesis 15:7.
16 Exodus 6:2–8.
17 Numbers 14:35.
18 Leviticus 18:2–5.

secondary reason, "that you will live by them," is also provided, the guarantee of this is the nature of God as the Lord [*Shem Havaya*].

Many commandments end with the words which indicate that God is eternal. For example, "None of you shall approach any that is near of kin to him, to uncover their nakedness: I am the Lord [*Shem Havaya*]."[19]

The Eternity of God's Attributes and Deeds

Just as the Lord is eternal, His attributes, too, are eternal. Many times the author of Psalms tells us that God's kindness exists forever.[20] So, too, His righteousness.[21] So, too, His truth.[22]

Whatever God does is for eternity. It is impossible to add to it or to subtract from it.[23]

• His Omnipotence

God's omnipotence is stated clearly. When Sarah heard the news that she would bear a son, she laughed, and God rebuked Abraham, saying, "Is anything impossible for the Lord?"[24] After Moses wondered if it was possible to supply meat and fish for all the Children of Israel, God said to him, "Has the Lord's hand grown short?"[25]

God's omnipotence is also described in the song which God wished to say to the Children of Israel before the death of Moses. "See now that I, even I, am He, and there is no god with Me: I kill and I make alive; I wound and I heal; neither is there any that can deliver out of My hand."[26]

God does as He wishes in the heavens and the earth.[27] Just as the skies are very high above the earth, so are God's ways far and distant from man's

---

19 Ibid., 18:6.
20 Psalms 136:1.
21 Ibid., 111:3.
22 Ibid., 117:2.
23 Ecclesiastes 3:14.
24 Genesis 18:13–14.
25 Numbers 11:23.
26 Deuteronomy 32:39.
27 Psalms 135:6.

ways. God's will is always fulfilled.[28] He has absolute control over the heavens and the earth and its inhabitants.[29]

God never grows weary.[30] God never stops doing.[31]

God's ability to punish the haughty and the wicked as opposed to Job's inability to do so, renders Job's complaints regarding God's justice as unacceptable. This ability reflects God's absolute right to characterize justice in the world.[32]

It is impossible to prevent acts planned by God. It is impossible to thwart His plans or to prevent Him from doing anything.[33] There is no one who can escape God's hand or who can annul His actions.[34]

• God's Knowledge and Wisdom

God Knows the Concealed

A description of God's knowledge is brought in different contexts throughout the Bible. In Deuteronomy we are told that "the secret things belong to the Lord our God."[35] Isaiah warned those who think that they can hide their plans from God, that the Creator knows the deeds of His creatures.[36]

It is useless to attempt to hide from God. God sees all people because He is in the heavens and the earth.[37]

God knows and remembers the evil deeds of people, even if they hide these in their hearts.[38] He knows all their sins.[39]

He knows every deed performed in secret, whether good or bad.[40]

---

28 Isaiah 55:8–11.
29 Ibid., 40:22–24.
30 Ibid., 40:28.
31 Psalms 121:4.
32 Job 40:6–14.
33 Isaiah 14:27.
34 Ibid., 43:13.
35 Deuteronomy 29:28.
36 Isaiah 29:15–16.
37 Jeremiah 23:24.
38 Hosea 7:2.
39 Psalms 90:8.

He Knows People's Thoughts

God knows everyone's innermost thoughts.[41] He knows man's thoughts (which are futile).[42] God knows who trusts in Him.[43]

God knows what King David thought, felt, and did.[44]

God's Thoughts are Substantively Different from the Thoughts of Humans

God's thoughts cannot be compared to those of people. God told the prophet Isaiah that just as the heavens are far above the earth, so are His thoughts loftier than those of people.[45] His wisdom is limitless.[46]

Remembering the Past and the Promises

God said to the prophet Jeremiah that He remembered how the People of Israel had gone into the wilderness, into a land not sown, as a kindness of their youth.[47]

When the Children of Israel cried out because of their hard labor in Egypt, God remembered His covenant with their forefathers.[48]

Knowledge of the Future

God has the ability to know what will happen in the future. All of history "is written" before Him before it occurs.[49] God can tell at the beginning of time what will occur at the end of time.[50] There is no one else who can say what will happen in the future.[51]

---

40 Ecclesiastes 12:14.
41 Psalms 44:22.
42 Ibid., 94:11.
43 Nahum 1:7.
44 Psalms 139 1–4.
45 Isaiah 55:8–9.
46 Psalms 147:5.
47 Jeremiah 2:2.
48 Exodus 2:24.
49 Psalms 139:16.
50 Isaiah 46:10.
51 Ibid., 44:7.

Thus, the fulfillment of a prophecy is the test to determine whether it came from God. If a person is unsure how he will know whether a prophecy came from God, when it is not fulfilled that is proof that it did not.[52]

On occasion, the Bible brings the words of God regarding events in the future which do not occur. After the Jewish People bowed down to the Golden Calf, God told Moses that He wished to destroy the entire nation and to make Moses himself into a great nation.[53] Moses pleaded to God not to do so. God assented to him and turned from the evil that He was going to do against the nation.[54]

After the report brought back by the spies to Moses, God said that He would destroy the nation and make Moses into a great nation.[55] Moses again appealed to God. God forgave the nation because of Moses's plea.[56]

God ordered Jonah to go to the city of Nineveh and to tell its inhabitants that the city was to be destroyed in forty days if they did not repent.[57] The people of Nineveh fasted, prayed, and repented their evil ways. God therefore annulled the evil which He would have brought upon them.[58]

The prophet Joel called upon the People to repent, because God is merciful and would not bring upon them the evil which He had planned.[59]

The sins of Noah's generation were so grievous that God decided to destroy all the people off the face of the earth, for He regretted that He had created them.[60]

David asked God if the people of Keilah would turn him over to Saul who was pursuing him. God told him that they would indeed do so. David and his men therefore left Keilah.[61] God told David about a "future" event and David acted to prevent it from occurring. There seems to be a problem

52 Deuteronomy 18:21–22.
53 Exodus 32:10.
54 Ibid., 32:14.
55 Numbers 14:11–12.
56 Ibid., 14:20.
57 Jonah 3:1–2, 4.
58 Ibid., 3:10.
59 Joel 2:13.
60 Genesis 6:5–7.
61 I Samuel 23:9–13.

here. If God knows what will happen in the future, how can we explain all of these "future" events which ultimately never took place? The fact that God Himself is directly involved in changes in the future does not mitigate the force of this question.

A possible answer is that God deliberately imparts incorrect information in order to affect the future. However, that is not a satisfactory answer. It contradicts "God's truth" (see p. 26). So, too, does it negate the definition of a true prophet as being one whose prophecies are always fulfilled, as stated in Deuteronomy. Furthermore, if God imparts information which is not correct, how can we accept as true that which He tells us?

A more logical answer is that there are a number of possible futures, and at the time that God speaks it has still not been determined which of these possible scenarios will actually take place. How can one reconcile that with the fact that God knows what will happen in the future? The answer is that God sees all the possibilities; many events can occur within all the possible futures, and these events are clearly known to Him.

One should note that all the events which God describes and which do not occur in the future are only annulled after prayers to God or by deeds in which one obeys or disobeys God's commandments. The fact that such activities are not determined in advance is clarified by the fact that these activities cause reward or punishment.

The existence of free will is stated clearly in Deuteronomy. God instructed the People that He gives each person the choice of life or death, blessing or curse, and they must choose life. By the fact that they love God, obey Him and cling to Him, they and their descendants will live on the land.[62] It follows from this that the free will which God gives man as to whether to observe or not observe His commandments prevents a situation of one determined future, and God saw all the possible futures.

In Keilah, David observed the commandment of "Take good heed for yourselves,"[63] which requires one to preserve human life. Saul pursued David

62 Deuteronomy 30:19–20.
63 Ibid., 4:15.

his whole life, but God did not deliver David into his hand.[64] (God did not want David to fall into Saul's hands, and He therefore gave David information which would enable him to choose to flee.) In addition, God had Balaam say, "God is not a man, that he should lie; neither the son of man, that He should repent: has He said, and shall He not do it? Or has He spoken, and shall He not keep it?"[65] God Himself does not change His mind, but He changes his deeds, as we saw, based on whether one obeys or disobeys His commandments (and sometimes after prayer and supplications), due to the free will which God chose to give to people.

• God's Relationship to the World and Mankind

Uniqueness

The recognition of God's uniqueness is expressed in the verse which Jews are required to say twice each day, "Hear O Israel, the Lord is our God, the Lord is One."[66] This verse is part of God's message as stated by Moses to the Children of Israel before they entered the Land of Canaan. So, too, was the nation told that it needed to know that the Lord is God in the heavens and on the earth, and there is none besides Him.[67]

God is incomparable.[68]

God differs substantively from humans. His thoughts are not like those of people and the way He acts is substantively different from the way people act.[69]

Presence

God is present in every place in the heavens and on the earth.[70]

---

64 I Samuel 23:14.
65 Numbers 23:19.
66 Deuteronomy 6:4.
67 Ibid., 4:39.
68 Isaiah 40:25–26.
69 Ibid., 55:8–9.
70 Jeremiah 23:24.

Superiority

There is no one who can describe (all) God's great deeds.[71]

God is exalted above all.[72] God's name is exalted. His glory is in the heavens and on the earth.[73] The Lord is God, in the heavens and on the earth.[74]

The universe belongs to God.[75] God created and gave each item of the universe its nature.[76] God rules over all.[77] God has always ruled the universe.[78] He will always rule it.[79] God will rule the entire universe and all will acknowledge that He is One and His name is One.[80]

God is the judge of all the inhabitants of the earth.[81] God is superior to everyone and everything in the universe. One cannot compare Him to anything people have devised as their god.[82]

• Other Qualities

God is described in terms of His attributes.

God revealed Himself to Moses and told him that He is compassionate and merciful, long-suffering, abundant in kindness and truth, showing love to thousands, forgiving iniquity and transgression and sin.[83]

Compassion and Mercy

God decides to whom He grants compassion and mercy.[84]

---

71 Psalms 106:2.
72 Isaiah 33:5.
73 Psalms 148:13.
74 Deuteronomy 4:39.
75 Exodus 19:5.
76 Isaiah 40:26.
77 Psalms 103:19.
78 Ibid., 93:2.
79 Lamentations 5:19.
80 Zechariah 14:9.
81 Psalms 94:2.
82 Ibid., 97:9.
83 Exodus 34:6–7.
84 Ibid., 33:19.

God is merciful to people to whom others would act without pity.[85]

His mercies are great.[86] God is merciful to everything which He created.[87]

Long-Suffering

God does not hurry to punish people.[88] This attribute of His is described in the Bible many times. The fact that it is mentioned in God's revealing of His attributes to Moses stressed its importance.

Kindness

God is full of kindness. His kindness is shown especially to those who love Him and who observe His commandments,[89] and to those who call in His name.[90]

God's kindness to people never ends.[91]

God's kindness fills the world.[92] His kindness is good.[93] It endures forever.[94]

Truth

God is a God of truth.[95]

God's truth fills the world.[96] It endures forever.[97]

Forgiving Sin

See Chapter 7.

---

85 Ibid., 22:25–26.
86 Psalms 119:156.
87 Ibid., 145:9.
88 Exodus 34:6.
89 Ibid., 20:6.
90 Psalms 86:5.
91 Lamentations 3:22.
92 Psalms 33:5.
93 Ibid., 69:17.
94 Ibid., 106:1.
95 Ibid., 31:6.
96 Ibid., 108:5.
97 Ibid., 117:2.

Punishing the Sins of the Fathers upon Later Generations

God will not forgive, and will punish the sins of the fathers upon their descendants up to the third and fourth generations.[98] This punishment will be added to that for the sins of the descendants themselves, should they be haters of God, but God will show kindness even to the thousandth generation to those who love God and observe His commandments.[99] To those who repent, the sins of the fathers are wiped out.

Faithfulness

God is a Faithful God, who fulfills His covenant and performs kindness to those who love Him and observe His commandments up to a thousand generations.[100] He is faithful to people in His deeds.[101] His faithfulness to people is apparent.[102] It continues from generation to generation.[103]

Good

God is good to all.[104] He is especially good to those who fear Him.[105]

When Moses asked to see God's ways, God showed him His goodness which is linked to His kindness.[106]

Justice

God is the God of justice.[107]

God's ways are just.[108] God's justice is free of favoritism or bribery.[109]

---

98 Exodus 34:7.
99 Ibid., 20:5–6.
100 Deuteronomy 7:9.
101 Psalms 33:4.
102 Ibid., 89:9.
103 Ibid., 100:5.
104 Ibid., 145:9.
105 Ibid., 31:20.
106 Exodus 33:19.
107 Isaiah 30:18.
108 Deuteronomy 32:4.
109 Ibid., 10:17.

Jealousy

In the Ten Commandments, God ordered the Children of Israel not to bow down to or to serve other gods, because the Lord their God is "a jealous God."[110] Before they entered the Land of Israel, Moses warned the Children of Israel not to serve other gods, the gods of the other nations in the land, because God is a "jealous God."[111] Moses warned the Children of Israel not to forget the covenant with the Lord their God and not to form any idol or picture, because God is a "jealous God."[112]

Vengeance

God is called a "God of vengeance," because He avenges those deserving of punishment.[113]

Holiness

In his vision, the prophet Isaiah saw that the *Seraphim* – fiery angels – in God's heavenly court call to one another and say, "Holy, holy, holy, is the Lord of Hosts."[114]

The Children of Israel are commanded to be holy because the Lord their God is holy.[115] God is holy and He sanctifies the priests who offer the sacrifices.[116]

God also demands that those who are close to Him must maintain their holiness. God is sanctified through those who are close to Him.[117]

God's name is holy.[118] God's holy name will not be profaned any more.[119]

---

110 Exodus 20:5.
111 Deuteronomy 6:14–15.
112 Ibid., 4:23–24.
113 Psalms 94:1–2.
114 Isaiah 6:3.
115 Leviticus 19:2.
116 Ibid., 21:8.
117 Ibid., 10:3.
118 Isaiah 57:15.
119 Ezekiel 39:7.

In addition to the integral holiness of God, He or His name are sanctified through His deeds. God is sanctified through acts of righteousness.[120] God is sanctified in the eyes of the other nations when He takes the Children of Israel out of their midst.[121] In the End of Days, God will be sanctified when He smites Gog as he comes to fight against Israel.[122]

Additional Attributes

God instills fear.[123] God is feared by all those around Him.[124]

God has the greatness and the power.[125]

God has all the glory.[126] God is the God of wonders.[127]

• Manifestations of God

God's Name

Moses asked God to show him His glory. In response to his request, God said to him that He would proclaim His name before him.[128]

God's Glory

God's glory reflects His presence, His deeds and His greatness.

The manna showed the people God's glory.[129] When the Tabernacle was completed, God's glory filled it and was revealed within the cloud.[130] When Moses ascended Mount Sinai, God's glory was seen on the mountain.[131]

---

120 Isaiah 5:16.
121 Ezekiel 20:41.
122 Ibid., 38:16.
123 Deuteronomy 10:17.
124 Psalms 89:8.
125 Deuteronomy 10:17.
126 Psalms 71:8.
127 Ibid., 89:6.
128 Exodus 33:19.
129 Ibid., 16:7.
130 Ibid., 40:34.
131 Ibid., 24:16–17.

God's glory is over the entire earth.[132] God's glory is great.[133] God's glory fills the earth.[134] Occasionally God's glory is expressed in a concealed manner.[135]

God's Face

When Moses wanted to see God's glory, God told him that he could only see His "back," for no person can see His "face" and live.[136]

God told Moses that His face (i.e., His presence) would accompany the Children of Israel.[137] However, if the nation would worship another god, God would conceal His face.[138]

The Light of God

God has (good) light.[139]

The Voice of God

God's voice is powerful and majestic (to rule over Nature).[140]

• Summary

God is characterized in terms of His eternal existence, His omnipotence, His wisdom and knowledge, His status vis-à-vis the world, and other attributes.

The Tetragrammaton reflects His eternal existence. It is God's eternity which is the most fundamental of His attributes which God wants people to recognize. His knowledge includes concealed information, knowledge of man's thoughts, remembering the past and His promises, and knowledge of the future in a way which does not preclude free will. God's thoughts are

132 Psalms 108:6.
133 Ibid., 138:5.
134 Numbers 14:21.
135 Proverbs 25:2.
136 Exodus 33:20, 23.
137 Ibid., 33:14.
138 Deuteronomy 31:16–18.
139 Psalms 36:10.
140 Ibid., 29:4.

substantively different from those of people, and the way He works is substantively different from the way people work. His status in regard to the world and to people is characterized by His uniqueness, His superiority, and His presence.

Other attributes include compassion and mercy, being long-suffering, kindness and truth, forgiving sin, visiting punishment upon future generations, faithfulness, goodness, justice, jealousy, vengeance, holiness, imposing reverence, greatness, might, and wondrous deeds.

Manifestations of God's presence in the world in different ways include His name, His glory, His face, His light, and His voice.

Chapter 3 – The Connection between God and the World

The connection between God and the world was determined by the very creation of the world by God, as well as by His full control of its course. This chapter also examines the relationship between man and the world as determined by God.

• Creation

The connection between God and the world was determined by the Creation of the world by Him.

In General

The heavens and the earth were created by God.[1] God has been present in the world ever since its Creation.[2]

The Process of the Creation

God describes the process of Creation. All phenomena were created by the command of God, who separated one from the other and assigned them their own characteristics. God called each stage "good." On each day, one or more stages of the creation was completed. Thus, light was created on the first day.[3]

---

1 Genesis 1:1.
2 Ibid., 1:2.
3 Ibid., 1:3–5.

On the second day, God divided the heavens and the earth.

On the third day, He ordered the dry land to become visible and that there be a separation between the land and the seas. Regarding this, the Torah states, "God saw that it was good." He also created the vegetation and trees on the land. Of this, too, "God saw that it was good."

On the fourth day, God created the luminaries of the heavens in order to distinguish between day and night, to illuminate the land and to determine the seasons. Of this, too, "God saw that it was good."[4]

On the fifth day, God created the sea creatures and the birds. Of this, too, "God saw that it was good."[5] God blessed them that they should be fruitful and multiply.[6]

On the sixth day, God created all the various land animals from the land.[7] On that same day, God created Man in His image. God gave Man and all the animals vegetation and trees to eat.[8]

When the creation had been concluded, God determined that everything which He had done was "very good."[9]

On the seventh day God rested from all of the tasks of creation. He blessed this day and sanctified it.[10]

Additional Details

The earth did not grow anything, because God had not yet caused rain to fall.[11] God caused a mist to come up from the ground to water it. God formed Man, whose first task was to work the land.[12]

---

4 Ibid., 1:6–19.
5 Ibid., 1:20–21.
6 Ibid., 1:22.
7 Ibid., 1:24–25.
8 Ibid., 1:26–30.
9 Ibid., 1:31.
10 Ibid., 2:1–3.
11 Nachmanides's view that שיח השדה and עשב השדה ("the plants of the field" and "the grasses of the field" Genesis 2:5) refers to fields worked by people appears to be more reasonable than that of *Bereshit Rabbah*, as brought by Rashi. The context of that verse is immediately after the creation of man and his being placed in the Garden of Eden, in order to work it. It is therefore reasonable to assume that this refers to fields which are

The animals and birds were created from the earth.[13] This fact had significance when God wanted to punish the earth at the time of the Flood.[14] Man was formed from the dust of the earth and from the living soul which God breathed into him.[15]

Implications

One cannot compare the Creator to those He created.[16]

Job (as well as anyone else) had no right to express astonishment at the way God manages the world, because he was not present when God created it.[17]

Each person must recognize that the ability to see and hear was given to him by God.[18] That is why God sees what every person does and hears whatever he says.[19]

Only God can say what will happen in the future, because He created the heavens and the earth and mankind.[20]

God is the Creator of the world and all that it includes. Therefore all belong to Him.[21]

---

being worked. To say that vegetation, in general, and trees had not yet grown and did not grow until the third day, as stated in *Bereshit Rabbah*, would appear to contradict the verse, "The earth brought forth grass, herbs yielding seed of the various kinds, and trees bearing fruit, with its seed in it, of various kinds." (Genesis 1:12)

12 Genesis 2:5-8, 15.

13 Ibid., 2:19.

14 Despite the discussion in Tractate *Chulin* 27b which states that according to Genesis 1:20, "Let the waters swarm with swarms of living creatures, and the birds fly above the earth" means that the birds were created also from the water, an analysis of the verse shows that the creatures created from the water were intended to live in the water and that the birds were created in order to fly over the earth. There is no reason to conclude from the verse that the birds were created from the water.

15 Genesis 2:7.

16 Isaiah 40:25–26.

17 Job 38:1–11.

18 Proverbs 20:12.

19 Psalms 94:9.

20 Isaiah 45:11–12. See Metzudot.

The rich man and the poor man are equal, as God created both.[22]

Characteristics of Those Created

The boundaries of land, summer, and winter were determined by God.[23]

The angels and the hosts of heaven were created by God.[24]

The qualities created by God include peace and evil.[25] He also established uprightness.[26]

God created people's souls.[27] He created the spirit in men.[28] He created people's hearts (which reflect their inclinations).[29]

God's Attributes which Are Revealed in the Creation of the World

God created the world with power, wisdom, and understanding.[30]

The Reasons for the Creation

God created the heavens and the earth so that people will live there.[31] Whatever God did, including the existence of evil people, was for His sake (that is, were created for His purposes).[32] For example, the leviathan was created to show the might of God.[33]

• God's Control and Providence

God has continued to control the world after its creation.

---

21 Psalms 24:1–2.
22 Proverbs 22:2.
23 Psalms 74:17.
24 Ibid., 148:2–6.
25 Isaiah 45:7.
26 Psalms 99:4.
27 Isaiah 57:16.
28 Zechariah 12:1.
29 Psalms 33:15.
30 Jeremiah 51:15.
31 Isaiah 45:18.
32 Proverbs 16:4.
33 Psalms 104:26.

Heavens and Earth

God does as He wishes in the heavens and the earth.[34]

God's word is eternally valid in the heavens and the earth.[35] The heavens and the earth, even after they were created, obey Him.[36]

God can shake the heavens and the earth.[37] If He wishes to, He can destroy everything which grows on the earth.[38]

The Nations

God watches all the nations.[39] God protects the People of Israel.[40]

The Land of Israel

God watches over the Land of Israel always, from the beginning of the year to the end of the year.[41]

The Actions of Men

Man has many thoughts and plans, but only God's plans will endure.[42]

God can turn a king's heart as He wishes.[43]

No city or house can be built or continue to remain without God's assistance.[44]

God also controls the results when lots are drawn.[45]

God can nullify the plans of nations.[46]

---

34 Psalms 135:6.
35 Ibid., 119:89–91.
36 Isaiah 48:13.
37 Haggai 2:6.
38 Isaiah 40:23–24.
39 Psalms 66:7.
40 Ibid., 121:4.
41 Deuteronomy 11:12.
42 Proverbs 19:21.
43 Ibid., 21:1.
44 Psalms 127:1.
45 Proverbs 16:33.
46 Psalms 33:10.

God's Control over the Processes of Nature

God controls the course of nature – the sun, the moon, and the ocean.[47] He controls the rainfall, lightning, and the wind.[48] He controls the clouds and makes all plants grow.[49]

God surrounds the world with light, and stretches the heavens around the earth. He controls the wind and the fire.[50]

God fills the rivers with water so that all the animals of the field can drink. He causes rain to fall on the mountains and waters the dry land. He causes the land to grow forage for animals, and food and drink for people. He causes the trees of Lebanon to grow, where birds nest. He causes the sun to be responsible for the change of night and day. He sets aside the night for animals of prey. When the sun rises, they go back to their places and people go out to work until evening.[51]

God gives creatures food at the proper times and in abundance. If He terminates their vitality, they die. If He causes them to have some of His spirit, they live. God renews the face of the earth.[52]

God made the mountains with His might. He quiets the sound of the waves of the seas. He remembers the land and waters it, and causes grain to grow for those who live on the land. He blesses the vegetation of the land. He causes grain to grow abundantly in the pastures of the wilderness, on the hills, in the pasture lands and in the valleys.[53]

God gives food to each one at the appropriate time for him.[54]

In the Book of Job, God describes His rule over the forces of nature and over the processes of nature, and contrasts this with the lack of knowledge

47 Jeremiah 31:34.
48 Psalms 135:7. Compare Jeremiah 51:16.
49 Psalms 147:8–9.
50 Ibid., 104:2–4.
51 Ibid., 104:10–23.
52 Ibid., 104:27–30.
53 Ibid., 65:7–14.
54 Ibid., 145:15–16.

and inability of Job to rule them, in order to emphasize that Job has no right to cast aspersions on the way God administers the world.[55]

God's Influence on the Forces of Nature

God can bring rain at its appointed time to make the earth give forth its vegetation, so that there will be food for animals and humans. He can stop the rain and the earth will not produce its yield.[56]

God sometimes stops rain from falling.[57] God can change the day into night.[58]

When God became angry, the entire world shook. He sent hail and coals of fire to the world, and His voice was heard in the heavens. The foundations of the world were laid bare at His rebuke.[59]

God gathers together the waters of the sea.[60] God stirs up a huge storm in the sea and when He wishes to He calms it down.[61]

God changes the sea to dry land.[62]

God can change rivers, places of plentiful water, into deserts and vice versa.[63] God can change rocks into pools of water.[64]

God can bring snow and ice to the world, and can melt them back to water.[65] God can make the earth quake.[66]

The Voice of God

The voice of God shatters the cedars, sends forth flames of fire, makes the desert tremble, and causes the deer to fear.[67]

---

55 Job 38:2–39:30.
56 Deuteronomy 11:14–15, 17.
57 Amos 4:7.
58 Ibid., 5:8.
59 Psalms 18:8–16.
60 Ibid., 33:7.
61 Ibid., 107:25–26, 29.
62 Ibid., 66:6.
63 Ibid., 107:33–35.
64 Ibid., 114:7–8.
65 Ibid., 147:16–18.
66 Ibid., 60:4.

Man's Abilities

God implanted in Man the ability to speak, listen, and see.[68]

God enables people to follow whichever path they wish.[69]

Setting the Order of the World

The natural order of the world was reset after the Flood. God ordered Noah to leave the ark and to free the animals in it so that they would spread throughout the world and would multiply.[70] God said that He would never again destroy the living creatures (which had been created from the earth) because of people's actions. All the natural systems and their laws, the plant seasons, summer and winter, day and night, would continue to exist as long as the earth exists. God made a covenant with Noah and his descendants. He would never again destroy all of life with a flood, and would not destroy the earth with a flood.[71]

• Man's Standing in the World

Man's standing in the world involves certain privileges and limitations as given to him by God.

His Ability

When mankind was created, God gave it rule over every living creature in the air, the sea, and on the land.[72] God blessed them that their descendants would fill the earth and would have dominion over everything on and in it.[73]

At first, they were given all plant life, trees and fruit to eat.[74] After the Flood, God told Noah and his sons that from that time on all creatures in the air, in the sea, and on the land would fear them. All living creatures were put

---

67 Ibid., 29:5–9.

68 Exodus 4:11.

69 Proverbs 16:9. See Rashi, Ibn Ezra, Metzudat David.

70 Genesis 8:15–17.

71 Ibid., 8:21–22, 9:11.

72 Genesis 1:26.

73 Ibid., 1:28.

74 Ibid., 1:29.

into the hands of man and man was permitted to eat them.[75] God will revenge Himself of any animal which kills a human.[76]

His Limitations

People are composed of matter, and God therefore limited the years of their lives to one hundred and twenty.[77]

Man's dominion over animals is not total. People are forbidden to eat any animal or part of it while it is still alive.[78]

Even though mankind was commanded to conquer the earth, people cannot control or even understand all the processes of nature. What people are able to do in the world does not even begin to approach the actions, abilities, and knowledge of God.[79] (See pp. 19–24 above.)

People can do very little in comparison to what God has done.[80]

There are many things which are beyond the comprehension of man.[81]

In summary, man has a high position within the framework of the world which was created, but it is lower than that of God.[82]

• Summary

The Bible describes the process of the Creation of the world by God. It also gives a number of reasons for the Creation of the world. The fact that God created the world has implications in terms of His standing in relationship to the world and Man, of the revealing of God's attributes reflected in the act of Creation, and of determining the relationship between His creatures. Reasons for the Creation are also mentioned.

---

75 Ibid., 9:1–3.
76 Ibid., 9:5.
77 Ibid., 6:3. See Malbim.
78 Ibid., 9:4.
79 Job 38:2–39:30.
80 Ecclesiastes 3:14.
81 Proverbs 25:3.
82 Psalms 8:5–9.

God constantly rules and supervises the heavens and the earth, the rules of nature, the nations and individuals. Only He enables people to act as they wish.

In the framework of the connection between God and the world, man's standing in the world was determined, including his rights and limitations.

Chapter 4 – Revelation

From time to time, God reveals Himself in various ways to people.

There are a number of aspects to the act of Revelation by God: the experience of Revelation whereby the person feels the presence of God, the purpose of the Revelation as expressed in its content, and covenants and signs, which are special cases of Revelation.

• The Types of Revelation Experiences

The Bible often tells us of events where God reveals Himself to people, where the content of the Revelation is the primary issue and the type of experience is not mentioned. Below are brought the cases where the type of experience of the Revelation is stated explicitly.

It is impossible to analyze completely the types of experience of Revelation as described in the Bible, because there are so many of them – depending on different situations and different periods of time. We will therefore limit ourselves to presenting examples.

Adam and His Wife

The first instance of Revelation mentioned in the Bible is after Adam and his wife ate of the forbidden fruit. They heard the voice of God walking about in the garden. Their reaction was an attempt to hide from God. God called to them and spoke to them about their sin.[1]

1 Genesis 3:8–13.

The Era of the Forefathers

During the era of the forefathers, God appeared in a vision, in a dream, or through an angel.

God appeared to Abram in a vision, and promised him that he would become a great nation, as numerous as the stars in the heavens, and that this nation would inherit the Land of Israel. God instructed him to take a heifer, a goat, a ram, a turtle-dove and a pigeon. Abram cut all of the animals in two. As the sun set, Abram fell into a deep sleep and terror overwhelmed him. God told him about the exile to Egypt and the slavery there, and of the return to the Land of Israel when the time would come. Within the darkness, Abram saw a smoking furnace and a burning torch passed between the pieces.[2]

An angel of God spoke to Hagar, Sarai's maidservant, after she had fled from her mistress. The angel told her to return to Sarai. She would give birth to a son, who would be called Ishmael, and a great nation would come out of him.[3]

God again appeared to Abraham. Three angels in the guise of men came to him, and told him that he would have a son born to him and Sarah.[4] After they left, Abraham remained standing before God.[5]

The "men" continued on to Sodom, spoke to Lot, blinded the people of the city who wished to harm Lot, and ordered him and his family to leave the city before it was destroyed.[6]

God appeared to Avimelech, King of Gerar, in a dream and warned him that if he did not return Sarah to Abraham, he would die.[7]

An angel of God appeared to Hagar a second time, after both Abraham and Sarah had sent her and her son Ishmael out of their home. The angel showed her a well of water, so that she could save her son from death.[8]

---

2 Ibid., 15:1–21.
3 Ibid., 16:7–12.
4 Ibid., 18:1–10. See Rashbam.
5 Ibid., 18:22.
6 Ibid., 19:1–22.
7 Ibid., 20:3–7.
8 Ibid., 21:17–19.

When Abraham took the knife to slaughter his son Isaac, an angel of God appeared to him to prevent him from doing so. The angel called him a second time and told him in the name of God that as he had been ready to slaughter his son, God would bless him and multiply his seed.[9]

When Jacob fled from his brother Esau, he dreamed of a ladder which reached heaven, with angels climbing up and down on it. In his dream, God told him that He would guard him and give him and his descendants the Land of Israel.[10]

When Jacob dwelled in Padan Aram, an angel of God appeared to him in a dream, and instructed him to return to the Land of Israel.[11]

God appeared to Laban in a dream, and warned him to be very careful when he spoke to Jacob.[12]

When Jacob left Laban and went on his way, angels of God met him.[13]

Before Jacob was to meet Esau, a "man" who had been sent by God struggled with him. The "man" blessed him for the fact that he had been successful in his struggle with God and with people.[14]

God appeared to Jacob at night in a vision, and told him not to fear to go down to Egypt, because God would make of him a great nation and would bring him up from there.[15]

The Exodus from Egypt

At the time of the Exodus from Egypt, God also appeared by means of signs to the residents of Egypt in order to emphasize His involvement.

An angel of God appeared to Moses in a flame of fire within a bush, which burned without being consumed. God called to Moses from the bush to take the Children of Israel out of the slavery of Egypt.[16]

---

9 Ibid., 22:10–18.
10 Ibid., 28:12–15.
11 Ibid., 31:11–13.
12 Ibid., 31:24.
13 Ibid., 32:1.
14 Ibid., 32:24–29.
15 Ibid., 46:2–4.
16 Exodus 3:2–22.

In order to allay Moses's fears that the Children of Israel might not listen to him, God gave him two signs. His staff was changed into a snake and then turned back into a staff. His hand became leprous, and then reverted to its former state.[17]

God told Moses to ask Aaron to cast his staff before Pharaoh, and it became a snake. When Pharaoh's sorcerers did the same, Aaron's staff swallowed all the staffs of the Egyptian sorcerers.[18]

God brought many plagues upon Egypt. In most cases, he warned Pharaoh in advance.[19]

At midnight, God smote all the Egyptian firstborn, as He had told Moses.[20]

In the Desert, until Mount Sinai

God, through His angel, went before the Children of Israel in the desert, in a pillar of cloud by day and a pillar of fire by night.[21]

When the Egyptians pursued the Children of Israel to the Sea of Reeds, God separated the Egyptian camp and that of Israel, changed the sea into dry land and drowned the Egyptians in the sea.[22]

At Mara, where the water was bitter (*mara* in Hebrew), God showed Moses a tree, in order to have Moses throw it into the water and make it potable.[23]

When the Children of Israel complained about a lack of food, Moses and Aaron told them that God had heard their complaints. God's glory appeared in a cloud.[24]

God sent the Children of Israel meat at night and special bread – the manna – in the morning. Regardless of how much manna was gathered, each

---

17 Ibid., 4:1–8.
18 Ibid., 7:8–12.
19 Ibid., 7:14–10:20.
20 Ibid., 12:29.
21 Ibid., 13:21–22; 14:19.
22 Ibid., 14:15–29.
23 Ibid., 15:25.
24 Ibid., 16:10.

person received the amount needed by him. Any leftover manna was spoiled by the following morning. On Friday, a double portion was gathered, and the second portion remained fresh for the following day. On the Sabbath, no manna fell.[25]

At Massa and Meriva, God extracted water from a rock after Moses struck it.[26]

At Mount Sinai

God told Moses that He would be revealed in a thick cloud so that the Children of Israel would hear that which God would say to Moses and would believe in Moses. God gave Moses instructions as to how the Children of Israel were to prepare themselves for the Revelation (not to ascend the mountain, not to touch it, and not to have conjugal relations for three days).

On the third morning there was thunder and lightning, a thick cloud and a loud *shofar* – a ram's horn – caused the Children of Israel who camped near the mountain to tremble. Moses took the nation out of the camp and placed them at the foot of the mountain, which was covered with smoke as God came down to it in fire. The sound of the *shofar* became even louder. Moses spoke and God answered him by a voice. God called Moses to go to the top of the mountain and instructed him and Aaron and the Priests to again warn the people not to come close to the mountain or ascend it.

God spoke to the Children of Israel, and the content of what He spoke was the Ten Commandments.[27] The nation was present when God spoke to them from the heavens.[28]

God told Moses that He would send an angel to guard the Children of Israel and to bring them to the place which He had prepared for them. The Children of Israel had to obey the angel's voice, because God's name was within him. He would not forgive the sins of the Children of Israel. The

---

25 Ibid., 16:11–27.
26 Ibid., 17:5–6.
27 Ibid., 19:9–20:14.
28 Ibid., 20:19.

angel would bring the Children of Israel to the land of the six nations of Canaan.[29]

Moses, Aaron, Nadav, Avihu and seventy of the elders of Israel saw the Revelation of God, characterized by clarity (like a paved work of sapphire stone) and purity. God did not harm them.[30]

God instructed Moses to ascend the mountain in order to receive the Tablets, the Torah and the commandments which He had written to instruct the Children of Israel. Moses ascended the mountain and waited for six days until God called to him from the midst of the cloud. God's glory appeared to be like fire on the top of the mountain to the eyes of the Children of Israel. Moses remained on the mountain for forty days and forty nights.[31]

While Moses remained on the mountain, God instructed him to construct a Tabernacle, based on the plan that God showed him.[32]

On Mount Sinai, God taught Moses the commandment of the Sabbatical Year and additional commandments.[33]

God told Moses that, in the future, He would speak to him between the two cherubs above the ark cover that was over the Ark of Testimony.[34]

God told Moses that He would commune with the Children of Israel in the Tent of Assembly, when He spoke to him there.[35]

God gave Moses the Two Tablets of Testimony, stone tablets written by the finger of God.[36] The tablets were made by God and written by His hand.[37]

After the Children of Israel sinned with the Golden Calf, God told Moses that He would send an angel before them, but His name would not be

29 Ibid., 23:20–23.
30 Ibid., 24:9–11.
31 Ibid., 24:12–18.
32 Ibid., 25:1–9.
33 Leviticus 25:1–2.
34 Exodus 25:22.
35 Ibid., 29:42.
36 Ibid., 31:18.
37 Ibid., 32:16.

within the angel, because the nation was stiff-necked and God was liable to destroy them on the way.[38]

In these verses, we have God's annulling His previous promise to them, that His name would be in their midst. Moses asked God to keep His promise. Moses said that if he had indeed found favor in God's eyes, God should explain to him His ways, so that he and the nation would find favor in His eyes. God answered him that His presence would lead them, and He would not destroy them because Moses had found favor in His eyes.

In order to understand God's ways, Moses asked God to show him His glory. God answered that He would show Moses all His good, would call before him God's name (*Shem Havaya*), and would show him the attribute of mercy. God told Moses that he could not see His face, because no person can see God's face and continue to live. Moses could see His back.

God instructed Moses to carve out two tablets of stone like the first ones. God would inscribe on them the words which had been on the first tablets. Likewise, did He instruct him to ascend Mount Sinai by himself. God descended in a cloud and Moses called out in the name of God. He passed over Moses and recited to him the Thirteen Attributes, with an emphasis on the attribute of mercy and on the way God relates to the sins of men. God also said that He would make a covenant with the nation. He would perform miracles so that the nation would see God's awe-inspiring acts. For them to inherit the land, they would need to observe God's commandments.[39] Moses remained on the mountain for another forty days and forty nights, and did not eat or drink. God wrote on the tablets the Ten Commandments as they had been on the first tablets. When Moses came down from the mountain, his face shone. When he did not speak to God, he covered his face.[40]

Moses, in his speech to the nation on the plains of Moab, again described the events on Mount Horeb (Sinai): God ordered Moses to assemble the nation so as to have them hear his words. Thus they would learn

38 Ibid., 33:1–3. See Ibn Ezra.
39 Ibid., 33:12–34:11.
40 Ibid., 34:28–35.

to fear Him all the days of their lives on the earth and to teach their children. They stood next to the mountain and saw on it fire, darkness, clouds and fog. God spoke to them from the midst of the fire. They heard the words, but did not see any image. God told them the message of the covenant – the Ten Commandments – which He commanded them to observe, and wrote them on two tablets of stone.[41]

God spoke to the Children of Israel, face to face, at Mount Sinai from within the fire. Moses stood between God and the Children of Israel to tell them God's word, because the Children of Israel were afraid of the fire.[42] [43] There has never again been such an event in the history of the nations, where God spoke to an entire nation from the midst of fire in order to teach it, or where God took out an entire nation from another with signs and wonders as occurred at the Exodus from Egypt. Thus all came to know that the Lord is God and there is none besides Him.[44] God had the entire nation hear the Ten Commandments at the mountain from the midst of the fire, the cloud and the fog in a loud voice. He wrote them on two stone tablets and gave them to Moses. The nation was afraid to hear God's words directly. They asked Moses to mediate between God and them. God looked favorably on this request, and He told Moses that He wished the nation would always fear Him and observe His commandments. God taught the other commandments to Moses and Moses taught them to the nation.[45] Moses ascended the mountain in order to receive the tablets of the covenant which God had made with the Children of Israel. On the tablets were inscribed with God's finger all that God had spoken on the mountain from the midst of the fire on the day of the assembly. These were given to Moses after forty days, during which he neither ate nor drank.[46] After the sin of the Golden Calf, God told Moses to carve two stone tablets like the first and to again ascend the

---

41 Deuteronomy 4:9–13.

42 Ibid., 5:4–5.

43 Moses's "telling" was evidently an explanation of what God had said, because the Children of Israel themselves heard God's word. See Exodus 20.

44 Deuteronomy 4:32–36. See the Aramaic translation by Onkelos.

45 Ibid., 5:19–28.

46 Ibid., 9:9–11.

mountain. God inscribed the second tablets, like the first ones, with the Ten Commandments which God had proclaimed to the nation on the mountain from the midst of the fire on the day of assembly, and gave them to Moses.[47]

The Revelation to Moses

When God spoke to Moses, the pillar of cloud came down to the entrance of the Tent of Assembly, which had been erected outside the camp. The nation saw the pillar of cloud.[48] When Moses came to the Tent of Assembly to speak to God, he heard the voice speaking to him from above the ark cover over the Ark of Testimony between the cherubs.[49]

God spoke to Moses face to face, as a person speaks to his fellow man.[50] God told Aaron and Miriam that He makes Himself known to most prophets in a vision and speaks to them in a dream. That was not the case with Moses. God spoke to him face to face, directly and not in riddles.[51]

Aaron and Miriam criticized Moses because he had separated himself from his wife. They thought that they were prophets similar to Moses, and that Moses had taken a step which was extraordinary, as if his degree of prophecy was greater than theirs.[52] God told them that Moses was indeed on a higher level of prophecy than they.[53] God could call upon Moses at any time. He was therefore always in a state similar to when God revealed Himself at Mount Sinai, at which time all the men had had to separate themselves from their wives.

The Dedication of the Tabernacle

Once the Tabernacle had been erected, God's glory filled it. Throughout all the travels of the Children of Israel in the desert, they saw above the

---

47 Ibid., 10:1–4.
48 Exodus 33:7–10.
49 Numbers 7:89
50 Exodus 33:11.
51 Numbers 12:6–8.
52 Ibid., 12:1–2. See the Aramaic translation by Onkelos and Rashi.
53 Ibid., 12:6–8.

Tabernacle the cloud of God during the day and fire at night.[54]

At the dedication of the Tabernacle, on the day following the seven days of the consecration offerings by Aaron, together with the offering of the sacrifices of the Priests and the nation, the glory of God appeared to the nation and a fire appeared and burned the burnt offering and the fat.[55] The sons of Aaron – Nadav and Avihu – brought unauthorized fire upon the altar, which God had not instructed them to do. God sent forth fire which consumed them.[56]

God told Moses that He would appear in the cloud above the ark cover.[57]

In the Desert after the Dedication of the Tabernacle

On the day the Tabernacle was erected, a cloud covered it. In the evening there was a fire above the Tabernacle until the morning. When the cloud ascended, the nation traveled, and when it descended the nation camped. The nation traveled and camped in accordance with what God indicated.[58]

Moses gathered seventy men from among the elders of Israel. God came down in a cloud, and imparted of the spirit which had been on Moses and put it on the elders, and they prophesied.[59]

After Aaron and Miriam had criticized Moses, God suddenly ordered the three of them to go out to the Tent of Assembly. God came down in a pillar of cloud and called to Aaron and Miriam, and explained to them the difference between Moses's degree of prophecy and that of the other prophets, and asked them how they had had the temerity to speak thus about Moses. When the cloud left them, Miriam was afflicted with a skin disease.[60]

---

54 Exodus 40:34–38.
55 Leviticus 9:23–24.
56 Ibid., 10:1–2.
57 Ibid., 16:2.
58 Numbers 9:15–23.
59 Ibid., 11:25.
60 Ibid., 12:4–10.

In different events during their travels in the desert, God reacted to the people's actions. God's glory appeared to the nation when Moses was called to the Tent of Assembly to speak with God.

When the spies returned from the Land of Israel, Caleb and Joshua rejected the harsh description reported by their colleagues. They told the nation that they needed to trust in God. The nation wanted to stone them. The glory of God then appeared in the Tent of Assembly before the eyes of the Children of Israel.[61]

Moses and Aaron, as well as Korah and his whole group prepared censers in which they put fire and incense. The nation assembled at the entrance to the Tent of Assembly, and the glory of God then appeared before the entire congregation.[62] God opened up the earth. Korah, Datan, Aviram, and their families and possessions were all swallowed up by it, so that the people would know that God had sent Moses.[63]

When the Children of Israel complained that Moses and Aaron had caused "God's nation" – Korah and his group – to be killed, God's glory appeared, and the cloud covered the Tent of Assembly.[64]

When the Children of Israel complained that they had been brought to the desert to die, the glory of God appeared to Moses and Aaron.[65]

After God became angry at Balaam for having gone to the king of Moab, He sent an angel to obstruct his way. Only his donkey saw the angel. After Balaam had beaten the donkey three times, God opened its mouth which asked Balaam why he was beating it. God opened Balaam's eyes and he also saw the angel. The angel told Balaam that he could continue on his way, but he was only to say that which God would tell him to say.[66]

When Balaam saw the tribes of Israel dwelling in peace, the spirit of God rested on him.[67]

---

61 Ibid., 14:10.
62 Ibid., 16:19.
63 Ibid., 16:28–33.
64 Ibid., 17:6–7.
65 Ibid., 20:4–6.
66 Ibid., 22:22–35.
67 Ibid., 24:2.

The Children of Israel asked God on the day of assembly at Mount Horeb not to hear His voice and to no longer see the great fire, so that they would not die. God therefore said that He would convey His words through the mouths of prophets.[68] The nation would be able to tell if the prophet was speaking in the name of God or not. If what the prophet had said did not materialize, God had not spoken to the prophet.[69]

God instructed Moses to summon Joshua and to stand alongside him at the entrance to the Tent of Assembly, so that God would appoint Joshua as Moses's successor. God then appeared in the Tent in a pillar of cloud.[70]

There will never arise another prophet for Israel like Moses, whom God knew face to face, and who was sent by Him to do the signs and wonders in the Land of Egypt before the eyes of all of Israel.[71]

The Era of Joshua

When the Children of Israel were about to cross the Jordan River, God ordered Joshua to command the Priests carrying the Ark of the Covenant to stand. God stopped the Jordan from flowing and the Children of Israel crossed it. After the Priests, too, had crossed the Jordan, the water in the river started flowing again. God did this in order to aggrandize Joshua's name in the eyes of the nation, and to show them that God was with him as He had been with Moses.[72]

In Jericho, a man with an unsheathed sword appeared before Joshua. He identified himself as a general of God's army. The man ordered Joshua to take off his shoes because the place where he stood was holy.[73] God instructed Joshua as to what actions he needed to take in order to conquer Jericho: to surround the walls of the city for seven days with the Ark of the Covenant, to blow the *shofar*, and on the seventh day to surround the wall

68 Deuteronomy 18:15–18.
69 Ibid., 18:21–22.
70 Ibid., 31:14–15.
71 Ibid., 34:10–12.
72 Joshua 3:7–4:18.
73 Ibid., 5:13–15.

seven times, to blow the *shofar* and to shout. The Children of Israel did as instructed and the wall collapsed.[74]

During the war with the five Emorite kings, God threw down large rocks from the heavens. In that way, many of the attackers were killed. God also acceded to Joshua's request to halt the progression of the sun in the heavens so that Joshua and his troops would be able to continue to fight.[75]

The Era of the Judges

After the death of Joshua, an angel of God appeared before the Children of Israel to rebuke them and to tell them what their punishment would be, because they had not obeyed God's instruction not to make a treaty with the residents of the land.[76]

An angel of God appeared to Gideon and appointed him to save Israel. He gave him a sign that he was indeed an angel of God. Fire came out of a rock and consumed Gideon's offering.[77]

God assented to Gideon's request and gave him a sign that he would save Israel – dew fell on a fleece of wool while the ground all around it remained dry. Another sign occurred when dew fell on the ground and the fleece remained dry.[78]

An angel of God appeared to Manoah's wife who was barren, and told her that she would bear a son, who would be a Nazirite (one who abstains from cutting his hair, etc.), and he would save Israel from the Philistines. The angel of God again appeared to Manoah's wife, who called her husband. The angel refused to eat of Manoah's bread, but told him to bring a burnt offering should he wish to. The angel also refused to reveal his name. Manoah brought a burnt offering and the angel of God disappeared in the flame.[79]

74 Ibid., 6:2–20.
75 Ibid., 10:10–14.
76 Judges 2:1–3.
77 Ibid., 6:11–23.
78 Ibid., 6:36–40.
79 Ibid., 13:2–21.

After the concubine of the Levite was killed by members of the tribe of Benjamin, the Children of Israel went to Bethel and asked by means of the *Urim* and *Thummim* (receptacle for signals from God on the breastplate of the High Priest) regarding waging battle against the tribe of Benjamin, and God answered them.[80]

When Samuel was a lad in the Tabernacle in Shiloh, God's words to people were very infrequent. God, however, called to Samuel three times. On the fourth time, God told Samuel that He was going to punish the house of Eli.[81] God continued to appear to Samuel in Shiloh.[82]

God spoke to Samuel in a pillar of cloud as He had done to Moses and Aaron.[83]

The Era of the Kings

Saul met a group of prophets. The spirit of God rested upon him, and he prophesied.[84]

When Saul heard how Nahash the Edomite wanted to humiliate the inhabitants of Jabesh Gilead, the spirit of God rested on him, and he spurred on the nation to fight against the Edomites.[85]

Samuel called to God in Gilgal, and God brought down rain with thunder at the time of the wheat harvest, in order to rebuke the nation for its wish to have a king rule over them.[86]

After Samuel anointed David, the spirit of God rested on David. The spirit of God departed from Saul, and an evil spirit from God upset his serenity and troubled him.[87]

Saul sent messengers to take David, who was with Samuel in Nayot. The spirit of God rested on them and they began to prophesy. This also happened

80 Ibid., 20:18–28. See Radak, Metzudat David.
81 I Samuel 3:1–14.
82 Ibid., 3:21.
83 Psalms 99:6–7.
84 I Samuel 10:10.
85 Ibid., 11:1–7.
86 Ibid., 12:16–18.
87 Ibid., 16:13–14.

to the second and third groups of messengers. When Saul came himself, the spirit of God rested upon him and he prophesied.[88]

Eviatar the Priest fled to David in Keilah, with the *Ephod* (priestly garment). When David wanted to ask God about what was liable to happen and what he should do, he asked Eviatar to bring him the *Ephod*. In this way, he asked God about remaining in Keilah. God answered him.[89]

David asked Eviatar to bring the *Ephod* so that he would be able to ask God whether he should pursue the Amalekites. God ordered him to do so.[90]

God appeared to the prophet Nathan in a vision at night and told him to tell David that he, David, would not build the Temple, but that his son would build the Temple for God.[91]

David counted the nation in spite of the prohibition to do so. Gad the Seer was sent by God to David to have him choose the punishment for this sin (famine, the sword, or a plague). David chose a plague to be brought upon the nation by an angel of God.. An angel of God appeared to David with his sword drawn and stretched out against Jerusalem. David prayed for God to remove the plague. An angel of God told Gad to tell David to set up an altar in the threshing floor of Ornan the Jebusite, to whom the angel appeared as well, in order to halt the plague. David built an altar, offering on it burnt offerings and peace offerings. He called to God, and God answered in fire from heaven onto the burnt offering altar. God ordered the angel to return his sword to its sheath.[92]

In Gibeon, God appeared to Solomon in a dream at night. God asked him to say what he, Solomon, wanted from God. Solomon asked for an understanding heart in order to judge justly, to know to differentiate between good and bad. This request was favorable to God, and God gave him that which he had asked, as well as wealth and honor.[93]

---

88 Ibid., 19:20–24.
89 Ibid., 23:6–12.
90 Ibid., 30:7–8.
91 II Samuel 7:4–17.
92 I Chronicles 21:1–2, 9–28.
93 I Kings 3:5–14.

After the Ark of the Covenant was placed in the Holy of Holies in the Temple built by Solomon in Jerusalem, and the Priests left the holy place, a cloud with the glory of God filled the House of God. The Priests were unable to stand and fulfill their duties.[94] After Solomon concluded his prayer at the time of the dedication of the Temple, fire came down from heaven and consumed the burnt offering and the sacrifices. The glory of God filled the House, and the Priests were unable to enter it. All of the Children of Israel saw the fire coming down and the glory of God on the House, and they bowed and prostrated themselves and thanked God for all His good.[95]

After the House had been built, God again appeared to Solomon at night, as He had appeared to him at Gibeon. God told him that the future of the House of God, his reign and the future of Israel would depend on him and the Children of Israel observing God's statutes and His ordinances.[96]

A man of God came from Judah to Bethel to the place of the altar where Jeroboam was going to offer incense. He prophesied that Josiah, a descendant of the House of David, would offer on that altar the priests of the high places. The sign that this would happen would be that the altar would be split apart and its ashes would be spilled. Jeroboam put out his hand in order to grab the man of God but his hand withered and he was unable to draw it back. The altar also split apart and all its ashes spilled. The king asked the man of God to pray to God so that his hand would be healed, and God granted his prayer.[97]

The man of God accepted the invitation of an old prophet to dine with him, even though God had forbidden this. God's word came to the prophet to say to the man of God that he would be punished. A lion killed him, but did not harm his body or his donkey.[98]

The spirit of God rested on Azariah, the son of Oded. He told Asa, the king of Judah, and the tribes of Judah and Benjamin that if they would seek

94 Ibid., 8:6–11.
95 II Chronicles 7:1–3.
96 I Kings 9:2–9.
97 Ibid., 13:1–6.
98 Ibid., 13:11–28.

God, they would find Him, but if they would forsake Him, He would forsake them.[99]

When Moab and Ammon came to wage war against Judah, King Jehoshafat declared a fast and prayer. The spirit of God rested on Jachaziel, the son of Zechariah, in the midst of the congregation. God told him that the people of Judah had no reason to be concerned, because the battle was not of the people of Judah but of God.[100]

After Elijah told Ahab that no rain would fall, God ordered him to hide by the river Cherith, and He ordered ravens to feed Elijah with bread and meat. [101]

During the years of famine, God instructed Elijah to go to Zarephath, which was close to Zidon, and to live there. A widow would supply him with his food. The woman had nothing and was only able to support her son and herself with great difficulty. Elijah promised her in the name of God that her jar of flour and her cruse of oil, both of which were almost empty, would not be depleted until God would cause rain to fall on the ground.[102] After the woman's son died, God listened to Elijah's prayer and brought the child back to life.[103]

In the confrontation between Elijah and the prophets of Baal on Mount Carmel, with the presence of the Children of Israel, the prophets of Baal prepared a single bull to sacrifice, while Elijah prepared another one. The prophets of Baal called upon Baal to send forth fire on their altar, and were not answered throughout the entire day. Elijah poured water on his bull and the altar that he built. He afterwards prayed to God, who listened to his prayer and sent forth fire which consumed the bull, the water, and the wood.[104]

After the event at Mount Carmel, Elijah fled from Jezebel, the wife of Ahab, who wanted to kill him. He walked for a day in the Judean Desert and

---

99 II Chronicles 15:1–7.
100 Ibid., 20:1–4, 14–17.
101 I Kings 17:2–6.
102 Ibid., 17:8–16.
103 Ibid., 17:17–22.
104 Ibid., 18:17–38.

afterwards lay down under a juniper tree, without food or water. An angel of God touched him and Elijah saw next to him a cake and a cruse of water. At the request of the angel, he ate and drank. From the energy provided by the food and drink, he walked in the desert for forty days and forty nights until he reached Mount Horeb.[105]

Elijah rested in a cave near Mount Horeb. God spoke to him and ordered him to leave the cave and to stand before it. God sent a strong wind, one which could destroy mountains – but God was not in that wind. God sent an earthquake – but God was not in that earthquake. God then sent a fire – but God was not in that fire. Afterwards there was a still, small voice. Elijah left the cave and God told him what to do in the future in order to cleanse the land of the prophets of Baal.[106]

One of the sons of the prophets asked his fellow man to beat him, as God had commanded. (He wanted to appear injured before Ahab, king of Israel.) When the other man refused to do so, he told him that a lion would tear him apart. That was what happened.[107]

Micaiah saw God sitting on His throne with the entire heavenly host standing before Him, on His right and left. He heard God say that a spirit that lies would come from the mouths of the Baal prophets of Ahab, in order to delude him and thus he would fall in battle.[108]

An angel of God instructed the prophet Elijah to go meet the messengers of Ahaziah, king of Samaria, who was ill. The king had sent them to inquire of Baalzebub, the god of Ekron, whether he would recover from his illness. Elijah told them in the name of God that Ahaziah would die.[109]

King Ahaziah sent fifty messengers to order Elijah to leave the mountain peak and to come to him. Elijah answered that if he was indeed a man of God, fire would come down from heaven and would consume them. The fire

---

105 Ibid., 19:2–8.
106 Ibid., 19:9–18.
107 Ibid., 20:35–36.
108 Ibid., 22:19–22.
109 II Kings 1:3–4

came down and consumed them. The same happened with the second group of messengers.[110]

An angel of God instructed Elijah to come down from the mountain and not to fear the king.[111]

God took Elijah up to heaven in a storm. A chariot of fire and horses of fire separated him from Elisha.[112]

When there was no drinking water for the army of Judah and Israel which was fighting against Moab and Ammon, God's hand rested upon Elisha when the minstrel played. He prophesied in the name of God that the river and its ditches would be filled with water, and that Judah and Israel would vanquish Moab and Ammon.[113]

Elisha, the man of God, performed miracles.[114]

The king of Aram wanted to seize the prophet Elisha. In response to Elisha's prayer, God opened the eyes of his lad, so that he saw horses and chariots of fire which filled the mountains around Elisha. Elisha again prayed, and God blinded the soldiers of Aram. Elisha led them into the city of Samaria, and there God restored their vision.[115]

The spirit of God rested on Zechariah, the son of Jehoiada the Priest. He turned to the people and said to them in the name of God that they would not succeed in what they were doing. They had again turned to other gods and had forsaken God. That was why He had left them.[116]

The king of Assyria besieged Jerusalem. An angel of God killed 185,000 of his soldiers.[117]

The prophet Isaiah gave King Hezekiah a sign from God that He had indeed listened to his prayer and that he would not die of his serious illness. The sign was that the shadow on his sundial went backwards ten degrees.[118]

---

110 Ibid., 1:9–12.
111 Ibid., 1:15.
112 Ibid., 2:1, 11.
113 Ibid., 3:14–19.
114 Ibid., 4:1–6:7.
115 Ibid., 6:17–20.
116 II Chronicles 24:20.
117 II Kings 19:35.

God's Revelation to the Prophets

The prophet Isaiah saw God sitting on a throne, high and lifted up in the palace. Fiery angels stood above Him and cried one to the other, "Holy, holy, holy is the Lord of Hosts; the whole world is filled with His glory." The sound of their voices shook the door frames, and the house was filled with smoke. One fiery angel flew and took a coal from the altar. He touched Isaiah's mouth, and told him that by that he had atoned for his sins. Isaiah accepted the duty of being a messenger of God to the nation.[119]

The spirit of God rested on him. He was anointed to bring good tidings, to proclaim liberty to those imprisoned, to free prisoners, to proclaim the year as one of God's favor, and a day of vengeance. He was anointed to comfort those in mourning, to bring them joy in place of mourning, praise instead of humiliation, and they would be the glory of God.[120]

Jeremiah was sanctified by God as a prophet for the nations even before he was born. God ordered him to go wherever He would send him, and to say that which God would command him. God stretched out His hand to touch Jeremiah's mouth so that he would be able to talk in God's name, and appointed him over the nations, to destroy and to build.[121]

Jeremiah, when speaking in the name of God to the false prophets, told them that God's word is not like a dream, but like fire, like a hammer smashing rocks.[122]

Ezekiel, when in exile along the river Chebar, saw the heavens open up, and he saw a vision of God. God's hand was on him. He heard God's word and saw a storm coming from the north, a large cloud, and a fire flashing with a brightness around it. In it was like the eye of a flame (pure of smoke).

Within the cloud, he saw four creatures, each with four faces (that of a man, a lion, an ox, and an eagle), and four wings. They went wherever they wanted, without turning. Their appearance was like coals of burning fire and like torches. They ran back and forth like flashes of lightning. Each creature

---

118 Ibid., 20:4–11.
119 Isaiah 6:1–8.
120 Ibid., 61:1–3.
121 Jeremiah 1:4–10.
122 Ibid., 23:28–29.

had a wheel which went with it. They were the color of beryl, and their rims were full of eyes. When they moved, the sound was like that of great waters. Above the sky, he saw the likeness of a throne, similar to the appearance of a sapphire. Above it was the image of a man. From its loins up, was like the eye of a flame similar to the appearance of fire surrounding it. Underneath there and below, it looked like a fire with a brightness around it, whose appearance was like the rainbow in a cloud – that was the appearance of the image of the glory of God.

God spoke to Ezekiel, who had fallen on his face. He told him that He was sending him to be a prophet to the Children of Israel, and that he should not fear them. They might listen to him and might not, but they would know that there was a prophet in their midst. God showed him a scroll, from which Ezekiel would speak to the House of Israel, and which included lamentations. God had him eat the scroll, which was sweeter than honey, and reappointed him as His messenger to the nation.

A wind carried Ezekiel, and he heard a very great sound: "Blessed is the glory of the Lord from His abode."[123]

God ordered Ezekiel to go out to the plain, where he would hear God's word. There he saw the appearance of the glory of God as he had seen it earlier by the river Chebar. Ezekiel fell on his face and a wind raised him up. God told him not to rebuke the nation, unless told to do so by Him. Whoever would listen to him would listen, and whoever would not listen to him would not listen.[124]

A year later, when Ezekiel was in his home in exile, he again saw the appearance of an image like that of fire. A hand came out and took him and a wind carried him between the heavens and the earth to Jerusalem. He saw the same image of the glory of God which he had seen in the plain. God showed him there different kinds of idol worship which were taking place around the Temple. He heard God call to the men, who were designated to destroy the city of Jerusalem. The glory of God went up above the cherubs in the Temple, and God instructed one of them, the man responsible for the

123 Ezekiel 1:1–3:14.
124 Ibid., 3:22–27.

destroying angels, who was dressed in linen with a pen holder by his side, to kill all those who practiced the abominations as well as the people of the city.

Ezekiel again saw the vision of the heavens above the heads of the cherubs and it was like a sapphire stone, with the likeness of a throne above them. God then instructed the man dressed in linen to take glowing coals from between the cherubs, and to throw them on the city. A cloud filled the inner court. The glory of God ascended above the cherubs, and the courtyard and the building were filled with the radiance of the glory of God. The sound of the cherubs' wings was heard as far as the outer court, like the voice of God when He spoke. God commanded the man to take fire from between the cherubs. The cherub thrust out its hand to the fire which was between the cherubs and gave it to the man. Ezekiel then saw the wheels by the cherubs, and the wheels accompanied the cherubs as they moved. The glory of God passed the threshold of the House and came to rest over the cherubs. The cherubs ascended before the eyes of the prophet and stopped next to the eastern gate of the House of God and the glory of God was above them. The cherubs were the creatures which Ezekiel had seen at the Chebar River.[125]

A wind carried Ezekiel to the eastern gate of the House of God. God showed him the leaders of the nation, who gave it evil counsel. God instructed Ezekiel to prophesy to them and to tell them that those who were involved in abominations would be punished, but those who observed God's statutes would be rewarded. The cherubs raised their wings, as did the wheels, and the glory of God appeared above them. The glory of God ascended from above Jerusalem. A wind carried Ezekiel back to the exile, and the vision disappeared.[126]

Even before a refugee arrived with the news of the destruction of Jerusalem, the hand of God was upon Ezekiel and opened his mouth. He was again able to prophesy and to tell God's word to the people.[127]

A number of years after the destruction of the Temple, God's hand brought Ezekiel, in a vision of God, to the Land of Israel and to a high

125 Ibid., 8:1–10:22.
126 Ibid., 11:1–25.
127 Ibid., 33:21–22.

mountain upon which was a city. He saw a man whose appearance was that of copper, who held a line of flax and a measuring reed (both used for measuring) in his hand standing at a gate. The man spoke to Ezekiel and told him to take careful note of whatever he would show him. Ezekiel saw a wall with a house. The man measured the house – the Temple – its halls, gates, doors, windows, courtyards, chambers, the wall and everything in it. He also measured the different utensils and even the Holy of Holies.[128]

The man led Ezekiel to the eastern gate, and he saw the glory of God and His voice like great waters and the land which shone from His glory. He again saw the vision he had seen at the Chebar River – and fell on his face. The glory of God came to the Temple and a wind carried the prophet to the inner courtyard. He heard the voice of God speaking to him from the Temple and the man stood by him. God told Ezekiel that in this House, He would dwell among the Children of Israel forever and that they would no longer make it ritually impure. God instructed him to tell the Children of Israel about the House so that they would repent of all their sins.[129]

God brought Ezekiel to the northern gate which faced the House, and the glory of God filled the House of God. God told Ezekiel to pay attention to all the laws of the House of God. The House of Israel needed to halt all their abominations, which the foreigners, uncircumcised of heart and flesh, had brought with them into the Temple in order to profane it.[130]

God showed Ezekiel the place where the Priests prepared the guilt offering, the sin offering, the meal offering, and the place where they would cook the people's sacrifices.[131]

God showed Ezekiel water which flowed out of the Temple and which became a stream. God told Ezekiel that every living thing which would come in contact with the water would be healed. There would be many fish in the water, and fishermen would fish them. On the bank of the stream, trees

128 Ibid., 40:1–42:20.
129 Ibid., 43:1–11.
130 Ibid., 44:4–8.
131 Ibid., 46:19–24.

would develop leaves which would never wither, and they would be medicinal. Their fruit would never end and would be for food.[132]

God told Joel that if the nation would repent, God would have His spirit over the entire nation and they would prophesy, including male and female slaves.[133]

The prophet Zechariah saw at night a man riding a red horse among myrtle trees with horses of different colors behind him. Zechariah asked the angel who was speaking to him: "What are these?" The man who stood among the myrtles answered the angel that God had sent these to wander about the land. The messengers reported to the angel of God that the land was quiet. The angel asked God for how long He would not have mercy on Jerusalem. God answered the angel with comforting words. The angel turned to Zechariah and told him that God was jealous for Jerusalem a great jealousy and that He was very angry at those nations which had harmed Israel more than they had been asked to do. He added that He would again build His house in Jerusalem, and would bring good to the cities of Israel, would console Zion and would choose Jerusalem.

God showed Zechariah four horns (which symbolized the nations) which had scattered Israel among the nations. He showed him four craftsmen, whose task was to terrify and to cast down the horns of the nations. Zechariah also saw a man carrying a measuring line, who had come to measure Jerusalem. Another angel came and instructed the first angel to tell the prophet that there would be a wall around Jerusalem because of the large number of people and animals which would be in it.[134]

God showed the following to the prophet Zechariah: Joshua the High Priest was standing before an angel of God and to his right was Satan, who stood to accuse him. God, who chose Jerusalem, was angry at Satan and told him that Joshua was a brand rescued from the fire. The angel ordered the people standing before him to remove the soiled clothes of the High Priest,

132 Ibid., 47:1–12.
133 Joel 3:1–2.
134 Zechariah 1:7–2:9.

and he removed all his sins. The angel ordered that Joshua the High Priest be dressed in clothes befitting the Priesthood.[135]

The angel who spoke to him showed Zechariah a golden candelabrum with seven lamps, and decorations of two olives next to each bowl of the candelabrum. He told him that Zerubabel needed to act not by might nor by power, but by the spirit of God.[136]

Zechariah saw two olive branches on both sides of the candelabrum, as well as two olive branches on the two golden spouts. They represented the two anointed ones who stand by the Lord of the Earth.[137]

Zechariah saw a flying scroll. The angel told him that that represented the curse which went out over the entire earth. Whoever steals or swears falsely would be punished according to the punishment prescribed in the scroll.[138]

The angel showed Zechariah an ephah measure, with a woman sitting inside it. Zechariah asked what this was, and the angel answered that it was Wickedness which had been cast into the basket. It was then closed with a lead weight. Zechariah saw her carried between heaven and earth by two women with wings. The angel told him that the women were taking the ephah to the land of Shinar so that it would remain there permanently.[139]

Zechariah saw four chariots with horses of different colors coming out between two copper hills. Zechariah asked the angel who was with him: "What are these?" The angel answered that these are the four winds of heaven which go forth from before the Lord of the Earth to the north, the south, and to move about the land. Those which go out to the north did God's will.[140]

The Visions of Daniel

In the first year of Belshazzar, king of Babylon, Daniel dreamed a dream at night. He saw the four winds of heaven breaking forth from the sea. Four

---

135 Ibid., 3:1–10.
136 Ibid., 4:1–7.
137 Ibid., 4:11–14.
138 Ibid., 5:1–4.
139 Ibid., 5:5–11.
140 Ibid., 6:1–8.

great beasts arose from the sea, all different from one another. The Ancient of Days sat on a throne, and a river of fire flowed from before Him. Many thousands ministered to Him, with many others standing before Him. The fourth beast was killed, while dominion was taken away from the others.

One who looked like a person came to the Ancient of Days, and He gave him eternal dominion over all the nations and languages. Daniel asked one of those standing there to explain what he was seeing. The man explained to him what he saw, and said that rule over the world would be given to the nation of the Most Holy One.[141]

In the third year of Belshazzar, Daniel had a vision. In his vision, he saw a ram with two horns, which was so strong that no animal could withstand it, until a young goat came from the west and vanquished it. A horn of the goat thrust part of the heavenly host to the earth and trampled them. In addition, it also removed the daily sacrifice from the prince of the host and cast down the Temple. One of the holy ones asked another: "For how long will the holy place and the host be trampled?" He was told that after two thousand three hundred days the holy one would be victorious. Daniel sought to understand this. He heard the voice of one man saying to the other, to Gabriel, to explain the vision. He was told that the vision was for the End of Days, when the ram would represent Persia and Media, and the male goat, Greece. The horn represents a king who would act against God, but would not succeed.[142]

In the first year of the reign of Darius, Daniel fasted and prayed to God to have mercy upon His nation, upon Jerusalem and upon the Temple. He saw the angel Gabriel, an angel whom he had already seen in his vision, flying to him. Gabriel told him that after the punishment was completed, Jerusalem would be rebuilt. Afterwards it would again be destroyed by a nation which would also be vanquished.[143]

In the third year of the reign of Darius, when Daniel stood by the bank of the Tigris River, he saw a man dressed in linen, with his loins girded with gold, his body was like beryl, his face had the appearance of lightning, his

141 Daniel 7:1–28.
142 Ibid., 8:1–27.
143 Ibid., 9:1–27.

eyes were like torches of fire, his hands and feet like copper, and his voice like a multitude of people. The people who were with Daniel did not see the vision, but a great fear fell upon them and they fled in order to hide. When Daniel saw the great vision, he became weak. When he heard the man's voice, he fell asleep. A hand touched him, which set him on his knees and the palms of his hands. The man told him to stand up and listen. Daniel stood, trembling. The man told him that he was about to inform him of what would happen to his nation in the End of Days.[144] The man told Daniel to write the words without any commentary, and to seal them until the time of the end arrived. Daniel saw two more men standing on both banks of the river. One of them asked the man dressed in linen who was above the waters of the river how long the end of the wonders would be. The man answered him that this would occur when they would finish to smash the hand of the holy people. Daniel did not understand and asked what would occur in the end. The man told him that these matters are closed and sealed until the end time, and Daniel would die and would receive his reward at the End of Days.[145]

• The Purposes of Revelation

For every revelation, whether the type of experience of the revelation is described or not described, there is a purpose. The purposes can be classified into the following groups: instructions and commands, rebuke, beneficence, and self-identification, as well as promises and warnings. In this chapter, examples of these are presented.

Instructions and Commands

God's first revelation was when He spoke to Adam immediately after his creation. God told him to multiply, to fill the land, and to conquer it. God gave Man permission to eat herbs and fruit.[146] (This was also a blessing.)

---

144 Ibid., 10:1–12:3.
145 Ibid., 12:4–13.
146 Genesis 1:28–29.

God instructed Noah to build an ark, so that he, his wife, his sons and their wives and the different types of animals would be saved from the Flood which would devastate the earth and destroy all the other people and animals.[147]

After the Flood, God appeared to him again, and told him to multiply and to fill the earth. God permitted him to eat animals but forbade him to eat any limb of a living animal. God warned him that one is forbidden to shed the blood of a human.[148] (These were blessings along with commandments.)

God appeared to Abram and told him to leave his land for a land which He would show him.[149]

An angel of God appeared to Hagar, who had fled from Sarai, and instructed her to return to Sarai and submit herself to Sarai's hands.[150]

When there was famine in the land, God appeared to Isaac and ordered him not to leave the Land of Israel (because it had been given to him and his descendants).[151]

In Padan Aram, God appeared to Jacob and instructed him to return to the land of his fathers, and promised him that He would be with him.[152]

After Jacob left Padan Aram, Laban pursued him. God appeared to Laban in a dream and told him not to say anything to Jacob, either good or bad.[153]

God first appeared to Moses in a vision of a burning bush which was not consumed, and told him to remove his shoes, because the earth on which he stood was holy.[154] He instructed him to go to Pharaoh and to take the Children of Israel out of Egypt.[155] Moses was commanded to say to the

---

147 Ibid., 6:13–21.
148 Ibid., 9:1–7.
149 Ibid., 12:1.
150 Ibid., 16:7–9.
151 Ibid., 26:2–3.
152 Ibid., 31:3.
153 Ibid., 31:24.
154 Exodus 3:2–5.
155 Ibid., 3:10.

Children of Israel that the God of their fathers had sent him. God ordered him to gather the elders of the nation and to say to them that God would take them out of Egypt. He was to go with the elders of Israel to Pharaoh to ask his agreement to go a distance of three days in the desert to offer sacrifices to God.[156] God ordered Moses to take with him his staff in order to perform signs as proof that God had spoken to him.[157]

God commanded Aaron to go to the desert to meet Moses.[158]

God told Moses to order the Children of Israel to take a lamb for each house, to keep it for four days, and to slaughter it on the fourteenth of the month, in the afternoon. They were to take of the blood of the slaughter and to place it on the doorposts and lintel of the house, as a sign that God would pass over the house when He would come to slaughter the firstborn in Egypt. That was the Passover sacrifice to God.[159] This day would be to them a memorial day, and they would celebrate it as a festival to God throughout all the generations. The Children of Israel were given other commandments related to the Festival of Unleavened Bread.[160]

God ordered Moses to tell the Children of Israel to go back and camp opposite the sea. Pharaoh would pursue them, but God would show Egypt His might.[161] After Pharaoh caught up with them, God told Moses to order the Children of Israel to enter into the sea. He ordered Moses to stretch out his hand over the sea and the sea would split, so that the Children of Israel would go through it on dry land.[162] After the Egyptians chased the Children of Israel into the sea, God instructed Moses to again stretch his hand towards the sea, and the water would return and cover the Egyptians.[163]

After the battle with Amalek at Refidim, God instructed Moses to write about the war as a memorial in a book. He is to tell Joshua that God would

156 Ibid., 3:14–18.
157 Ibid., 4:17.
158 Ibid., 4:27.
159 Ibid., 12:1–11.
160 Ibid., 12:14–20.
161 Ibid., 14:1–4.
162 Ibid., 14:15–16.
163 Ibid., 14:26.

wipe out the memory of Amalek from under the heavens, and that there is a war between God and Amalek in every generation.[164]

At Mount Sinai, God told Moses to tell the Children of Israel that if they listened to His voice and observed His covenant, they would be a Holy Nation to God.[165] After the Children of Israel agreed to obey God's word, God instructed Moses to sanctify them, to give them instructions to prepare for the third day and to warn them against approaching the mountain.[166] On the third day God called Moses and instructed him to go down and again to warn the Children of Israel not to approach the mountain, except for Aaron.[167]

God spoke to the Children of Israel and said the following to them: They may not have other gods or worship them. They may not take God's name in vain. They must remember the Sabbath day to sanctify it and may not perform any work on that day. Each person must honor his father and mother. One is forbidden to murder, to commit adultery, to steal (i.e., kidnap) a person, to give false testimony, or covet anything belonging to another person.[168]

God told Moses to tell the nation that He had spoken to them from heaven. Moses was to warn the nation not to make a god of silver or a god of gold. They were to erect an earthen or stone altar to offer sacrifices to God on them.[169] God instructed Moses about the laws that the Children of Israel must observe.[170] God told him to tell the Children of Israel that they must observe everything which God said and must not worship the gods of the nations of the land to which God was bringing them.[171] They must destroy and demolish them.[172]

---

164 Ibid., 17:14, 16.
165 Ibid., 19:3–6.
166 Ibid., 19:10–13.
167 Ibid., 19:20–22, 24.
168 Ibid., 20:1–14.
169 Ibid., 20:19–23.
170 Ibid., 21:1–23:19.
171 Ibid., 23:22–25.
172 Ibid., 23:32.

God told Moses to ascend to Him on the mountain, in order to receive the stone tablets, upon which God wrote the Torah and the commandments.[173]

God told Moses to tell the Children of Israel to donate towards the building of the Tabernacle based on a plan which He would show them, so that He would dwell among them.[174] God gave Moses instructions regarding the structure of the Tabernacle, its vessels, the clothes of the Priests, the process of the dedication of the Tabernacle and some of the worship procedures in the Tabernacle.[175]

When the nation started worshipping the Golden Calf, God ordered Moses to descend from the mountain.[176]

After the Children of Israel were punished, God ordered Moses to carve out new tablets. God would write on them the text which had been on the first tablets. He also ordered him to ascend the mountain by himself.[177]

God spoke to Moses from the Tent of Assembly and instructed him regarding the laws of offering sacrifices.[178]

God told Aaron the Priest that the Priests are forbidden to drink wine or other alcoholic beverages when they come to the Tent of Assembly, so that they will be able to differentiate between the holy and the profane, and between the ritually impure and ritually pure. It is their duty to teach the Children of Israel the laws which God gave through Moses.[179]

God told Moses and Aaron to inform the Children of Israel which creatures are permissible as food and which are not, as well as all the laws of ritual impurity to humans and to various types of vessels which are caused by creeping things and animal carcasses.[180]

173 Ibid., 24:12.
174 Ibid., 25:1–9.
175 Ibid., 25:10–30:10.
176 Ibid., 32:7–8.
177 Ibid., 34:1–3.
178 Leviticus 1:1–3:17.
179 Ibid., 10:8–11.
180 Ibid., 11:1–47.

After Aaron and Miriam spoke against Moses, God told Moses, Aaron, and Miriam to go to the Tent of Assembly.[181]

An angel of God told Balaam that he could continue to go with the elders of Moab to Balak, but he could only say what God instructed him to say.[182]

God told Joshua to cross the Jordan with the nation and to enter the land which was set aside for the Children of Israel, to be strong, and observe all the laws of the Torah as commanded to him by Moses and study it constantly in order to observe it.[183]

God instructed Gideon to destroy the altar of Baal and to cut down the *asherah* there. An *asherah* is a tree next to the altar of Baal which was meant to honor the mother-goddess Asherah. He was also to build an altar for God, to take a bull of his father's and to offer it as a burnt offering with the wood of the *asherah*.[184]

An angel of God told the wife of Manoah not to drink wine or any alcoholic drink or to eat anything which was ritually impure during her pregnancy, and not to cut the hair of the son which she would bear, because he would be a Nazirite (one who abstains from cutting his hair, etc.) from birth.[185] The angel gave the same instructions to Manoah.[186]

The Children of Israel went up to Bethel to ask God who should lead them in the war against the tribe of Benjamin, and God answered that the tribe of Judah should lead them.[187]

After the tribe of Benjamin vanquished the other tribes on the first days of battle, Phineas, the son of Elazar the Priest, asked God whether they should continue to do battle against the tribe of Benjamin. God told him to

181Numbers 12:4.
182 Ibid., 22:35.
183 Joshua 1:1–9.
184 Judges 6:25–26.
185 Ibid., 13:3–5.
186 Ibid., 13:13–14.
187 Ibid., 20:18.

continue, and he would deliver the tribe of Benjamin into the hands of the other Children of Israel.[188]

God instructed Samuel to listen to the voice of the elders of Israel who wanted a king over them, but to warn them regarding the results of appointing a king and his ruling the nation.[189]

God answered David's questions and instructed him to smite the Philistines and to save Keilah.[190]

An angel of God told Gad that David should erect an altar to God in the threshing floor of Ornan the Jebusite.[191]

God's message to Shemaiah the man of God was to instruct Rehoboam the king of Judah not to fight against his brethren the Children of Israel, because the division of the kingdom was from God.[192]

God ordered Elijah to hide by the Cherith stream, near the Jordan.[193]

God order Jeremiah to go to whichever place God would send him and to say that which God would command him to say.[194]

Rebuke

After Adam and Eve ate of the forbidden fruit, God rebuked them and punished them.[195]

After Cain killed Abel, God rebuked him and told him his punishment.[196]

When Sarah did not believe when the angel said that she would have a son, God told Abraham of His discontent.[197]

God appeared to Avimelech in a dream, and told him that he would soon die because he had taken Sarah, and that she was a married woman.[198]

188 Ibid., 20:28.
189 I Samuel 8:7–9, 22.
190 Ibid., 23:2,4.
191 I Chronicles 21:18.
192 I Kings 12:22–24.
193 Ibid., 17:2–4.
194 Jeremiah 1:7.
195 Genesis 3:9–19.
196 Ibid., 4:9–12.
197 Ibid., 18:13–14.

In the desert, God rebuked the Children of Israel through Moses because there were those who had gone out to gather the manna on the Sabbath.[199]

God admonished Aaron and Miriam because they had not hesitated to speak disparagingly about Moses, even though the level of his prophecy exceeded that of all other prophets.[200]

God told Moses and Aaron that they would not bring the people into the Land of Israel, because they had not believed in Him to sanctify him before the Children of Israel (when Moses smote the rock for water).[201]

An angel of God came to Bochim and said to the Children of Israel that God would not expel the inhabitants of the land speedily from it, because the Children of Israel had not listened to God's voice.[202]

The Children of Israel cried out to God because of Midian. God sent a prophet who rebuked them because they had not listened to His voice and had worshipped the gods of the Emorites.[203]

A man of God came to the old man Eli and rebuked him because his sons scorned the sacrifices which the people brought to offer. As a result, his sons would not live to an old age, and other Priests would serve in the Temple. The sign for that would be that both his sons would die on the same day. The other members of his family would come to bow down to the newly anointed High Priest, and would beg to receive the rights of the priesthood.[204]

God told Samuel that He regretted that He had made Saul the king because Saul had not kept his word.[205]

God sent the prophet Nathan to rebuke David because he had brought about the death of Uriah and had taken Uriah's wife from him. Nathan told

---

198 Ibid., 20:3.
199 Exodus 16:28–29.
200 Numbers 12:5–8.
201 Ibid., 20:12.
202 Judges 2:1–3.
203 Ibid., 6:7–10.
204 I Samuel 2:27–36.
205 Ibid., 15:10–11.

David that even though God had given him the monarchy and the wives of Saul, David had despised God's word and had done evil in His eyes when he had caused Uriah to be killed by the sword of the Ammonites and had taken Uriah's wife, Bathsheba, as his wife. Therefore the sword would never depart from his house. God would raise up against him evil from within his house and would take his wives and give them to his neighbors before the eyes of Israel.[206]

God rebuked Solomon because he had not observed His covenant and His laws. God would therefore divide his kingdom and give it to his servant.[207]

God told the man of God who came to Bethel (to rebuke Jeroboam) that he would not be buried in the burial place of his ancestors, because he had not observed God's commandment not to eat bread or drink water in Bethel.[208]

God told Achiyahu the prophet regarding the arrival of Jeroboam's wife and instructed him what to say to her. She was to go back to Jeroboam and to tell him in the name of God that he was more wicked than all others who had preceded him when he had made other gods to provoke Him. He had sinned and caused Israel to sin. As a result, God would destroy the house of Jeroboam.[209]

God told Jehu, the son of Chanani, to tell Baasha the king of Israel that God had appointed him as the ruler of Israel, but he had caused the nation to sin and had angered God. God would therefore destroy the house of Baasha, as He had done to the house of Jeroboam.[210]

God instructed Elijah to go to Ahab in the vineyard of Naboth and to tell him in God's name: "Have you murdered and then taken possession? In the place where the dogs lapped up the blood of Naboth, the dogs will also lap up your blood." God would kill him and the members of his household,

206 II Samuel 12:1–12.
207 I Kings 11:11–13.
208 Ibid., 13:21–22.
209 Ibid., 14:5–16.
210 Ibid., 16:1–4.

because he had angered God and caused Israel to sin. The dogs would kill his wife Jezebel by the wall of Jezreel.[211]

An angel of God ordered Elijah to go to meet the messengers of King Ahaziahu, who was ill, and to ask them why they were going to the god of Ekron to ask if the king would live, and to tell them that Ahaziahu would die.[212]

Prophets were sent to the ministers of Judah to warn them not to forsake the God of their forefathers and not to worship idols.[213]

The spirit of God rested upon Zechariah, the son of Jehoiada the Priest. He turned to the nation and said to them in the name of God that they would not succeed because they had again turned to foreign gods. They had forsaken God and God had therefore forsaken them.[214]

God sent a prophet to rebuke King Amaziah (who after his victory over the Children of Seir had begun to worship the god of Seir). The prophet asked the king why he now worshipped the god of a nation who had not succeeded in saving his nation in battle.[215]

The prophet Oded told the soldiers of the army of Samaria that their victory over the army of Judah was because God was angry at the sins of Ahaz the king of Judah and his nation. They were therefore forbidden to take the Children of Judah captive as male and female slaves, because they, too, had sinned against God.[216]

The prophet Micah said in the name of God to those prophets who led the nation astray by saying there would be peace, that they would not have any more visions from God and that they would be ashamed because God would not answer them. Micah, however, was given the spirit of God and the ability to tell the Children of Israel their transgressions.[217]

---

211 Ibid., 21:17–24.
212 II Kings 1:3–4.
213 II Chronicles 24:18–19.
214 Ibid., 24:20.
215 Ibid., 25:15.
216 Ibid., 28:9–11.
217 Micah 3:5–8.

King Ahaz refused to choose a sign from God. God, therefore, reproved him and chose the sign that he would have a son who would be called Immanuel. Even before the child could differentiate between good and bad, God would bring the king of Assyria to destroy and conquer the land.[218]

Through His prophets, God said that He would bring evil upon Jerusalem and Judah because of the abominations of Menasseh and because he had caused Judah to sin. Jerusalem would receive the same punishment which Samaria had received. God would abandon the remnant of the nation, and would deliver them into the hands of their enemies, for they had done evil in the eyes of God and had provoked Him.[219]

Jeremiah told the Jews in Egypt that they had sinned when they brought to Egypt the people of Judah while continuing to offer incense to other gods. God would punish them like the inhabitants of Jerusalem and would destroy the remnants of Judah who were in Egypt. Only a few refugees would return to Judah and they would know that God's word had been fulfilled. The sign would be that the king of Egypt would be delivered into the hands of his enemies.[220]

Beneficence

After the Flood, God made a covenant with Noah and his descendants, and with all the creatures who left the ark that He would never again destroy them with a flood.[221]

When Abram went to the Land of Canaan, God appeared to him and promised him that He would give him and his descendants the land.[222]

God sent angels to Lot to rescue him and his family from the overturning of Sodom and Gomorrah.[223]

---

218 Isaiah 7:10–17.
219 II Kings 21:10–15.
220 Jeremiah 44:1–30.
221 Genesis 9:8–17.
222 Ibid., 12:7.
223 Ibid., 19:12–13.

An angel of God called to Hagar from heaven and told her that Ishmael would become a great nation. God opened her eyes and she saw a well from which she gave the boy water to drink.[224]

God told (the pregnant) Rebecca that there were twins in her womb.[225]

God appeared to Isaac and told him that because of the merits of Abraham, He would be with him, bless him, and multiply his seed.[226]

God promised Jacob that He would give the Land of Israel to him and that his descendants would be as the dust of the earth. God would protect him wherever he would go and would not leave him until He had fulfilled His promise.[227]

God told Moses that Pharaoh would send out the Children of Israel with a mighty hand.[228]

God told Moses that He would appear in a pillar of cloud, and that He would speak to him so that the nation would hear and believe in him forever.[229]

God told Joshua that He would magnify him in the eyes of Israel, and the nation would know that God was with him as He had been with Moses.[230]

After the death of Joshua, the Children of Israel asked God who should lead them in their battle against the Canaanites. God answered that the tribe of Judah should lead them, and the land would be delivered into their hands.[231]

An angel of God appeared to Gideon and said to him: "The Lord is with you, O mighty man of valor."[232]

---

224 Ibid., 21:17–19.
225 Ibid., 25:23.
226 Ibid., 26:24.
227 Ibid., 28:13–15.
228 Exodus 6:1.
229 Ibid., 19:9.
230 Joshua 3:7.
231 Judges 1:1–2.
232 Ibid., 6:11–12.

An angel of God appeared to the wife of Manoah and told her that even though she was barren, she would bear a child who would save Israel from the Philistines.[233]

God told Samuel that He would send him a man to anoint a man as the ruler of Israel, to rescue the nation which was suffering under the Philistines. God pointed out Saul, and told Samuel that he was the man.[234]

When David wanted to build a House for God, God sent him Nathan to tell him that he would establish his kingdom. However, the House would be built by his son, from whom God's mercy would never depart.[235]

After the Temple was dedicated, God appeared to Solomon at night and told him that He had heard Solomon's prayer. God would listen to the nation's prayers in this place, and would forgive their sins if they would humble themselves before Him, pray, and turn away from their evil ways.[236]

God told Elijah that Ahab had humbled himself before God, and He would therefore not bring evil in his days but in the days of his son.[237]

God said to Jehu that he had acted properly in the eyes of God regarding the house of Ahab. Therefore four generations of his descendants would sit on the throne of Israel.[238]

God instructed Isaiah to tell King Hezekiah that He had heard his prayer and seen his tears, and that He would heal him on the third day. He would then ascend to the House of God. God would add fifteen years to his life, and would rescue him and the city from the king of Assyria.[239]

God told Ezekiel after showing him the Temple in a vision that He would dwell there among the Children of Israel forever.[240]

God said to the angel who spoke to Zechariah that He would return to Jerusalem in mercy and His house would be built there. He would protect

---

233 Ibid., 13:3–5.
234 I Samuel 9:15–17.
235 II Samuel 7:4–17.
236 II Chronicles 7:12–16.
237 I Kings 21:28–29.
238 II Kings 10:30.
239 Ibid., 20:4–6.
240 Ezekiel 43:7.

Jerusalem. The cities of Israel would again be full of people, due to God's goodness. God would console Zion and would again choose Jerusalem.[241]

Self-Identification

At the Covenant between the Pieces, God identified Himself to Abram as the Lord (*Shem Havaya*) who had taken him out of Ur of the Chaldees to give him the Land of Canaan so that he would inherit it.[242]

Before God changed his name from Abram to Abraham, God identified Himself to Abram as "El Shaddai" (God of Power).[243]

God identified Himself to Isaac as the God of Abraham his father.[244]

God identified Himself to Jacob in the dream of the ladder, as the Lord (*Shem Havaya*), the God of Abraham and Isaac.[245]

Before Jacob went down to Egypt, God identified Himself to him again and presented himself as the God of his fathers.[246]

At the burning bush, God identified Himself to Moses as the God of his father, the God of Abraham, Isaac and Jacob.[247]

Moses asked God to tell him what he was to answer the nation when they would ask him what the name was of the God of their fathers, in whose name he spoke. God told Moses to tell the Children of Israel that His name was "I will be that which I will be, the Lord [*Shem Havaya*], the God of their fathers, the God of Abraham, Isaac and Jacob," and that is how He would be remembered forever.[248]

When Pharaoh, king of Egypt increased his demands of the Children of Israel, God identified Himself to Moses as the Lord (*Shem Havaya*). He identified Himself to Abraham, Isaac and Jacob as "El Shaddai" (God of Power). Even though He had revealed Himself to our forefathers as "I am the

---

241 Zechariah 1:16–17.
242 Genesis 15:7.
243 Ibid., 17:1.
244 Ibid., 26:24.
245 Ibid., 28:13.
246 Ibid., 46:3.
247 Exodus 3:6.
248 Ibid., 3:13–15.

Lord" (*Shem Havaya*), they were not yet able to understand the significance of the name.[249]

When God spoke to the Children of Israel at Mount Sinai, He identified Himself to them as the Lord (*Shem Havaya*) their God, who had taken them out of Egypt.[250]

Promises and Warnings

At Mara, God told the Children of Israel that if they would obey His voice and do that which was correct in His eyes, He would not bring upon them any of the afflictions with which the Egyptians had been afflicted.[251]

God told Moses that when the Children of Israel would worship other gods, forsake Him and violate His covenant, God would forsake them. He would hide His face from them, and they would be destroyed. Many evils and troubles would come upon them.[252]

When Solomon began to build the Temple, God told him that if he would follow in God's statutes, keep His laws and observe His commandments, God would dwell among the Children of Israel in the House which he was building, and would not forsake His nation.[253]

The spirit of God rested on Azariah, the son of Oded. He told Asa, the king of Judah, and the tribes of Judah and Benjamin that God would be with them when they are faithful to Him. If they would seek God, they would find Him, but if they would forsake Him, He would forsake them.[254]

• Covenants

The most significant relationship between God and Man is that of covenants. Covenants are entered into by God with people and they reflect long-term

249 Ibid., 6:2–3. See Rashi, Ibn Ezra.
250 Ibid., 20:2.
251 Ibid., 15:26.
252 Deuteronomy 31:16–18.
253 I Kings 6:11–13.
254 II Chronicles 15:1–2.

commitments. Sometimes signs accompany the entry into a covenant. We will examine the different covenants described in the Bible.

With Noah

The first covenant in the Bible was an implicit one between God and Noah. Noah was a righteous man in a corrupt generation. God promised him that He would keep His covenant with him and would rescue him and his family from the Flood.[255]

The second covenant was explicit. God made a covenant with Noah and all his descendants, and with all the animals which came out of the ark, that He would never again destroy all flesh by means of a flood. God also gave a sign of the covenant between Him and humans throughout the generations, as a remembrance before Him – the rainbow.[256]

With the Forefathers (including Circumcision)

God made a covenant with Abram that the Land of Israel would be given to him and his descendants. The covenant was made: Abram fell into a deep sleep and a smoking furnace and a burning torch passed between the pieces of the animals that Abram had prepared according to God's commandment. God told Abram that his descendants would be strangers in a land which was not their own, and they would be subject to slavery and persecution. After this period, they would return to the Land of Israel to inherit it.[257]

God appeared to Abram and told him that He was making a covenant with him. Abram would be the father of many nations, and his seed would be numerous. God made an eternal covenant with him and his descendants, that He would be their God. The land would be given to them in perpetuity. The sign of the covenant for all generations would be the circumcision of every male on the eighth day from his birth, including slaves. A male who was not

255 Genesis 6:18.
256 Ibid., 9:8–17.
257 Ibid., 15:1–21.

circumcised would be violating the covenant and would be cut off from his nation.[258]

God told Abraham that He would maintain His covenant with Isaac and his descendants as an everlasting covenant.[259]

God remembered His covenant with Abraham, Isaac and Jacob, when the Children of Israel cried out because of their slavery in Egypt.[260]

When Moses was on his way back to Egypt, God wanted to kill him. God spared him only after Tzipporah, Moses's wife, circumcised his son.[261]

After Moses's complaint to God that his attempts to take the nation out of Egypt had only resulted in added burdens upon the people, God told him that He had made a covenant with Abraham, Isaac and Jacob, to give them the Land of Canaan. He had heard the cry of the Children of Israel and remembered the covenant. He would therefore redeem them from Egypt. They would be His nation and He would be their God, and He would bring them to the land which He had promised to their fathers.[262]

Someone who is uncircumcised is forbidden to eat of the Passover sacrifice. Therefore a slave or convert may only eat of the Passover sacrifice if he has been circumcised.[263]

God instructed Moses to tell the Children of Israel that they were to circumcise their sons on the eighth day from their birth.[264]

At Sinai

At Mount Sinai, God told Moses to tell the Children of Israel that if they would listen to His voice and observe His covenant, they would be special to Him among all the nations, a kingdom of priests and a holy nation.[265] The content of the covenant is the Ten Commandments.[266]

---

258 Ibid., 17:1–14.
259 Ibid., 17:19, 21.
260 Exodus 2:24.
261 Ibid., 4:24–26.
262 Ibid., 6:2–8.
263 Ibid., 12:43–48.
264 Leviticus 12:3.
265 Exodus 19:5–6.

Moses descended from the mountain and gave the Children of Israel God's words and His commandments. They agreed to observe them. Moses wrote God's words and built an altar. The young men of the Children of Israel offered burnt sacrifices. Moses placed half of the blood in bowls and sprinkled the other half on the altar. He read to the Children of Israel the words of the covenant and they responded, "We will do and listen to God's words." Moses sprinkled on them of the blood of the sacrifices as a confirmation of the covenant made between them and God.[267]

Moses ascended to the mountain and God gave him two stone tablets upon which were written the words of the covenant – the words which God had spoken to the nation, on the mountain from the midst of the fire, on the day of assembly. They were given to Moses after forty days, during which he neither ate nor drank.[268] The covenant was not only with the Children of Israel who were present at Mount Horeb, but with all the Children of Israel throughout history.[269]

An eternal covenant between God and the Children of Israel is the observance of the Sabbath by the Children of Israel throughout its generations. The observance of the Sabbath is the sign that God created the heavens and the earth in six days and rested from His work on the seventh day.[270]

After God revealed His attributes to Moses, He told Moses that He would make another covenant with the Children of Israel and would do wondrous deeds which would arouse fear. The Children of Israel had to observe that which God would command.[271] God instructed Moses to write down the details of these matters as a condition of the covenant.[272]

---

266 Deuteronomy 4:13.
267 Exodus 24:1–8.
268 Ibid., 31:18; Deuteronomy 4:13; 9:10–11.
269 Deuteronomy 5:3.
270 Exodus 31:16–17.
271 Ibid., 34:10–11.
272 Exodus 34:27. See Rashbam.

If the Children of Israel observe God's commandments, He will keep His covenant with them.[273]

If the Children of Israel do not observe God's commandments and violate the covenant, God will bring terror upon them, diseases, and calamities, and their enemies will eat the produce of the land.[274]

If the Children of Israel confess their sins and that of their fathers and humble their hearts, God will remember His covenant with their forefathers.[275] When the Nation of Israel returns to God, God will not punish it and will not forget the covenant He made to its forefathers.[276] Even at the time that the nation is in exile in the lands of its enemies, God will not destroy it. He will remember His covenant with the nation, the covenant of its ancestors, when He took them out of Egypt, in sight of the other nations, to be their God.[277]

The Children of Israel must ensure that they do not forget the covenant which God made with them and must not turn to other gods.[278]

God is faithful to keep the covenant and the kindness which He swore to the forefathers and to those who love Him for a thousand generations. This is so, as long as the Children of Israel listen to His commandments and keep them.[279] The Children of Israel must remember that God alone is the One who gives them the ability to act and be successful in all their ventures, in order to keep the covenant which He swore to their forefathers.[280]

Salt is a sign of the covenant between God and His nation. One must therefore put salt on every meal offering.[281]

---

273 Leviticus 26:3–9.
274 Ibid., 26:14–17.
275 Ibid., 26:40–42.
276 Deuteronomy 4:30–31.
277 Leviticus 26:44–45.
278 Deuteronomy 4:23–24.
279 Ibid., 7:9, 12.
280 Ibid., 8:18.
281 Leviticus 2:13.

In the Land of Moab

In Moab, before the Children of Israel entered the Land of Israel, God commanded Moses to make another covenant between Him and the Children of Israel in addition to the covenant which He had made with them at Horeb.[282] The conditions of this covenant are the observance of the commandments written in the Torah. If the Children of Israel observe them, they will be blessed. If not – they will be cursed. The reciting of the blessings and the curses will take place on Mount Gerizim and Mount Ebal.[283]

If the Children of Israel keep the covenant, they will succeed in whatever they do.[284] All of the Children of Israel who were in the Land of Moab before the entry into the Land of Israel were included in God's covenant and in the curses (for not keeping the covenant). God will be their God and they will be His people. The covenant and the curse were made not only with those who were present, but also with all those who were not present (the future generations).[285] If an individual or a tribe turns away from God and worships other gods, the curse will apply to that individual or tribe., The other nations will say that the reason for this was that the individual or tribe did not keep the covenant.[286] If the Children of Israel leave God and turn to other gods, this will be a violation of the covenant. God will abandon the nation and will ignore it. Many evils and troubles will befall it.[287]

With the Priests

A covenant was made between God and the Priests. All the special gifts given to Aaron will belong to him and his descendants eternally, an everlasting covenant of salt.[288]

The covenant with the Priests will not be violated.[289]

---

282 Deuteronomy 28:69.
283 Ibid., 27:1–28:68.
284 Ibid., 29:8.
285 Ibid., 29:9–14.
286 Ibid., 29:17–27.
287 Ibid., 31:16–17.
288 Numbers 18:19.
289 Jeremiah 33:20–22.

With Phineas

Phineas, Aaron's grandson, was zealous for God and turned away God's wrath from the Children of Israel when they started being licentious with the daughters of Moab to worship Baal Peor. He killed an Israelite leader and a Midianite woman who had violated God's commandments publicly. God therefore gave him a covenant of peace and an eternal covenant of priesthood.[290]

After Entering the Land of Israel

At the time of the conquest of the Land of Israel, Achan took of the booty of Jericho and violated the prohibition which Joshua had declared about the city. He was burned by fire along with everything of his, because he had violated God's covenant.[291]

After Joshua's death, an angel of God came to the Children of Israel and reminded them that God's agreement never to violate His covenant with them depended on their not making any covenant with the inhabitants of the land. It was their duty to destroy these peoples' altars. As they had already violated the covenant, God would not evict the inhabitants of the land from before them, and the inhabitants would be a source of trouble.[292]

The Era of the Kings

God made a covenant with David and swore to him that his kingdom would continue to his children.[293] God therefore did not want to destroy the House of David at the time when Jehoram was king.[294] The covenant with the House of David and with the Priests and Levites would not be violated as long as day and night would still come in rotation.[295]

God told Solomon that He would take his kingdom away from him, except for the tribe of Judah, as he had not observed God's covenant and His statutes.[296]

---

290 Numbers 25:10–13.
291 Joshua 7:10–15, 18.
292 Judges 2:1–3.
293 Psalms 89:4–5.
294 II Chronicles 21:6–7.
295 Jeremiah 33:20–22.
296 I Kings 11:11.

After Jehoash was anointed as King of Judah and after the killing of Ataliah, Jehoiada the Priest renewed the covenant between God and the king and nation: the nation would be God's nation.[297]

God was compassionate to Israel in the days of Jehoash, because of the covenant with their forefathers. Therefore, at that time, He did not want to destroy them, to cast them away from His presence.[298]

The nations brought to Samaria by the king of Assyria after the destruction of the Kingdom of Israel were God-fearing, but also worshipped other gods. This was unlike the covenant which God had made with the Children of Israel not to worship other gods, which obligates all those who fear God not to worship other gods.[299]

After Josiah, king of Judah, read before the elders of the nation, all the people of Judah and the residents of Jerusalem, the Priests and the Levites, old and young, the words of the Book of the Covenant which was found in the House of God, he made a covenant before God to observe His commandments with all his heart and all his soul and to keep all the words of the covenant written in the book, he and all the people of Judah with him.[300]

After the Return to the Land of Israel

Ezra persuaded the nation to make a covenant with God and to send away all the foreign wives and their children, by the advice of God and according to the Torah.[301]

In the Words of the Prophets

Isaiah conveyed the words of God to the nation, where God stated that at a favorable time He would make a covenant with the Children of Israel to be His nation. God would lead them and would bring them from all places to have them inherit the Land of Israel, and would safeguard their welfare

297 II Kings 11:17.
298 Ibid., 13:23.
299 Ibid., 17:32–39.
300 II Chronicles 34:31–33.
301 Ezra 10:2–5.

and redemption.[302] When the Children of Israel listen to God's voice, God will make with them an eternal covenant. He will establish the monarchy of the House of David as testimony to all the nations that God's word was kept, and they will come to the nation of Israel because God had glorified His nation.[303] God will make a covenant with the nation of Israel: His spirit and words will be with the nation eternally.[304] God will make an eternal covenant with the nation of Israel and all the other nations will recognize that the nation of Israel is the nation which God blessed.[305]

The prophet Jeremiah prophesied about a new covenant between God and the nation of Israel (after the nation had violated the previous covenant): the Torah will be written in the hearts of the Children of Israel, God will be their God and they will be His nation. Everyone will know and recognize that it is God who forgives them and who will no longer remember their sins.[306] God will make an eternal covenant with them. He will do good to them and will put His fear in their hearts.[307]

The prophet Ezekiel prophesied in the name of God that God will remember the covenant which He made with the nation of Israel. He will make an eternal covenant with Jerusalem and the nation will acknowledge God and be ashamed of its sins.[308]

In the future, God will make a covenant of peace with His nation, which will live in its land in security.[309]

The prophet Hosea said in the name of God that He would make a covenant with the nation and remove from them idol worship and the threats of wild animals and of a state of war, so that they can live in security. This would occur when the nation obeys God as it did when they left Egypt.[310]

302 Isaiah 49:8–12.
303 Ibid., 55:3–5.
304 Ibid., 59:21.
305 Ibid., 61:8–9.
306 Jeremiah 31:30–33.
307 Ibid., 32:40.
308 Ezekiel 16:60–63.
309 Ibid., 34:25.
310 Hosea 2:16–20.

The Implications of Keeping the Covenant or Violating It during the Era of the Prophets

The prophet Isaiah noted that God had preserved the nation of Israel and had made a covenant with it so that it would be a light to the nations to remove them from their darkness.[311]

He said in the name of God that those eunuchs who observe God's covenant and keep the Sabbath would have an everlasting place and name in God's House. And for those foreigners who keep God's covenant, God would cause them to rejoice in Jerusalem and the Temple and would favorably accept their sacrifices.[312]

The prophet Ezekiel prophesied in the name of God that when God would gather together Israel from among the other nations, He would judge the Children of Israel one by one, and bring into the bond of the covenant all those who are not rebellious and sinners.[313]

God told the prophet Haggai to tell Zerubavel, Joshua the High Priest and the entire nation that they should not hesitate to build the House, because God made a covenant with them when they left Egypt and His spirit is in their midst.[314]

God told the prophet Zechariah that because of the merit of the covenant, He would send out the prisoners of Zion from exile.[315]

The prophet Malachi said in the name of God that He would send the angel of the covenant to God's Palace. He would purify the Children of Levi who would offer a meal offering to God in righteousness. Then the meal offering of Judah and Jerusalem would be pleasing to God as in the past.[316]

In his psalm, Assaf said that God would gather together His righteous ones, who had made a covenant with Him with sacrifices.[317]

---

311 Isaiah 42:6–7.
312 Ibid., 56:4–7.
313 Ezekiel 20:34–38.
314 Haggai 2:4–5.
315 Zechariah 9:11.
316 Malachi 3:1–4.
317 Psalms 50:5.

God remembered His covenant with Abraham, Isaac and Jacob that the Land of Israel would be given to the Children of Israel as an eternal covenant.[318]

At a difficult time for the nation of Israel, God heard their prayer and remembered His covenant with them, and saved them.[319]

God supplies the needs of those who fear Him and frees His nation, because He always remembers the covenant which He made with them.[320]

If David's descendants keep God's covenant and His commandments, they will sit on David's throne forever.[321]

Jeremiah rebuked the people of Judah and Jerusalem who had violated God's covenant which He had made with them when Israel left Egypt (to listen to His voice and to keep His commandments, so that they would be His nation and He would be their God). They had not listened to His voice and thus the words of the covenant (and the curses) would apply to them.[322]

The prophet Jeremiah prophesied in the palace of the king of Judah that after the destruction, the other nations would say that God had destroyed the city because the people of the city had forsaken God's covenant and had worshipped other gods.[323]

The Children of Israel, who had enslaved their slaves again after six years had passed, had violated the covenant between them and God. God would therefore bring upon them the sword, pestilence and famine. The king and his ministers would be delivered into the hands of their enemies and the land would be laid waste.[324]

God instructed Ezekiel to remind Jerusalem (and its inhabitants) that God would make a covenant with it, and the city would be His.[325] Jerusalem

---

318 Ibid., 105:8–11.
319 Ibid., 106:44–46.
320 Ibid., 111:5,9.
321 Ibid., 132:12.
322 Jeremiah 11:1–8.
323 Ibid., 22:8–9.
324 Ibid., 34:13–22.
325 Ezekiel 16:8.

had violated the covenant. Much suffering would come on it because of the abominations and sins which it had perpetrated.[326]

God told Ezekiel that the king of Babylon had made a covenant with a person of the royal dynasty. However the new king had rebelled, and had sent messengers to Egypt asking for aid. Therefore the new king, who had violated the oath of the previous king would die with him in Babylon. God would punish him because he had violated the covenant with Babylon, as if it had been a covenant with God.[327]

God instructed Ezekiel to speak to the nation and to tell them that they had desecrated His house through their abominations. They had brought into the Temple foreigners, of uncircumcised heart and flesh. They had violated His covenant because of their abominations. They had not guarded the holiness of the Temple by themselves, but had placed there foreign guards.[328]

The prophet Hosea said in the name of God that an enemy would come up upon the House of God, because the Children of Israel had violated God's covenant and had sinned against His Torah.[329]

The prophet Malachi brought God's word to the Priests. God had made a covenant with the tribe of Levi, a covenant of life and peace, because they were God-fearing. They spoke the Torah of truth, with uprightness and the knowledge of God. The nation sought Torah from them, for they were like messengers of God. However, the Priests of his days had turned away from the proper path and had caused others to err. They had violated the covenant of the tribe of Levi. God would therefore make them contemptible and base in the eyes of the nation.[330]

The prophet also rebuked the people of Israel and told them that all have a single Father, and a single God created them. Every person is therefore forbidden to act treacherously to another and to profane the covenant of the fathers. God's altar would be covered with tears, because God would no

326 Ibid., 16:57–59.
327 Ibid., 17:11–21.
328 Ibid., 44:6–8.
329 Hosea 8:1–3.
330 Malachi 2:4–9.

longer accept their meal offerings, for He was a witness to their treachery against the covenant of their youth.[331]

• Signs

Signs by God express a special relationship between Him and those who receive these signs.

The rainbow in the cloud is a sign of the covenant between God and Noah –that He would not destroy all life by means of a flood.[332]

Circumcision is a sign of the covenant between God and Abraham – that God would give him and his descendants the Land of Israel and He would be their God.[333]

God instructed the Children of Israel that on the night that the Egyptian firstborn were to be killed, they should take of the blood of the lamb which they had slaughtered, and daub it on the doorposts and lintels of their homes. The blood would be a sign to God, and none of the Children of Israel would be harmed.[334]

Moses instructed the Children of Israel in the name of God to place a sign on their arms and a memorial above their eyes so that God's Torah would be with them eternally, as well as a memorial of the Exodus from Egypt.[335]

The sign which must be bound on the arm and above the eyes includes the verses which state that God is the God of Israel, that He is One, and that the Children of Israel must love Him with all their hearts, all their souls, and all their possessions.[336] It also includes verses which describe the reward for observing God's commandments, the love of God, and serving Him with all one's heart and soul, and the punishment for worshipping other gods.[337]

---

331 Ibid., 2:10–16.
332 Genesis 9:12–17.
333 Ibid., 17:1–14.
334 Exodus 12:3–13.
335 Ibid., 13:9.
336 Deuteronomy 6:4–8. See Mechilta (Exodus 13:9).
337 Deuteronomy 11:13–18.

Observing the Sabbath is a sign for all generations that God sanctified the Children of Israel, as well as that God created the world in six days and rested on the seventh day.[338]

God instructed Elazar, the son of Aaron the Priest, to make of the censers which the two hundred and fifty members of Korah's group had brought plates for the altar. It would be a sign and memorial to the Children of Israel that one who is not a Priest is forbidden to offer up incense, so that his fate should not be like that of Korah and his group.[339]

Aaron's rod, which had blossomed, was brought into the Tent of Testimony as a sign that God had chosen him, the purpose of this being to prevent any future rebellion.[340]

On the day that Egypt leaves Judah, they will erect an altar in the Land of Egypt and a pillar on its border as a sign and witness that God will rescue Egypt when they turn to Him because they recognize Him and serve Him.[341]

• SUMMARY

God's revelations to people are evidence of His presence in the world and His involvement in its course. These revelations are mentioned at different periods, from Adam until the prophets and Daniel. In some of these, the experience of the Revelation is described, and in others there is no description, but only a statement that God spoke to a person. There are many types of experiences of Revelation: visions, images, voices, the receiving of the Tablets, angels, clear signs and wonders, Divine inspiration, the *Urim* and *Thummim* of the High Priest, and signs by the prophets.

The purposes of the revelations are variegated: commands, instructions as to how to act, reproof, beneficence, self-identification, and promises and warnings.

Within the framework of the revelations, there were also covenants made between God and man. In most cases, the covenant involved actions by

338 Exodus 31:12–17.
339 Numbers 17:1–5.
340 Ibid., 17:25.
341 Isaiah 19:19–21.

people, either before or after the making of the covenant. Covenants were made with Noah, with the forefathers, and with the Nation of Israel at Mount Sinai and in Moab. Special covenants were made with the Priests and with Phineas. Even after the Children of Israel entered the Land of Israel, at the time they lived there and after they returned to it, covenants were made. Some of these were mentioned by the prophets. God will act kindly to the Children of Israel if they keep their part in the covenants, but He will punish them if they violate them.

Within the framework of some of these revelations, God gave various signs in order to express the relationship between Him and those who received the sign.

Chapter 5 – God's Commandments and His Demands

God's commandments and demands as specified in the Bible may be divided into two types: those limited to a specific time and those intended to be kept at all times.

• Instructions for a Specific Time

To Adam

Adam was forbidden to eat of the tree of knowledge of good and evil.[1,2] This commandment was given in order to clarify to Adam that God expected him to listen to Him.

To Noah

Noah was commanded to build an ark and to bring inside it his entire family and representatives of all the animals that lived on the earth, in order to save them from the Flood.[3]

During the Era of the Forefathers

Abram was commanded to go to the land which God would show him.

---

1 Genesis 2:16–17.

2 Originally, the commandment not to eat of the tree of knowledge was not limited to a specific time period. However, it did not remain as a commandment for future generations, and that is why it is brought here.

3 Genesis 6:13–7:4.

(The effectiveness of the blessing to his descendants was dependent on his obeying this instruction.)[4]

To confirm that Abram and his descendants would inherit the Land of Israel, God ordered Abram to prepare a heifer, a goat, a ram, a turtle-dove and a pigeon as a sacrifice.[5]

Hagar was commanded to return and to submit to Sarai. God promised her that her descendants would be so numerous that they could not be counted.[6]

God commanded Abraham to circumcise himself, all his descendants, and all those who were born in his household, as a sign of the covenant between him and God.[7]

Lot was commanded by the angels to leave the city with his family in order to be saved from the destruction of Sodom and Gomorrah. Likewise, Lot was told that he and his family were forbidden to look backward as they were fleeing, because it was essential to cut themselves off from the sin there.[8]

God commanded Abraham to bring Isaac as an offering on a mountain which God would show him – another test of Abraham).[9] God instructed him not to slaughter Isaac.[10] The aim of the test of Abraham was achieved. That was why there was the need to save Isaac.

God commanded Isaac not to leave the Land of Israel, even though there was a famine in the land.[11]

God instructed Jacob to leave Aram Naharayim and to return to the land of his fathers. If he would do so, God would be with him.[12]

When Laban pursued Jacob, God told him not to speak to Jacob, either positively or negatively.[13]

---

4 Ibid., 12:1–3.
5 Ibid., 15:9–21
6 Ibid., 16:9–12.
7 Ibid., 17:9–13.
8 Ibid., 19:12–17.
9 Ibid., 22:1–2.
10 Ibid., 22:11–12.
11 Ibid., 26:2–3.
12 Ibid., 31:3.
13 Ibid., 31:24.

God commanded Jacob to go to Bethel, to live there and to erect an altar as a sign of thanks that God had answered him when he had fled from Esau.[14]

At the Time of the Exodus from Egypt

God said to Moses, who was standing by the burning bush which was not consumed to take off his shoes, because he was standing on holy ground.[15]

God gave various orders as part of His overall plans for history.

God instructed Moses to gather the elders of the nation and to tell them that the Lord, the God of their fathers had appeared to him, and told him of the end of the enslavement in Egypt and the ascent of the Children of Israel to the Land of Israel. Moses and the elders of the nation would have to go to the king of Egypt and ask him for permission to go on a three-day journey into the desert to offer sacrifices to God.[16]

God ordered Moses to go as His messenger to Pharaoh and He would tell Moses what to say.[17] When Moses refused, God ordered him to tell His words to Aaron. He would talk in Moses's name in accordance with the instructions which they would receive from God.[18] God ordered Aaron to go meet Moses in the desert.[19]

God also ordered Moses to take his staff for signs[20] and to return to Egypt[21] to perform these miracles before Pharaoh.[22]

God told Moses to tell Pharaoh that he had to send Israel away, and if he would not do so, God would kill his firstborn son.[23]

---

14 Ibid., 35:1.
15 Exodus 3:5.
16 Ibid., 3:16–18
17 Ibid., 4:12.
18 Ibid., 4:14–16.
19 Ibid., 4:27.
20 Ibid., 4:17.
21 Ibid., 4:19.
22 Ibid., 4:21.
23 Ibid., 4:22–23.

After Pharaoh's first negative reply, God ordered Moses to go to Pharaoh again and to tell him God's word with the aid of Aaron, who would speak directly to Pharaoh.[24] Many times God ordered Moses to come to Pharaoh, to show him signs, to demand that the nation be sent away, and to bring various plagues upon Egypt.[25]

Before the plague of hail, God told Moses to tell Pharaoh to bring back all the people and cattle from the fields, so that they would not be killed by the hail.[26] Only those in Egypt who feared God saved their own lives and their property.[27]

Before the last plague, God instructed the Children of Israel to borrow silver and gold vessels from their neighbors.[28] He ordered every family among the Children of Israel to prepare a one-year-old male animal, either a lamb or a goat, to keep it for four days, and to slaughter it on the fourteenth of the month, at twilight. They had to take of the blood of the slaughtered animal and use it to mark the doorposts and lintels of their doors. God commanded them to eat the meat that night, grilled over a fire, with unleavened bread and bitter herbs, to eat it in haste while they were ready to leave, and in the morning to burn up whatever meat was left. Obeying these orders would be considered as a sacrifice (the Passover sacrifice) to God.[29] The blood of the Passover sacrifice would be a sign that God would pass over that house when He struck the firstborn of Egypt.[30]

God told Moses that the Children of Israel had to return and camp before the sea so that Pharaoh would pursue them, and God would make it difficult for Pharaoh and his army; then Egypt would know that God is the Lord.[31] God told Moses to order the Children of Israel to enter into the sea because of the Egyptians who were pursuing them. Moses had to raise up his

---

24 Ibid., 6:29; 7:2.
25 Ibid., 7:8–9, 14–18, 19, 26–29; 8:1, 12, 16–19; 9:1–5, 8–9, 13–19, 22; 10:1–6, 12, 21.
26 Ibid., 9:19.
27 Ibid., 9:20–21.
28 Ibid., 11:1–2.
29 Ibid., 12:3–11.
30 Ibid., 12:12–13.
31 Ibid., 14:1–4.

staff and then the sea would split into two and the Children of Israel would cross it on dry land.[32] After the Children of Israel had passed through, God told Moses to raise his hands toward the sea so that the sea would return and cover the Egyptian army which was pursuing the Children of Israel. This was so that the Children of Israel would fear God and would believe in Him and His servant Moses.[33]

In the Desert before the Events at Mount Sinai

God told Moses that He would bring down bread from heaven – manna. The people were told to collect it daily. Through this, God would test them to see if they would obey His Torah.[34] Moses commanded the nation in God's name not to leave over any manna until the following morning.[35] On the Sabbath, they were forbidden to go out to collect the manna.[36] God commanded Moses to place manna in a jar, as a memorial for future generations.[37]

God instructed Moses to write as a memorial in a book and to tell Joshua that God would erase the memory of Amalek from underneath the heavens and that there is a war of God against Amalek from generation to generation.[38]

At Mount Sinai

When the Children of Israel reached Mount Sinai, God told Moses to remind them how they had left Egypt, and to say that if they would listen to His voice and keep His covenant, they would be a special nation to Him among the nations.[39]

---

32 Ibid., 14:15–16.
33 Ibid., 14:26, 31.
34 Ibid., 16:4–5.
35 Ibid., 16:19.
36 Ibid., 16:25–29.
37 Ibid., 16:32–34.
38 Ibid., 17:14, 16.
39 Ibid., 19:3–6.

God told Moses to gather together the nation to hear God's words, so that they would learn to fear God all the days that they would live on the earth and so that they would teach their children. God also commanded Moses to teach all the statutes and ordinances which they had to keep in the land which they would inherit.[40]

He ordered Moses to tell the Children of Israel to prepare for the third day and to wash their clothes. They were forbidden to climb the mountain or to touch it lest they die – until the sound of the blowing of the *shofar*.[41]

God gave Moses orders for the nation and for the Priests about standing next to Mount Sinai and warned them not to approach it.[42] After the Children of Israel heard the word of God, He instructed Moses and Aaron, Nadav and Avihu and seventy of the elders of Israel to come close and to bow down from a distance.[43] God ordered Moses to ascend the mountain to receive the stone tablets upon which God had inscribed the Torah and the commandments to teach them to the Children of Israel.[44]

The Children of Israel feared that they might die in the wake of the sights and sounds at Mount Sinai. They asked to hear God's word indirectly. God instructed them to return to their tents while Moses would stand before God to hear His words, and afterwards would teach the nation all the statutes, commandments, and ordinances.[45]

Towards the Conquest of the Land

God told Moses that it was forbidden for the Children of Israel to make a covenant with the Seven Nations of the Land of Israel or to take pity on them.[46] The Children of Israel were forbidden to take silver and gold from

40 Deuteronomy 4:10–14.
41 Exodus 19:10–13.
42 Ibid., 19:20–22, 24.
43 Ibid., 24:1–2.
44 Ibid., 24:12.
45 Deuteronomy 5:19–28.
46 Ibid., 7:2.

these nations, so that they should not be guilty of idol worship. The Children of Israel had to detest them because they were an abomination to God.[47]

Towards the Preparation of the Tabernacle

God told Moses to speak to the Children of Israel and to tell them to contribute, each according to his heart,, and to build the Tabernacle and its utensils based on the pattern which God had shown to Moses.[48]

God ordered Moses to make holy garments for Aaron. They would be for his glory and splendor.[49]

God instructed Moses on how to compound the anointing oil.[50] He gave instructions to Moses how to sanctify the Priests who would officiate before God, with the anointing oil, with the priestly garments, and with special sacrifices.[51]

God instructed Moses to make a basin for washing, to place it between the Tent of Assembly and the altar, and to fill it with water.[52]

God instructed Moses to anoint the Tabernacle and its utensils, as well as Aaron and his sons with the anointing oil.[53]

God instructed Moses on how to compound the incense.[54]

God told Moses that Betzalel and Oholiav, together with other skilled craftsmen in whose hearts God had given skill, were to build the Tabernacle and its utensils as commanded by God to Moses.[55]

After the Golden Calf

When the Children of Israel worshipped the Golden Calf, God instructed Moses to go down to them from the mountain.[56, 57]

---

47 Ibid., 7:25–26.
48 Exodus 25:1–9.
49 Ibid., 28:2.
50 Ibid., 30:22–25.
51 Ibid., 29:1–37.
52 Ibid., 30:17–18.
53 Ibid., 30:26–30.
54 Ibid., 30:34–36.
55 Ibid., 31:1–11.
56 Ibid., 32:7–8.

God instructed Moses to continue to lead the people.[58] God instructed Moses and the nation to ascend to the land which had been promised to their forefathers.[59] Moses was to go before them and to bring them to the land which God had sworn to their forefathers to give to them and to inherit it.[60] The Children of Israel were to remove the jewelry which they had worn at Mount Horeb.[61]

After Moses requested that God remain with the Children of Israel, God instructed him to carve out two stone tablets so that God would inscribe on them the words which had been inscribed on the first tablets,[62] to go up to the mountain alone,[63] and to write the words of the covenant between Him and the Nation of Israel (see p. 48).[64] God commanded that a wooden box be made into which the second tablets were to be placed.[65]

The Completion of the Erecting of the Tabernacle

God instructed Moses to erect the Tabernacle of the Tent of Assembly, to place inside it its utensils and to anoint them, to bring Aaron and his sons to the entrance of the Tent of Assembly, to wash them with water, to dress them in the holy garments, and to anoint them.[66]

Moses told Aaron and his sons, after they had been anointed with the anointing oil, to remain in the Tent of Assembly for seven days, by God's command, and to perform guard duty for God.[67] On the eighth day, the day of the dedication of the Tabernacle, Aaron and his sons were to offer a sin

57 God's words to Moses that Moses should allow Him to destroy the nation (Exodus 32:9–10) were not an instruction to Moses. God did not need Moses's permission. They were phrased as a request, and that is why they invited a response (Exodus 32:11–13).

58 Exodus 32:34.

59 Ibid., 33:1–3.

60 Deuteronomy 10:11.

61 Exodus 33:5.

62 Ibid., 34:1.

63 Ibid., 34:2–3.

64 Ibid., 34:27.

65 Deuteronomy 10:1–2.

66 Exodus 40:1–15.

67 Leviticus 8:33–35.

offering and a burnt offering, and the Children of Israel were to offer a sin offering, two burnt offerings, two peace offerings, and a meal offering, for on that day God would appear to them.[68]

God instructed Moses to give the Levites, as required for their work, the wagons and the cattle which the tribal leaders of Israel had brought on the day the Tabernacle was dedicated.[69]

God told Moses that each tribal leader was to offer the sacrifice of the dedication of the Tabernacle with a different tribal leader each day, based on the order of the way the tribes camped and traveled in the desert.[70]

In the Desert

God commanded Moses and Aaron to count, by family, every male among the Children of Israel from the age of twenty years and up who would be able to serve in the army.[71]

God instructed Moses not to count the Levites (in the census of those who would go out to the army), but to appoint them over the Tabernacle and its utensils, and over carrying the Tabernacle and its utensils when the Children of Israel traveled. They were to camp around it.[72]

God instructed the Children of Israel about the order of how they would camp by tribes around the Tent of Assembly.[73]

God instructed Moses to count every male a month old or older of the tribe of Levi.[74] He also instructed him to count all the firstborn males a month old or older among the Children of Israel. The Levites would serve God in place of them, and the firstborn cattle of the Levites would be in place of the firstborn cattle of the Children of Israel.[75] The firstborn among the Children of Israel exceeding the number of Levites would be redeemed

---

68 Ibid., 9:1–4.
69 Numbers 7:4–5.
70 Ibid., 7:11.
71 Ibid., 1:1–3.
72 Ibid., 1:48–53.
73 Ibid., 2:1–31.
74 Ibid., 3:14–15.
75 Ibid., 3:40–41.

for five shekels for each firstborn. The money of the redemption would be given to the Priests.[76]

Moses and Aaron were to count, by family, all the Levites from the ages of thirty to fifty to serve in the Tent of Assembly.[77] The Levites were to serve from age twenty-five to age fifty. After that, they would help their fellow Levites to watch over the Tent of Assembly.[78]

God instructed Moses and Aaron how the Priests were to cover all the Tabernacle utensils before the Levites of the family of Kehat came to carry them. This was so members of the family of Kehat would not touch them, lest they die.[79] God told Moses and Aaron that the Priests were to be very careful in covering the Tent of Assembly (so that the members of the family of Kehat would not be harmed when they came to carry them).[80] The Priests would be responsible for the work of the family of Gershon.[81] God ordered the work that was to be carried out by the family of Merari.[82]

God instructed Moses about the process of purifying the Levites before sanctifying them for work in the Tabernacle. They had to be sprinkled with the water of the sin offering. Afterwards they were to shave their entire bodies and to wash their garments. They had to prepare two bulls with their meal offerings, one for a sin offering and one for a burnt offering. Moses would bring the Levites before the Tent of Assembly, and the entire community of Israel which was gathered around would place their hands on the Levites. Aaron would offer the Levites before God, and they would place their hands on the bulls. The Priests would sacrifice the bull of the sin offering and the bull of the burnt offering before God to atone for the Levites. Aaron and his sons would offer the Levites before God, would separate them from the Children of Israel and would offer them again as a redemption of the

76 Ibid., 3:44–48.
77 Ibid., 4:1–3, 21–23, 29–30.
78 Ibid., 8:23–26.
79 Ibid., 4:4–15.
80 Ibid., 4:17–20.
81 Ibid., 4:24–28.
82 Ibid., 4:31–33.

firstborn of the Children of Israel. The Levites would be given to God and with their service they would atone for the Children of Israel.[83]

God instructed Moses to make two silver trumpets to be blown as a sign for the nation to gather by the Tent of Assembly or as a sign for the camps to start moving.[84]

God told the Children of Israel at Horeb that they had rested enough at the foot of the mountain. They had to leave and go to the Land of Canaan to inherit the land which God had sworn to their forefathers to give to them.[85]

When Moses complained to God that he could not carry the burden of the nation alone, God instructed him to gather together seventy of the elders of Israel and to bring them to the Tent of Assembly. God would impart of the spirit which was on Moses to them, and they would be able to carry the burden of the nation with him.[86]

After the criticism by Miriam and Aaron of Moses, God instructed Moses, Aaron and Miriam to come to the Tent of Assembly. God called to Aaron and Miriam in order to tell them that they were not on the same level of prophecy as Moses.[87]

God ordered Moses to send one man from each tribe to spy out the Land of Canaan.[88] After the negative report of the ten spies and the reaction of the nation, God instructed Moses to return the nation to the desert.[89]

When the Children of Israel regretted their reaction and hastened to go out in a war to conquer the land, God told Moses that they should not go out to war because He was not in their midst.[90] God told Moses and Aaron to inform the nation that they would not enter the land until forty years had passed in the desert.[91]

---

83 Ibid., 8:5–19.
84 Ibid., 10:1–8.
85 Deuteronomy 1:6–8.
86 Numbers 11:16–17.
87 Ibid., 12:4–5.
88 Ibid., 13:1–2.
89 Ibid., 14:25.
90 Deuteronomy 1:42.
91 Numbers 14:26–35.

God instructed Moses to kill by stoning the man who had been gathering wood on the Sabbath.[92]

At the time of the revolt by Korah and his band, God told Moses and Aaron to move away from the Children of Israel, because He wished to destroy all of them.[93] After Moses and Aaron beseeched God not to kill all, God instructed the Children of Israel to distance themselves from the dwelling places of Korah, Datan and Aviram.[94] After the deaths of Korah and his band, God instructed Moses to order Elazar the Priest to coat the altar with the metal censers of Korah, Datan, and Aviram as they had become sanctified. They would be a sign to the Children of Israel.[95] When the Children of Israel complained that Moses and Aaron were to blame for the deaths of Korah and his band, God ordered Moses and Aaron to again distance themselves from them so that God could destroy them.[96]

God ordered Moses to take twelve staffs of the leaders of the tribes, one from each tribe, and to write on each the name of the leader. These staffs were to be placed in the Tent of Assembly. The staff of the leader whom God had chosen to perform His service in the Tabernacle of the Tent of Assembly, would blossom.[97] After Aaron's staff blossomed, God ordered Moses to return Aaron's staff to the Tent of Assembly as a sign to the Children of Israel that they should never again rebel, lest they die.[98]

Towards the Entry into the Land

God instructed Moses to command the Children of Israel to turn from Mount Seir northward when they passed on their way near the border of the Children of Esau. They were warned not to provoke them and not to do battle with them, because God had given Mount Seir as an inheritance to the Children of Esau. The Children of Israel had to pay them for food and water,

92 Ibid., 15:32–35.
93 Ibid., 16:20–21.
94 Ibid., 16:22–24.
95 Ibid., 17:1–3.
96 Ibid., 17:6–10.
97 Ibid., 17:16–20.
98 Ibid., 17:25.

because God had blessed the Children of Israel in all the work of their hands.[99]

When the Children of Israel complained about a lack of water, God instructed Moses to take a staff and to gather together the congregation. He and Aaron were to speak to the rock, and water would gush from it.[100]

At Aaron's impending death, God instructed Moses to bring Aaron and his son Elazar up to the mountain, to remove the priestly garments from Aaron and to dress Elazar with them.[101]

When the Children of Israel spoke against God and against Moses, God sent snakes to kill many of them. They asked Moses to pray for them. God instructed Moses to make a copper snake and to place it on a long pole, so that whoever was bitten would look at it and would live.[102]

God instructed Moses to gather together the entire nation, so as to give them water from the well.[103]

God told Moses that the Children of Israel were not to battle against Moab, because Ar had been given as an inheritance to the Children of Lot.[104] God instructed the Children of Israel to pass over the brook Zared.[105] God commanded the Children of Israel not to provoke the Children of Ammon, because their land had been given to them as an inheritance.[106] He commanded Moses also that the Children of Israel were not to enter the land of the Children of Ammon.[107] God commanded Moses to wage war against Sichon (so that the other nations would fear the Children of Israel).[108] Before the battle against Og, king of Bashan, God told Moses not to fear, because God would deliver him and his nation and his land into Moses's hand.[109]

---

99 Deuteronomy 2:2–7.
100 Numbers 20:7–8.
101 Ibid., 20:23–26.
102 Ibid., 21:5–8.
103 Ibid., 21:16.
104 Deuteronomy 2:9.
105 Ibid., 2:13.
106 Ibid., 2:19.
107 Ibid., 2:37.
108 Ibid., 2:24–25.
109 Numbers 21:34.

God instructed Balaam not to go with the elders of Moab and not to curse the Nation of Israel, because it is a blessed nation.[110] When Balak's messengers came a second time, God told Balaam that he was permitted to go with the elders of Moab, but he was to do only what God instructed him to do.[111] An angel of God also told Balaam (after his donkey had spoken) that he could continue to go with the elders of Moab, but he could only say that which he was permitted to.[112] God instructed Balaam what to say before Balak.[113] God appeared to Balaam again and instructed him what to say before Balak.[114]

God instructed Moses to kill the leaders of the nation who had worshipped Baal Peor (to remove God's anger from Israel).[115]

God instructed Moses and Elazar to count the Children of Israel from age twenty and up who could go out to war, as a preparation for the division of the Land of Israel.[116]

God instructed Moses to divide up the country. Each tribe would receive its inheritance according to its size. He was to divide the inheritances of the tribes according to their families, by means of casting lots.[117]

God instructed Moses to give the daughters of Zelophechad the inheritance of their father.[118] God instructed the daughters of Zelophechad and all daughters who inherited from their fathers to marry someone from their own tribe, so that the tribe's inheritance should not be transferred to another tribe.[119] [120]

God instructed Moses not to ask again to enter the Land of Israel.[121]

---

110 Ibid., 22:12.
111 Ibid., 22:20.
112 Ibid., 22:35.
113 Ibid., 23:5.
114 Numbers 23:16.
115 Ibid., 25:3.
116 Ibid., 26:1–2.
117 Ibid., 26:52–56.
118 Ibid., 27:6–7.
119 Ibid., 36:5–9.
120 This was not a commandment for future generations. See *Bava Batra* 120a.
121 Deuteronomy 3:26–27.

At Moses's request to have a worthy leader for the nation to be appointed in his place, God instructed him to lay his hands on Joshua in the presence of Elazar the Priest and the Children of Israel. Joshua was to ask Elazar the Priest for the decisions of the *Urim*.[122]

God instructed Moses to harass the Midianites and to smite them, because they were responsible for having caused Israel to sin with Baal Peor.[123] He was to take revenge of the Children of Israel of against the Midianites (and afterwards Moses would die).[124]

Elazar the Priest instructed the soldiers who fought against Midian how to purify the booty of the battle: whatever could be passed through fire was to be passed through fire and then immersed in water. Whatever could not be passed through fire was to be immersed in water. They were to wash their clothes on the seventh day before they came into the camp.[125]

God instructed Moses to count all the booty taken by the soldiers – people and animals. The booty was to be divided: half to the soldiers and half to the Children of Israel. A tax was to be exacted from the soldiers, one of every five hundred, and that was to be given to Elazar the Priest. The Children of Israel should give of their portion one-fiftieth to the Levites.[126]

The tribes of Reuben, Gad, and half the tribe of Menasseh were to be the first ones to cross into the land, before the rest of the Children of Israel, and only their wives, children and cattle were to remain across the Jordan – until their brothers would inherit the land.[127]

God told Moses to tell the Children of Israel that they were to inherit the land from all the residents of Canaan and to destroy their gods and high places, so that they would live in the land which God had given them.[128]

God told Joshua and the Children of Israel not to be afraid of the other nations, because God would fight for them.[129]

---

122 Numbers 27:18–21.
123 Ibid., 25:16–18.
124 Ibid., 31:1–2.
125 Ibid., 31:21–24.
126 Ibid., 31:25–30.
127 Deuteronomy 3:18–20.
128 Numbers 33:50–53.

God told Moses to command the Children of Israel to give of their inheritance cities to the Levites for the Levites to dwell in, along with fields around these cities. Six cities would be cities of refuge to which a killer could flee. In addition, there would be another forty-two cities. The number of cities which would be given to the Levites would be proportional to the size of each tribe's inheritance.[130]

Across the Jordan, in the land of Moab, Moses spoke to the Children of Israel as commanded to him by God.[131]

The nation was instructed to place large rocks in the Jordan when the Children of Israel crossed it. The rocks were to be covered with plaster and the words of the Torah were to be written on them. These rocks would be brought to Mount Ebal, where an altar for God was to be built, without the use of iron, to offer up burnt offerings and peace offerings to God. In that place they would read the Torah and explain it fully.[132] Six tribes were to stand on Mount Gerizim and would confirm the blessings, while six tribes would stand on Mount Ebal and would confirm the curses.[133]

God instructed Moses to write the words of the Song (Deuteronomy 32:1-43) and to teach it to the Children of Israel, so that it would be a witness.[134] Moses instructed the Levites to place the Torah scroll in the Ark of the Covenant as a witness.[135]

God instructed Moses to strengthen Joshua's hands, as he would lead the nation when they went to inherit the land.[136] God told him to call Joshua and to stand with him in the Tent of Assembly so that God would command Joshua.[137]

---

129 Deuteronomy 3:21–22.
130 Numbers 35:1–8.
131 Deuteronomy 1:3.
132 Ibid., 27:1–8.
133 Ibid., 27:11–13.
134 Ibid., 31:19.
135 Ibid., 31:25–26.
136 Ibid., 3:28.
137 Ibid., 31:14.

God told Joshua to strengthen himself, because he would bring the Children of Israel into the Land of Israel.[138]

God instructed Moses to ascend to Mount Abarim to see the land which God had given to the Children of Israel before his death. He would not enter the land because he had not obeyed God's voice at the waters of Meriva.[139]

After the Entry into the Land

After the death of Moses, God instructed Joshua to cross the Jordan River and to enter with the Children of Israel into the land which He had given them.[140] God instructed him to be strong and of good courage in order to have the Children of Israel inherit the land. God also commanded him to strengthen himself and to be very courageous in observing the Torah which Moses had commanded him, not to turn from it and to always study it. God also commanded Joshua to strengthen himself and not to be afraid of anything – because God would be with him in whatever he did.[141]

God instructed Joshua to command the Priests to carry the Ark of the Covenant before the camp and to walk before the nation. When they would come to the Jordan, they were to halt.[142] The Children of Israel were to choose one representative from each tribe – twelve men.[143] After the Children of Israel passed on dry land over the Jordan, God instructed Joshua to order each of the twelve men chosen to take one of the rocks which had been under the feet of the Priests (when the waters of the Jordan had halted), and to bring the rocks to where they would remain that night.[144] God commanded Joshua to command the Priests to ascend from the Jordan. The water then returned to its original course.[145]

138 Ibid., 31:23.
139 Numbers 27:12–14.
140 Joshua 1:1–2.
141 Ibid., 1:6–9.
142 Ibid., 3:7–8.
143 Ibid., 3:12.
144 Ibid., 4:1–3.
145 Ibid., 4:15–18.

God instructed Joshua to make flint knives, in order to circumcise the Children of Israel who had been born in the desert.[146]

At Jericho, the commander of God's host told Joshua to take off his shoes because of the sanctity of the place.[147]

When the time came to conquer Jericho, God instructed Joshua how to cause the walls of the city to fall. All of the members of the army were to walk completely around the city wall once a day for six days. Seven Priests would carry *shofarot* – rams' horns – in front of the Ark of the Covenant, which was carried by Priests who were in the midst of the procession. The Priests who carried the *shofarot* were to blow them, while everyone else was to remain silent. On the seventh day, they were to circle the city seven times. On the seventh circuit, the Priests were to blow the *shofarot* and everyone else was to shout at Joshua's command and the wall would fall.[148]

After the defeat at Ai, God told Joshua to arise from his mourning and to cease his pleading. He was to prepare the nation to capture the person who had violated the sanctified goods.[149]

After the death of Achan, God instructed Joshua not to be afraid and to go up with the soldiers to conquer Ai. They were permitted to take booty, and they had to prepare an ambush behind the city.[150] During the time of the battle, God instructed Joshua to indicate with the spear in his hand when the people in the ambush were to enter and conquer the city.[151]

God told Joshua not to fear the kings of the north who had assembled together with their armies to fight Israel, because by the next day all would be killed by the Children of Israel. God also instructed Joshua to hamstring their horses and to burn their chariots.[152]

146 Ibid., 5:2.
147 Ibid., 5:13–15.
148 Ibid., 6:2–5.
149 Ibid., 7:10–15.
150 Ibid., 8:1–2.
151 Ibid., 8:18.
152 Ibid., 11:6.

God instructed Joshua to divide up the land among the nine tribes and half the tribe of Menasseh, even though the conquest of the entire land had not yet been achieved.[153]

God told Joshua to instruct the Children of Israel to allocate cities of refuge for people who had killed unintentionally.[154]

The Era of the Judges

After the death of Joshua, the Children of Israel asked God's word as to which tribe should be the first which would wage war against the Canaanites. God's reply was that the tribe of Judah should be first.[155]

God commanded Barak, the son of Avinoam, through Deborah the prophet, to assemble ten thousand men on Mount Tabor to wage battle against Sisera, the general of Yavin king of Canaan, in order to draw Sisera and his army to the Kishon stream for battle. Thus God would deliver them into the hands of Barak.[156]

God told Gideon to go in his might, as he always sought the good of Israel, to save Israel from servitude to Midian.[157] Gideon asked for a sign from God to confirm that God had indeed spoken to him. An angel of God told him to take that which he had set aside as an offering – meat and unleavened bread – and put them on a rock, and to pour the broth over them. (Fire came up from the rock and burned everything).[158] God instructed Gideon to take the two bulls of his father and to destroy his father's altar to Baal. So, too, was he to destroy the *asherah* tree which was above the altar. He was to build an altar to God and to take one of the bulls and offer it as a burnt offering, while the wood of the *asherah* tree was to be used to burn it.[159]

When volunteers were needed to fight Midian, Amalek and the children of the east, too many people volunteered. God wanted to decrease the

153 Ibid., 13:1–7.
154 Ibid., 20:1–6.
155 Judges 1:1–2.
156 Ibid., 4:6–7.
157 Ibid., 6:14.
158 Ibid., 6:17–21.
159 Ibid., 6:25–26.

number of people, so that they should not boast that it was their superior force which had won the battle. God therefore instructed Gideon to announce in the camp that whoever was afraid should go back to his home.[160] God instructed Gideon to again decrease the number of fighters by a test of having them drink water from the stream. Some scooped out water in their hands and licked it with their tongues, while others bent on their knees to drink. The number of those who drank the water from their hands was three hundred, and these were chosen to fight against Midian and Amalek.[161] God instructed Gideon to fight against Midian, as He would deliver them into his hand, but if he was still afraid he could come with his young lad to hear what was they were talking about, so that he would be strengthened and go out to battle.[162]

An angel of God appeared to the wife of Manoah, who was barren, and instructed her to refrain from wine and alcoholic drinks and not to eat anything which was ritually impure. The son who would be born to her would be a Nazirite from birth and would not cut the hair on his head. He would save Israel from the Philistines.[163] The angel of God repeated his directions to Manoah as well.[164]

The Children of Israel asked God who should go out first to wage war against the tribe of Benjamin (because of the concubine of the Levite who had been tortured and killed by members of the tribe of Benjamin). God's reply was that Judah should go out first to wage war.[165] God instructed the Children of Israel to continue the battle on the second day even though they had been beaten by the tribe of Benjamin.[166] On the third day, God instructed them to go out again to war, and this time they were victorious.[167]

---

160 Ibid., 7:2–3.
161 Ibid., 7:4–7.
162 Ibid., 7:9–11.
163 Ibid., 13:3–5.
164 Ibid., 13:13–14.
165 Ibid., 20:18.
166 Ibid., 20:23.
167 Ibid., 20:28.

The Era of the Kings

God instructed Samuel to listen to the voice of the elders of Israel and the nation who wanted a king, but to warn them of the results of anointing a king and his rule of the nation.[168, 169]

God instructed him to anoint Saul as the ruler over Israel, so that he would save them from the Philistines.[170]

Samuel told Saul, by God's command, to wait for him before he would offer a burnt offering.[171]

God told Samuel to instruct Saul to go out to war against Amalek and to kill the entire nation of Amalek and their cattle – not to take pity on any of them.[172]

As Saul had not obeyed God's word, God instructed Samuel not to mourn for him any more and to go to Jesse of Bethlehem and to anoint one of his sons as king.[173] God told Samuel to take a heifer with him and to tell his men that he was going to offer a sacrifice to God. He was to invite Jesse to the sacrifice, and there God would tell him what to do, and whom to anoint.[174] God instructed Samuel to anoint Jesse's youngest son as king.[175]

David asked what to do. God instructed him to smite the Philistines and to save the people of Keilah.[176]

God instructed Nathan the prophet to tell David not to build the House of God, but that his son should.[177]

---

168 I Samuel 8:7–9, 22.

169 In Deuteronomy 17:14–20, it states that the selection of a king will be by God, who is the true King. Samuel was asked by the elders of Israel to appoint a king who would be their (true) judge. The request was a rebellion against God. God wanted Samuel to try to dissuade them from appointing a king. God agreed to appoint a king because this is not forbidden.

170 I Samuel 9:15–17.

171 Ibid., 10:8; 13:13.

172 Ibid., 15:1–3.

173 Ibid., 16:1.

174 Ibid., 16:2–3.

175 Ibid., 16:12.

176 Ibid., 23:2,4.

177 II Samuel 7:4–13.

After David counted the people in an improper way and chose the punishment of a plague by God, the prophet Gad instructed him in the name of God to build an altar in the threshing floor of Aravnah the Jebusite in order to stop the plague.[178]

God told Shemayahu, a man of God, to instruct Rehoboam and all the people of Judah and Benjamin not to fight against the Kingdom of Israel, in order to return it to the Kingdom of Judah, and for each person to return to his home, because the division of the kingdom had been a decree by God.[179]

After Elijah told Ahab that no dew or rain would fall, God instructed Elijah to hide in the Cherith stream near the Jordan. He would drink from the stream and ravens would bring him food.[180] There God instructed Elijah to go to Zarephath which was in Sidon and to stay in the home of a widow, because God had commanded the widow to support him.[181] In the third year, God instructed Elijah to return to Ahab.[182]

In order to settle the dispute between Elijah and those who worshipped Baal, Elijah built an altar to God on Mount Carmel and placed wood and a bull as a sacrifice on it. In response to Elijah's prayer, God sent a fire which burned his sacrifice. Thus it became known that Elijah had acted in accordance with God's word.[183]

The prophet Elijah fled to the desert because Jezebel, Ahab's wife, wanted to kill him. An angel of God instructed Elijah to eat and drink of the food which appeared at his head. The angel again asked him to eat, explaining that he still had a long way to go.[184] When Elijah reached a cave in the Mountain of God, He instructed him to go out and stand before Him.[185] God instructed him to return to the desert of Damascus to anoint Hazael as

---

178 Ibid., 24:18.
179 II Chronicles 11:2–4.
180 I Kings 17:2–4.
181 Ibid., 17:8–9.
182 Ibid., 18:1.
183 Ibid., 18:17–38.
184 Ibid., 19:2–7.
185 Ibid., 19:11.

king of Aram, Jehu as king of Israel, and Elisha as a prophet in his place.[186] They would carry out God's plans to kill the worshippers of Baal.

One of the sons of the prophets asked his fellow man to beat him, as God had commanded. (He wanted to appear injured before Ahab, king of Israel.) [187]

When King Ahab came to inherit the vineyard of Naboth the Jezreelite who had been killed by the orders of his wife Jezebel, God instructed Elijah the prophet to come to Ahab and to tell him that his death would be like that of Naboth – because he had murdered Naboth and afterwards inherited his vineyard.[188]

Before the war against Moab, when there was no water for the troops, God told the kings of Judah, Israel, and Edom to dig pits in the stream so that God would fill them with water.[189]

In reply to the question of King Jehoshaphat and the nation about what they should do against the multitudes of Moab and Ammon who had come to battle against them, the spirit of God rested on Jahaziel, the son of Zecharyahu. He instructed them not to fear, but to stand up and see God's deliverance.[190]

Amaziah, the king of Judah, gathered warriors from Judah and Benjamin. In addition, he hired one hundred thousand warriors from Israel. A man of God warned the king not to go out to war, because God would make him fail because his army had mercenaries from Israel.[191]

A prophet of God named Oded warned the army of Israel, after they had vanquished the army of Judah, not to take any of the people of Judah as male or female slaves, because they, too, were not blameless. They needed to return the captives, because God was angry at them.[192]

---

186 Ibid., 19:15–18.
187 Ibid., 20:35–36.
188 Ibid., 21:17–19.
189 II Kings 3:16.
190 II Chronicles 20:14–17.
191 Ibid., 25:7–8.
192 Ibid., 28:9–11.

When the Children of Israel sinned against God by worshipping other gods, following the statutes of the nations whose land God had given them to inherit, saying things about God secretly which were not true, and building high places, monuments, and *asherah* trees in every place and worshipping them – all these actions angered God. God warned Israel and Judah through the prophets. He told them to repent from their evil ways and to observe God's commandments which He had commanded their forefathers and had sent through the prophets.[193]

God told King Hezekiah, through the prophet Isaiah, that he should not fear the curses of the servants of the king of Assyria.[194]

God instructed Isaiah to return to King Hezekiah and to tell him that God was going to add fifteen years to his life and would also save the city from the king of Assyria.[195]

Instructions to the Prophets

After Isaiah agreed to be a messenger of God's word, God instructed him to tell the nation that they would hear His words but would not relate to them at all.[196]

When Rezin, the king of Aram, and Pekah, the son of Remalyahu, the king of Israel, went to wage war against Ahaz, the king of Judah, God instructed Isaiah to go to Ahaz and to tell him that he should not fear these two kings.[197]

God instructed Isaiah to write on a sheet that the looting of Damascus and Samaria by Assyria would take place very soon.[198]

God told Isaiah not to be afraid, but to sanctify God and to fear Him.[199]

God instructed Isaiah to remove the sackcloth and his shoes and to go naked and barefoot, as a sign of what would happen to Egypt and Cush.[200]

---

193 II Kings 17:7–13.
194 Ibid., 19:6.
195 Ibid., 20:4–6.
196 Isaiah 6:9–10.
197 Ibid., 7:3–4.
198 Ibid., 8:1–4.
199 Ibid., 8:11–13.

God instructed Isaiah to to go to Shebna, who was responsible for the king's house and to prophesy that God would punish him because of his intention to hand over Jerusalem to the king of Assyria.[201]

When Jeremiah was sanctified to be a prophet, God told him that He would direct him where to go and what to say to the nation. Jeremiah should not fear them because God would save him.[202] God spurred him on to say to the nation everything which He would command him and that he should not fear them.[203]

God instructed Jeremiah to say to the inhabitants of Judah and Jerusalem that whoever would not observe the words of the covenant which God had made with their forefathers when He took them out of Egypt was cursed. God would bring upon them a great evil and would not listen to their prayer. God also instructed Jeremiah not to pray for them.[204] Their sin was so severe that God would not answer them even if they fasted, prayed or offered sacrifices.[205]

God's word came to Jeremiah to warn Israel not to trust in Egypt or Assyria, because God had rejected Israel, and the assistance of other nations would not help.[206]

God instructed Jeremiah not to marry and not to have sons or daughters, because they would all die by famine or be killed by the sword and would not even be buried.[207]

God instructed Jeremiah to go to the king of Judah and to tell him and his entire nation to act justly and righteously. The nation should rescue one who had been robbed from his oppressor, should not oppress the stranger,

200 Ibid., 20:2–3.
201 Ibid., 22:15–25.
202 Jeremiah 1:7–8.
203 Ibid., 1:17.
204 Ibid., 11:1–14.
205 Ibid., 14:11–12.
206 Ibid., 2:36–37.
207 Ibid., 16:1–4.

orphan, and widow, and not shed innocent blood. If they would do so, his kingdom would survive, and if not – the king's house would be destroyed.[208]

At the beginning of the reign of Jehoiakim, God instructed Jeremiah to stand in the courtyard of the House of God and to speak to those who came there as God instructed him. If they would repent from their sins, God would not punish them as He had planned to do, but if they did not follow the ways of the Torah and did not listen to the prophets, the city would be destroyed.[209]

In the fourth year of the reign of Jehoiakim, God instructed Jeremiah to write on a scroll that which God had spoken about Israel, Judah, and the nations, from the beginning of his prophecy, so that the people of Judah would repent from their evil ways.[210] After the scroll was burned, in the presence of the king and his ministers, God instructed Jeremiah to write everything on a new scroll.[211]

God instructed Jeremiah to prepare bonds and yokes, to put them around his neck, and afterwards give them to the messengers of the kings of Edom, Moab, Ammon, Tyre and Sidon who had come to King Zedekiah. Jeremiah was to tell them to bring to their masters the word of God, that they had to submit to Nebuchadnezzar, king of Babylon, because God, to whom all the earth belongs, had delivered them into his hands. Any kingdom which would not submit would be destroyed.[212]

God instructed Jeremiah to come to Hananiah who had prophesied falsely (on freeing themselves from the yoke of the king of Babylon), and to tell him that he would die that very year.[213]

Jeremiah sent a scroll from Jerusalem to the nation exiled to Babylon in which was written the word of God which instructed them to build houses and to plant vineyards, to marry wives and to have children, and to pray for the welfare of the city to which they had been exiled – because their welfare

208 Ibid., 22:1–4.
209 Ibid., 26:1–6.
210 Ibid., 36:1–3.
211 Ibid., 36:27–28.
212 Ibid., 27:1–11.
213 Ibid., 28:12–17.

depended on its welfare. They should not listen to the false prophets, but their exile would end only after seventy years.[214]

God instructed Jeremiah to tell King Zedekiah that the army of Pharaoh which had come to help Zedekiah would return to Egypt, whereas the Chaldeans would return, capture Jerusalem and burn it.[215]

God instructed Jeremiah to say directly to King Zedekiah that if he surrendered, he should leave Jerusalem and go to the ministers of the king of Babylon. This way, he and his family would remain alive and the city would not be burned.[216]

God instructed Jeremiah to tell Eved Melech the Cushite that when the city was destroyed, he would be saved, because he believed in God.[217]

During the siege of Jerusalem, God instructed Jeremiah to redeem a field from his relative in Anatot as a sign to the people of Judah that God would return them to the land, and they would yet buy fields and houses.[218]

God instructed Jeremiah to write in a scroll everything which he had prophesied about the return of Israel to its land.[219]

God instructed Jeremiah to tell the remnants of the nation who were still in Judah, after they had asked him to pray for them, to remain in the country and not go down to Egypt to dwell in it, because they would die there by the sword, famine, or pestilence.[220] God instructed Jeremiah to take large rocks and to place them at the door of Pharaoh's house before the eyes of the Jews who lived in Egypt. Jeremiah was to tell them that Nebuchadnezzar would come to conquer Egypt, would kill its inhabitants and destroys its idols.[221] God instructed him to rebuke the Jews of Judah who had taken others with them to Egypt and engaged in idolatry.[222]

---

214 Ibid., 29:1–10.
215 Ibid., 37:6–10.
216 Ibid., 38:17.
217 Ibid., 39:15–18.
218 Ibid., 32:6–8, 14–15.
219 Ibid., 30:1–3.
220 Ibid., 42:7–22.
221 Ibid., 43:8–13.
222 Ibid., 44:7–8.

God told Ezekiel that He had appointed him as a prophet to warn the House of Israel.[223]

God informed the prophet Ezekiel that He was sending him to the Children of Israel to warn them about their sins and that he should not fear them.[224] He commanded Ezekiel to eat a scroll which He was giving to him, which was entirely full of lamentations (about the destruction).[225]

God instructed Ezekiel to go to the Children of Israel in the exile of Babylon and to prophesy to them.[226]

God instructed Ezekiel to warn the wicked to return from his evil ways and the righteous not to sin.[227]

God instructed Ezekiel to go out to a plain in order to hear the word of God.[228]

God instructed Ezekiel not to rebuke the nation unless God ordered him to.[229]

God instructed Ezekiel to take a tile and to portray on it the city of Jerusalem. He was to lay siege on it, as a sign to the Children of Israel. He was to lie on his left side for 390 days as a symbol of the years that the House of Israel had sinned, and to lie on his right side for forty days, as a sign of the years that the House of Judah had sinned. He was to take various grains and to bake a bread of all of them, and to eat it on those days he would lie on his side. He should drink a minimal amount of water. The bread would symbolize the food which the Children of Israel would eat when they were in exile, and the bread and water would symbolize what they would eat and drink in Jerusalem.[230]

Ezekiel was to take a razor and shave his head and beard. He was to take a balance-scale and divide the hairs. At the end of the siege period, he was to burn

---

223 Ezekiel 33:7–9.
224 Ibid., 2:3–7.
225 Ibid., 2:8–3:3.
226 Ibid., 3:10–11.
227 Ibid., 3:16–21.
228 Ibid., 3:22.
229 Ibid., 3:25–27.
230 Ibid., 4:1–17.

up with fire a third of the city which he had built, a third was to be struck by a sword, and a third to be scattered to the wind, and God would send a sword after them. He was to take a few of the hairs and save them. Afterwards he was to throw some of them into the fire so that they would be burned up. All of this was evidence of what was to happen to the people of Jerusalem.[231]

God instructed Ezekiel to turn to the mountains of Israel and to prophesy about them that a sword would come upon them.[232]

God instructed Ezekiel to clap with his hand, kick with his foot, and shout as a sign of mourning because of the abominations of Israel and their troubles.[233]

God instructed Ezekiel to tell the Nation of Israel His word to the inhabitants of Jerusalem that the land would be totally destroyed. Then they would know that "I am the Lord."[234]

God instructed Ezekiel to tell the inhabitants of the land that the time of the fulfillment of the prophecies was drawing near.[235]

God instructed Ezekiel to tell the prophets who were prophesying without being sent by God that their prophecy about peace would not be realized, and that they would be punished severely.[236]

God told Ezekiel to inform Jerusalem about its abominations.[237]

God instructed Ezekiel to say to the nation that when the king violated the covenant which he had made with the king of Babylon, it was as if he had violated a covenant with God. Therefore, he and his men would be punished.[238]

God instructed Ezekiel to say to the elders of the nation who had come to the prophet to seek God while they violated His commandments, that God would not answer them.[239]

---

231 Ibid., 5:1–17.
232 Ibid., 6:1–3.
233 Ibid., 6:11–12.
234 Ibid., 12:17–20.
235 Ibid., 12:21–28.
236 Ibid., 13:1–16.
237 Ibid., 16:1–2.
238 Ibid., 17:11–21.
239 Ibid., 20:2–4.

God instructed Ezekiel to tell the inhabitants of the city of blood (Jerusalem) that because of its many sins which had led to bloodshed, God would scatter them among the nations.[240]

God instructed Ezekiel not to mourn nor to weep for the apple of his eye (his wife). Similarly, the House of Israel should not mourn and weep when the Temple was desecrated and their sons and daughters would be killed by the sword.[241]

God instructed Ezekiel to prophesy to the exiles in different lands and to say to them that God would be with them and would gather them from the lands where they had been scattered to the Land of Israel. They needed to remove the idolatry from the land. God would even give them a new heart, so that they would observe His statutes and commandments.[242]

God instructed Ezekiel to tell the nation that God is not interested in the death of the sinner but in his repenting. A righteous person who is sure of his righteousness and sins will be punished for his sin, and his earlier righteousness will not help him. If a wicked person repents from his ways and does what is just and right – his earlier sins will not be an impediment and will not be remembered further. God judges every person according to his way and his deeds in the present.[243]

God instructed Ezekiel to pay attention to everything that God would show him, and to tell the House of Israel everything he had seen. God showed him the Temple with all its details.[244] He had to tell the Children of Israel everything which he had seen about the Temple – the description might cause them to be embarrassed about their sins.

If indeed that would be their reaction, the prophet was to write down the plans of the House and all the statutes of the service in it.[245] God instructed Ezekiel to warn the Children of Israel who violated the laws of the

240 Ibid., 22:1–16.
241 Ibid., 24:15–27.
242 Ibid., 11:14–21.
243 Ibid., 33:10–20.
244 Ibid., 40:1–42:20.
245 Ibid., 43:10–11.

Temple and allowed foreigners and those of uncircumcised hearts to enter the House.[246]

God instructed Ezekiel how to dedicate the altar so that it would be ready to offer burnt offerings on it and to sprinkle blood on it. A bull as a sin offering was to be given to the Priests who were descendants of Zadok, who were close to God and who served Him. They were to take of its blood and to place it on its four corners, the four corners of the Temple courtyard, and the border around it. The Priests would cleanse the altar and would make atonement upon it. They would take the bull of the sin offering and burn it outside the Temple. On the second day, they would offer a male goat as a sin offering and would cleanse the altar, as they had done with the bull. Afterwards they would offer a bull without blemish and a ram without blemish. The Priests would sprinkle salt on them and offer them as burnt offerings. This was to be done for seven days. On the eighth day, the Priests could offer burnt offerings and peace offerings, which would be accepted by God.[247] When the Children of Israel returned to the Land of Israel and divided it up again according to tribes, they would need to set aside land for God – for the Temple and for the Priests, as well as land for the leaders.[248] The nation would have to bring an offering of wheat, barley, flax and a lamb for a meal offering, for a burnt offering and for a peace offering to atone for themselves, including the leader.[249]

God further instructed Ezekiel how to consecrate the Temple in the first year by means of sacrifices. On the first day of the first month, they were to take an unblemished bull to cleanse the Temple. The Priest would have to take of the blood of the sin offering and place it on the doorpost of the House and on the four corners of the Temple courtyard for the altar, and on the doorpost of the gate of that courtyard. On the seventh day of the month, one who had sinned unintentionally would have to bring a sin offering, in order to atone for the House. On the fourteenth day of the month would be

246 Ibid., 44:5–8.
247 Ibid., 43:18–27.
248 Ibid., 45:1–8.
249 Ibid., 45:13–16.

the Passover sacrifice. Afterwards they would celebrate for seven days, during which they would eat unleavened bread. On that day, the leader would bring a bull as a sin offering for himself and for the nation. On the seven days of the festival he would bring a burnt offering to God, seven unblemished bulls and similarly seven unblemished rams, each day, as well as a sin offering of a male goat, a meal offering of an ephah measure for each bull and each ram, and a hin measure of oil for each ephah. In the seventh month, on the fifteenth day of the month, they would again bring sacrifices for seven days.[250]

God also instructed Ezekiel about how the land was to be redivided for the Twelve Tribes, and their borders. In the tract which is the inheritance of the tribe of Judah, land is to be set aside for God, a place for the Temple to be built as well as a place for the Priests and the Levites. Similarly, a tract will be given to the leader. The grain of the areas around the city will belong to its workers, who will come from all the tribes. The gates are to be named after the tribes, and the name of the city will be "The Lord is there."[251]

God told Hosea to take an adulterous woman and children of adultery as a sign that the land had committed adultery against God.[252]

God told Hosea to name the son who would be born to him from her Jezreel, as a sign that God would revenge the blood of Jezreel (the destruction of the House of Ahab) on the House of Jehu.[253]

God told Hosea to name the daughter who would be born to him from her Lo Ruhamah ("not pitied"), because God would not continue to take pity on the House of Israel.[254]

God told Hosea to name his son Lo Ami ("not my nation"), because Israel is not His nation.[255]

God told Hosea to love another adulterous woman as a sign that God loved the Children of Israel, but they had turned to other gods.[256]

---

250 Ibid., 45:18–25.
251 Ibid., 47:13– 48:35.
252 Hosea 1:2.
253 Ibid., 1:3–4.
254 Ibid., 1:6.
255 Ibid., 1:9.

God instructed the prophet Joel to tell the Priests to mourn that the meal offerings and wine libations were no longer being brought to the House of God. They were to proclaim a fast and a solemn assembly and to cry to God.[257]

God instructed the prophet Amos to prophesy to the Nation of Israel.[258]

God instructed the prophet Jonah to go to Nineveh and to rebuke its inhabitants.[259] After Jonah failed in his attempt to flee, God again instructed him to go to Nineveh and to proclaim the message that He had put in his mouth.[260]

God instructed Zechariah to tell the nation that if they returned to God, He would return to them.[261]

God instructed Zechariah to tell the people of the land and the Priests that they had to observe those matters which they had been asked to do by the earlier prophets, when Jerusalem was still tranquil.[262]

God instructed Zechariah to take the staff of a foolish shepherd as a sign that God would raise up a shepherd for the nation who would abandon them.[263]

God instructed Haggai to tell Zerubabel, Joshua, and the nation that the time had come for building the House of God.[264] God told Haggai to tell Zerubabel, Joshua and the rest of the nation to be strong and not to fear. They are to continue to build the House of God because God had been with them ever since the covenant He had made with them at the Exodus from Egypt.[265]

---

256 Ibid., 3:1.
257 Joel 1:13–14.
258 Amos 7:15.
259 Jonah 1:2.
260 Ibid., 3:1–2.
261 Zechariah 1:1–3.
262 Ibid., 7:4–7.
263 Ibid., 11:15–17.
264 Haggai 1:7–8.
265 Ibid., 2:1–5.

God told Haggai to ask the Priests how well they knew the laws in the Torah of ritual purity and ritual impurity.[266]

God instructed Zechariah to take silver and gold from those who were in the exile in order to make crowns and to place them on the head of Joshua the High Priest.[267]

God instructed Malachi to tell the nation to bring the tithe and heave offering to the Temple.[268]

In the Scriptures

God told Eliphaz the Temanite and his fellow men to take seven bulls and seven rams to offer as a burnt offering to appease God, and Job would pray for them – so that they should not be punished for not having given Job a proper answer regarding the way God acts in the world.[269]

Daniel was told to write the things he had heard in a book, in an unclear way and without an explanation. They would remain so until the End.[270]

• Commandments and Demands for All Generations

The commandments and demands for all generations mentioned in this section may be divided into two parts:

a) Those given directly.
b) Those which can be deduced from the reward of their observers, and the punishment of those who do not observe them. The assumption is that the mention of reward and punishment indicates that the actions or attitudes involved are required or are forbidden, as the case may be.

The listing below does not, of course, seek to determine authoritatively

266 Ibid., 2:11–14.
267 Zechariah 6:9–11.
268 Malachi 3:10.
269 Job 42:7–8.
270 Daniel 12:4.

the way the commandments and demands for all generations must be observed, but merely to list them in a very general way.

One may characterize the commandments which apply to all generations as belonging to a number of groups, some of which overlap. The groups are:

a) General commandments and demands regarding the relationship between man and God.
b) Commandments and demands to negate improper methods of relating to God.
c) General commandments and demands regarding human behavior.
d) Commandments and demands which teach one how to serve God.
e) Commandments related to mentioning the Exodus from Egypt.
f) Commandments related to specified times.
g) General commandments and demands regarding maintaining holiness.
h) Commandments related to marriage and unacceptable sexual relationships.
i) Commandments related to eating and drinking.
j) Commandments related to one's behavior (towards oneself).
k) General commandments and demands regarding behavior towards others, including the functioning of courts.
l) Commandments related to working the land in the Land of Israel and dealing with its produce.
m) Commandments related to living creatures.
n) Commandments as to how to relate to those with special holiness.
o) Commandments of a national character.

In this sub-chapter the term "one" or "a person" refers to an Israelite.

Man's Relationship to God

In General

One is commanded to fear God.[271]

271 Deuteronomy 10:12.

Every person must submit to God.[272]

One is commanded to love God with all his being.[273]

The Children of Israel are commanded not to forget God who took them out of Egypt.[274] One must remember God before his death.[275]

One must believe God.[276]

One must trust in God and not in people.[277] One must trust in God with all one's heart.[278] He must trust in God's salvation.[279]

One must believe in God.[280] One must believe in God's wonders.[281]

One must find refuge in God.[282] He must place his trust in God.[283] One must draw his strength from God.[284] One must throw on God the solution to his burdens and the fulfillment of his hopes.[285]

One must place his hopes in God.[286] He must yearn for God's kindness.[287] It is good for a person to yearn for deliverance by God.[288]

One must prepare his heart to seek God.[289] One must call to God.[290]

God expects people to call upon Him as a father.[291]

One must turn to God to seek counsel.[292] One must wait for His advice.[293]

---

272 II Kings 22:18–19.
273 Deuteronomy 6:5.
274 Ibid., 6:12.
275 Ecclesiastes 12:1–8.
276 Deuteronomy 9:23.
277 Jeremiah 17:5,7.
278 Proverbs 3:5.
279 Psalms 78:22.
280 Ibid., 78:22.
281 Ibid., 78:32.
282 Ibid., 118:8–9.
283 Ibid., 78:7.
284 Ibid., 84:6.
285 Ibid., 55:23.
286 Isaiah 40:31.
287 Psalms 147:11.
288 Lamentations 3:26.
289 II Chronicles 12:14.
290 Psalms 145:18.
291 Jeremiah 3:19.

The nation must strive to receive direction from God.[294]

One must honor God.[295] One must honor God with one's wealth and with the fruit of one's land.[296]

One must praise God[297] and sing praises in His honor.[298] One must always relate the kindness of God and His keeping of His promises.[299]

One must rejoice that he relies on God.[300]

One must seek to be close to God.[301]

One must thank God.[302]

People must have knowledge of God (to know what God wants of them).[303] They must seek it.[304]

One must know God's ways.[305] He must be aware and know that God acts with kindness, justice, and righteousness in the land.[306]

One must tell the truth about God's actions in the world.[307]

One must remember God's kindness.[308] He must remember God's might, and the day God redeemed the people from Egypt.[309]

One must relate to God's wonders in the world.[310] One must think about what God brings about.[311]

---

292 Isaiah 30:1.
293 Psalms 106:13.
294 Ibid., 81:12.
295 Ibid., 22:24.
296 Proverbs 3:9.
297 Psalms 146:1.
298 Ibid., 147:1.
299 Ibid., 92:3.
300 Ibid., 37:4.
301 Ibid., 91:14.
302 Ibid., 92:2.
303 Hosea 4:1.
304 Proverbs 2:5.
305 Psalms 95:10.
306 Jeremiah 9:23.
307 Job 42:7.
308 Psalms 106:7.
309 Ibid., 78:42.
310 Ibid., 106:7.
311 Isaiah 5:12.

Our Sages determined that there should be prayers three times a day: the *Shaharit* prayer in the morning, the *Minhah* prayer in the afternoon, and the *Arvit* prayer in the evening.

They also determined that prayers should be said publicly with a quorum of at least ten adult men, and that there should be a place set aside for prayer – a synagogue. Our Sages determined that blessings should be recited in praise of God – before one performs commandments, before one eats, and on other special occasions.

Relating to God's Name

One must think about God's name,[312] know it,[313] and honor it.[314]

One must praise God's name,[315] bless it,[316] and love it.[317]

A person should swear in God's name only.[318] When a person swears by God, he must do so in truth, in judgment, and in righteousness.[319]

Relating to the Words of God

The words which God commanded must be inscribed on the hearts of the Children of Israel. They must teach them to their sons and speak about them (by reading the paragraphs of the *Shema* prayer, Deuteronomy 6:4-9 and 11:13-21) each evening and morning. Verses with the words of God must be tied to the arm (as the *tefillin* of the arm – a leather box with leather straps containing those verses handwritten by a scribe) and placed on the top of the head (as the *tefillin* of the head). Verses from the words of God must be placed on the doorposts of the house and of the gates.[320]

---

312 Malachi 3:16.
313 Psalms 91:14.
314 Malachi 2:2.
315 Psalms 92:2.
316 Ibid., 100:4.
317 Ibid., 5:12.
318 Deuteronomy 6:13.
319 Jeremiah 4:2.
320 Deuteronomy 6:6–9. See Mechilta on Exodus 13:9.

One must adopt God's commandments.[321] One must take interest in God's statutes.[322]

One must study the Torah (God's teaching) by day and by night.[323] It must always be in one's heart.[324] The nation must remember the Torah which God commanded Moses, its statutes and its ordinances.[325] One must remember God's commandments in order to observe them.[326]

One must desire God's Torah.[327] One must desire its commandments.[328]

One must love God's Torah.[329]

It is good to teach the nation the Book of God's Torah.[330]

Our Sages determined that one must read from the Torah scroll on Sabbaths at the morning *Shaharit* prayer, and the custom is to complete the entire Torah in the course of a single year (on the eighth day from the beginning of the festival of Tabernacles in Israel and on the ninth day elsewhere). Our Sages also determined that the Torah should be read on festivals, New Moons, at the afternoon *Minhah* service of the Sabbath, and on Mondays and Thursdays.

Proper Behavior

One must serve God with all one's heart and with all one's soul.[331] One must follow in God's ways.[332]

One must walk modestly with God.[333] One must be confident that God will solve all his problems.[334] One must ensure that his entire life will be in keeping with God's word.[335]

---

321 Proverbs 10:8.
322 Psalms 119:155.
323 Ibid., 1:2.
324 Ibid., 37:31.
325 Malachi 3:22.
326 Psalms 103:18.
327 Ibid., 1:2.
328 Ibid., 112:1.
329 Ibid., 119:165.
330 II Chronicles 17:9.
331 Deuteronomy 10:12.
332 Ibid.

One must live in accordance with God's Torah,[336] His ordinances,[337] and His commandments.[338]

One must seek God with all his heart[339] and draw close to Him.[340]

One must cling to God[341] and feel that he is always with Him.[342]

One must be faithful to God[343] and upright with Him.[344]

Relating to God's Commandments

The Children of Israel must observe God's commandments and His statutes.[345] They must observe and keep all of God's words.[346] They must keep His ordinances and statutes.[347]

Israel must keep the Torah, which was given to them by God through Moses.[348]

One must observe God's covenant and His testimonies,[349] to be scrupulous in observing that which God commanded,[350] and to observe God's testimony.[351]

All of the Children of Israel must observe God's commandments with all their hearts and with all their souls, and observe the words of the covenant

---

333 Micah 6:8.
334 Psalms 37:5.
335 II Chronicles 27:6.
336 Psalms 78:10.
337 Ibid., 89:31.
338 II Chronicles 17:4.
339 Jeremiah 29:13.
340 Zephaniah 3:2.
341 Deuteronomy 30:20.
342 Psalms 73:23.
343 Ibid., 78:8.
344 Deuteronomy 18:13.
345 Ibid., 10:13.
346 Exodus 23:13.
347 Leviticus 18:4.
348 II Chronicles 33:8.
349 Psalms 25:10.
350 Ibid., 119:4.
351 Ibid., 19:8.

written in the Torah.[352]

One must listen to God's voice, and do that which is proper in God's eyes.[353]

One must return to God.[354] First, one must examine his deeds.[355]

One must confess his sins and not repeat them.[356] One must return to God with all one's heart.[357] One must return to God by fasting, weeping, and mourning.[358] The wicked person must forsake his wicked ways.[359]

One must fear God's commandments.[360]

Proper Actions in Special Circumstances

One must bow down to God facing His holy mountain (the Temple).[361] One must come to Him in song.[362] God's nation must come to the Temple with words of thanksgiving and praise to God.[363] The nation must gather and cry to God.[364] The nation must call to God on a day of distress.[365] At a time of distress, the nation must submit to God, pray, seek His face, and return from its evil ways.[366]

It is better to listen to God's voice than to offer sacrifices.[367] Kindness and the knowledge of God are more important than sacrifices and burnt offerings.[368] Righteousness and justice are preferable to sacrifices.[369] Singing

---

352 II Chronicles 34:31.
353 Exodus 15:26.
354 Deuteronomy 30:2.
355 Lamentations 3:40.
356 Proverbs 28:13.
357 Jeremiah 24:7.
358 Joel 2:12.
359 Isaiah 55:7.
360 Proverbs 13:13.
361 Psalms 99:9.
362 Ibid., 100:2.
363 Ibid., 100:4.
364 Joel 2:16–17.
365 Psalms 50:15.
366 II Chronicles 7:12–14.
367 I Samuel 15:22.
368 Hosea 6:6.

to God and offering thanks are preferable in God's eyes to offering a sacrifice.[370]

Improper Ways to Relate to God

General Prohibitions

The nation is forbidden to leave God,[371] to distance itself from Him or to turn away from Him.[372]

One may not part from God.[373]

One is forbidden to forget God[374] and His deeds.[375]

One is forbidden to ignore God's words.[376]

One is forbidden to reject God's counsel[377] or to scorn His word.[378]

One is forbidden to be rebellious towards God,[379] to rebel against God's word,[380] to be against Him or to think of schemes against Him.[381]

One is forbidden to complain about God.[382]

One is forbidden to quarrel with God.[383] One is forbidden to argue with God regarding His justice,[384] or to stand before Him in a dispute.[385]

One is forbidden to test God.[386]

One is forbidden to hate God.[387] One is forbidden to scorn God's ways.[388]

---

369 Proverbs 21:3.
370 Psalms 69:31–32.
371 Deuteronomy 31:16–17.
372 Psalms 73:27.
373 Proverbs 18:1.
374 Deuteronomy 8:11.
375 Psalms 78:7.
376 Ibid., 50:17.
377 Ibid., 107:11.
378 Proverbs 13:13.
379 Deuteronomy 9:7.
380 Psalms 107:11.
381 Ibid., 21:9–12.
382 Ibid., 106:25.
383 Isaiah 45:9.
384 Job 40:8.
385 Ibid., 41:2.
386 Deuteronomy 6:16.
387 Psalms 81:16.

One is forbidden to cast doubts on God's capabilities.[389]

One is forbidden to say (secretly) things which are not correct about God.[390] One is forbidden to say anything unseemly about God.[391]

One is forbidden to say that evildoers are good in God's eyes, or that He is not a just judge.[392]

One is forbidden to add to what God has commanded or to subtract from it.[393]

One is forbidden to worship other gods. One is forbidden to make an idol or the likeness of anything,[394] and so too is one forbidden to bow down to it.[395] One is forbidden to bow down to the sun, the moon, the stars or the heavenly hosts or to worship them.[396]

Explicit Prohibitions

One is forbidden to make himself a god of silver or gold.[397] One is forbidden to make a cast idol.[398] One is forbidden to erect a monument (for purposes of worship).[399] One is forbidden to erect altars or high places for other gods.[400]

One may sacrifice only to God.[401] One is forbidden to eat of a sacrifice made to other gods.[402]

---

388 Proverbs 19:16.
389 Isaiah 5:19.
390 II Kings 17:9.
391 Job 1:22.
392 Malachi 2:17.
393 Deuteronomy 13:1.
394 One is permitted to paint two-dimensional pictures of most creatures, except for complete images in special cases, such as people, angels, and heavenly bodies. See *Rosh Hashanah* 24b.
395 Exodus 20:3–5.
396 Deuteronomy 4:19.
397 Exodus 20:20.
398 Ibid., 34:17.
399 Deuteronomy 16:22.
400 II Chronicles 28:24–25.
401 Exodus 22:19.
402 Ibid., 34:15.

One is forbidden to follow other gods[403] or to turn to them.[404] One is forbidden to turn to idols[405] or to place one's trust in them.[406]

One is forbidden to sacrifice his sons or daughters to Molech.[407] One is forbidden to burn his sons or daughters in fire on the high places.[408]

One is forbidden to mention or to talk about other gods.[409]

One may not swear by other gods (rather than by God).[410]

The Children of Israel are commanded to destroy all places where idols are worshipped.[411] They are commanded to destroy the idols, the altars, and the monuments of the people of the land of Canaan.[412]

The Children of Israel must destroy all types of idol worship.[413]

One is forbidden to secretly entice a family member or friend to serve other gods.[414]

A prophet or dreamer of dreams is forbidden to give a sign or show a wonder in order to persuade others to worship other gods. One is forbidden to listen to them.[415]

One is forbidden to worship God as the nations of Canaan worshipped their gods, because they did all types of abominations of God, including burning their sons and daughters.[416] One is forbidden to plant an *asherah* (a form of idol worship) tree next to an altar to God.[417]

---

403 Deuteronomy 6:14.
404 II Chronicles 25:15.
405 Leviticus 19:4.
406 Psalms 115:4, 8.
407 Leviticus 18:21.
408 Jeremiah 7:31.
409 Exodus 23:13.
410 Jeremiah 5:7.
411 Deuteronomy 12:3.
412 Exodus 23:24; 34:13.
413 Ezekiel 11:18.
414 Deuteronomy 13:7–12.
415 Ibid., 13:2–6.
416 Ibid., 12:30–31.
417 Ibid., 16:21.

One is forbidden to set up a stone floor (except in the Temple) and to bow down on it.[418]

One is forbidden to learn the ways of the other nations, which are afraid of signs from heaven and worship these signs, because their idols are made of wood and are unable to do bad or good.[419] One is forbidden to mix with the other nations and to learn from their deeds.[420]

One is forbidden to engage in any type of magic.[421] One is forbidden to turn to necromancers or spiritists.[422]

One is forbidden to curse God.[423]

One is forbidden to swear falsely in the name of God.[424] One is forbidden to use God's name in vain.[425] One is forbidden to swear in God's name untruthfully and unjustly.[426] One is forbidden to swear deceitfully.[427] One is forbidden to violate an oath by God.[428]

A witness is forbidden to deny under oath that he can provide relevant testimony.[429] One is forbidden to swear to do something and then to not do it. It is forbidden to swear not to do something and then to do it.[430]

Actions which Are Forbidden in Regard to the Torah

One is forbidden to forsake God's Torah.[431] One is forbidden to stop listening to the words of the Torah.[432]

One is forbidden to violate any of God's commandments.[433]

---

418 Leviticus 26:1. See Sifra.
419 Jeremiah 10:1–5.
420 Psalms 106:35.
421 Leviticus 19:26.
422 Ibid., 19:31.
423 Exodus 22:27.
424 Leviticus 19:12. See Rashi, based on *Sanhedrin* 66a.
425 Exodus 20:7.
426 Isaiah 48:1–2.
427 Psalms 24:4.
428 II Chronicles 36:13.
429 Leviticus 5:1.
430 Ibid., 5:4. See Rashi based on *Shevuot* 19a.
431 Proverbs 28:4.
432 Ibid., 28:9.

One is forbidden to violate God's statutes and to act as if it were unintentional.[434] One is forbidden to turn away from God's way and to lie.[435]

One is forbidden to forget God's Torah and His commandments.[436]

Actions of Human Behavior

General

One must emulate the life style of the righteous.[437] One must act wisely.[438] One must seek the proximity of the wise.[439]

One must fear God. Then he will not sin.[440]

One who is faithful and upright should pray to God.[441]

It is good for a man to bear the yoke of his youth in acquiescence .[442]

One must do that which is good and upright in the eyes of God.[443]

One must have clean hands (i.e., one must be blameless).[444] One must speak pleasantly.[445]

One must have a pure heart.[446]

One must seek righteousness.[447] One must act with justice.[448]

One must seek faith.[449] One must love the truth.[450]

One must be humble.[451]

---

433 II Chronicles 24:20.
434 Psalms 119:118.
435 Ibid., 44:18–19. See Metzudat David.
436 Proverbs 3:1.
437 Ibid., 4:18.
438 Ibid., 28:26.
439 Ibid., 13:20.
440 Psalms 4:5.
441 Proverbs 15:8.
442 Lamentations 3:27–28.
443 Deuteronomy 6:18.
444 Psalms 24:4.
445 Proverbs 15:26.
446 Psalms 24:4.
447 Zephaniah 2:3.
448 Jeremiah 5:1.
449 Ibid.
450 Zechariah 8:19.
451 Zephaniah 2:3.

One must love kindness.[452] One must love peace.[453]

One must always be careful.[454]

One must rule over his spirit.[455] One must be modest.[456] One must hold his peace.[457]

One must be diligent.[458]

Relating to Wisdom, Understanding and Instruction

One must remember that fear of God is the beginning of wisdom.[459]

One must learn matters of wisdom.[460] One must acquire wisdom[461] and love it.[462]

One must listen to the words of the wise, pay attention to them,[463] and review and recite them.[464]

One must speak words of wisdom.[465]

It is preferable to have understanding.[466]

One must know holy matters.[467]

One must have knowledge.[468] One must acquire it,[469] and keep that which he acquired.[470]

---

452 Micah 6:8.
453 Zechariah 8:19.
454 Proverbs 28:14.
455 Ibid., 25:28.
456 Ibid., 11:2.
457 Ibid., 11:12.
458 Ibid., 10:4.
459 Psalms 111:10.
460 Proverbs 1:2.
461 Ibid., 4:5.
462 Ibid., 29:3.
463 Ibid., 22:17.
464 Ibid., 22:18.
465 Ibid., 10:31.
466 Ibid., 12:8.
467 Ibid., 9:10.
468 Ibid., 17:27.
469 Ibid., 18:15.
470 Ibid., 10:14.

One should understand words of wisdom,[471] love wisdom, strive for it[472] and acquire it.[473] One must have an understanding heart.[474]

One must understand what righteousness, justice, honest ways, and a proper path are.[475]

One must know how to plan his life.[476]

One must know matters of moral instruction (education).[477] One must accept words of instruction of wisdom.[478]

A son must listen to the words of moral instruction of his father,[479] and must accept the words of moral instruction.[480] One must relate seriously to moral instruction (the education he received).[481] One must internalize the ways of moral instruction.[482]

One must listen to the voice of his teachers.[483]

One must listen to words of rebuke.[484]

A son must pay attention to his father's ways.[485]

One must offer his son moral training when he is young.[486] One must use a rod of discipline for a youth.[487] The father must discipline his son.[488] A person is forbidden to banish his son from his home, but must rebuke him.[489]

471 Ibid., 1:2.
472 Ibid., 8:17.
473 Ibid., 4:5.
474 Ibid., 8:5.
475 Ibid., 2:9.
476 Ibid., 8:5.
477 Ibid., 1:2.
478 Ibid., 1:3.
479 Ibid., 1:8.
480 Ibid., 19:20.
481 Ibid., 4:13.
482 Ibid., 23:12.
483 Ibid., 5:13.
484 Ibid., 15:32.
485 Ibid., 23:26.
486 Ibid., 13:24.
487 Ibid., 22:15.
488 Ibid., 29:17.
489 Ibid., 29:15.

One must instruct the child according to the child's tendencies.[490]

A person must know what to answer.[491]

One must rebuke his fellow man in such a way that his rebuke will be effective.[492] It is better to rebuke openly than to love in secret.[493] One should rebuke a person who has understanding.[494]

It is desirable to listen to advice.[495]

Relating to Various Types of People

One must honor those who fear God.[496]

One must detest vile people.[497]

A person must hate evil and haughtiness.[498]

It is proper to point out to a fool his foolishness, so that he should not consider himself wise.[499]

One should smite a scorner, in order to teach him.[500]

A person must think before he answers.[501]

One must obey the king.[502] One must also fear him.[503]

A Good Name

A good name is more desirable than wealth.[504]

It is good for a person not to praise himself.[505]

---

490 Ibid., 22:6.
491 Ibid., 24:26.
492 Ibid., 25:12.
493 Ibid., 27:5.
494 Ibid., 19:25.
495 Ibid., 12:15.
496 Psalms 15:4.
497 Ibid.
498 Proverbs 8:13.
499 Ibid., 26:5. See also n. 590 in this chapter.
500 Ibid., 19:25.
501 Ibid., 15:28.
502 Ecclesiastes 8:2.
503 Proverbs 24:21.
504 Ibid. 22:1.
505 Ibid., 27:2.

Effective Action

One must be speedy in his work.[506]

It is desirable to work in a group. It is also desirable to work alone, and not to rely on others.[507]

The Roles of the Woman

A woman must be a woman of valor.[508] She must do well for her husband throughout her life, to be efficient and diligent, to manage her household well, to bring home income and to act wisely and compassionately towards others.[509]

Comparing Values

Wisdom is better than might.[510] Wisdom has greater value than wealth and property.[511]

Recommended Actions Regarding the Family

One must be wary of a woman who is not his wife.[512] A man must distance himself from her.[513]

One is forbidden to keep company with prostitutes.[514]

A man must rejoice with his wife, always love her, and not turn to other women.[515] A man is forbidden to covet in his heart an evil woman.[516]

It is good for a man to find himself a wife.[517] It is desirable for a man to have children while he is still young.[518]

---

506 Ibid., 22:29.
507 Ibid., 30:25, 27.
508 Ibid., 12:4.
509 Ibid., 31:10–27.
510 Ecclesiastes 9:16–18.
511 Proverbs 8:11.
512 Ibid., 22:14.
513 Ibid., 5:8.
514 Ibid., 29:3.
515 Ibid., 5:15–20.
516 Ibid., 6:24–25.
517 Ibid., 18:22.

Recommended Actions to Improve One's Material Status

It is advisable to prepare an economic infrastructure before one builds a home.[519]

It is advisable to prepare in advance food for difficult times.[520]

One must treat his flock properly,[521] work his land,[522] and harvest his field at the proper time.[523]

One should eat only what he needs.[524]

Forbidden Behavior

One is forbidden to emulate the ways of Egypt or Canaan, or to live according to their laws.[525]

One is forbidden to be involved with wickedness.[526]

The sacrifice brought by a wicked person is an abomination to God.[527]

One may not commit sins repeatedly.[528]

One may not turn away from the path of understanding.[529]

One may not turn his thoughts away from God.[530]

A person should refrain from pursuing pleasure[531] and is forbidden to act wantonly.[532]

One should not be obstinate.[533]

---

518 Psalms 127:4–5. See Ibn Ezra, Metzudat David.
519 Proverbs 24:27.
520 Ibid., 30:24.
521 Ibid., 27:23.
522 Ibid., 12:11.
523 Ibid., 10:5.
524 Ibid., 25:16.
525 Leviticus 18:3.
526 Proverbs 10:2.
527 Ibid., 15:8.
528 Ibid., 17:9. See Ibn Ezra.
529 Ibid., 21:16.
530 Psalms 95:10.
531 Proverbs 21:4.
532 Psalms 5:6.
533 Ibid., 95:8.

One should distance himself from evil,[534] and should close his eyes from seeing evil.[535] One may not ask for evil to befall his fellow man.[536]

One should keep away from crooked[537] and evil[538] paths. One is forbidden to hurry to unsuitable places.[539] One is forbidden to hasten to do evil.[540]

One is forbidden to have any thoughts of sinning.[541] One is forbidden to have thoughts of harming others.[542]

One is forbidden to plan evil deeds.[543]

One may not praise himself for the evil which he did.[544] One is forbidden to hint at doing evil deeds.[545]

One is forbidden to be an agent for an evil deed.[546] One is forbidden to be rebellious.[547]

One is forbidden to cause the righteous to go astray.[548] One is forbidden to acquire anything by deceit.[549]

One should not hide his sins (but should admit them).[550] [551] One is forbidden to say that he has been cleansed of his sins, even though he knows that nothing is concealed before God.[552]

534 Proverbs 3:7.
535 Isaiah 33:15.
536 Proverbs 11:27.
537 Ibid., 22:5.
538 Ibid., 22:3.
539 Ibid., 19:2. See Metzudat David, Ibn Ezra, Ralbag.
540 Ibid., 1:16.
541 Psalms 66:18. See Ibn Ezra.
542 Proverbs 15:26.
543 Ibid., 12:20.
544 Psalms 52:3–7.
545 Proverbs 10:10.
546 Ibid., 13:17.
547 Psalms 68:7. See Ibn Ezra.
548 Proverbs 28:10.
549 Ibid., 12:27.
550 Ibid., 28:13.
551 But one is forbidden to publicize them. See Psalms 32:1.
552 Proverbs 20:9.

Forbidden Attitudes to Wisdom and Knowledge

One is forbidden to be distracted from wisdom.[553] One may not sin against wisdom.[554] One is forbidden to go in the path of the foolish.[555]

One is forbidden to hate knowledge.[556]

Forbidden Attitudes towards Moral Instruction

One is forbidden to hate moral instruction (education).[557] One is forbidden to reject moral instruction.[558] One is forbidden to loathe God's moral instruction.[559] One is forbidden to loathe his father's moral instruction.[560]

One is forbidden to hear moral instruction leading to false views.[561]

One is forbidden to hate words of reproof[562] or to ignore them.[563] One may not stubbornly refuse to listen to words of reproof.[564]

One is forbidden to depart from the ways of his fathers.[565] One is forbidden to depart from the teaching of his mother.[566]

One may not spare the rod of moral instruction from his son.[567]

Forbidden Behavior and Attitudes towards Those with Specific Qualities

One is forbidden to hate the righteous person[568] or to hold him guilty.[569]

---

553 Ibid., 3:21.
554 Ibid., 8:36.
555 Ibid., 9:6.
556 Ibid., 1:22.
557 Psalms 50:17.
558 Proverbs 13:18.
559 Ibid., 3:11.
560 Ibid., 15:5.
561 Ibid., 19:27.
562 Ibid., 12:1.
563 Ibid., 10:17.
564 Ibid., 29:1.
565 Ibid., 5:7.
566 Ibid., 1:8.
567 Ibid., 13:24.
568 Psalms 34:22.
569 Proverbs 17:15.

One is forbidden to punish the righteous or to strike the generous.[570]

One is forbidden to scorn the prophets of God.[571]

One is forbidden to follow the advice of the wicked.[572] A person is forbidden to enable sinners to entice him.[573]

One is forbidden to envy those who perform evil deeds.[574] One is forbidden to envy those who are violent towards others.[575] One is forbidden to justify the wicked.[576]

One is forbidden to give honor to the foolish.[577]

The righteous are not to submit to the wicked.[578]

One is forbidden to join the ways of the wicked.[579] One is forbidden to wish to befriend those who do evil deeds.[580]

One is forbidden to befriend the scornful.[581] One should chase away the scorners.[582] One is forbidden to befriend thieves or adulterers.[583] One is forbidden to befriend the foolish[584] or to come close to them.[585] A wise man should not argue with the foolish.[586]

One should not befriend those who are lustful.[587]

One is forbidden to befriend a quick-tempered person, in order not to learn from his ways.[588]

570 Ibid., 17:26.
571 II Chronicles 36:16.
572 Psalms 1:1.
573 Proverbs 1:10.
574 Ibid., 24:1.
575 Ibid., 3:31.
576 Ibid., 17:15.
577 Ibid., 26:8.
578 Ibid., 25:26.
579 Ibid., 4:14.
580 Ibid., 24:1.
581 Psalms 1:1.
582 Proverbs 22:10.
583 Psalms 50:18.
584 Proverbs 13:20.
585 Ibid., 14:7.
586 Ibid., 29:9. See Rashi.
587 Ibid., 28:7.

There is no talking with fools.[589] One should not answer their foolishness, in order not to be like them.[590]

One should not have a fool carry a message.[591]

One should not eat with a miserly person.[592]

Behavior from which to Refrain

One is forbidden to go on a path which is not straight.[593]

One must hate lies.[594]

One should not talk without knowledge.[595]

One is forbidden to have a deceptive tongue.[596]

One is forbidden to falsify.[597]

One is forbidden to express words of evil.[598]

One is forbidden to curse without cause.[599]

A person must be careful with his speech.[600]

One is forbidden to be a scorner.[601]

One is forbidden to be a fool.[602]

Sometimes one should refrain from joking and joy.[603] One should not like feasts and parties.[604]

---

588 Ibid., 22:24–25.
589 Ibid., 23:9.
590 Ibid., 26:4.
591 Ibid., 26:6.
592 Ibid., 23:6.
593 Ibid., 10:9.
594 Ibid., 13:5.
595 Job 38:2.
596 Proverbs 10:31.
597 Ibid., 11:3.
598 Ibid., 15:28.
599 Ibid., 26:2.
600 Ibid., 18:21.
601 Ibid., 3:34.
602 Ibid., 3:35.
603 Ibid., 14:13.
604 Ibid., 21:17. See Rashi, Ibn Ezra, Metzudat David.

One is forbidden to be quick-tempered.[605] A person must be tolerant.[606] One is forbidden to be hot-tempered.[607]

One may not act in a way which causes shame or brings reproach.[608]

One must refrain from jealousy.[609]

One is forbidden to seek wealth. One should not exert himself in order to become wealthy.[610]

One is forbidden to wander from his place to other places.[611]

One should not chase after worthless actions.[612]

Refraining from Haughtiness and from Relying on Oneself and Others

One is forbidden to be proud of his possessions.[613] One is forbidden to be haughty,[614] and should not seek honor excessively.[615]

One is forbidden to be so proud as to reach a situation where he has nothing to eat.[616]

One is forbidden to boast about what will happen tomorrow.[617]

One is forbidden to be a wise man in his own eyes.[618]

One is forbidden to boast about his strength.[619]

One is forbidden to rely on one's understanding.[620] One is forbidden to rely on himself (more than necessary),[621] and one may not rely on his wealth.[622]

---

605 Ibid., 14:17.
606 Ibid., 14:29.
607 Ibid., 29:22.
608 Ibid., 19:26.
609 Ibid., 27:4.
610 Ibid., 23:4–5.
611 Ibid., 27:8.
612 Ibid., 12:11.
613 II Kings 20:12–18.
614 Jeremiah 13:15.
615 Proverbs 25:27.
616 Ibid., 12:9.
617 Ibid., 27:1.
618 Isaiah 5:21.
619 Amos 6:13.
620 Proverbs 3:5.
621 Ibid., 28:26.

One is forbidden to rely on any person or on generous people.[623]

One is forbidden to believe everything.[624]

One should be careful of free gifts from rulers.[625] One should beware of smooth talk.[626]

One is forbidden to listen to lies or slander.[627]

Refraining from Bad Traits

One is forbidden to engage excessively in talking.[628]

One must not be lazy[629] or slothful while at work.[630] One should not like to sleep.[631] One should not fall asleep during the harvesting season.[632]

One should not be too swift.[633] One should not speak quickly.[634]

Inappropriate Behavior at a Specific Time

One is forbidden to rejoice at a time of mourning.[635]

Forbidden Behavior for Women

A woman is forbidden to leave her husband. She is forbidden to forget the covenant of God.[636] A woman is forbidden to act in a disgraceful way.[637]

---

622 Ibid., 11:28.
623 Psalms 118:8–9.
624 Proverbs 14:15.
625 Ibid., 23:3.
626 Ibid., 26:23.
627 Ibid., 17:4.
628 Ibid., 10:19.
629 Ibid., 6:6–11.
630 Ibid., 18:9.
631 Ibid., 20:13.
632 Ibid., 10:5.
633 Ibid., 21:5.
634 Ibid., 29:20.
635 Isaiah 22:12–14.
636 Proverbs 2:17.
637 Ibid., 12:4.

Forbidden Behavior for Those in Specific Positions

The teachers of the nation, such as the Priests, are forbidden to instruct the people about the laws of God after they drink wine or liquor.[638]

A prophet is forbidden to say anything in God's name which he is not commanded to or to say anything in the name of other gods.[639]

The Way to Serve God

In General

One must mention God's name in those places where God ordered His name be mentioned there.[640]

The Children of Israel are to build a Holy Place (a Tabernacle or Temple) for God, that He might dwell in their midst.[641, 642] (This commandment, which was given at a specific time, is also applicable for the future.) They must remain in awe of God's Holy Place.[643]

The Holy Place

The Tabernacle had a courtyard whose length was one hundred cubits and whose width was fifty cubits.[644] The length of the Tabernacle was thirty cubits from east to west and its width was nine cubits from north to south.[645] The building was divided by a curtain between the Holy area and the Holy of Holies.[646] At the entrance to the tent a screen was put up on the eastern side.[647]

---

638 Leviticus 10:8–11.

639 Deuteronomy 18:20.

640 Exodus 20:21.

641 Ibid., 25:8.

642 The structure erected in the desert is referred to as the Tabernacle, the Tent of Assembly, or the Holy Place. The structure built in Jerusalem is referred to as the House; the Temple, or the Holy Place.

643 Leviticus 19:30.

644 Exodus 27:18. The courtyard of the Temple had different dimensions. See Ezekiel 40:47.

645 Exodus 26:15–16, 18, 22. The Temple had different dimensions. See, for example, I Kings 6:2–3.

646 Exodus 26:33.

647 Ibid., 26:22, 36.

Within the Holy Place, an altar was erected. It could be made of earth or of stone.[648] The altar could not be built of hewn stones, because the stones had been profaned by the sword.[649] In the first Tabernacle, it was made of wood overlaid with copper.[650] On the top half of the altar was a copper grating.[651] The altar was placed in the courtyard, in front of the entrance to the Tent of Assembly (or the Temple).[652]

One is forbidden to ascend the altar by means of steps, so that one's private parts should not be exposed.[653]

The Ark was placed within the Holy of Holies.[654] The Tablets of the Covenant were placed within the Ark.[655] The Torah scroll written by Moses was placed alongside it.[656] Above the Ark was a gold cover.[657] On both sides of the cover and above it were two cherubs of gold.[658]

One is forbidden to look at the Ark of God.[659] One is forbidden to hold onto it without having received permission to do so.[660] One is forbidden to stretch out one's hand and to touch the Ark.[661]

On the northern side within the Holy area, a table was placed.[662] Dishes made specially for placing the loaves of bread were connected to it.[663]

On the southern side, opposite the table, was the candelabrum.[664] The candelabrum had six branches, three on each side, and seven lamps.[665] In

648 Ibid., 20:21–22.
649 Ibid., 20:22.
650 Ibid., 27:1–2.
651 Ibid., 27:4–5.
652 Ibid., 40:6.
653 Ibid., 20:23.
654 Ibid., 26:34.
655 Ibid., 25:16.
656 Ibid., 31:25–26. According to another view: within it. See *Bava Batra* 14a.
657 Ibid., 25:21.
658 Ibid., 25:18–20.
659 I Samuel 6:19.
660 II Samuel 6:6–7.
661 I Chronicles 13:10.
662 Exodus 26:35.
663 Ibid., 25:29. See Rashi's explanation, based on *Menachot* 96a.
664 Ibid., 26:35.

front of the curtain, within the Holy area, was a special altar for incense.[666] This altar was overlaid with gold.[667]

Within the courtyard, between the Tent of Assembly (or the Temple) and the altar, was a copper basin with a copper foot, and water was put in it.[668]

In the Temple as described by Ezekiel, the gate facing the east was always closed. One was forbidden to enter through it, because God would come through that way. A prince might sit next to it and eat before God, but he could not enter via that entrance.[669]

The House of God must be regarded with sanctity.[670] One is forbidden to take apart the vessels of the House of God. One is forbidden to close the doors.[671] One is forbidden to defile the House of God.[672]

Offering Sacrifices

The offering of sacrifices is carried out in a number of ways. Many of the sacrifices are burnt offerings and peace offerings of cattle or flocks (sheep or goats) on the altar.[673]

If a person offers a burnt offering to God of cattle or flocks, the animal must be an unblemished male. The person will offer it of his own free will before God at the entrance to the Tent of Assembly (to the courtyard of the Tabernacle/Temple). The one who offers it must rest his hand on the head of the burnt offering, and he will receive atonement. The one who offers the animal must slaughter it "before the Lord" (in the north), and the Priests sprinkle the blood on the altar. The carcass is flayed and is then cut up into parts. It is burned totally on the altar. The burnt offering is considered to be

665 Ibid., 25:31–32, 37.
666 Ibid., 30:1, 6.
667 Ibid., 30:3.
668 Ibid., 30:18.
669 Ezekiel 44:1–3.
670 II Chronicles 29:5.
671 Ibid., 28:24–25.
672 Ibid., 36:14.
673 Exodus 20:21.

a sweet fragrance before God (i.e., it is acceptable to Him).[674] It must be burned up completely on the altar during the night until the morning.[675] The hide of the burnt offering is given to the Priests who were responsible for offering that animal.[676]

A person may offer a burnt offering of a fowl. In such a case, the head is nipped off and the blood drips onto the altar. The Priest removes the crop with the feathers, and throws these into the pile of ashes. He tears the fowl by its wings, and burns it on the altar.[677]

A peace offering may be offered from cattle or flocks, male or female. The one who offers it lays his hands on it and slaughters it. Afterwards the Priests sprinkle the blood. The fat which covers the entrails, the fat which is on the entrails, the fat on the kidneys on the loins, as well as the kidneys and the protruding lobe of the liver are all burned on the altar. In the case of a sheep, the tail must also be burned. The peace offering is considered to be a fire offering, with a sweet fragrance before God.[678]

If one offers a peace offering as a thanksgiving offering to God, he must offer it of his own free will.[679] Along with the sacrifice, he must offer unleavened cakes mingled with oil, unleavened wafers anointed with oil, cakes mingled with oil, of fine flour, scalded in water, all of this along with leavened bread. One of each of these kinds of bread is a heave offering to God, given to the Priests responsible for sprinkling the blood. The meat of a thanksgiving offering may be eaten only on the day that the sacrifice was brought, and one must not leave over anything until the morning.[680]

It is fitting to give a thanksgiving offering to God.[681]

A person who offers a peace offering as an oath or vow can eat the meat on the first day and the following day. Whatever remains over to the third

---

674 Leviticus 1:2–9. See Rashi.
675 Ibid., 6:2.
676 Ibid., 7:8.
677 Ibid., 1:14–17. See Rashi.
678 Ibid., 3:1–16.
679 Ibid., 22:29,
680 Ibid., 7:12–15.
681 Psalms 50:14.

day must be burned. If one plans to eat the meat on the third day, the sacrifice is not acceptable. Whoever eats of that sacrifice will be punished for his sin, for he desecrated that which is holy to God.[682]

One must fulfill his vows to God.[683] In certain circumstances a person should vow to bring sacrifices and must then carry out these pledges to God.[684]

Meat of a sacrifice which comes into contact with something which is ritually unclean must be burned up.[685]

Any person who is ritually clean may eat of the meat of the peace offering. If a person is ritually unclean, or touched something which was ritually unclean, he may not eat of the meat.[686]

One who brings a peace offering must bring the fat with the breast as a wave offering before God. The Priest will burn the fat on the altar, while the breast is for the Priests. The right thigh is to be given as a heave offering to the Priest who sprinkles the blood and burns the fat of the peace offering. These portions are given to the Priests as they were anointed to serve God.[687]

The Priests are forbidden to take of the meat of the sacrifice until the fat has been offered.[688]

One may bring a meal offering of fine flour, with oil and frankincense. The Priests take half a handful and offer it on the altar. The meal offering is also considered to be a fire offering with a sweet fragrance before God.[689]

The leftover of the meal offering is given to the Priests and is considered to be Most Holy.[690] The Priests must bake it without any fermentation like unleavened bread – in a holy area – in the court of the Tabernacle/Temple. It

---

682 Leviticus 7:16–18. See Sifra.
683 Psalms 50:14.
684 Ibid., 76:12.
685 Leviticus 7:19.
686 Ibid., 7:20–21.
687 Ibid., 7:29–36.
688 I Samuel 2:15–17, 29.
689 Leviticus 2:1–2.
690 Ibid., 2:3.

is their portion, given to them by God. It may only be eaten by males who are descendants of Aaron.[691]

One may bring a meal offering which was baked.[692] So too can one bring a meal offering baked in a pan, and then it must be cut up into pieces.[693] One can bring it deep-fried in a pan.[694] The actions taken by the Priest in each of the meal offerings is the same.[695]

The leftover part of the meal offering, whether baked in an oven, in a pan, or deep-fried, is given to the Priest who offers the sacrifice. The leftover part of the other meal offerings is divided among the Priests.[696] The meal offering of a Priest is totally burned up.[697]

The meal offering may not be leavened. One cannot, therefore, offer along with it leaven or honey as an offering made by fire to God. One may bring it as a first-fruit offering, like the two loaves of bread on the Pentecost festival, but one may not offer it on the altar as a sweet fragrance.[698]

Whatever touches the meal offering must be dealt with at the same level of sanctity as the meal offering.[699]

The High Priest must bring a meal offering each day, half in the morning and half in the evening. The offering is made of fine flour on a pan. It is burned completely to God on the altar.[700]

Offering Sacrifices because of Sins

One who violates a serious negative commandment unintentionally must bring a sin offering.[701]

---

691 Ibid., 6:9–11.
692 Ibid., 2:4.
693 Ibid., 2:5–6.
694 Ibid., 2:7. See Rashi based on Sifra.
695 Ibid., 2:8–10.
696 Ibid., 7:9–10.
697 Ibid., 6:16.
698 Ibid., 2:11–12. See Rashi based on Sifra.
699 Ibid., 6:11. See Rashi based on Sifra (Leviticus 6:20).
700 Ibid., 6:12–15. See Sifra.
701 Ibid., 4:2, 13, 22, 27. See Sifra.

If the High Priest sins unintentionally, he must bring a bull for a sin offering. He must lay his hand on its head and slaughter it. Afterwards he must dip his finger in the blood and sprinkle some of the blood seven times in the direction of the curtain. He must also sprinkle some of the blood on the corners of the incense altar. He must pour the rest of the blood on the base of the burnt offering altar. He must offer up the same parts of the animal as in the peace offering. He must burn the rest in the place where the ashes are placed outside the camp.[702]

If the supreme religious court causes the nation to sin unintentionally following a ruling, the elders must lay their hands on the sacrifice and slaughter it. The Priest brings the blood of the sin offering to the Tent of Assembly (or the Temple), sprinkles some of the blood, pours it, offers parts of the animal on the altar, and afterwards burns it – precisely what is done with the sin offering of the High Priest.[703]

One is forbidden to eat of a sin offering whose blood is brought into the Tent of Assembly (or the Temple) for atonement, but it must be burned.[704]

If a ruler sins, he must bring a male goat as a sin offering, must lay his hand on its head, and must slaughter it. There is no need to sprinkle the blood or put it on the curtain or on the incense altar. The blood must be placed on the corners of the burnt offering altar and the rest must be poured on the base of the altar. [705]

An Israelite who sins must bring a female goat or sheep. The method of bringing the sin offering of an individual is the same as that of a ruler.[706]

If the congregation sins by unintentionally engaging in idol worship, it must bring a bull for a burnt offering and a male goat as a sin offering.[707] The atonement is for the entire congregation.[708]

---

702 Ibid., 4:3–12.
703 Ibid., 4:13–21. See Sifra.
704 Ibid., 6:23.
705 Ibid., 4:24–26.
706 Ibid., 4:27–35.
707 Numbers 15:22–24. See Sifri.
708 Ibid., 15:26.

If an individual unintentionally engages in idol worship, he must bring a goat as a sin offering.[709]

The Priest, through his service for the sin offering, will atone for the one who brings the offering, and his sin will be forgiven.[710]

A person must bring a sin offering of a female sheep or goat in the following cases: If a witness denies under oath that he knows relevant testimony, or touches something which is ritually unclean, and forgets and eats something holy (sacrificial), or enters the Tabernacle/Temple, or if he swears and forgets his oath and violates it.[711]

If he cannot afford to bring a lamb, he must bring two turtle-doves or two young pigeons, one for a sin offering and one for a burnt offering. The first bird will be for a sin offering and he nips its neck, without totally severing the head, and sprinkles of its blood on the altar, while the rest of the blood is wrung out on the base of the altar. When he brings the burnt offering, the Priest will atone for the sin and he will be forgiven.[712]

If he cannot afford to bring a fowl, he must bring a tenth of an ephah measure of fine flour as a sin offering. One does not place any oil or frankincense on it. The Priest takes half a handful of it and burns it on the altar. The rest of the meal offering goes to the Priests.[713]

If a person improperly uses holy articles of God, is not sure whether he sinned or not, or swears falsely regarding the fact that he has in his possession an object belonging to another person, he must bring a ram as a guilt offering.[714] Similarly, if a man lives with a female slave who is betrothed to another and was not entirely free, he must bring a ram as a guilt offering.[715]

The sin and guilt offerings are considered to be Most Holy.[716] The sin offering and the guilt offering are to be slaughtered in the same place as the

709 Ibid., 15:27–29.
710 Leviticus 4:20, 26, 31, 35; Numbers 15:25, 28.
711 Leviticus 5:1–6. See Sifra.
712 Ibid., 5:7–9.
713 Ibid., 5:11–13.
714 Ibid., 5:14–26.
715 Ibid., 19:20–21. See Sifra.
716 Ibid., 6:10.

burnt offering. The Priest who offers them can only eat of their meat in a holy area, in the courtyard of the Tabernacle/Temple. Everything which touches it has the same level of sanctity. If the blood of the sacrifice falls on a garment, it must be washed in a holy area. If the meat of the sacrifice is cooked in a pottery vessel, the vessel must be broken. If it is cooked in a copper vessel, it must be thoroughly cleaned and washed in water. Only male Priests are permitted to eat it. The Priest sprinkles some of the blood of the sacrifice on the altar and burns those parts of the animal which must be burned, like the peace offering, as a fire offering to God. The rest of the meat of the sacrifice belongs to the Priest who does the atonement.[717]

Details of Offering the Sacrifices

With each sacrifice, salt must be added.[718]

One is forbidden to offer an animal with a blemish, and so too is one forbidden to bring an animal with a blemish which was brought by a non-Israelite.[719] Such an animal is an abomination to God.[720]

Animals may only be offered from the eighth day since their birth.[721] A firstborn animal may only be offered from the eighth day since its birth.[722]

When a person sacrifices a burnt offering of cattle, sheep or goats, or other sacrifice as a fire offering to God, or on the holidays, he must also bring a meal offering of fine flour and wine for a libation. The amount of fine flour, the oil mixed into it, and the quantity of wine varies, depending upon whether the animal was a sheep or goat, ram or bull.[723]

The nation must bring its sacrifices to God. They must bring a daily sacrifice of two sheep as burnt offerings, one in the morning and one in the afternoon, with meal offerings and wine for libations.[724]

---

717 Ibid., 6:17 – 7:7. See Sifra (Leviticus 6:20).
718 Ibid., 2:13.
719 Ibid., 22:17–25.
720 Deuteronomy 17:1.
721 Leviticus 22:26–27.
722 Exodus 22:28–29. See Mechilta.
723 Numbers 15:1–16.
724 Ibid., 28:1–8.

In the morning, before the daily sacrifice, the Priest must wear his linen clothes and remove the ashes from the altar and place them next to the altar. After he changes his clothes, he must take the ashes out of the camp to a ritually clean place.[725] One must ensure that the fire on the altar never goes out.[726]

The altar is considered to be Most Holy. Whatever touches it becomes holy (and it must remain on the altar if it is proper for it to be there).[727]

The Lamps

The public must bring refined olive oil for the perpetual lamp that Aaron and his sons light each evening so it will burn until the morning.[728] When lighting the candelabrum, the Priest will light all seven lamps.[729]

The Incense

The Priest must light the incense on the golden altar each morning when he prepares the lamps. So, too, will he light it at twilight when he lights the lamps. No foreign incense, sacrifice or libation may be offered on the golden altar. Once a year, the High Priest will atone on it from the blood of the sin offering of the Day of Atonement. The golden altar is Most Holy to God.[730] The composition of the incense is defined very specifically. One may not make it or use it except for use on the altar. The incense is Most Holy.[731]

Anyone who is not a Priest is forbidden to offer up the incense.[732]

The Showbread

The Priests must bake twelve loaves of bread of a uniform size using fine flour. They are to be placed in two rows of six loaves each, on the table before

725 Leviticus 6:3–4.
726 Ibid., 6:5–6.
727 Exodus 29:37. See *Zevachim* 83a, b.
728 Exodus 27:20–21.
729 Numbers 8:1–2.
730 Exodus 30:7–10.
731 Ibid., 30:34–38.
732 Numbers 17:5.

God. One must place on each row pure frankincense next to it as a remembrance for the bread – and it is offered as a fire offering to God. The showbread is to be set up by a Priest on the Sabbath. The showbread is Most Holy.[733] The showbread is placed on the table before God perpetually.[734]

The Blessing of the Priests

The Priests are to bless the Children of Israel with the following words: "May the Lord bless you and keep you. May the Lord have His face shine upon you and be gracious to you. May the Lord turn His face to you and grant you peace." The Priests must place God's name upon the Children of Israel, and God will bless them.[735]

First Fruits

Those of the Children of Israel who live in the Land of Israel must take some of their first crops, put them in a woven basket, and bring them to the place that God will choose to have His name dwell there (in the Temple in Jerusalem). The one who brings the first fruits will come to the Priest and say the following to him: "I declare today to the Lord your God that I have come to the land that the Lord promised to our ancestors to give us." The Priest takes the basket and places it next to the altar. The one who brought the first fruits then must relate the story of the Exodus from Egypt and the coming of the Children of Israel to the Land of Israel in order to explain the reason for the bringing of the first fruits. He must bow down before God and rejoice in all the good which God gave him. Levites and converts also must bring first fruits.[736] One is forbidden to delay the bringing of the first fruits.[737]

The Second Tithe

The Children of Israel who live in the Land of Israel must tithe their crops – their grains, wine and olive oil (here we refer to the Second Tithe,

733 Leviticus 24:5–9.
734 Exodus 25:30.
735 Numbers 6:23–27.
736 Deuteronomy 26:1–11. See Sifri.
737 Exodus 22:28.

which is brought in the first, second, fourth, and fifth years of the seven-year Sabbatical cycle). This tithe is to be eaten in the place which God chooses to have His name dwell there (in Jerusalem) so that the Children of Israel will always fear God. If a person is unable to carry the tithe to the place chosen by God because of the distance, he must redeem it with money, go to that place, use that money to buy edibles, and eat these in joy with his family, before God.[738] This tithe is Holy to God.[739]

The Priests and the Levites

God chose Aaron and his sons to be Priests in order to serve Him.[740] A Priest who has a blemish is forbidden to perform any of the functions in the Temple. He is forbidden to approach the curtain and the altar so as not to profane the holy service of God. However he is permitted to eat of the Most Holy (the leftover of the meal offering and the meat of the sin and guilt offerings) and of the Holy (the meat of peace offerings and similar) like the other Priests.[741] So too is one who is uncircumcised forbidden to enter the Temple.[742]

The Priests carry the iniquity of the Temple and the iniquity of their Priesthood. They must keep charge of the Temple and the altar, so that God will not be angry at the Children of Israel. One who is not a Priest may not approach.[743]

Levites (i.e., Priests) who engaged in idolatry are forbidden to perform the Priestly functions such as at the altar, but can be responsible for the gates of the Temple, can slaughter the sacrifices, and can keep charge of the House.[744]

The Levites were given by God to the Priests to work in the Temple. They have to accompany the Priests and serve them. The Levites are to keep

738 Deuteronomy 14:22–26. See Sifri and Rashi.
739 Leviticus 27:30.
740 Exodus 28:1.
741 Leviticus 21:16–23. See Rashi.
742 Ezekiel 44:9.
743 Numbers 18:1–5.
744 Ezekiel 44:10–14. See Radak, Rashi, Metzudat David.

charge of the Priests and of the Temple, but they are forbidden to approach the utensils of the Temple or the altar.[745]

The Levites have to do the service of the Children of Israel in the Temple and to make atonement for the Children of Israel.[746]

The High Priest must wear holy garments, for glory and splendor, as the servant of God. These garments include a breastplate, an *Ephod*, a robe, a checkered shirt, a mitre, and a sash.[747] The other Priests must wear a shirt, a sash, and a headband for glory and for splendor, as servants of God.[748]

On the *Ephod* are two precious stones with the names of the Children of Israel on them, as a memorial before God.[749] On the breastplate were the *Urim* and *Thummim*, which represented the justice of the Children of Israel. The High Priest was to wear them over his heart when he came before God.[750] On the robe of the High Priest bells were attached, so one could hear when he came into the Holy area.[751]

The High Priest must wear a gold plate as a sign of atonement for the sins related to holy articles. On it is engraved, "Holy to the Lord."[752]

The Priests are also to wear linen trousers from their waists to their thighs out of respect and modesty.[753] The Priests are to wear their clothes when they come to the Tent of Assembly (or to the Temple) or when they approach the altar to serve in the Holy area.[754]

The Priests are forbidden to shave their heads or to let their hair grow wild, but to have it of modest length.[755]

---

745 Numbers 18:6–7.
746 Ibid., 8:19.
747 Exodus 28:2–4.
748 Ibid., 28:40.
749 Ibid., 28:9–12.
750 Ibid., 28:30.
751 Ibid., 28:33–35.
752 Ibid., 28:36–38.
753 Ibid., 28:42.
754 Ibid., 28:43.
755 Ezekiel 44:20.

Preparations before Entering the Holy Place

The Priests and the utensils of the Tabernacle are to be anointed with the anointing oil whose composition is described in detail. It is Holy to God for all generations. One is forbidden to use it as a lotion. One is also forbidden to make a preparation which resembles it.[756]

The Priests must wash their hands and feet in the water in the basin when they come to the Tent of Assembly (or the Temple) or before they approach the altar to serve, to offer fire offerings to God.[757]

Priests are forbidden to drink wine or other alcoholic beverages before they come to the Holy Place, so that they will be able to distinguish between the holy and the profane, and between the ritually unclean and the ritually clean.[758]

The Children of Israel must keep away from ritual uncleanliness in order not to make God's Tabernacle/Temple ritually unclean.[759]

The High Priest is forbidden to enter beyond the curtain except when he offers the incense on the Day of Atonement.[760]

The following may not enter the Temple: non-Israelites, those with uncircumcised hearts (who do not wish to know God), the uncircumcised, or Levites who turned away from God along with some of the nation.[761]

In the Temple described in the Book of Ezekiel, when the ruler brings a voluntary sacrifice, whether a burnt offering or a peace offering, he will need to open the gate facing east to offer his burnt offering or his peace offering, as on the Sabbath (see p. 172). When he leaves, he will close the gate after him.[762]

The Place which God Chose

One is forbidden to set up any altars except in the place which God chose to put His name (in the Temple in Jerusalem), so that the Children of

---

756 Exodus 30:22–33.
757 Ibid., 30:19–21.
758 Leviticus 10:8–10.
759 Ibid., 15:31.
760 Ibid., 16:2, 13, 29–30.
761 Ezekiel 44:9–10.
762 Ibid., 46:12.

Israel will come to the chosen place. The Children of Israel must bring their offerings there: their sacrifices, tithes, heave offerings, pledges, pledged items, and their firstborn animals to eat and rejoice before God for His blessing of the work of their hands.[763] One is forbidden to slaughter an animal as a sacrifice except in the courtyard of the Temple.[764] One is forbidden to offer a sacrifice in any other place than the courtyard of the Temple.[765]

Three times each year all of the males of the Children of Israel must come to the place which God chose, on the Festival of Unleavened Bread, on the Festival of Pentecost, and on the Festival of Tabernacles. Each person is to bring his gifts, in accordance with the blessing given him by God.[766]

One is to serve God on His holy mountain.[767]

One is forbidden to erect high places.[768] One must remove existing high places.[769]

Sacrifices Related to Festivals

On the fourteenth day of the first month, each family is to slaughter an unblemished one- year-old male sheep or goat in the afternoon. If there are not enough people to consume an entire lamb, a neighbor can be included.[770] One is forbidden to slaughter it before all the leaven has been disposed of.[771] It must be slaughtered in the place chosen by God.[772] The meat is to be eaten that night, roasted on a fire, with unleavened bread and bitter herbs. It is to be consumed by the morning, and whatever is left must be burned. This is the Passover sacrifice to God.[773] Non-Israelites are forbidden to eat of it. Slaves are permitted to eat of it only if they were circumcised. One who is not

763 Deuteronomy 12:4–7. See Sifri.
764 Leviticus 17:1–5. See Sifra.
765 Ibid., 17:8–9.
766 Deuteronomy 16:16–17.
767 Ezekiel 20:40.
768 II Chronicles 21:10–11.
769 Ibid., 20:33.
770 Exodus 12:3–6, 25.
771 Ibid., 23:18. See Mechilta.
772 Deuteronomy 16:2.
773 Exodus 12:8–11.

of the Children of Israel is forbidden to eat of it. It is to be eaten in one place. The meat may not be taken outside, and one is forbidden to break any bone of it. Every member of the Children of Israel must offer the Passover sacrifice, while a convert may offer it and eat of it only if he was circumcised. One who is uncircumcised is forbidden to eat of it. The laws of the native-born and the convert are identical.[774]

If a man is ritually clean and is not far away, he must bring the Passover sacrifice. If he becomes ritually unclean by coming in contact with a dead body or is far away, he must offer the sacrifice on the fourteenth of the second month, and eat it with unleavened bread and bitter herbs. He is forbidden to leave any of the meat until the morning or to break any bone of it. He must observe all the laws of the Passover sacrifice.[775]

On the day after the first day of the Festival of Unleavened Bread, the Children of Israel must bring the sheaf, which is the first of the harvest, to the Priest. The Priest must wave the sheaf before God. On that day, a sheep is to be offered as a burnt offering, fine flour for a meal offering, and wine as a libation. One is forbidden to eat from the new crop of grain until this sacrifice is brought.[776] The sheaf, also referred to as the "meal offering of the new crop," is similar to other meal offerings, but it is made of crushed barley rather than of fine wheat flour.[777]

On the fiftieth day from the bringing of the sheaf sacrifice, one is to bring a new meal offering to God of two loaves made of fine flour, baked leavened. These are the first crop of wheat to God. Along with the bread they must sacrifice seven sheep, a bull, and two rams as a burnt offering with their meal offerings and libations, as well as a goat for a sin offering and two sheep for peace offerings. The Priest must wave the peace offerings with the first-crop bread before God. They will be holy to God, and will be given to the Priest.[778]

---

774 Ibid., 12:43–49.
775 Numbers 9:10–13.
776 Leviticus 23:10–14. See Sifra.
777 Ibid., 2:14–16. See Sifra.
778 Ibid., 23:15–20.

On the Festival of Pentecost, one is to rejoice (with peace sacrifices) in the place chosen by God.[779]

In the seventh month on the tenth day of the month, on the Day of Atonement, before the High Priest enters the Holy of Holies behind the curtain, he must bring a bull as a sin offering and a ram as a burnt offering. He must immerse himself in a ritual bath, and then put on the linen garments. He is to take two goats for a sin offering and a ram for a burnt offering from the Children of Israel, and is to stand them in the courtyard of the Temple. He must cast a lot as to which of the goats will be a sacrifice to God and which will be the scapegoat. Afterwards he sacrifices the goat to God as a sin offering, whereas he keeps the scapegoat standing alive before God in order to send it into the desert.

The High Priest sacrifices the bull which is a sin offering. He takes a censer with burning coals from the altar and a full handful of incense and brings them beyond the curtain. He must place the incense on the fire. The cloud of the incense will cover the ark-cover. He must sprinkle of the blood of the sin offering on the ark-cover one time and before the ark-cover seven times. That way he atones for himself and for his family. Afterwards he slaughters the goat, the sin offering of the nation. He must sprinkle the blood inside the curtain just as he did with the blood of the bull to atone for the Children of Israel for all their sins, trespasses, and ritual uncleanliness. He must also atone on the curtain from the outside. No other person is permitted to be in the Temple when the High Priest is inside the Holy of Holies to atone.

The High Priest must go out to the golden altar and atone upon it, by sprinkling the blood of the two sin offerings on the corners of the altar seven times. Thus the altar will be cleansed of the ritual uncleanliness of the Children of Israel and will be sanctified.

The High Priest must take the scapegoat, lay his hands on it, and confess the sins of the Children of Israel. Afterwards he will send it to the desert with a man designated to do so.

The High Priest then removes the linen garments which he was wearing, immerses himself and then dons the priestly garments. He has to sacrifice the

779 Deuteronomy 16:10–11. See Sifri.

two rams, his own and that of the Children of Israel, as a burnt offering. He must offer the fat of the sin offering on the altar.

Afterwards the High Priest must again don the linen garments and go behind the curtain (to remove the spoon and the censer). He must again take off the linen garments, immerse himself, and then don the priestly garments.

The man who sent the scapegoat to the desert must immerse his clothes in a ritual bath and immerse himself before he returns to a place which is ritually clean. The sin offerings whose blood was used for atonement in the Holy of Holies must be taken outside the camp or the city and their hides and flesh and dung must be burned. The one who burns them must immerse his garments and immerse himself.[780]

On the Festival of Tabernacles one celebrates joyfully (by bringing peace offerings of joy and peace offerings of the festival) for seven days in the place chosen by God.[781, 782] During the days of the festival, water is to be poured onto the altar as a libation in the morning.[783]

On the festivals, a fire offering is to be offered to God, burnt offerings, meal offerings, sacrifices and libations, each on its day, in addition to those brought on the Sabbath and in addition to the meal offerings, pledges and pledged offerings which will be given to God.[784]

On the festival, burnt offerings are to be sacrificed along with their meal offerings and libation. These are in addition to the daily burnt offering.[785]

On the Sabbath, two sheep are offered as burnt offerings.[786] On the New Moon, two bulls, one ram and seven sheep are sacrificed as burnt offerings, as well as a goat as a sin offering.[787] On the Festival of Unleavened Bread and on the Festival of Pentecost the offerings are the same as on the New Moon.[788]

---

780 Leviticus 16:2–28. See Sifra (Leviticus 16:9, 17, 18, 23, 26).

781 Deuteronomy 16:15.

782 They are to be brought on at least one of the days, preferably the first day. See Sifri.

783 See *Ta'anit* 2b.

784 Leviticus 23:37–38.

785 Numbers 28:1–29:38.

786 Ibid., 28:9–10.

787 Ibid., 28:11–15.

788 Ibid., 28:16–31.

On the Day of the Blowing of the Shofar (the New Year), one brings one bull, one ram and seven sheep as burnt offerings, and a goat as a sin offering in addition to the burnt offerings of the New Moon.[789]

On the Day of Atonement, one brings as burnt offerings one bull, one ram, and seven sheep, as well as a goat as a sin offering.[790]

On the first day of the Festival of Tabernacles, one brings thirteen bulls, two rams, and fourteen sheep as a burnt offering, along with a goat as a sin offering. On each day thereafter of the festival, the number of bulls is decreased by one so that on the seventh day only seven bulls are offered. The number of rams and sheep remains identical for each day of the festival.[791] On the eighth day, one bull, one ram, and seven sheep are offered as burnt sacrifices, as well as a goat as a sin offering.[792]

These sacrifices, which are brought by the nation on the festivals, are in addition to their pledges and pledged objects, their burnt offerings, meal offerings, libations, and their peace offerings.[793]

Our Sages determined that an additional prayer be said on the Sabbaths, festivals, and New Moons, in which the additional sacrifices of those days are mentioned.

The fat of the peace offering of the festival may not remain off the altar until morning.[794]

In the Temple as described by Ezekiel, the ruler must bring burnt offerings, the sin offering, the meal offering, the libations and the peace offerings on the festivals, the New Moons, and the Sabbaths, in order to atone for the House of Israel.[795]

The gate of the inner courtyard which faces east will be closed on the six days of work, and will be opened on the Sabbaths and New Moons. The ruler will come through the hall of the gate from outside and will stand at the

---

789 Ibid., 29:1–6.
790 Ibid., 29:7–11.
791 Ibid., 29:12–34.
792 Ibid., 29:35–38.
793 Ibid., 29:39.
794 Exodus 23:18. See Mechilta.
795 Ezekiel 45:17.

doorpost of the gate. The Priests will offer his burnt offering and peace offerings. The ruler must bow down at the threshold of the gate and leave. The gate will not be closed until the evening. The nation must bow down before God at the entrance of this gate on the Sabbaths and New Moons.[796]

When the ruler comes to the Temple, he must enter via the hall of the main gate to the eastern gate of the inner courtyard, and leave that way as well. On festivals – when the nation enters via the northern gate and leaves via the southern gate, while those who come in through the southern gate leave through the northern gate – the ruler, too, will come and leave as they do.[797]

On the festivals and New Moons, trumpets are to be blown when the burnt offerings and peace offerings are sacrificed. Through this blowing, the Children of Israel will be remembered by God.[798]

Sacrifices in Special Circumstances

A woman who gave birth, after the period of her ritual cleanliness ends, must bring a one-year-old sheep as a burnt offering and a pigeon or turtle-dove as a sin offering. The Priest will sacrifice them before God and will atone for her. If she cannot afford it, she can bring two turtle-doves or two young pigeons, one as a burnt offering and one as a sin offering, and the Priest will atone for her and remove her ritual uncleanliness from her.[799]

On the eighth day of his becoming clean, one who has recovered from a specific skin ailment must bring two male sheep and a one-year-old female sheep, three tenths of a measure of fine flour mixed with oil and a log quantity of oil. The Priest who performs the purification will stand the man before God at the entrance to the Temple. The Priest will wave one sheep and the oil. He must offer the sheep as a guilt offering. The Priest will take of the blood of the guilt offering and place it on the left ear lobe of the one becoming ritually clean, and on his right thumb and his right big toe.

796 Ibid., 46:1–3.
797 Ibid., 46:8–10.
798 Numbers 10:10.
799 Leviticus 12:1–8.

Afterwards the Priest will pour some of the oil on the palm of his left hand, dip his right hand in it, and sprinkle seven times before God. The Priest will place some of the oil on those places where the blood of the guilt offering was placed. The remaining oil is to be poured on the man's head – and he will atone for him before God. The second sheep is to be offered as a sin offering, the female sheep as a burnt offering, and the fine flour for a meal offering – and he will atone for the man and he will become ritually clean.

If the man cannot afford it, he may bring two turtle-doves or two young pigeons, one for a sin offering and the other for a burnt offering in place of the male sheep for a sin offering and the female sheep for a burnt offering.[800]

A man who is becoming ritually clean after having been ritually unclean as a result of a specific abnormal male emission (a *zav* – see p. 181) must bring, on the eighth day, two turtle-doves or two young pigeons to the Priest, one as a sin offering and the other as a burnt offering. The Priest will atone for him.[801]

A woman who had a bloody discharge, not at the time of her regular monthly period or beyond the time of her monthly period (a *zavah* – see p. 182), after counting seven days without any emission, on the eighth day must bring two turtle-doves or two young pigeons, one as a sin offering and the other as a burnt offering. The Priest will atone for her.[802]

If a husband warns his wife not to be alone with another man, whether she was unfaithful to him or not, he must bring her to the Priest and bring a meal offering for her, without oil or frankincense, a meal offering of jealousy, a memorial of iniquity. The Priest must place water that had been sanctified in the basin into an earthenware vessel and place in it also dust of the Tabernacle (the Temple). He must uncover the woman's hair and place in her hand the meal offering of jealousy. He must hold in his hands the earthenware vessel with the water – the water of the curse. The Priest must have the woman swear. He says to her that if she was not unfaithful to her husband, the water she drinks would not do anything to her, but if she was unfaithful to him, her belly would swell and her thigh would fall away. The woman is to answer, "Amen, amen." The

800 Ibid., 14:10–32.
801 Ibid., 15:13–15.
802 Ibid., 15:29–30. See Sifra.

Priest must write these words and erase them into the water, must wave the meal offering in the woman's hand and sacrifice half a handful. Afterwards he has the woman drink the water.[803] If she was unfaithful, her belly will swell and her thigh will fall away and she will be a curse among the nation. If not – she is guiltless of any sin.[804, 805]

If a Nazirite becomes ritually unclean through exposure to a dead body, after seven days of ritual uncleanliness, on the eighth day, he must bring two turtle-doves or two young pigeons, one for a sin offering and one for a burnt offering. He must also bring a sheep as a guilt offering, and the Priest will atone for him.[806]

On the day that the Nazirite completes his Nazirite days in ritual cleanliness, he must bring a male sheep as a burnt offering, a female sheep as a sin offering, and a ram as a peace offering, along with their meal offerings and libations.[807] He must also bring a basket of unleavened bread made of fine flour, cakes mixed with oil and thin wafers coated with oil. The Priest will sacrifice the sin offering and the burnt offering. He will offer the ram as a peace offering along with the basket of unleavened bread, and then the Nazirite will shave the hair of his head and place it in the fire of the peace offering. The Priest will take the shoulder of the ram along with one wafer of unleavened bread and place them on the Nazirite's palms. The Priest must wave them, and they will be sanctified to the Priest. From then on, the Nazirite may once again drink wine.[808, 809] The Nazirite can add to these sacrifices according to whatever vow he took.[810]

---

803 According to another view, the water was drunk before offering the half a handful. See *Sotah* 19a.

804 Numbers 5:11–31.

805 Previous merits and sins can also affect the outcome. See *Sotah* 20a, and *Sotah* 3:2 in the Palestinian Talmud.

806 Numbers 6:9–12.

807 The Nazirite brings a sin offering because he left the sanctity of being a Nazirite. According to views brought in the Talmud (*Nedarim* 10a), the sin of the Nazirite is the distress he caused himself by refraining from wine.

808 Numbers 6:13–20.

809 According to another view, the Nazirite may drink wine after one of the sacrifices is offered. See *Nazir* 46a.

810 Numbers 6:21.

Limitations Related to Bringing Sacrifices

One is forbidden to sacrifice the proceeds of a prostitute or of the sale of a dog as a pledge to God, because these are an abomination to Him.[811]

One may not offer something which was stolen as a burnt offering.[812]

One may not place any idolatry in the House of God.[813]

God does not want sacrifices, of any kind, when the nation's hands are full of blood. It would be better if they ceased doing evil and judged the oppressed, the orphans, and the widows fairly.[814]

One is forbidden to desecrate the holy things of God.[815]

The Ritually Unclean and Ritually Clean

The Children of Israel must refrain from entering God's Tabernacle (or the Temple) when they are ritually unclean. Similarly, one is forbidden to eat of the meat of the sacrifices or the leftover of the meal offerings when one is ritually unclean.[816]

To purify a person, utensils, or clothing from ritual uncleanliness requires immersion in a spring or a ritual bath at the time specified for purification.[817]

The carcasses of forbidden animals (see p. 197) who live on the land, in the sea, or who fly make one ritually unclean. Whoever touches any of these carcasses is ritually unclean until the evening. Whoever holds or carries such a carcass is ritually unclean until the evening and must immerse his clothes in order to remove the ritual uncleanliness from them.[818]

Similarly, one who touches one of the carcasses of the swarming things mentioned, including the weasel, the mouse, the great lizard, the gecko, the land-crocodile, the lizard, the sand-lizard, and the chameleon becomes

---

811 Deuteronomy 23:19.
812 Isaiah 61:8.
813 Jeremiah 7:30.
814 Isaiah 1:10–17.
815 Ezekiel 22:26.
816 Leviticus 22:2–7. See Sifra.
817 Leviticus.,11:36. See Sifra (ibid. and Leviticus 15:5, 13).
818 Ibid., 11:1–28. See Sifra.

ritually unclean. If a dead creature of this kind falls on a wooden utensil or on a garment or on leather or on a sack, as long as work can be done with it, the item must be immersed, and it remains ritually unclean until the evening. If the carcass of such a swarming thing falls into an earthenware vessel, anything in the vessel will become ritually unclean, and one must break the vessel in order to remove its ritual uncleanliness.[819]

All food which comes into contact with potable water or any liquid in a vessel can become ritually unclean.[820]

If a carcass falls on an oven or stove, they are to be broken in order to remove their ritual uncleanliness.[821]

If a carcass touches seeds, they remain ritually clean. However, if the seeds are made wet with water before the carcass touches them, they become ritually unclean.[822]

One who touches the carcass of a type of animal which is permitted to be eaten is ritually unclean until the evening. In addition, one who eats of it or who carries it is required to immerse his clothes in order to remove his ritual uncleanliness.[823]

If one eats the meat of a permitted bird which was not slaughtered ritually, or after it was slaughtered ritually, was found to have a defect making it forbidden, he must immerse his clothes and himself in order to remove his ritual uncleanliness. He remains ritually unclean until the evening.[824]

A spring or well remain ritually clean – they do not acquire ritual uncleanliness. However, if a person inside touches a carcass which is in the spring or well, he becomes ritually unclean.[825]

One who touches a dead body becomes ritually unclean for seven days. Similarly, if a person dies in a tent, everyone who enters the tent and everything inside it becomes ritually unclean for seven days. Every

819 Ibid., 11:29–33. See Sifra.
820 Ibid., 11:34. See Sifra.
821 Ibid., 11:35. See Sifra.
822 Ibid., 11:37–38.
823 Ibid., 11:39–40.
824 Ibid., 17:15.
825 Ibid., 11:36.

earthenware vessel which is not covered becomes ritually unclean. Whoever touches a dead body or the bone of a person in an open place or in a grave is ritually unclean for seven days.[826]

In order to remove the ritual uncleanliness of a dead person, the person who became ritually unclean must purify himself on the third day and on the seventh day.[827] In the process of purification, the Priest will use the water of separation (or sprinkling water): The Priest must take an unblemished red heifer which never had a yoke on it outside the camp, where it is slaughtered. The Priest takes of the blood and sprinkles it seven times towards the Temple. The heifer must be burned before his eyes. The Priest must take cedar wood, hyssop and scarlet, and throw them into the fire. Afterwards the Priest must immerse his clothes and his own body, and can then come to the camp. He and the one who burned the heifer are ritually unclean until the evening. A person who is ritually clean must gather the ashes and place them outside the camp in a place which is ritually clean. This is to be preserved by the Children of Israel as the water of separation for a sin offering. The one who gathers the ashes must also immerse his clothes and remains ritually unclean until the evening.[828]

Some of the ashes of the red heifer are to be taken and placed in a vessel. Then water from a spring is to be poured on it – fresh water. A man who is ritually clean is to dip the hyssop in the water, and to sprinkle it on everything which became ritually unclean through contact with the dead. The person who is ritually unclean must immerse his clothes and immerse himself, and he remains ritually unclean until the evening. The one who sprinkles the water with the ashes must immerse his clothes and whoever touches the water is ritually unclean until the evening. Whoever touches a person who touched a dead body is ritually unclean until the evening.[829, 830]

---

826 Numbers 19:11, 14–16.
827 Ibid., 19:12.
828 Ibid., 19:2–10.
829 Ibid., 19:17–22. See Sifri.
830 One should note that one who was ritually unclean due to contact with the dead does not leave that status until the evening of the seventh day, just as those who dealt with these waters. Thus the sprinkling of the water causes purification but, in itself, does not

A woman who gives birth to a boy is ritually unclean for seven days, just as for the monthly period (see p. 182). For an additional thirty-three days she is forbidden to touch anything holy or to enter the Temple. A woman who gives birth to a girl is ritually unclean for fourteen days. For an additional sixty-six days she is forbidden to touch anything holy or to enter the Temple. After she immerses herself and offers her sacrifices (see p. 173), she gains atonement and becomes ritually clean.[831] Nowadays, a woman who gives birth to either a boy or a girl must count seven days during which there is no discharge of blood, like a woman who had such a discharge not during her monthly period, in order to become ritually clean. (See p. 182.)

If a person has a rising in the skin of his flesh, or a scab or bright spot of a specific affliction of a skin ailment, so that the hair in it turns white, and the affliction appears deeper than the skin of the flesh, the Priest must proclaim that the person is ritually unclean (with the specific skin ailment). If the spot is white whereas the rest of the hair did not turn white or it does not look deeper than the skin, the Priest must confine the person for two periods of seven days each. After each period he must check to see if it spread. If the affliction is darker after the second time, the Priest must proclaim that the person is ritually clean after he immerses his clothes. If the affliction spreads in the skin, the Priest must proclaim that he is ritually unclean.[832]

If there is a white rising in the skin and the hair in it is white or there is flesh-colored skin inside it, the Priest must proclaim that he is ritually unclean. If the affliction covers all his body, the Priest must proclaim that he is ritually clean. If flesh color again appears, the Priest must proclaim that he is ritually unclean until it turns white.[833]

If a person has a boil on its skin and it heals, and in the place of the boil there is a white or reddish white rising so that the hair turned white and it appears deeper than the skin, the Priest must proclaim that he is ritually unclean. If there is no white hair or the spot does not appear to be deep, the

---

make one ritually clean.

831 Leviticus 12:2–7.

832 Ibid., 13:2–8.

833 Ibid., 13:9–17.

Priest is to confine the person for seven days, and then check if the affliction has spread in the skin.[834]

If a person has a burn on his skin and the raw area of the burn develops a bright spot or a rising, so that the hair is white and it appears deeper than the skin, the Priest must proclaim that he is ritually unclean. If there is no white hair and the skin does not appear to be deep, the Priest is to confine the person for seven days, and then to examine if the affliction has spread in the skin.[835]

If an affliction in the head or the beard of a man or a woman appears deeper than the skin, and yellow hair is seen, the Priest must proclaim that he is ritually unclean. If it does not appear to be deeper than the skin, but there is no black hair, the Priest is to confine the person for seven days. If it has not spread in the skin and there is no yellow hair, the person must shave around the affliction and remain confined for another seven days. If it has still not spread, the Priest is to proclaim that he is ritually clean after he immerses his clothes. If after the person was proclaimed to be ritually clean, the affliction begins to spread on the skin, the Priest must immediately proclaim him to be ritually unclean. He will be proclaimed to be ritually clean when black hair appears.[836]

If bright white spots appear on the skin, the man is ritually clean.[837]

If the hair on a man's head or his beard has fallen out, he is ritually clean. If a reddish-white affliction spot appears on his head or face which appears like a skin ailment, the Priest will proclaim that the man is ritually unclean.[838]

One who has the skin ailment must tear his clothes like a mourner, leave his head uncovered, cover himself up to his upper lip, and proclaim himself ritually unclean. He must remain alone outside the camp.[839] The instructions

834 Ibid., 13:18–23.
835 Ibid., 13:24–28.
836 Ibid., 13:31–37.
837 Ibid., 13:38–39.
838 Ibid., 13:40–44.
839 Ibid., 13:45–46.

of the Priests are to be followed scrupulously in regard to the affliction of the skin ailment.[840]

After the affliction has been healed, the Priest will verify this. The Priest must take two birds of a ritually clean species and slaughter one of them above an earthenware vessel in which there is spring water. The Priest must dip the live bird, cedar wood, scarlet, and hyssop in the blood of the slaughtered bird. He must sprinkle the blood on the person who is becoming ritually clean seven times and release the live bird. The person who is becoming ritually clean must immerse his clothes, shave off all his hair, and immerse himself so that he will be able to enter the camp. He must sit outside his tent for seven days. On the seventh day he must again shave off all his hair, immerse his clothes and himself, and on the eighth day must bring his sacrifices (see p. 173). After these are sacrificed, he is completely ritually clean.[841]

If a man has a specific abnormal emission two or three times, he becomes ritually unclean.[842] Such a person is known as a *zav*.

Whatever place or object a *zav* sits on becomes ritually unclean. Whoever touches anything upon which a *zav* lay, or sits on something upon which he sat must immerse his clothes and immerse himself. He is ritually unclean until the evening. The same is true for anyone who touches a *zav* or upon whom a *zav* spat. Whatever a *zav* rides on becomes ritually unclean. Whoever touches anything which was under a *zav* is ritually unclean until the evening. If he carries any such object, he must immerse both his clothes and himself. If a *zav* does not immerse himself to become ritually clean and he touches another person, the latter must immerse his clothes and himself, and remains ritually unclean until the evening. Earthenware vessels touched by a *zav* must be broken, while wooden vessels touched by a *zav* must be immersed in order to remove the ritual uncleanliness.[843]

In order to become ritually clean, the *zav* must count seven days without emissions, and must immerse his clothes and himself in the water of a spring.

---

840 Deuteronomy 24:8.
841 Leviticus 14:2–32.
842 Ibid., 15:2–3. See Sifra.
843 Ibid., 15:4–12. See Sifra.

On the eighth day (if he saw three emissions), he must bring a sacrifice (see p. 174), and afterwards he becomes ritually clean.[844]

If a man has an emission, he must immerse himself and remains ritually unclean until the evening. Every article of clothing or leather upon which there is semen must be immersed, and it remains ritually unclean until the evening. A woman who had relations with a man must immerse herself, and she is ritually unclean until the evening.[845]

A woman who is having her monthly period is called a *niddah*. She is ritually unclean for seven days and then must immerse herself. (Today, a woman who sees blood is considered to be a *zavah*. See below.) Whoever touches her is ritually unclean until the evening. Whatever she lies on during her period becomes ritually unclean. Whatever she sits on becomes ritually unclean. One who touches something upon which she had lain or sat must immerse his clothes and himself, and is ritually unclean until the evening. If a person sat on the bed where the woman lay or upon something where she had sat, even if he did not touch it, he is ritually unclean until the evening. Whoever lies with such a woman becomes ritually unclean for seven days, and whatever he lies on becomes ritually unclean.[846]

If a woman has a bloody discharge not at the time of her monthly period or beyond the time of her monthly period, she is called a *zavah*, and is ritually unclean and makes others ritually unclean as does a woman at the time of her monthly period. After she stops having a discharge, she must count seven days without any discharge. She becomes ritually clean after she immerses herself.[847]

If within a woolen or linen garment, in the warp or the woof, or in leather, or in any leather garment, a reddish or greenish spot appears, the Priest must place it in confinement for seven days. If the spot spreads, the item is ritually unclean and the Priest must burn it. If it does not spread, it is to be washed and put in quarantine for another seven days. If the spot does

844 Ibid., 15:13–15. See Rashi (Ibid., 15:3) based on *Megillah* 8a.
845 Ibid., 15:16–18.
846 Ibid., 15:19–24.
847 Ibid., 15:25–28.

not change, the item is ritually unclean and the Priest must burn it. If the spot becomes darker, the Priest must tear it out of the garment or from the warp or woof. If the spot again appears on it, it is to be burned. If a garment or the warp or woof threads or a leather garment are washed and the spot disappears, it is to be washed a second time in order to render it ritually clean.[848]

If a person is afraid that there is an affliction in his home, he must empty out everything from the house, and the Priest will examine it. If the affliction is greenish or reddish and appears to be deeper than the wall, the Priest must leave the house and close it up for seven days. If the affliction spreads, he must remove the stones involved and throw them to a ritually unclean place outside the city. The place of the affliction must be scraped clean and the scrapings must be thrown into a place which is ritually unclean. The old stones are to be replaced by new stones. The house is then to be replastered. If after these actions the affliction reappears, the Priest must proclaim the house to be ritually unclean. The house is to be demolished, the stones of the house are to be smashed along with its wood, and these along with the dust are to be taken outside the city to a place which is ritually unclean.[849] If the Priest finds that the affliction does not reappear, he must atone for the house (see p. 329) and proclaim that the house is ritually clean.[850]

One who enters the house during the time when it was closed up becomes ritually unclean until the evening. One who lies or eats within the house must also immerse his clothes.[851]

Consecrated Property

Whatever is used in the service of the sacrifices and the Temple receives the status of consecrated property. Under certain conditions, it is possible to redeem items which were consecrated and thereby permit them for general use once again.

---

848 Ibid., 13:47–58.
849 Ibid., 14:35–45.
850 Ibid., 14:48–53.
851 Ibid., 14:46–47.

A male firstborn of cattle, sheep or goats is holy to God. It must be set aside for God.[852] One cannot consecrate a firstborn of cattle, sheep or goats for another type of sacrifice, because it already belongs to God.[853, 854] One is forbidden to work with a firstborn ox, or to shear a firstborn sheep. The meat of the firstborn is to be eaten in the place which God chose. If it has a blemish, one is forbidden to sacrifice it to God, but one may eat it in within one's gates, like a gazelle or a deer.[855]

If a person consecrates an animal from which one may bring a sacrifice, it becomes consecrated to God. One may not exchange it for another, even if the other one is better. If one does exchange it, both of the animals are considered to have been consecrated to God.[856]

Every tenth animal, whether an ox, a sheep, or a goat is consecrated to God. One may not differentiate between a good one and a bad one (even if it has a blemish), and one is forbidden to exchange another animal for that one. If one does exchange it, both of the animals are considered to have been consecrated and cannot be redeemed.[857]

If one consecrates an animal of a species which may be used as a sacrifice, but in itself cannot be sacrificed – the Priest will evaluate its value for a person who would want to buy it. If the one who consecrated it wishes to redeem it, he must add a fifth (i.e., a quarter) of its value.[858]

One who consecrates an animal of a species which cannot be used as a sacrifice must redeem it and add a fifth (i.e., a quarter) of its value. If he does not redeem it, it can be sold for its value.[859]

---

852 Exodus 13:2,12.

853 Leviticus 27:26.

854 The instruction to sanctify a firstborn (Deuteronomy 15:19) means to proclaim his sanctity. See Rashi based on Sifra.

855 Deuteronomy 15:19–22.

856 Leviticus 27:9–10.

857 Ibid., 27:32–33. See *Bechorot* 36b.

858 Leviticus 27:11–13. See Sifra. See also *Bava Metzia* 54a.

859 Leviticus 27:27.

If a house was consecrated to God, a Priest must evaluate its value to whoever wishes to buy it. If the one who consecrated it wishes to redeem it, he must add a fifth (i.e., a quarter) of its value.[860]

If a field has been handed down in a family by inheritance ever since the division of the land during the time of Joshua is now consecrated, the evaluation of its worth is made by a Priest based on the number of years of sowing remain until the Jubilee year. If the one who consecrated it redeems it, he must add a fifth (i.e., a quarter) of its value. If he does not redeem it and the Priest sells it to another person, the one who consecrated it can no longer redeem it, but in the Jubilee year it will return to the Priest as being holy to God.[861]

If other fields not handed down by inheritance from the time of Joshua are consecrated, they return to their original owners in the Jubilee year.[862]

One who pledges to give to God the value of a specific person is to give the amount specified by the Torah based on the person's age and sex. If he is unable to give the amount specified, the Priest is to determine how much the person who pledged can afford to pay.

For a male from the ages of twenty until sixty, the amount is fifty shekels. For a female in that age group, the amount is thirty shekels.

For a male from the ages of five until twenty, the amount is twenty shekels. For a female in that age group, the amount is ten shekels.

For a male from the age of one month until five years, the amount is five shekels. For a female in that age group, the amount is three shekels.

For a male from age sixty and above, the amount is fifteen shekels. For a female in that age group, the amount is ten shekels.[863] All of these figures are according to the value of the shekel of the Holy Place.[864]

---

860 Ibid., 27:14–15.
861 Ibid., 27:16–21.
862 Ibid., 27:22–24.
863 Ibid., 27:2–8.
864 Ibid., 27:25,

One is forbidden to sell or redeem a specific kind of consecrated items, because it is Most Holy to God.[865] One is forbidden to redeem a person who has been sentenced to death, because he has no value.[866]

When there is a census of the Children of Israel, each person must give a fixed sum of money as a donation to God as atonement for his soul, and that will spare the nation from a plague. The money of atonement is to be used for the service of the Holy Place, and it will be a remembrance before God to atone for the souls of the Children of Israel.[867]

One who unintentionally makes use of things consecrated to God must bring a sacrifice. He must pay the cost of the use and add a fifth (i.e., a quarter) and give this amount to a Priest.[868]

Sanctity and Redemption

The second tithe (see p. 164) is holy to God. If its owner redeems it, he must add a fifth (i.e., a quarter).[869] Similarly, the fruit of the fourth year of a new tree is holy.[870]

Every firstborn son is holy to God.[871] He must be redeemed.[872]

The firstborn of a donkey is holy to God.[873]

Every firstborn donkey must be redeemed with a lamb. If it is not redeemed, its neck must be broken.[874]

Remembering the Exodus from Egypt

When the Children of Israel come to the land which God promised them, they will have to observe the Passover sacrifice as a remembrance that God passed over the houses of the Children of Israel in Egypt when He

865 Ibid., 27:28.
866 Ibid., 27:29. See Rashi.
867 Exodus 30:11–16.
868 Leviticus 5:15–16.
869 Ibid., 27:30–31.
870 Ibid., 19:24.
871 Exodus 13:2.
872 Ibid., 13:13.
873 Ibid., 13:2.
874 Ibid., 13:13.

smote Egypt and saved the firstborn of the Children of Israel. This is a commandment for all generations.[875]

For seven days, the Children of Israel can eat unleavened bread and the seventh day will be a festival to God. On these days, unleavened bread or yeast may not be seen throughout their boundaries. The Children of Israel must tell their children on the first evening of the festival that it was because of the observance of the Passover sacrifice that God took them out of Egypt.[876]

One must rejoice on the Festival of Pentecost, as a remembrance of the fact that the Children of Israel were slaves in Egypt.[877]

The Children of Israel are to dwell in booths for seven days in order to have the future generations know that God had the Children of Israel live in booths when He took them out of Egypt.[878]

The Children of Israel must place a sign on their arm and a memorial at the top of the head (the *tefillin* of the hand and of the head) so that God's Torah will be in their mouths, because He took them out of Egypt with a strong hand.[879]

The firstborn were sanctified as a remembrance of the fact that God killed the firstborn in Egypt.[880]

The Children of Israel must observe the Sabbath, because they were slaves in Egypt, and God took them out with a strong hand.[881]

The Children of Israel are forbidden to cheat or oppress a stranger, because they were strangers in Egypt.[882] One is forbidden to be unjust in a judgment or to cheat with measurements or weights. One's balance-scales, weights, and measuring instruments must be calibrated and precise, because

---

875 Ibid., 12:24–27.
876 Ibid., 13:6–8. See Mechilta.
877 Deuteronomy 16:9–12.
878 Leviticus 23:42–43.
879 Exodus 13:9. See Mechilta.
880 Ibid., 13:14–15.
881 Deuteronomy 5:15.
882 Exodus 22:20.

it is God who took the Children of Israel out of Egypt.[883] The Children of Israel must love the stranger, because they too were strangers in a foreign land.[884] One is forbidden to pervert the judgment of a stranger or orphan or to take the clothing of a widow as a security, as a remembrance of the fact that the Children of Israel were slaves in Egypt and God redeemed them.[885] When olives are being harvested, one is forbidden to take all of them, but must leave over some for the stranger, the orphan and the widow. So too is one forbidden to take the last grape clusters after the harvest. These prohibitions are a reminder that the Children of Israel were slaves in Egypt.[886]

When a Hebrew slave is freed in the seventh year, his master must give him of everything with which God blessed him, because the Children of Israel were slaves in Egypt, and God redeemed them.[887]

At Specified Times

The Sabbath

The Children of Israel must remember the Sabbath day to sanctify it. (Our Sages determined that the sanctification should be over wine. They also determined that candles be lit before the Sabbath for pleasure, that one eat three meals during the course of the day, and that one have a separation ceremony at the end of the day.) All work is to be done during the six weekdays and the seventh day is a Sabbath to the Lord. It is forbidden for the Children of Israel, their families, servants, animals, and strangers who live in their settlements to do any work (of the thirty-nine defined categories of work), because God created the heavens and the earth in six days and rested on the seventh day. God blessed the seventh day and sanctified it.[888] We must observe the Sabbath day and thus sanctify it.[889] Plowing and harvesting are

---

883 Leviticus 19:35–36.
884 Deuteronomy 10:19.
885 Ibid., 24:17–18.
886 Ibid., 24:20–22.
887 Ibid., 15:12–15.
888 Exodus 20:8–11. See *Shabbat* 73a.
889 Deuteronomy 5:12.

among the categories of work forbidden on the Sabbath.[890] One is forbidden to light a fire on the Sabbath.[891] When people rest from work on the Sabbath, their cattle, servants, and strangers are able to rest as well.[892] The Sabbath is also the sign for the future generations that God sanctified the Children of Israel.[893] On the Sabbath, one must refrain from one's normal pursuits, to delight in it and to honor it because it was honored by God.[894] Our Sages also forbade one to move various items and to engage in activities characteristic of weekdays.

The Festival of Unleavened Bread

The day that the Children of Israel left Egypt is a festival for all future generations. The Children of Israel can eat unleavened bread for seven days. Leavened bread may not be found in their homes. They are forbidden to eat leavened bread from the first day until the end of the seventh day. The first day and the seventh day are holy. Only work connected to the preparation of food is permitted. The unleavened dough must be kept from fermenting. The Children of Israel, including converts, are forbidden to eat any leavened bread throughout the seven days. They must eat unleavened bread in all their settlements (on the first evening).[895] The first day and the seventh day are referred to as "Holy Days of Assembly," and one is forbidden to perform any work on them except for that pertaining to preparing food.[896] The festival is also called the Festival of Passover. Our Sages set a special Seder ceremony for the first evening of the festival, in order to tell the children about the Exodus from Egypt (see about telling this to the children, on p. 187) as well as the eating of the Passover sacrifice, unleavened bread and bitter herbs. They added rabbinic commandments of drinking four cups of wine and reciting the *Hallel* – thanksgiving psalms. After the destruction of the Temple, our Sages determined that one should eat unleavened bread as a

---

890 Exodus 34:21.
891 Ibid., 35:2–3.
892 Ibid., 23:12.
893 Ibid., 31:13.
894 Isaiah 58:13.
895 Exodus 12:14–20. See Mechilta.
896 Leviticus 23:7.

dessert in place of the Passover sacrifice, and the eating of bitter herbs even without the Passover sacrifice.

The Festival of Pentecost

After the first day of the Festival of Unleavened Bread, one must count seven full weeks (forty-nine days).[897] The fiftieth day is a Holy Day of Assembly, and one is forbidden to perform any work except for that needed in preparing food. This is an everlasting commandment in all the settlements of the Children of Israel, for all generations.[898]

The New Year

The first day of the seventh month of the Hebrew year, the month of Tishrei, is a Sabbatical day for the Children of Israel, as a remembrance of the blowing of the horn, a Holy Day of Assembly. One is forbidden to perform any work except for that needed in preparing food.[899] It is a day of blowing of the horn, and the ram's horn is blown.[900] Our Sages determined a special additional prayer, with verses relating to God's sovereignty, a remembrance of God's actions in the world, and the blowing of the ram's horn. It is the custom everywhere to observe a second day of the New Year.

The Day of Atonement

The tenth day of the seventh month is a Holy Day of Assembly for all generations. One must fast and is forbidden to do any work on that day. That is an eternal law for all generations in every place where the Children of Israel live. The day lasts from the evening of the ninth day to the following evening.[901] The commandments of the day obligate both the native-born Israelite and the convert. On this day, God atones for the Children of Israel for all their sins, and they purify themselves before God. The Day of

897 Ibid., 23:15. See Sifra.
898 Ibid., 23:21.
899 Ibid., 23:24–25.
900 Numbers 29:1.
901 Leviticus 23:27–32.

Atonement is called the Sabbath of Sabbaths.[902] Our Sages added other prohibitions for that day. They also determined special prayers which ask God for forgiveness and atonement, as well as a special final concluding prayer at the end of the day known as the *Ne'ilah* prayer.

The Festival of Tabernacles

From the fifteenth day of the seventh month, for seven days, the Children of Israel are to celebrate the Festival of Tabernacles, as a festival to God. The first day is a Holy Day of Assembly, upon which work, except for food preparation, is forbidden. The eighth day is also a Holy Day of Assembly, with the same restrictions on work.[903]

On the first day, the Children of Israel must take the fruit of a citrus tree (the citron), branches of date palms, branches of a myrtle tree, and willows of the brook. They must bring these four species to the Temple and rejoice with them for seven days. (After the destruction of the Temple, our Sages determined that these four species be taken in every place, on the seven days of the festival.) They are also to dwell in booths for these seven days, so that the future generations will know that God had the Children of Israel dwell in booths when He took them out of Egypt.[904] Our Sages determined that willow branches should be on the sides of the altar in the Temple, and that the people make a circuit around the altar during the seven days of the festival. On the seventh day, known as "Hoshana Rabbah," they made seven circuits around the altar. After the destruction of the Temple, it is the custom to make a circuit around the central platform of the synagogue, while carrying the four species, as a remembrance of the circuit around the altar. It is also the custom to recite special prayers for rain on the eighth day. It is a custom to make circuits around the central platform on the eighth day (the ninth day in the Diaspora) while carrying Torah scrolls.

After the seven-year Sabbatical cycle (six years and the Sabbatical year) ends, on the following Festival of Tabernacles, the entire nation is to gather,

---

902 Ibid., 16:29–31.
903 Ibid., 23:34–36.
904 Ibid., 23:39–43.

including men, women, and children in the place which God chose to hear the reading of the Torah, so that people will hear, fear, learn, and observe everything written in it.[905]

Regulations for the Festivals

Our Sages determined that the *Hallel* – (psalms of praise) should be recited on the festivals, as well as the sanctification over wine, candle-lighting, two meals, and a separation ceremony, similar to the Sabbath. Outside the Land of Israel, it is the custom to add a second day during which work is forbidden to every day upon which the Torah mandates a cessation of work on the festivals of Unleavened Bread, Pentecost, and Tabernacles. One should practice all the commandments of the holiday applicable to the previous day.

Purim

There are two days called Purim which are celebrated each year for all generations in every place where the Children of Israel live, and they are to be remembered always. The two days which are the fourteenth and fifteenth of the month of Adar, are to be kept as days of feasting and joy, and the sending of gifts to one another and charity to the poor. These days were set aside after Haman tried to kill all the Jews, but Esther caused him to receive the fate that he had planned for the Jews, with him and his sons being hanged.[906] Our Sages determined that the scroll of Esther be read on the fourteenth day of the month of Adar in cities and villages which do not have a wall around them, and on the fifteenth of the month in the cities which do have a wall around them.

Additional Regulations

Our Sages also determined eight days of Chanukah, beginning with the twenty-fifth day of the month of Kislev, during which candles are lit and *Hallel* is recited. The holiday publicizes the miracle of the cruse of oil which should have had enough oil to light the candelabrum in the Temple for one day and which nevertheless lasted for eight days.

---

905 Deuteronomy 31:10–13.
906 Esther 9:20–28.

The prophets and the sages determined that people should fast on days upon which the people suffered calamities, including the ninth of the month of Av. They also determined various mourning practices for that day and for the period preceding it.

Preserving Holiness

The Children of Israel must be holy, because the Lord their God is holy.[907] The Children of Israel must be holy, because the Lord their God separated them from the other nations to be a nation which belongs to God.[908] God brought the Children of Israel up from Egypt to be their God, and they must therefore be holy like Him.[909] The Children of Israel must be holy by observing all the commandments.[910] They must sanctify themselves by differentiating between animals and birds which are permitted and forbidden species, and must refrain from eating forbidden animals, including swarming creatures.[911] They are forbidden to eat an animal which died on its own.[912] They are forbidden to eat an animal which was slaughtered ritually but was found to have a fatal defect.[913] One is forbidden to inflict a wound on himself as a sign of mourning.[914]

One who has a specific skin ailment, or a man who has a specific abnormal emission, and one who became ritually unclean by contact with the dead, must be sent out of the camp in order not to make the camp in which God rests ritually unclean.[915, 916]

---

907 Leviticus 19:2.
908 Ibid., 20:26.
909 Ibid., 11:45.
910 Numbers 15:40.
911 Leviticus 20:25; 11:43–44.
912 Deuteronomy 14:21.
913 Exodus 22:30.
914 Deuteronomy 14:1–2. See Sifri.
915 Numbers 5:2–3.
916 A person with a specific skin ailment is sent outside the camp of Israel (or the city), while a man with a specific abnormal emission is sent outside the Levite camp (or the Temple Mount). One who became ritually unclean by coming into contact with the dead is sent out of the Tabernacle (or the Temple). See Sifri.

When the Children of Israel go out to battle against their enemies, a man who is ritually unclean because of an emission must leave the camp and immerse himself. He will become ritually clean when the sun sets.[917]

A place must be set up outside the camp as a latrine. A spade must be left there so that people can dig a hole and cover their excrement. The camp of Israel may not have anything which is ritually unclean, loathsome or indecent. God is there with them to save them from their enemies, and the camp must therefore be holy.[918]

Forbidden Marriages and Sexual Relationships

The Children of Israel are forbidden to marry the inhabitants of the Land of Canaan, because this marriage can lead their sons astray into idol worship.[919] One may not marry non-Israelite women.[920]

One is forbidden to emulate the actions of the people of Egypt or those of the people of Canaan. One is forbidden to follow in their paths, but must observe the laws of the Lord, the God of Israel.[921] One is forbidden to contaminate oneself with the abominations of the nations of the land.[922]

One is forbidden to have sexual relations with his mother, his father's wife, his sister on either his father's or mother's side, his granddaughter, his father's sister, his mother's sister, the wife of his father's brother, his daughter-in-law, his brother's wife, his wife's daughter, his wife's granddaughter, two sisters when both are still alive, a woman during her monthly period (or who had a bloody discharge not during her regular monthly period), or another man's wife.[923] One is forbidden to have sexual relations with his mother-in-law.[924] A man is forbidden to lie with a man as he does with a woman. A man is forbidden to lie with an animal, and a

917 Deuteronomy 23:10–12.
918 Ibid., 23:13–15. See Sifri.
919 Exodus 34:16.
920 Ezra 10:3.
921 Leviticus 18:2–5.
922 Ibid., 18:26–30.
923 Ibid., 18:7–20.
924 Ibid., 20:14.

woman is likewise forbidden to do so.[925] All of these actions are considered to be abominations.[926] One is forbidden to take any actions which might lead to sexual relations with forbidden women.[927] Our Sages forbade sexual relations with additional relatives. They also determined that husband and wife must separate close to the onset of the woman's monthly period.

One is forbidden to lie with a woman slave who is assigned to another man, when the former has not yet been completely freed.[928]

A father is forbidden to cause his daughter to become a prostitute.[929]

One is forbidden to lie with a woman who is betrothed (who needs a divorce from her husband, even though she is not yet completely married).[930]

One is forbidden to rape an unmarried woman.[931]

A person of the Children of Israel is forbidden to be a male or female prostitute.[932]

A man is forbidden to destroy his seed.[933]

A woman is forbidden to act haughtily and in a provocative manner.[934] A woman is forbidden to leave her husband.[935] A woman must build her home, and not destroy it.[936] A woman is forbidden to lack discretion.[937]

A castrated man is forbidden to marry a daughter of Israel.[938] One born of an incestuous relationship or of a woman's adultery may not marry a daughter or son of Israel, even after ten generations.[939] An Ammonite or

---

925 Ibid., 18:22–23.
926 Ibid., 18:26.
927 Ibid., 18:19. According to another view, this prohibition is not by Torah law but by rabbinic decree.
928 Ibid., 19:20. See Sifra.
929 Ibid., 19:29.
930 Deuteronomy 22:23–27.
931 Ibid., 22:28–29.
932 Ibid., 23:18.
933 Genesis 38:9–10.
934 Isaiah 3:16.
935 Proverbs 2:17.
936 Ibid., 14:1.
937 Ibid., 11:22.
938 Deuteronomy 23:2. See Sifri.
939 Ibid., 23:3.

Moabite may not marry a daughter of Israel, even after ten generations.[940] An Edomite or Egyptian, in the third generation from the conversion, may marry one of Israel.[941]

There are two stages to enter marriage. In the first stage – *kiddushin* ("betrothal"), a man dedicates for himself a woman by one of three methods: money, a written contract, or sexual relations.[942] After the *kiddushin*, the relationship can be terminated only by having the man give the woman a divorce document (*get*), but they still cannot live as a couple. The second stage – the *nissuin* (marriage) takes place when the groom brings his bride under the marriage canopy, and then she is his wife in every way.[943] Our Sages determined that, within the framework of marriage, the husband must give his wife a document known as a *ketubah*, which obligates him (or his heirs) in the event of divorce or his death.

If a man married a woman and found in her something loathsome, he must divorce her. If she then married someone else and was divorced or widowed from the second husband, she may not remarry her first husband, because that is an abomination in God's eyes.[944]

If a man's married brother died without having any children, the widow is forbidden to remarry. The living brother is to marry her so as to perpetuate his brother's name by having children. If the brother does not want to marry the widow, he must state this fact to the elders of the city and perform the ceremony of *chalitzah* – literally "removal" – where the widow removes the brother's shoe and spits towards him, saying, "Thus shall be done to the man who does not build his brother's house." The brother's family will be known as "the house of the one whose shoe was removed."[945]

Eating and Drinking

One is forbidden to eat the meat of an animal which died without

940 Ibid., 23:4–7.
941 Ibid., 23:8–9. See Sifri.
942 See *Kiddushin* 2a.
943 See *Kiddushin* 5b.
944 Deuteronomy 24:1–4. See Sifri.
945 Ibid., 25:5–10. See Sifri.

having been ritually slaughtered, because the Children of Israel are a holy nation to God. One may give the meat to a person who has accepted the seven Noahide laws or sell it to one who has not accepted these laws.[946]

One may ritually slaughter and eat meat in the place where one lives.[947]

If a person catches an undomesticated animal or bird for food, after it is slaughtered its blood must be covered, so that it is not eaten.[948]

One is forbidden to eat the meat of an animal or fowl which had a fatal defect. It may be given to dogs.[949]

One is forbidden to eat the fat (that portion offered on the altar as a result of a peace offering) of any animal species which could be used as a sacrifice. One may use the fat of such an animal which died without ritual slaughter or which had a fatal defect, for various purposes.[950]

One is forbidden to ingest the blood of any fowl or animal.[951] It is an eternal law applicable to all generations and places that one is forbidden to ingest fat or blood.[952]

One is forbidden to eat meat without the preparation needed for the blood (such as the ritual slaughtering of the animal and waiting until it has died or the sprinkling of the blood on the altar).[953]

The Children of Israel do not eat the sciatic nerve, because the angel who struggled with Jacob injured the sciatic nerve in his thigh so that he limped on it.[954]

One is forbidden to cook (or to eat) the meat of an animal in milk.[955] Our Sages determined that this should also apply to meat of a fowl in milk.

---

946 Ibid., 14:21.
947 Ibid., 12:20–22. See Sifri.
948 Leviticus 17:13–14.
949 Exodus 22:30.
950 Leviticus 7:23–25.
951 Ibid., 7:26.
952 Ibid., 3:17.
953 Ibid., 19:26. See *Sanhedrin* 63a.
954 Genesis 32:24–25, 31–32.
955 Exodus 23:19. See Mechilta.

One is only permitted to eat the meat of an animal which has the following characteristics: it has true hooves which are cloven, and it chews its cud. Other animals may not be eaten.[956]

One may eat creatures of the seas only if they have fins and scales.[957]

One is forbidden to eat types of fowl from the list mentioned in the Torah.[958] Our Sages determined that one may not eat any species of fowl for which there is no tradition of its being permitted.

Any flying creature which has four legs is considered to be a swarming creature, and is forbidden. Among those are flying creatures which have, in addition to four legs, jointed legs which enable them to jump. Some of these species are permitted.[959] Every swarming creature or one which has more than four legs is forbidden.[960]

If a person plants a fruit-bearing tree in the Land of Israel, he may not eat its crops for the first three years.[961]

One is forbidden to eat bread or any other food from the various grains of that year's crop before the sheaf sacrifice is brought.[962]

After the entry into the Land of Israel, before a person may eat bread, he has to offer the first part of the dough as a heave offering to God. This is a commandment for all generations.[963]

Metal vessels which contained forbidden food can be made fit for use by passing them through fire. If the vessel was used by a non-Israelite, it must also be immersed in water. Those vessels which cannot be passed through fire can be passed through boiling water to make them fit for use.[964] Our Sages also determined that glass vessels must be immersed in water.

---

956 Leviticus 11:2–8.
957 Ibid., 11:9–12.
958 Ibid., 11:13–19.
959 Ibid., 11:20–23.
960 Ibid., 11:41–42.
961 Ibid., 19:23.
962 Ibid., 23:14. See Sifra.
963 Numbers 15:18–21.
964 Ibid., 31:23. See Sifra.

One is forbidden to indulge excessively in wine or other liquor.[965] One is forbidden to indulge excessive quantities of meat.[966] One is forbidden to indulge excessively in oil.[967]

Personal Behavior

A son is to be circumcised on the eighth day from his birth.[968]

After the Children of Israel eat and are satisfied, they must thank God for the good land which He gave them.[969]

One is forbidden to wear clothing which is made of both wool and linen.[970]

For all generations, the Children of Israel must place fringes with a blue thread on each corner of their clothes. When one sees the fringes, he will remember God's commandments and observe them, and thus he will not follow his heart or his eyes. He must be holy to God.[971] If a blue thread cannot be obtained, one can place the fringes without it.

A man is forbidden to remove the hair at the juncture of the jaw and of the head, located next to the ear. He is forbidden to shave a corner of his beard with a razor.[972]

One is forbidden to cut himself because of mourning for a deceased person.[973] One is forbidden to injure himself because of mourning for a deceased person, because the Children of Israel are children of God and a holy nation. God chose them to be a special people to Him from all the nations.[974]

One is forbidden to tattoo himself.[975]

965 Isaiah 5:22.
966 Proverbs 23:20.
967 Ibid., 21:17.
968 Leviticus 12:3.
969 Deuteronomy 8:10.
970 Leviticus 19:19; Deuteronomy 22:11.
971 Numbers 15:38–41.
972 Leviticus 19:27. See Rashi based on *Makkot* 20b.
973 Leviticus 19:28. See Sifra.
974 Deuteronomy 14:1–2. See Sifri.
975 Leviticus 19:28.

A man may not wear women's clothing, nor may a woman wear men's clothing, because these are an abomination to God.[976]

One is forbidden to leave the carcass of a man who had been judged hanging on a tree (after execution) overnight, because the curse of God is hanging.[977]

If a man makes a vow to God or takes an oath to forbid something upon himself, he must keep that vow. If a girl makes a vow to God when she is in her father's house in her youth (until age twelve and a half), if her father hears her making that vow and remains silent, her vow must be kept. If, on the day her father hears it he annuls it, the oath is annulled. God will forgive her (for not having kept her vow), because her father annulled it. Similarly, if she is betrothed (see p. 195), her father and husband can together annul her vow. The vow of a widow or divorcee remains valid. The husband of a married woman can annul his wife's vow, but only on the day that he heard about her vow.[978]

If a man makes a vow to God, he is forbidden to delay in implementing it – to do so is considered a sin in the eyes of God. One is not required to make an oath, but if he does so – he must keep what he said.[979]

A Torah scholar or three men can release vows under certain conditions.[980]

Behavior towards Others

Forbidden Behavior and Forbidden Actions

One is forbidden to murder.[981] One is forbidden to beat someone to death.[982] One is forbidden to refrain from saving a person who is in danger of losing his life.[983]

---

976 Deuteronomy 22:5.
977 Ibid., 21:23.
978 Numbers 30:2–17. See Sifri.
979 Deuteronomy 23:22–24.
980 See *Nedarim* 77b, 78a.
981 Exodus 20:13.
982 Ibid., 21:12.
983 Leviticus 19:16. See Sifra.

One is forbidden to dig a pit which will be an obstacle, or to roll a stone (to cause injury).[984]

One is forbidden to kidnap a person.[985] It is especially serious if one kidnaps a person and then sells him.[986] One is forbidden to hit another person.[987] When two men are fighting, the wife of one is forbidden to grab the private parts of the other, even if it is to help her husband.[988] One is forbidden to cause an injury to another person.[989]

One is forbidden to commit adultery.[990]

One is forbidden to steal.[991] One is forbidden to defraud his fellow man or to rob him.[992] One is especially forbidden to rob a poor person.[993] One is forbidden to evict women and their children from their home.[994]

One is forbidden to trust in oppression and robbery.[995]

One is forbidden to be a partner with a thief.[996]

One is forbidden to cheat his fellow man in buying or selling.[997] One is forbidden to cheat in measurements and weights. One's balance-scales, weights, and measuring instruments must be calibrated and precise.[998] One is forbidden to use two sets of weights or measuring instruments so as to cheat his fellow, but must have one accurate set.[999]

---

984 Proverbs 26:27.
985 Exodus 20:13.
986 Ibid., 21:16. See Mechilta.
987 Deuteronomy 25:3.
988 Ibid., 25:11–12.
989 Leviticus 24:19.
990 Exodus 20:13.
991 Leviticus 19:11.
992 Ibid., 19:13.
993 Proverbs 22:22.
994 Micah 2:9.
995 Psalms 62:11.
996 Proverbs 29:24.
997 Leviticus 25:14, 17.
998 Ibid., 19:35–36.
999 Deuteronomy 25:13–15.

One's soul must be clean of deception.[1000] One may not deal with acts of deception.[1001]

One is forbidden to trick his fellow man, and to claim that it was only a joke.[1002]

One is forbidden to move his fellow man's boundary line.[1003] One is forbidden to move a boundary line as established in the time of his ancestors.[1004] One is forbidden to move the boundary line of an orphan.[1005]

One is forbidden to covet something belonging to someone else.[1006] One must loathe the acquisition of money in an illegal manner.[1007] One must refrain from doing so.[1008]

One is not to demand and receive donations.[1009]

One is forbidden to take interest on money, food or anything else from his fellow man.[1010]

One is forbidden to take as a security utensils used for preparing food.[1011] One is forbidden to enter the home of a borrower to take a security, but the lender must remain outside until the borrower comes outside and gives it to him. If the borrower is poor and needs the security, the lender is forbidden to go to sleep before he returns it to the lender before sunset.[1012]

One is forbidden to hate his fellow man secretly in his heart.[1013] One is forbidden to deal with hatred.[1014] One is forbidden to scorn his fellow man.[1015] One is forbidden to plan a robbery.[1016]

1000 Psalms 32:2.
1001 Proverbs 12:27.
1002 Ibid., 26:18–19.
1003 Deuteronomy 19:14.
1004 Proverbs 22:28.
1005 Ibid., 23:10.
1006 Exodus 20:14.
1007 Proverbs 28:16.
1008 Jeremiah 6:13.
1009 Proverbs 29:4.
1010 Deuteronomy 23:20–21.
1011 Ibid., 24:6.
1012 Ibid., 24:10–13.
1013 Leviticus 19:17.
1014 Proverbs 10:12.

One is forbidden to ply his fellow man with wine in order to embarrass him.[1017]

One is forbidden to gloat at his enemy's downfall.[1018] One is forbidden to rejoice at calamities.[1019]

One is forbidden to be sorry that wicked people repented and were not destroyed, when they turned away from their evil ways.[1020]

One is forbidden to tell someone who is suffering that this is because he certainly sinned.[1021]

One is forbidden to give false testimony.[1022]

One is forbidden to deny the truth or to lie to his fellow man.[1023] One is forbidden to accept a lie as the truth.[1024]

One must distance himself from lies.[1025]

One is forbidden to be a tale-bearer.[1026] One is forbidden to slander his fellow man.[1027] One is forbidden to do this secretly.[1028]

One should refrain from complaining.[1029] One is forbidden to slander a slave to his master.[1030]

One is forbidden to curse a judge or ruler.[1031] One is forbidden to curse a deaf person.[1032]

1015 Ibid., 11:12.
1016 Ibid., 24:2.
1017 Habakkuk 2:15.
1018 Proverbs 24:17.
1019 Ibid., 17:5.
1020 Jonah 3 10.
1021 Job 4:1–5:27; 8:1–22; 11:1–20; 15:1–35; 18:1–21; 20:1–29; 22:1–30; 25:1–6; 42:7.
1022 Exodus 20:13.
1023 Leviticus 19:11.
1024 Exodus 23:1.
1025 Ibid., 23:7.
1026 Leviticus 19:16.
1027 Proverbs 10:18.
1028 Ibid., 25:23.
1029 Ibid., 16:28.
1030 Ibid., 30:10.
1031 Exodus 22:27. See Mechilta.
1032 Leviticus 19:14.

One is forbidden to place a stumbling block before the blind. Similarly, one may not cause a person to commit a sin.[1033]

One is forbidden to be a flatterer.[1034]

One must guard his tongue from speaking evil or deceit.[1035]

One must refrain from distorting the truth when speaking.[1036]

One is forbidden to be haughty.[1037] One must not reprove a poor person.[1038] One must not mock a poor person.[1039]

One is forbidden to reveal the secret of another person.[1040]

One is forbidden to take credit for a gift which was not given.[1041]

One is forbidden to praise his fellow man too frequently, when others can hear it.[1042]

One may not answer before listening.[1043]

One is forbidden to persuade his fellow man to follow an evil path.[1044]

One is forbidden to leave hanging overnight the body of a person who was hanged. It must be buried that day.[1045]

One is forbidden to sell one of the Children of Israel into slavery.[1046, 1047]

One is forbidden to oppress the righteous or the poor.[1048] One is forbidden to oppress or rob the poor.[1049]

One is forbidden to oppress the poor.[1050]

1033 Ibid., 19:14. See *Pesachim* 22b.
1034 Proverbs 11:9.
1035 Psalms 34:14.
1036 Proverbs 15:4.
1037 Ibid., 29:23.
1038 Ibid., 13:8.
1039 Ibid., 17:5.
1040 Ibid., 25:9.
1041 Ibid., 25:14.
1042 Ibid., 27:14. See Metzudat David.
1043 Ibid., 18:13.
1044 Ibid., 16:29.
1045 Deuteronomy 21:22–23.
1046 Leviticus 25:42.
1047 See p. 212 on how a slave who was sold must be treated.
1048 Amos 5:12.
1049 Proverbs 30:14.

One is forbidden to do acts of wickedness and violence.[1051] One may not cause unjust actions.[1052]

One is forbidden to think in his heart about carrying out an evil deed against his fellow man.[1053] A person may not plan evil against his fellow man, especially when that person trusts him and when that person has never done anything bad against him.[1054]

One is forbidden to prepare deceitful plans.[1055]

One is forbidden to betray his fellow man.[1056] One is forbidden to wait in ambush by the home of a righteous person. One is forbidden to rob him.[1057]

One may not repay good with evil.[1058]

One is forbidden to love quarrels.[1059] One is forbidden to enter into a quarrel.[1060] One must refrain from quarreling.[1061] A woman must refrain from quarreling.[1062] One is forbidden to hasten to quarrel.[1063] One is forbidden to cause a quarrel between brothers.[1064]

One is forbidden to get involved in a quarrel of others.[1065]

One must keep out of quarrels before they start.[1066]

1050 Ibid., 28:3.
1051 Ibid., 10:29.
1052 Ibid., 22:8.
1053 Zechariah 7:10.
1054 Proverbs 3:29–30.
1055 Ibid., 12:5.
1056 Malachi 2:10.
1057 Proverbs 24:15.
1058 Ibid., 17:13.
1059 Ibid., 17:19.
1060 Ibid., 18:6.
1061 Ibid., 20:3.
1062 Ibid., 19:13.
1063 Ibid., 25:8.
1064 Ibid., 6:16–19.
1065 Ibid., 26:17.
1066 Ibid., 17:14.

One is forbidden to take revenge or to bear a grudge.[1067] One is forbidden to say about his fellow man, "I will do to him what he did to me."[1068] A person may not himself punish a person who did evil to him.[1069]

Actions of Benefit to Others

One who builds a house must put up a fence around its roof.[1070]

If one sees a lost object, he must return it to its owner. If the person who lost it is not in the area or the finder does not know who lost it, he must take the lost object and look after it until its owner comes to look for it.[1071] One is commanded to return a lost object even to an enemy.[1072]

One must support another person who has declined financially.[1073] One must give generously to the poor based on their needs.[1074] One may not block his ears in order not to hear the cries of the poor.[1075] One may not ignore the distress of the poor, but should given whatever they need.[1076] A woman should give to the poor.[1077] One should give generously to aid others.[1078]

In the Sabbatical Year of Remission (the year which is referred to as a "Remission for God"), one may not demand from a debtor the paying back of a loan.[1079] A person is not to refrain from making a loan to his fellow man when the Year of Remission approaches.[1080]

1067 Leviticus 19:18.
1068 Proverbs 24:29.
1069 Ibid., 20:22.
1070 Deuteronomy 22:8.
1071 Ibid., 22:1–3.
1072 Exodus 23:4.
1073 Leviticus 25:35.
1074 Deuteronomy 15:7–8, 11. See Sifri.
1075 Proverbs 21:13.
1076 Ibid., 28:27.
1077 Ibid., 31:20.
1078 Ibid., 11:25.
1079 Deuteronomy 15:1–3. See Sifri.
1080 Ibid., 15:9–10.

After every three years of the Sabbatical cycle, one must take a tenth of his produce of that year and remove it from his house. The Levite, the stranger, the orphan, and the widow can take of it, eat and be satisfied.[1081]

At the time of the wheat and grape harvest, one is forbidden to harvest everything, but must leave the corner unharvested. One is forbidden to pick up stalks which fell during the harvesting. One is forbidden to go back and take the remaining grape clusters after the original grape harvest, as well as those grapes which fell during the harvesting. These are to be left for the poor and the stranger.[1082] When olives are picked, one is forbidden to take all of them, but must leave some of them for the stranger, the orphan and the widow.[1083] If bundles of wheat were forgotten in the field during the harvesting, the owner of the field is forbidden to go back and retrieve them. He must leave them for the stranger, the orphan and the widow.[1084]

One who receives a garment as a security during the day must return it by sunset.[1085]

One who has in his possession something not belonging to him must return it to its owner and add a fifth (i.e., a quarter) of its value. If the owner dies and has no heirs, he must give to a Priest (in addition to a sacrifice).[1086] A borrower must return whatever he borrowed.[1087]

The value of a field, at the time it is bought or sold, is to be established based on how many years remain until the next Jubilee year.[1088]

One must give of what belongs to him to others.[1089]

One must love his fellow man as he loves himself.[1090] One must love his fellow man at all times, and especially if the person is in distress.[1091]

1081 Ibid., 14:28–29.
1082 Leviticus 19:9–10. See Sifra and Rashi based on Mishnah *Pe'ah* 4:10; 7:3.
1083 Deuteronomy 24:20. See Sifri.
1084 Ibid., 24:19.
1085 Exodus 22:25.
1086 Numbers 5:5–8. See *Bava Metzia* 54a.
1087 Psalms 37:21.
1088 Leviticus 25:15–16.
1089 Proverbs 18:16.
1090 Leviticus 19:18.
1091 Proverbs 17:17.

One must know the condition of the poor.[1092] One must have consideration for the poor.[1093]

One must honor the poor.[1094] One must pity them.[1095] One must treat the humble kindly and affectionately.[1096] One must act benevolently towards the simple.[1097]

It is desirable to think about doing justice.[1098]

One should speak in such a way that his words will be a balm to his fellow man.[1099] It is desirable for a person not to be rude in his answers.[1100]

People must speak the truth to one another.[1101]

Every person must be a true witness.[1102]

Instead of hating one's fellow man in the heart, a person must rebuke the other person but must not sin by doing so in a way which is inappropriate (as in public).[1103]

One must desire peace and do everything possible to achieve it.[1104] One must offer advice to others as to how to be at peace.[1105]

The Children of Israel are to live together and in brotherhood.[1106]

It is appropriate to conceal shame.[1107] One must conceal his friend's secrets.[1108] It is advisable for a person to restrain himself and not to react to his fellow man's transgression.[1109]

1092 Ibid., 29:7.
1093 Psalms 41:2.
1094 Proverbs 14:31.
1095 Ibid., 19:17.
1096 Ibid., 14:21.
1097 Ibid., 29:10.
1098 Ibid., 12:5.
1099 Ibid., 15:4.
1100 Ibid., 15:1.
1101 Zechariah 8:16.
1102 Proverbs 14:25.
1103 Leviticus 19:17. See *Arachin* 16b and Rashi there.
1104 Psalms 34:15.
1105 Proverbs 12:20.
1106 Psalms 133:1.
1107 Proverbs 12:16.
1108 Ibid., 11:13.

It is advisable to give gifts secretly, so as to assuage the anger of the person who receives them.[1110]

One should offer food and drink – even to one's enemy.[1111]

People must perform acts of kindness and have mercy on each other.[1112] One must be full of kindness.[1113]

It is proper for a person to be humble and to befriend the humble, and not to attain achievements by associating with the arrogant.[1114]

One should always do righteous acts.[1115]

One should not deprive a deserving person of good, when this can be provided.[1116]

One is forbidden to prevent the supply of food.[1117]

One must be a trusty messenger.[1118]

It is advisable for people to be together in order to improve their understanding.[1119]

One is forbidden to abandon one's friend or a father's friend (when they are in trouble).[1120]

Our Sages set various mourning customs after the deaths of relatives for periods of seven days, thirty days, and twelve months. They also determined that people must comfort mourners.

Our Sages determined that one is to visit the sick.

Recommended Actions for One's Own Benefit

One must hate gifts.[1121]

1109 Ibid., 19:11.
1110 Ibid., 21:14.
1111 Ibid., 25:21.
1112 Zechariah 7:9.
1113 Proverbs 11:17.
1114 Ibid., 16:19.
1115 Psalms 106:3.
1116 Proverbs 3:27–28.
1117 Ibid., 11:26.
1118 Ibid., 13:17.
1119 Ibid., 27:17.
1120 Ibid., 27:10.

One should not give gifts to a wealthy person.[1122]

It is not advisable to visit one's friend too frequently.[1123]

It is not advisable to be a guarantor.[1124] This is especially true when one does not have the necessary money to pay the guarantee.[1125] One should not be a guarantor for a stranger.[1126]

Behavior towards Various People

One must honor his father and mother.[1127] One must fear them.[1128] One is forbidden to hit them.[1129] One is forbidden to curse them.[1130]

A son must obey his father.[1131]

One is forbidden to rob his father or mother.[1132] One is forbidden to mock his father or his mother.[1133]

One is forbidden to scorn his mother in her old age.[1134] One must bless her.[1135] One is forbidden to stray from the path which she taught him.[1136]

A man is forbidden to deprive his wife of food, clothing, or conjugal relations.[1137] If a man marries, it is forbidden to draft him into the army or to

1121 Ibid., 15:27.
1122 Ibid., 22:16.
1123 Ibid., 25:17.
1124 Ibid., 6:1–5.
1125 Ibid., 22:26–27.
1126 Ibid., 11:15.
1127 Exodus 20:12.
1128 Leviticus 19:3.
1129 Exodus 21:15.
1130 Ibid., 21:17.
1131 Proverbs 23:22.
1132 Ibid., 28:24.
1133 Ibid., 30:17.
1134 Ibid., 23:22.
1135 Ibid., 30:11.
1136 Ibid., 1:8.
1137 Exodus 21:10. See the commentaries of Rashi and Rashbam based on Mechilta. According to Nachmanides, food and clothing are not mentioned in the verse, but only bed coverings.

have him have to deal with military related issues. He must remain in his home for a full year and cause his wife to rejoice.[1138]

A man is forbidden to malign his wife and to say that she was not a virgin.[1139]

A woman of valor must only benefit her husband and not harm him, her entire life.[1140]

If a man has two wives, one whom he loves and one whom he hates, he is forbidden to give his son from the beloved wife the portion belonging to the firstborn unless he is indeed the firstborn. The genuine firstborn receives a double portion of everything.[1141]

One is especially forbidden to hit a pregnant woman, because she might give birth prematurely.[1142]

One is forbidden to neglect the Levite, and must give him that to which he is entitled.[1143]

One must arise before an old man and honor a wise man.[1144]

One is forbidden to cheat or oppress a stranger.[1145] The Children of Israel must love the stranger.[1146]

One is forbidden to oppress a widow or orphan.[1147] One is forbidden to take a widow's garment as a security.[1148]

One is forbidden to delay the payment of a worker (who works by the day) until the following morning.[1149] A poor person (who works at night) must be paid his daily wage before sunset.[1150]

1138 Deuteronomy 24:5. See Sifri.
1139 Ibid., 22:13–19.
1140 Proverbs 31:12.
1141 Deuteronomy 21:15–17.
1142 Exodus 21:22.
1143 Deuteronomy 12:19.
1144 Leviticus 19:32. See Sifra.
1145 Exodus 22:20.
1146 Deuteronomy 10:19.
1147 Exodus 22:21–23.
1148 Deuteronomy 24:17.
1149 Leviticus 19:13. See Sifra.
1150 Deuteronomy 24:14–15. See Sifri.

If a person works at harvesting grapes, he may eat of the grapes, but is forbidden to put any of the grapes in his utensil. A worker who works in the grain harvest may take of the grain for himself, but only if he harvests it with his hand and not with a scythe.[1151]

A Hebrew slave works for six years and is set free the seventh year. When he leaves, he regains the same marital status that he had before being sold as a slave. If his master gave him a wife of his non-Israelite female slaves and she bears children to him, they remain with his master. If the slave wants to continue to be a slave, his master must pierce his ear and he remains a slave.[1152] A Hebrew slave may not be given servile work to perform. He must be treated like a hired hand or a resident and must work until the Jubilee year. He then goes out with his children to his family and to his ancestors' land holdings.[1153] The fiftieth year is the Jubilee year.[1154]

One is forbidden to oppress a Hebrew slave or to treat him harshly.[1155]

When a Hebrew slave is freed in the seventh year, his master must give him from everything with which God blessed him.[1156]

The slave must be loyal to his master.[1157]

If a man sold his daughter as a slave, she does not go free under the same conditions as the Canaanite slaves. If her master does not marry her and does not bring about her redemption, he may not sell her to a non-Israelite. If the master's son marries her, he must treat her as his wife in every way. If he does not marry her and does not cause her to be redeemed, she is freed at whatever time comes first: the end of six years or when she reaches the age of puberty.[1158]

If an Israelite is sold as a slave to a wealthy resident non-Israelite or to an idol worshipper, he must make every effort to be freed. One of his brothers,

1151 Ibid., 23:25–26.
1152 Exodus 21:2–6.
1153 Leviticus 25:39–41.
1154 Ibid., 25:10.
1155 Ibid., 25:43, 46.
1156 Deuteronomy 15:12–14.
1157 Proverbs 27:18.
1158 Exodus 21:7–11. See Mechilta, Rashi.

his uncle, his cousin, or another relative must redeem him and pay the amount needed, or he should acquire the necessary money by himself. The amount needed is based on the number of years remaining until the Jubilee year. If he is not redeemed, he goes free in the Jubilee year.[1159]

If an Israelite needs a male or female slave, he should take one of the surrounding nations, or of the residents of the land, and not of his brother Israelites. He can bequeath them to his sons.[1160]

A master is forbidden to inflict deadly blows on a slave.[1161] A master is forbidden to blind the eye of his slave or knock out his tooth.[1162]

One is forbidden to spoil a slave in his youth.[1163] One must not punish a slave only with words.[1164]

If an Israelite wishes to take a comely female war prisoner as a wife, he must bring her to his home, where she must shave off her hair and allow her fingernails to grow.[1165] She must remove the dress of her captivity and mourn her parents for a month. Afterwards she can be his wife. If he does not want her as a wife, he must set her free and may not sell her for money.[1166]

One is not to seek the welfare and good of the Ammonites and Moabites, as they did not offer the Children of Israel bread and water then they left Egypt, and even sent Balaam to curse the Children of Israel.[1167]

One must remember what Amalek did to the Children of Israel when they were in the desert on the way from Egypt, tired and weary. Amalek attacked the weak and helpless, because the Amalekites did not fear God.[1168]

One may not goad a king into becoming angry.[1169] It is advisable to appease the king.[1170] It is not worthwhile for a person to curse a king, even in his thoughts.[1171] One should not exalt himself before a king.[1172]

1159 Leviticus 25:47–54. See Sifra.
1160 Ibid., 25:44–46.
1161 Exodus 21:20.
1162 Ibid., 21:26–27.
1163 Proverbs 29:21.
1164 Ibid., 29:19.
1165 Another opinion: cut her fingernails.
1166 Deuteronomy 21:10–14. See Sifri.
1167 Ibid., 23:4–7.
1168 Ibid., 25:17–19. See Rashi and Siftei Chachamim.

One must not befriend those who do not listen to their leaders.[1173]

When one dines in the presence of a ruler, he must understand the intentions of the ruler.[1174]

Actions of the Courts of Law

General Instructions

The Children of Israel must appoint judges and policemen who pursue justice in order to judge the nation justly.[1175]

One who judges between people in conflict must judge fairly.[1176] The judge must issue an honest verdict.[1177] He must judge and bring about peace.[1178] One is forbidden to cause injustice in one's verdict.[1179]

One is forbidden to favor a poor man in judgment.[1180] One is forbidden to pervert the judgment of a poor man to his detriment.[1181] A judge is forbidden to pervert a ruling in favor of any person.[1182] One is forbidden to pervert the judgment of a convert or orphan.[1183] A judge is forbidden to fear any person.[1184] A judge is forbidden to take a bribe.[1185] A convert and a native Israelite must both be treated equally.[1186]

1169 Proverbs 20:2.
1170 Ibid., 16:14.
1171 Ecclesiastes 10:20.
1172 Proverbs 25:6.
1173 Ibid., 24:21.
1174 Ibid., 23:1.
1175 Deuteronomy 15:18, 20.
1176 Ibid., 25:1.
1177 Zechariah 7:9.
1178 Ibid., 8:16.
1179 Leviticus 19:15.
1180 Exodus 23:3.
1181 Ibid., 23:6.
1182 Deuteronomy 1:17.
1183 Ibid., 24:17.
1184 Ibid., 1:17.
1185 Exodus 23:8.
1186 Leviticus 24:22.

One must maintain the rules of justice in judgment.[1187] One must show that in Israel there is justice in judgment.[1188]

The demand for just decisions, for easing the conditions of those undergoing hardships, and for fair judgment for the orphan and the widow are more important than sacrifices, festival gatherings, and prayers.[1189]

The judge must save the one who was robbed from his oppressor.[1190]

One is forbidden to favor a wicked person and to pervert the judgment against the righteous.[1191]

For a death sentence against a person, there must be two witnesses. One witness is insufficient.[1192]

Only by the testimony of two or three people can a person be convicted.[1193]

False witnesses are given the punishment that they plotted to have imposed on their fellow men.[1194]

When a person is sentenced to lashes, he is not to receive more than forty lashes (in reality, no more than thirty-nine).[1195]

If the body of a person who was killed is found in the field and it is not known who killed him, the elders of the people and the judges must measure the distance from the place the body was found to the nearest cities. The elders of the closest city must take a heifer, which was never used for plowing or for carrying any load, to a valley with a running river, where the land is not worked, and break its neck. They must wash their hands above the heifer and declare that they did not contribute to the death of this person and did not see the murder and must beg forgiveness for the nation of Israel for the sin of bloodshed.[1196]

1187 Psalms 106:3.
1188 Amos 5:15.
1189 Isaiah 1:10–17.
1190 Jeremiah 22:3.
1191 Proverbs 18:5.
1192 Numbers 35:30.
1193 Deuteronomy 19:15.
1194 Ibid., 19:16–19.
1195 Ibid., 25:2–3. See Sifri.
1196 Ibid., 21:1–8.

If a judge is unable to decide in a case, he must go to the place which God chose and ask the Priests, the Levites, and the judges of that era. They will instruct him how to rule. He must accept their ruling and cannot stray from it. In general, one must obey the words of the Sages.[1197]

Enforcing Payment

One who injures his fellow man must compensate him.[1198]

If one strikes his fellow man and the one who was struck does not die and recovers from the blows, the former must pay the wages of the latter, and all of his medical expenses.[1199]

If during a quarrel between two men, a pregnant woman was struck and as a result she gave birth to stillborn children (she did not die), the one who struck her must pay her husband as determined by the court of law. If the woman died or was injured, the one who struck her is punished accordingly.[1200]

If two men fight and the wife of one grabs the private parts of the other, she must pay him for the embarrassment.[1201]

If an ox gores a person to death, the ox is to be stoned and its meat may not be eaten, but the owner of the ox is not responsible. If the ox is known as one which gores and its owner, despite being warned, does not guard it properly and it kills someone, its owner is liable for death (from Heaven). The owner of the ox must pay the redemption of the person who was killed. The same is true with a son or daughter. If a slave is killed by such an ox, the owner of the ox must pay thirty shekels to its owner.[1202]

If an ox gores the ox of his fellow man, the owner of the goring ox must pay half the value of the damages. However, if that ox was known as a goring

1197 Ibid., 17:8–11. See *Shabbat* 23a.
1198 Leviticus 24:19–20. See Sifra.
1199 Exodus 21:18–19. See the Aramaic translation by Onkelos, Rashi based on *Bava Kama* 83b.
1200 Exodus 21:22–25. See *Mechilta.*
1201 Deuteronomy 25:11–12. See Rashi based on Sifri.
1202 Exodus 21:28–32. See *Mechilta.*

ox, and it was not guarded properly, the owner must pay the full amount of the damages beyond the value of the dead ox.[1203]

If a person leaves a pit open and an animal falls into it, he must pay the damages to the owner of the animal, and the carcass remains in the possession of the animal's owner.[1204]

If a person sends his animal to graze in someone else's field, the owner of the animal must reimburse the owner of the field with the best of his land.[1205]

If a person lights a fire and it spreads and burns part of his neighbor's field, he must pay the damages.[1206]

If a person kills an animal, he must pay its owner its value.[1207]

If one blinds the eye of his slave or knocks out his tooth, the slave must be set free.[1208]

If a thief comes into a home stealthily and the owner of the house kills him, the owner is exempt from punishment. If it is clear that the thief only intended to steal and not to kill, the person who killed him deserves the death penalty. If the thief is not killed, he must pay for the theft. If the thief does not have the resources from which to pay, he is sold to slavery in order to pay. If the stolen object is still in the thief's possession, he must pay double its value.[1209]

If a thief stole and sold or slaughtered an ox or sheep, he must pay five times the value of the ox or four times the value of the sheep.[1210]

If a man seduces a girl who is not betrothed to a man, he has to marry her and to pay the amount of money included in her marriage contract. If her father refuses to give her to him, the man must pay the appropriate amount for the dowry of a virgin.[1211]

1203 Ibid., 21:35–36. See *Mechilta.*
1204 Ibid., 21:33–34. See *Mechilta.*
1205 Ibid., 22:4.
1206 Ibid., 22:5.
1207 Leviticus 24:18.
1208 Exodus 21:26–27.
1209 Ibid., 22:1–3. See Mechilta.
1210 Ibid., 21:37.
1211 Ibid., 22:15–16. See Mechilta.

One who rapes a woman who was not betrothed must pay her father an amount of money, must marry her (if she agrees) and may never divorce her.[1212]

If a man falsely claimed that his new wife was not a virgin, and her father and mother bring proof that she was, the husband receives lashes and must pay her father. He may never divorce her. (If she was indeed not a virgin, she is to be killed by stoning for having committed adultery).[1213]

If a person gives another person money or goods to guard for him (as an unpaid guard) – and they are stolen, if the thief was found, he must pay double. If he was not found, the guard must swear that he did not use the property, and he is exempt. If it becomes clear that the object was not stolen by another person, the court must determine that the guard must pay double.[1214]

If a person gives another person an animal to guard (for pay) and it dies or is taken captive without witnesses, the guard must swear that he did not use the property, and he is exempt. However, if it was stolen from him, he must pay. If the animal was torn apart and he has witnesses to that effect, he is exempt from paying.[1215]

If someone borrows an object or animal from another and the object is broken or the animal dies, the borrower has to reimburse the owner. If the owner worked alongside the borrower at the time that it was borrowed, he is exempt. If the object or animal was rented, he is not considered to be a borrower.[1216]

Punishment by a Court of Law for Harm to People

If a person beats his fellow man to death, he receives the death penalty. If he lies in wait for a person and kills him, even if he serves as a Priest, he is

1212 Deuteronomy 22:28–29. See *Ketubot* 39b, *Makkot* 15a.
1213 Deuteronomy 22:13–21. See Sifri.
1214 Exodus 22:6–8. See Mechilta (Exodus 22:11), Rashi.
1215 Ibid., 22:9–12. See Mechilta.
1216 Ibid., 22:13–14. See *Bava Metzia* 95b, Mechilta.

to be put to death.[1217] The avenger of the blood (a relative of the murdered person) may kill the murderer.[1218]

If a person kills another unintentionally, he may flee to a place set aside for this purpose.[1219] Cities of refuge are to be set up, three on each side of the Jordan River. One who killed another unintentionally may flee there from the avenger of the blood, until he is tried. If the court rules that he indeed killed the person unintentionally, he remains in the city of refuge until the High Priest dies, and at that time he may leave and the avenger of the blood no longer has the right to kill him. If he leaves the city of refuge before the death of the High Priest, he may be killed. If a person kills another because of hate or deliberately, the avenger of the blood has the right to kill him. If he kills unintentionally, the judges of the people will protect him from the avenger of the blood and he will remain in the city of refuge until the High Priest dies.[1220]

One is forbidden to take a money settlement in order to not kill a person who was sentenced to the death penalty. One is not permitted to take a money settlement from a person who killed another unintentionally so that he will not need to flee to the city of refuge.[1221]

One who hits his mother or father is to be put to death.[1222] One who curses his mother or father is to be put to death.[1223]

If a person kidnaps an Israelite and sells him, and this is proven, he receives the death penalty.[1224]

Punishments by Courts of Law for Various Offenses

If a person curses God, he is to be put to death by stoning.[1225]

1217 Exodus 21:12, 14. See Mechilta.
1218 Numbers 35:21. See *Makkot* 11b.
1219 Exodus 21:13.
1220 Numbers 35:9–29.
1221 Ibid., 35:31–32.
1222 Exodus 21:15.
1223 Ibid., 21:17.
1224 Ibid., 21:16. See Mechilta.
1225 Leviticus 24:15.

A person who tries to get involved with witchcraft is to be put to death.[1226] If a man or woman is involved in the practices of necromancers or spiritists, the punishment is death by stoning.[1227]

If a person offers up his child as a sacrifice to Molech, he is to be put to death by stoning.[1228]

If a man commits adultery with a married woman, both are to be put to death.[1229]

If a man lies with a betrothed woman in the city (she has not yet been married but requires a bill of divorce before marrying anyone else), both are to be stoned. The man is to be stoned because he afflicted the woman, and the woman, because she did not cry out.[1230] If a man rapes a betrothed woman in the field, he is to be put to death but the woman is not to be punished, because even if she had cried out, no one would have heard her.[1231]

If a betrothed or married daughter of a Priest commits adultery and desecrates the honor of her father, she is to be put to death by fire.[1232]

If a man lies with a female slave who is designated for another man, and she has not yet been entirely freed, there is no death penalty but she is punished (with lashes).[1233]

If a man lies with his father's wife or with his daughter-in-law or with another man like with a woman, both are liable for the death penalty.[1234]

If a man marries a woman and also lies with her mother – both are liable for the death penalty by burning. If a man marries a woman and also lies with her daughter, both are liable for the death penalty by burning.[1235]

If a man or woman lies with an animal, the person is liable for the death penalty and the animal must also be killed.[1236]

1226 Exodus 22:17.
1227 Leviticus 20:27.
1228 Ibid., 20:2.
1229 Ibid., 20:10.
1230 Deuteronomy 22:23–24.
1231 Ibid., 22:25–27.
1232 Leviticus 21:9.
1233 Ibid., 19:20. See Sifra.
1234 Ibid., 20:11–13.
1235 Ibid., 20:14.

If a person desecrates the Sabbath, he is to be stoned to death.[1237]

If a man has a rebellious son who does not listen to the voices of his father and mother, and even after receiving lashes still does not listen to them, his parents are to take him to the elders of their city and to say to them that their son is a rebellious son (and is also a glutton and drunkard). His punishment is death by stoning by the people of the city.[1238]

If after intensive investigation, it is proved that a man or woman has served other gods or bowed down to them, their punishment is stoning. The first ones responsible for inflicting the punishment are the witnesses, and afterwards the entire nation.[1239]

If a family member or friend incites one secretly to worship other gods, one is forbidden to listen to him. He is to be stoned. The first person responsible for inflicting this punishment is the one whom the inciter tried to incite, and thereafter the entire nation.[1240]

If a rumor comes that in one of the cities evil people incited the members of the city to worship other gods, one has to undertake a thorough investigation. If the rumor is true, all the members of that city are to be put to death by the sword, including even its animals. All the booty is to be gathered into a single place and burned together with the entire city. One is forbidden to rebuild it or to take any of the booty.[1241]

If a prophet provides a sign or performs a miracle to persuade the people to worship other gods, he is to be put to death.[1242]

A prophet who says in God's name something which God did not command him to say, or says something in the name of other gods is to be put to death.[1243]

1236 Ibid., 20:15–16.
1237 Numbers 15:35.
1238 Deuteronomy 21:18–21. See Sifri.
1239 Ibid., 17:2–7.
1240 Ibid., 13:7–12.
1241 Ibid., 13:13–18.
1242 Ibid., 13:2–6.
1243 Ibid., 18:20.

One is forbidden to kill the fathers for the sins of their sons or vice-versa. Each person is to be put to death for his own sin.[1244]

After a person is killed for having cursed God, his body is to be hanged on a tree.[1245]

The Land of Israel and Its Produce

One works his land for six years and gathers its produce. In the seventh year he should rest. During this year, the poor of the nation can eat of its produce. The rest is to be eaten by animals.[1246] For six years a person can work his land and gather its produce. The seventh year is a Sabbatical year for God. One is forbidden to sow, prune, or harvest grain or grapes. However the person and all who accompany him may eat of whatever grows from the ground.[1247]

The Children of Israel must count seven times seven years. On the Day of Atonement of the fiftieth year they must blow the ram's horn and sanctify the fiftieth year. In the fiftieth year, the Jubilee year, all the laws regarding working the land on the Sabbatical year apply as well.[1248] The Children of Israel are forbidden to sell the land in perpetuity, because it belongs to God, and the Children of Israel are like strangers and residents in it.[1249]

Throughout the land which is an inheritance to the Children of Israel, a person who sold land has the right to redeem it. If a person became destitute and was forced to sell part of his inheritance, a close relative should come and redeem that which was sold. If the seller has no one who can redeem the land, when he can afford it he can redeem it by paying the buyer the value of the land until the next Jubilee year and receive it back immediately. If he is

---

1244 Ibid., 24:16.

1245 Ibid., 21:22–23. There is a dispute whether this applies only to those who worship other gods or to all those who are killed by stoning. See Sifri.

1246 Exodus 23:10–11.

1247 Leviticus 25:2–7.

1248 Ibid., 25:8–11.

1249 Ibid., 25:23.

not able to obtain enough money to buy the land back, the land will return to him in the Jubilee year.[1250]

If a person sells a house in a walled city, he has one year during which he can redeem it. After that time, the house remains permanently in the hands of the buyer.[1251]

Houses in unwalled cities are considered like fields in terms of redemption.[1252]

The houses of the Levites in their cities may be redeemed immediately after they are sold. In any event, they return to their owners in the Jubilee year. The same is true for the open spaces which surround their cities.[1253]

During the grain and grape harvest seasons, one is forbidden to harvest everything, leaving a corner unharvested. One is forbidden to gather whatever fell during the harvest and may not return to take grape clusters not taken the first time, as well as the grapes which fell during the harvest. They are to be left for the poor and the stranger.[1254]

During the harvesting of olives, one is forbidden to take all of them, but must leave some of them for the stranger, the orphan, and the widow.[1255] If bundles of wheat were forgotten in the field at the time of a harvest, the owner of the field is forbidden to go back and collect them. He must leave them for the stranger, the orphan, and the widow.[1256]

One is forbidden to plant two kinds of seeds together.[1257] One is forbidden to plant a vineyard together with other crops.[1258]

The Children of Israel who live in the Land of Israel must take of their first fruits, put these in a woven basket, and bring them to the place which God chose to have His name dwell there.[1259]

1250 Ibid., 25:24–28.
1251 Ibid., 25:29–30.
1252 Ibid., 25:31.
1253 Ibid., 25:32–34.
1254 Ibid., 19:9–10. See Sifra, Rashi based on *Pe'ah* 4:10 and 7:3.
1255 Deuteronomy 24:20. See Sifri.
1256 Ibid., 24:19.
1257 Leviticus 19:19. See the Aramaic translation by Onkelos.
1258 Deuteronomy 22:9. See *Kiddushin* 39a.
1259 Deuteronomy 26:1–2.

The Children of Israel must give their first olive oil, wine, and grain to God for the Priests, as a heave offering.[1260] Our Sages determined that other fruits and vegetables must also be given as a heave offering.[1261]

The tithe is to be given to the Levites.[1262]

A tenth of the crops (the second tithe, see p. 164) is holy to God. If its owner redeems it, he must add a fifth (i.e., a quarter) of its value.[1263]

After a person finishes tithing his crops in the third year of the Sabbatical year cycle and gives the tithe to the Levite, the stranger, the orphan, and the widow, he must declare the following before God: He has cleared out all his tithes from his home and given them to those to whom He commanded to give them, that he has not eaten of the tithe when he was in mourning before the burial, did not separate it in ritual uncleanliness, and has not used it for the purposes of a dead person, and that he did that which God commanded him.[1264]

The crops of the fourth year of a new tree are holy to God (and are treated like a second tithe, which must be eaten in Jerusalem or redeemed with the money used brought to Jerusalem).[1265]

If a person dies without leaving a son, his inheritance goes to his daughter. (The issue of inheritance is originally brought up relating to the Land of Israel.) If he has no daughter, it passes to his father or his brothers. If he has no father or brothers, it passes to his father's brothers. If his father has no brothers, it passes to his closest relative.[1266]

If a man has two wives, one beloved and one hated, he cannot give to his son of his beloved wife that which belongs to his firstborn son, if he is not the firstborn. The firstborn receives two portions of everything.[1267]

1260 Numbers 18:12.
1261 According to another view, the obligation of other types of fruit is also by Torah law.
1262 Numbers 18:24.
1263 Leviticus 27:30–31. See *Bava Metzia* 54a.
1264 Deuteronomy 26:12–14.
1265 Leviticus 19:24. See Rashi based on *Ma'aser Sheni*, Ch. 5.
1266 Numbers 27:8–11. See Sifri.
1267 Deuteronomy 21:15–17.

Ezekiel said in the name of God that a ruler can give as a gift to his sons only from his inheritance. If he gives part of his inheritance to one of his servants, it returns to him in the Jubilee year. A ruler is forbidden to take from the inheritance belonging to the nation and to give it to his sons, as a result of which land owners will be visited from their land.[1268]

Animals

If a person sees the donkey of his fellow man falling down under its burden, he must help to remove the burden.[1269] He must help him load it up again.[1270]

One may not prevent an ox from eating of the crop on which it is working.[1271]

One is forbidden to plow with an ox and a donkey together.[1272]

A person must recognize the nature of his animal.[1273]

One is forbidden to castrate animals.[1274] One is forbidden to cross-breed two kinds of animals.[1275]

If one sees a bird's nest and wishes to take the chicks or the eggs, he must first drive the mother away.[1276]

One is forbidden to slaughter an ox and its young, or a sheep and its young on the same day.[1277]

People with Special Sanctity

Aaron and his sons are to receive the heave offerings of the Children of Israel to God. They are to receive a portion of each sacrifice. The meal offering, the sin offering, and the guilt offering are Most Holy. Each male

1268 Ezekiel 46:16–18.
1269 Exodus 23:5.
1270 Deuteronomy 22:4.
1271 Ibid., 25:4.
1272 Ibid., 22:10.
1273 Proverbs 12:10.
1274 Leviticus 22:24.
1275 Ibid., 19:19.
1276 Deuteronomy 22:6–7.
1277 Leviticus 22:28.

Priest can eat these in the courtyard of the Temple. Each ritually clean Priest can eat of all the heave offerings of the Children of Israel. The first oil, wine, and grain are to be given to them. Each ritually clean Priest can eat of the first fruits of the land. Every consecrated item in Israel of a specific kind belongs to them. Each firstborn male among people and animals belongs to them. However, the firstborn male child is to be redeemed when he is a month old for five shekels, and the firstborn of a ritually unclean animal species is to be redeemed. The firstborn ox, sheep, and goat are to be sacrificed, with their blood sprinkled and their fat sacrificed on the altar, while the Priests can eat the meat. All these contributions will belong to them, for all eternity, as an eternal covenant before God.[1278] The Levite (i.e., the Priest) who comes to the place which God chose on one of the pilgrimage festivals, but not during the time period of the year assigned to him, and serves there, will receive an equal portion of the sacrifices (of the pilgrimage festival), but not of the standard sacrifices.[1279] The Priests will not receive a portion or an inheritance in the land, because God gives them their portion and inheritance.[1280]

The foreleg, the jaw, and the stomach of each animal which is slaughtered are to be given to the Priests. The same applies to the first shearing of sheep.[1281]

The Priests are to keep God's charge. One who is a non-Priest, resident, or employee of a Priest may not eat of the heave offering. The slave or one born into the Priest's home are permitted to eat it. The daughter of a Priest who married a non-Priest is forbidden to eat it. However, if she is widowed or divorced and has no descendants, she can return to her father's house and eat it. If a person eats it unintentionally, he must add a fifth (i.e., a fourth) of its value and give it to the Priest.[1282]

1278 Numbers 18:8–19. See Sifri.
1279 Deuteronomy 18:6–8. See Sifri.
1280 Numbers 18:20.
1281 Deuteronomy 18:3–4. See Sifri.
1282 Leviticus 22:9–14. See Sifra, *Bava Metzia* 54a.

One is forbidden to be late in bringing the first fruits or heave offering.[1283]

A Priest is forbidden to become ritually unclean by contact with the dead except for his wife, mother, father, son, daughter, brother or sister who is a virgin. A Priest may not become ritually unclean to his wife if the marriage to her was a forbidden one. He must be holy to God. A Priest may not take as his wife a prostitute, the daughter of a Priest from a forbidden marriage, or a divorcee. He must be holy, because he offers up God's bread.[1284]

The High Priest is forbidden to let his hair grow long or to tear his clothes as a sign of mourning. He is forbidden to become ritually unclean even to his father or mother. He is forbidden to leave the Temple to escort a dead body. By not doing so he will not desecrate the honor of God's holy place, because the anointing oil of God were poured on his head. He must take a virgin as a wife. He is forbidden to take any other type of woman – a widow, divorcee, the daughter of a Priest who was from a forbidden marriage, or a prostitute – in order not to desecrate his progeny.[1285]

A Priest who has a physical deformity is forbidden to offer sacrifices, but may eat of the Most Holy. He is forbidden to come to the curtain or the altar, in order not to desecrate the Holy Place of God, which God consecrated.[1286]

A Priest who is ritually unclean is forbidden to eat of the Holy. He must immerse himself in a ritual bath or in a spring and remain ritually unclean until the evening. Afterwards he can eat of the Holy.[1287]

The words of the Priest must be the words of the true Torah. The Priest must walk before God, acting in the ways of uprightness and peace. He must move people not to sin.[1288]

1283 Exodus 22:28. See Mechilta.
1284 Leviticus 21:1–8. See Sifra.
1285 Ibid., 21:10–15. See Sifra.
1286 Ibid., 21:16–23.
1287 Ibid., 22:2–7.
1288 Malachi 2:6.

The words of the Priest must reflect knowledge of God and His ways. The nation must seek Torah from him, for he is the messenger of God.[1289]

A Priest is forbidden to favor a person basing himself on words of the Torah.[1290]

God gave the Levites the tithes of the Children of Israel as a substitute for land inheritance, in return for their work in the Holy Place. They have the responsibility to warn people. They must ensure that a non-Priest does not approach the Holy.[1291]

The Levites must give a tithe of their tithe as a heave offering to God. It is to be given to the Priest. The Levites may eat the tithe in any place.[1292]

God chose the Levites to serve Him eternally.[1293]

If a person takes a vow to be a Nazirite to God, he must abstain from wine, strong drink, and grape products. He is also forbidden to shave. Throughout the time that he is a Nazirite, he may not cut his hair. He is forbidden to become ritually unclean by contact with the dead, because the consecration of God is on his head, and he is holy to God.[1294] If a Nazirite becomes ritually unclean by contact with the dead, after the seven days of being ritually unclean and the bringing of sacrifices on the eighth day, he must begin the count of his Nazirite days anew.[1295]

One is forbidden to give wine to a Nazirite.[1296]

Of a National Character

The Nation

The nation of Israel is forbidden to make a treaty with the nations who inhabit the Land of Israel.[1297] The six Canaanite nations are to be destroyed

---

1289 Ibid., 2:7.
1290 Ibid., 2:9.
1291 Numbers 18:21–24.
1292 Ibid., 18:25–32.
1293 I Chronicles 15:2.
1294 Numbers 6:2–8.
1295 Ibid., 6:9–12.
1296 Amos 2:12.
1297 Exodus 34:15.

and none of them is to be left alive, so that the Children of Israel will not learn to act in their depraved ways.[1298] (If they are willing to give up these ways, one is permitted, at a time of war, to call to them for peace. See below.)[1299]

At a time of war in the land, two silver trumpets must be blown.[1300]

When the nation of Israel goes out to war against a larger enemy army and with better weapons, they should not fear them, because God, who took them out of Egypt, is with them. The Priest must encourage the people and tell them not to fear because God will be with them to save them. The officials of the nation are to announce that whoever has built a house and not dedicated it, has planted a vineyard and not benefited from it, has betrothed a woman but not married her, and whoever is afraid – are all to return to their homes (and not go out to battle) Afterwards the officials will appoint the military commanders.[1301]

During the war, when the army of Israel approaches a city to wage war against it, it must call upon that city to surrender peacefully. If the city heeds the call, its residents will pay taxes and will be subservient to the Children of Israel. If they do not respond to the call for peace, the city is to be besieged and God will deliver it into their hands. The Children of Israel are to kill all the adult males. The women, the children and the cattle will be booty. These provisions only apply to the cities of distant nations, but not to the six nations of the Land of Israel. (See above also.)[1302]

When a city is placed under siege, one is forbidden to destroy fruit-bearing trees for the purpose of the siege. One can only cut down non-fruit-bearing trees for that purpose.[1303]

One is forbidden to carry out a census of the population (using normal counting methods).[1304]

1298 Deuteronomy 20:16–18.
1299 Sifri *ad loc.*
1300 Numbers 10:9.
1301 Deuteronomy 20:1–9.
1302 Ibid., 20:10–15.
1303 Ibid., 20:19–20.
1304 I Chronicles 21:7. See Exodus 30:11–12.

When the Children of Israel come to the land and settle in it, and they want a king like the other nations, they must anoint a king whom God has chosen. They must choose one of their people to be the king, and not a non-Israelite.[1305]

The nation is forbidden to spurn the monarchy of the house of David.[1306] The nation must strive to renew the monarchy of the house of David.[1307]

After the Children of Israel conquer the Land of Israel, settle in it, and God has given them rest from all their enemies, they are to destroy the memory of Amalek from underneath the heavens.[1308]

The nation of Israel is to be the witness before all the nations of the world that the Lord is God – there was none before Him and there will be none after Him.[1309] The nation of Israel is to relate the praise of God.[1310]

The nation of Israel must know that the Torah comes forth from God and that His laws are the light of the nations.[1311]

King and Leader

The king is forbidden to have a large number of horses, or to take back the nation of Israel to Egypt for that purpose, because God commanded the Children of Israel not to return to Egypt the same way they came. He may not have a large number of wives, so that they do not lead him astray from God. He may not accumulate gold and silver. He must write a Torah scroll in the presence of the Priests and Levites, and it is to be with him always, so that he can read in it and learn to fear God and to obey that which is written in it, and also so that he should not exalt himself over the members of the nation.[1312]

1305 Deuteronomy 17:14–15.
1306 Isaiah 8:5–8.
1307 Hosea 3:5.
1308 Deuteronomy 25:19.
1309 Isaiah 43:9–10.
1310 Ibid., 43:21.
1311 Ibid., 51:4.
1312 Deuteronomy 17:16–20.

The king must go in the ways of God.[1313]

The king who arises from the House of David must judge each person with righteousness, uprightness, and faith.[1314]

The king must judge righteously and, in that way, remove evil.[1315] The king and leaders must rule through the power of wisdom and understanding.[1316] The wise king must banish the wicked and pay them their just deserts.[1317]

A ruler is forbidden to listen to lies.[1318]

The king must judge the poor with an honest verdict.[1319] He must judge justly and must be the voice of the poor and the speechless.[1320]

The king must perform acts of kindness and truth.[1321]

The leaders must seek the good of the members of the nation, and not exploit them for their own personal needs.[1322]

A ruler of Israel may not impose such excessive taxes on the nation that it causes them to leave the country.[1323]

A leader is forbidden to abandon his nation.[1324]

Leaders are forbidden to become drunk on wine.[1325]

A king is forbidden to drink wine and chase after women. He must act as is proper for a king.[1326]

1313 II Chronicles 6:16.
1314 Isaiah 11:4–5.
1315 Proverbs 20:8.
1316 Ibid., 8:14–15.
1317 Ibid., 20:26.
1318 Ibid., 29:12.
1319 Ibid., 29:14.
1320 Ibid., 31:8–9.
1321 Ibid., 20:28.
1322 Ezekiel 34:1–10.
1323 Ibid., 45:9.
1324 Zechariah 11:17.
1325 Hosea 7:5.
1326 Proverbs 31:3–5.

• Commandments and Demands of the Nations of the World

Relationship to the Basic Order of the World

When Adam was created, God told him that he was to be fruitful and multiply, to fill the earth and to rule over everything on it.[1327] After the Flood, God again told Noah and his sons that they were to be fruitful and multiply.[1328]

One is forbidden to eat meat taken from a living animal.[1329]

The nations of the world are to refrain from abominations. These abominations include sexual relations with forbidden relatives (see p. 194) or with a married woman, offering children to Molech, a man's lying with another man like with a woman or lying with an animal.[1330] They must refrain from dealing in witchcraft.[1331]

Relationship to People

One is forbidden to murder another person and is forbidden to commit suicide, because Man was made in the image of God. On the other hand, one can kill a murderer.[1332]

One is forbidden to rob.[1333]

One is forbidden to act with violence.[1334]

One is forbidden to take revenge, and to destroy because of hatred.[1335]

One is forbidden to burn people's bones.[1336]

One is forbidden to desire war.[1337]

1327 Genesis 1:28.
1328 Ibid., 9:1.
1329 Ibid., 9:4. See Rashi based on *Sanhedrin* 59a.
1330 Leviticus 18:6–28.
1331 Deuteronomy 18:9–12.
1332 Genesis 9:5–6.
1333 See *Sanhedrin* 56b, 57a.
1334 Genesis 6:11.
1335 Ezekiel 25:15.
1336 Amos 2:1.
1337 Psalms 68:31.

One is forbidden to attempt to acquire things which do not belong to him.[1338] One may not take booty from other nations.[1339]

One is forbidden to act treacherously and to loot.[1340]

One is forbidden to give his friend wine to drink, in order to embarrass him later.[1341]

One may not cheat or lie.[1342]

One is forbidden to violate a covenant between nations.[1343]

The nations must set up courts of law.[1344]

Relationship to God

One is forbidden to be conceited and to claim that whatever he has accomplished was done purely by his own efforts.[1345]

One is forbidden to think himself greater than God.[1346]

One is forbidden to think that he is God.[1347]

One is forbidden to claim that he created anything in the world.[1348]

One is forbidden to think arrogantly towards God.[1349]

One is forbidden to stand before God in any way but with total submission.[1350]

One is forbidden to question God's authority.[1351]

One must feel lowly and submissive before God.[1352]

One is forbidden to challenge God.[1353]

1338 Habakkuk 2:5–7.
1339 Nahum 2:9, 13–14.
1340 Isaiah 21:2.
1341 Habakkuk 2:15–16.
1342 Nahum 3:1.
1343 Amos 1:9.
1344 See *Sanhedrin* 56b.
1345 Isaiah 10:12–13.
1346 Jeremiah 48:26.
1347 Ezekiel 28:1–2, 6–7.
1348 Ibid., 29:3.
1349 Jeremiah 50:29.
1350 Job 41:2.
1351 Genesis 11:4, 6.
1352 Daniel 5:22.

One is forbidden to reproach and blaspheme God, and to boast that his might and power are all his own.[1354]

One is forbidden to speak against God.[1355]

One is forbidden to sin with his lips.[1356]

The nations are forbidden to try to change the festivals of Israel and the laws of the Torah.[1357] The nations are forbidden to defile the Temple, to abolish the daily sacrifice or to bring an idol into the Temple.[1358]

Other nations are forbidden to enter the Temple.[1359]

The other nations are forbidden to take God's treasures.[1360] The kings of the other nations are forbidden to take the utensils from the House of God and to drink wine from them, along with their people.[1361]

The nations must know that God is the Lord (*Shem Havaya*).[1362]

The nation must recognize that the Lord is God and that there is no God beside Him, and that He is righteous and saves.[1363]

The other nations must understand that it was God who caused them to be victorious over Israel and to defeat it.[1364]

The nations must understand that God's name is renowned by His greatness.[1365] They must understand that His name is awe-inspiring.[1366] They must understand that God is exalted.[1367]

The nations are forbidden to forget God.[1368]

1353 Jeremiah 50:24.
1354 II Kings 19:22–24.
1355 Daniel 7:25.
1356 Job 2:10.
1357 Daniel 7:25.
1358 Ibid., 11:31.
1359 Lamentations 1:10.
1360 Joel 4:5.
1361 Daniel 5:23.
1362 Exodus 7:5.
1363 Isaiah 45:20–21.
1364 Deuteronomy 32:27–30.
1365 Malachi 1:11.
1366 Ibid., 1:14.
1367 Psalms 46:11.
1368 Ibid., 9:18.

The nations must understand that God is holy.[1369] The nations must know that the Lord is God and that He is holy in Israel.[1370] They must recognize that He is the Redeemer of Israel.[1371]

One may not say incorrect statements about God.[1372] One may not talk about God without proper knowledge.[1373] One may not criticize God's justice in order to justify oneself.[1374]

One may not speak disparagingly about God.[1375]

All nations must know that God reigns over all human rulers, and gives rule to those whom He chooses.[1376]

All nations must know that God will perform justice soon and will not delay in rescuing Israel.[1377]

One is forbidden to make idols, to trust in them,[1378] or to praise them.[1379]

If a nation has sinned, it must return to God.[1380]

All nations must listen to God's voice.[1381]

All nations of the world must serve God with fear and joy.[1382]

Every person must strive to be guileless, honest, fearing of God, and to turn away from evil.[1383]

All nations must sing a song of praise to God and honor Him.[1384] All nations must accept upon themselves the yoke of the Kingdom of God.[1385]

1369 Ezekiel 20:41.
1370 Ibid., 39:7.
1371 Isaiah 49:26.
1372 Job 42:7.
1373 Ibid., 38:2.
1374 Ibid., 40:8.
1375 Ibid., 1:22.
1376 Daniel 4:29.
1377 Isaiah 46:13.
1378 Psalms 115:4–8.
1379 Daniel 5:23.
1380 Jeremiah 18:8.
1381 Micah 5:14.
1382 Psalms 2:10–11.
1383 Job 1:8.
1384 Isaiah 42:10–12.

The House of God must be a house of prayer for all nations.[1386] In the future, all nations will ascend in a pilgrimage to Jerusalem, to bow down to God and to celebrate the Festival of Tabernacles.[1387]

All nations must trust in God.[1388] They must turn to Him.[1389] All nations must request God's judgment.[1390]

All nations must come to God.[1391]

All nations must cry out to God to save them.[1392]

All nations must serve God through sacrifices and through fulfilling vows to God.[1393] However one may not sacrifice an animal of a non-Israelite if it has a blemish.[1394]

The nations must swear in the name of God.[1395]

All nations must cooperate with God's plans. They therefore had to acquiesce to the rule of Nebuchadnezzar, the king of Babylon, and his descendants, until the time of the destruction of the Babylonian kingdom.[1396]

The Relationship to the Nation of Israel

The other nations are forbidden to try to destroy Israel.[1397] They are forbidden to gather together for war against Israel.[1398] The armies of the other nations are forbidden to lay siege to Israel.[1399]

1385 Ibid., 45:23.
1386 Ibid., 56:7.
1387 Zechariah 14:16.
1388 Psalms 2:12.
1389 Zechariah 9:1. See Radak, Metzudat David.
1390 Isaiah 51:5.
1391 Zechariah 2:15.
1392 Isaiah 19:20.
1393 Ibid., 19:21.
1394 Leviticus 22:25.
1395 Jeremiah 12:16.
1396 Ibid., 27:6–11.
1397 Daniel 11:16–17.
1398 Micah 4:11.
1399 Zechariah 14:12.

The other nations are forbidden to wage war against the nation of Israel.[1400] They are forbidden to act with violence against the nation of Israel.[1401]

They are forbidden to attack the nation of Israel when it is in a weak state.[1402]

The other nations are forbidden to pursue the nation of Israel.[1403]

The other nations are forbidden to divide the Land of Israel among themselves.[1404] The other nations are forbidden to inherit the Land of Israel.[1405] The other nations are forbidden to expand their territory at the expense of tracts of the Land of Israel.[1406]

The other nations are forbidden from harming the nation of Israel more than God planned for them.[1407] They are forbidden to take revenge upon Israel.[1408] They are forbidden to afflict Israel.[1409]

The other nations are forbidden to curse Israel.[1410]

The other nations are forbidden to take booty from Israel.[1411]

The other nations are forbidden to shed innocent blood of the Children of Israel.[1412]

The other nations are forbidden to exile Israel from its land.[1413]

The other nations may not sell a member of the Children of Israel.[1414] They may not sell a member of the Children of Israel to a nation which resides far from the boundaries of the Land of Israel.[1415]

1400 Amos 1:11.
1401 Obadiah 1:10.
1402 Deuteronomy 25:18.
1403 Ibid., 30:7.
1404 Joel 4:2.
1405 Ezekiel 36:5.
1406 Zephaniah 2:8.
1407 Zechariah 1:15.
1408 Ezekiel 25:12.
1409 Zephaniah 3:19.
1410 Numbers 22:12.
1411 Zechariah 2:12.
1412 Joel 4:19.
1413 Amos 1:6.
1414 Zechariah 11:5.

The other nations are forbidden to hand over refugees of the Children of Israel to their enemies.[1416]

The other nations are forbidden to harm the anointed of God, or to harm God's prophets.[1417]

The other nations are forbidden to humiliate or curse the nation of Israel.[1418]

No nation may have an eternal hatred towards the Children of Israel.[1419]

No nation may rejoice at the defeat of Israel.[1420] No nation may think it will be built up at the expense of the destruction of Jerusalem.[1421]

The other nations are forbidden to rejoice over taking booty from Israel (where even taking booty from Israel will bring about a punishment from God).[1422]

The other nations are forbidden to say that the nation of Israel is a nation like all other nations.[1423] The other nations are forbidden to treat the nation of Israel disparagingly.[1424]

The other nations must have mercy towards the nation of Israel.[1425]

The other nations should have welcomed the Children of Israel when they left Egypt with bread and water.[1426]

They must protect Israel.[1427]

The other nations must praise God's nation.[1428]

1415 Joel 4:6.
1416 Obadiah 1:14.
1417 Psalms 105:15.
1418 Zephaniah 2:8.
1419 Ezekiel 35:5–6.
1420 Ibid., 25:3–4.
1421 Ibid., 26:2.
1422 Jeremiah 50:11.
1423 Ezekiel 25:8.
1424 Jeremiah 48:25–27.
1425 Isaiah 47:5–6.
1426 Deuteronomy 23:5.
1427 Song of Songs 8:11–12. See Rashi.
1428 Deuteronomy 32:43.

The other nations must come to the nation of Israel.[1429] They must learn from it.[1430]

• Summary

The demands upon and commandments required of the Children of Israel encompass all realms of life. They include general demands and specific commandments. The demands and commandments are divided into instructions at a specific time, and those which are for all generations. Instructions for a specific time were given at various periods of time. All such instructions were the result of the situation in which they were given and were intended for a specific purpose. The commandments and demands for all generations are binding for all times. (See the introduction to the sub-chapter of Commandments and Demands for All Generations, p. 130.)

The commandments and demands determine the way an Israelite must relate to God, his actions in the world, and how he relates to other people. Some of them are positive commandments which require one to take certain actions. Others are negative commandments, which require one to refrain from certain actions.

The commandments and demands of the other nations in the world relate to the order of the world, to people in general, to the nation of Israel, and to God.

1429 Isaiah 55:5.
1430 Ibid., 60:3.

Chapter 6 – Reward and Punishment

The message of the Bible is unequivocal. Good deeds are rewarded, whereas bad deeds are punished. The reward and punishment involved may affect all of mankind, nations, various groups, or individuals.

• For All of Mankind, Nations, and Groups of People

For Mankind

God commanded Adam, the first man, not to eat from the Tree of Knowledge of Good and Evil. If he would eat from it, he would become mortal and subject to death.[1] The woman, who ate from the tree, was punished: her pregnancies and births would be with great suffering and pain. She would desire her husband, and he would rule over her.[2] The punishment of the man for eating from the forbidden fruit: the earth would be cursed for him. He would have to work hard to produce from it his food, and at the end of his life he would return to the earth that he came from.[3] God banished man from the Garden of Eden so that he should not also eat from the Tree of Life, which would make him immortal.[4]

When God found that the deeds of people and their thoughts were only to do evil, He said that He would destroy everything which He had created,

---

1 Genesis 2:16–17.
2 Ibid., 3:16.
3 Ibid., 3:17–19.
4 Ibid., 3:22–24.

including people and all animals.[5] The violence and destructiveness were another reason for destroying them.[6]

The people sought to build a city and tower which would reach to the heavens in order to express their might. God, therefore, did not permit them to continue to speak and understand one another in the same language, and dispersed them throughout the earth.[7]

Reward for the Nation of Israel

In General

If the Children of Israel observe God's commandments, He will be good to them and their descendants.[8]

Closeness to God

If the Children of Israel listen to the voice of God and observe His covenant, they will be a nation to Him, a kingdom of Priests and a holy nation.[9] He will be their God and they will be His nation.[10]

If the Children of Israel keep God's ordinances, God will keep the covenant and the kindness which He swore to their forefathers, will love them and bless them.[11] He will glorify Israel.[12] The Holy Place of God will be among them[13] and they will know that God is in their midst and is their God.[14]

If the Children of Israel feed and clothe the hungry and poor, God will answer them when they call to Him.[15]

When the nation walks in God's ways, they will always rejoice in Him

---

5 Ibid., 6:5–7.
6 Ibid., 6:13.
7 Ibid., 11:5–9.
8 Deuteronomy 4:40.
9 Exodus 19:5–6.
10 Leviticus 26:12.
11 Deuteronomy 7:12–13.
12 Isaiah 55:5.
13 Leviticus 26:11.
14 Joel 2:27.
15 Isaiah 58:7–9.

and will be strengthened by Him.[16]

The prophet Zechariah prophesied that if the nation would listen to the voice of God, God's House would be rebuilt.[17]

The Nation's Material Condition on Its Land

If the Children of Israel do that which is good and upright in the eyes of God, they will inherit the good land which God swore to give to their forefathers.[18]

If the Children of Israel internalize God's words, bind them as a sign on their arm and above their eyes, teach them to their children so that they will always be with them, and write them on the doorposts of their houses and gates, they will live for a long time on the land which God swore to give to them.[19]

If the Children of Israel observe God's statutes and ordinances, they will live on their land in security.[20]

If the nation of Israel obeys God's commandments, it will be repaid with peace.[21] When the Children of Israel seek God in truth, the nations around them will not harm them.[22]

Those who offer blessings in the name of the God of Truth and swear in His name will have great joy. They will build houses and dwell in them, will plant vineyards and enjoy their fruit. There will be no destruction on the Holy Mountain.[23]

If the Children of Israel observe God's commandments, there will be peace in the land. If necessary, they will pursue their enemies and defeat them.[24]

---

16 Psalms 89:16–17.
17 Zechariah 6:12–15.
18 Deuteronomy 6:18.
19 Ibid., 11:18–21. See Mechilta, Exodus 13:9.
20 Leviticus 25:18.
21 Isaiah 48:18.
22 II Chronicles 15:14–15.
23 Isaiah 65:16–25.
24 Leviticus 26:6–8.

They will inherit all the nations, even those which are great and mighty. Wherever they tread will be theirs – from the desert and the Lebanon, from the Euphrates River until the Mediterranean will be their border. No one will oppose them and all the other nations will fear them.[25]

If the Children of Israel observe the commandment of releasing loans in the Sabbatical year, they will be lenders and not borrowers. They will rule over nations and none will rule over them.[26]

The tribe of Judah vanquished the other tribes in war because they turned to God and trusted Him.[27]

If the Children of Israel observe God's commandments, He will bring rain in its appointed season, and they will gather the produce of their land. There will also be grass in their fields for their cattle. The Children of Israel will eat and be satisfied.[28] The land will yield its crops in abundance.[29] God will bless and increase their animals.[30]

There will be no poor people among the Children of Israel.[31]

God will multiply them and bless their progeny. There will not be any barren women among them.[32]

God will remove all illness from them – even the illnesses of the Egyptians.[33]

When the Children of Israel repent at a time that they are scattered in exile among the nations, God will gather them from among the nations and will bring them back to the Land of Israel.[34]

---

25 Deuteronomy 11:22–25.
26 Ibid., 15:6.
27 II Chronicles 13:18.
28 Deuteronomy 11:13–15.
29 Leviticus 26:3–4.
30 Deuteronomy 7:13–14.
31 Ibid., 15:4. The statement in Deuteronomy 15:11 that "the poor will not cease from the earth" refers to a time in which Israel will not observe the commandments. See Rashi on ibid., 15:4.
32 Ibid., 7:12–14.
33 Ibid., 7:15.
34 Ibid., 30:1–5.

Respect from the Other Nations

If the Children of Israel return to God, remove their idol worship and swear to God in truth, justice, and righteousness, the other nations will be blessed because of them and will praise them.[35]

Escaping from Evil

Whoever calls in the name of God can escape on the great and awesome day of God to Mount Zion and Jerusalem.[36]

Those who repent will be redeemed.[37]

If the Children of Israel obey God's commandments, they will not be destroyed.[38]

If all of the Children of Israel fast and come to a solemn assembly, and the Priests cry and plead to God, they will not be shamed among the nations.[39]

At the beginning of the reign of Jehoiakim, Jeremiah prophesied in the name of God to the people of Judah: if they would repent from their evil ways, God would not visit upon them the evil which He had planned for them.[40]

God will send the prophet Elijah, before the coming of the great and awesome day of God, to return the hearts of the fathers and of the children. Should they repent, He will not smite the inhabitants of the land.[41]

Rehoboam and his ministers submitted to God, and that is why He did not destroy them.[42]

King Hezekiah and the inhabitants of Jerusalem submitted to God, and that is why He did not punish them.[43]

---

35 Jeremiah 4:1–2.
36 Joel 3:4–5.
37 Isaiah 59:20. See Metzudat David.
38 Ibid., 48:18–19.
39 Joel 2:15–19.
40 Jeremiah 26:1–3.
41 Malachi 3:23–24.
42 II Chronicles 12:6–7, 12.
43 Ibid., 32:26.

Reward for the Levites

God gave the Levites the tithe of the fruit of the land of the Children of Israel instead of an inheritance in the land.[44] The Levites can eat the tithe in any place, because it is their reward for their work.[45]

Reward for the Nations

Nations which turn to God will be saved.[46]

If a nation acts with righteousness, its importance will grow.[47]

If the nations which neighbor the land of Israel learn to swear in the name of God, they will be built up among God's nation.[48]

Those nations which protect the nation of Israel will receive a reward. [49]

If a nation repents its evil ways, God will annul the punishment which He had planned for it.[50]

When the people of Nineveh and its king repented their evil ways, God did not bring upon them the punishment which had been planned for them.[51]

The humble of the land who seek God and act justly will be saved from punishment on the day earmarked by God for punishment.[52]

The Children of Israel are required not to treat Egyptians negatively, because they were strangers in their land.[53]

When five cities in Egypt swear in the name of God and their inhabitants destroy every city whose inhabitants do not so; when an altar to God is erected in Egypt and a memorial to God is put up on its border as testimony that the Egyptians turn to God and afterwards cry to Him to save

44 Numbers 18:24.
45 Ibid., 18:31.
46 Isaiah 45:22.
47 Proverbs 14:34.
48 Jeremiah 12:16.
49 Song of Songs 8:11–12.
50 Jeremiah 18:8.
51 Jonah 3:10.
52 Zephaniah 2:3.
53 Deuteronomy 23:8.

them, God will send someone to save them.[54] When the people of Egypt return to God, He will listen to their prayers and heal them.[55] On that day, God will bless Egypt.[56]

Punishments for the Nations

A nation which sins against God will be punished. The land upon which it dwells will not be able to support its inhabitants, and it will become a wasteland, while its sons will be killed by the sword or by pestilence.[57]

God will take vengeance on those nations which are His enemies and will bear a grudge against them. He will not forgive them.[58]

God visits the sins of the fathers upon the sons up to the third and fourth generation, when they continue to hate Him.[59] Sometimes God avoids punishing for a sin, until the repetition of the sin brings about a greater punishment at a later stage. This is true also for nations.

Even though God plans to do good to a specific nation, if that nation does evil in His eyes and does not listen to His voice, God will annul the good which he planned for it.[60, 61]

A nation which takes booty after war from other nations through bloodshed and violence will receive its punishment when other nations will take booty from it.[62]

---

54 Isaiah 19:18–20.
55 Ibid., 19:22.
56 Ibid., 19:24–25.
57 Ezekiel 14:12–19.
58 Nahum 1:2–3.
59 Exodus 20:5.
60 Jeremiah 18:9–10.
61 It is written that if a prophet makes a statement about something which does not happen, that statement could not come from God (Deuteronomy 18:21–22). Jeremiah clarified that if a prophet prophesies peace, only the fact that that is what happens will be proof that God indeed sent him (Jeremiah 28:6–9). It is known that repentance can annul a prophecy of destruction, as happened with Jonah. (See p. 333). See also Maimonides, *Mishneh Torah, Laws of the Principles of the Torah*, 10:4. It thus appears that in order to preserve the ability to differentiate between a true prophet and a false prophet, one must understand that a plan of God which can be annulled is a plan of God Himself, and is not a plan which is expressed within the prophecy of a prophet.

A nation which builds a city through bloodshed and injustice will receive its punishment through fire and working in vain.[63]

Punishments for the Nation of Israel

Material Condition

If the Children of Israel do not listen to God's voice, do not observe His commandments and the statutes which He gave them, and thus annul the covenant which He made with them, He will bring upon them confusion and terrible diseases. Their enemies will eat the fruit of their land. They will be vanquished by their enemies, and will flee even though no one is pursuing them.[64]

If they still do not listen to His voice, the earth will not yield its produce.[65]

If they still do not listen to His voice, God will send the wild beasts of the field to kill them and their animals, and as a result the roads throughout the country will be desolate.[66]

If they still do not listen, God will send the sword and pestilence against them. They will be delivered into the hands of their enemies and will suffer starvation.[67]

If they still do not listen, God will cause them to eat the flesh of their sons and daughters, kill many of them, and destroy their cities and Holy Place. He will not accept their sacrifices, will make the land desolate and disperse them among the nations.[68]

They will be exiled among the nations also as a punishment for not observing the laws of the Sabbatical and Jubilee years.[69]

---

62 Habakkuk 2:8.
63 Ibid., 2:12–13.
64 Leviticus 26:14–17.
65 Ibid., 26:18–20.
66 Ibid., 26:21–22.
67 Ibid., 26:23–26.
68 Ibid., 26:27–33.
69 Ibid., 26:34–35.

God will make the remnants of the nation fear, and they will flee even though there is none pursuing them. They will fall as if by the sword and will not be able to contend with their enemies. They will be lost among the nations in the land of their enemies.[70]

Those who remain alive will suffer in the lands of their enemies because of their sins and the sins of their fathers.[71]

If the Children of Israel do not obey God's commandments, they will be cursed. The curse will accompany them whether in the city or the field. It will affect their children, their crops, their animals, and all their actions.[72]

God will destroy them from upon the face of the earth.[73]

Whatever they possess will be taken from them: their wives, sons, daughters, property, animals, houses, fields, and vineyards.[74] They will grope around like a blind person in the dark, oppressed and robbed.[75]

They will be subservient to their enemies and will suffer hunger, thirst, and nakedness.[76]

Their carcasses will be food for the birds of the field and the wild animals of the land.[77]

They will be visited by diseases and blows which are not written in the Torah.[78]

They will be an example, as a nation which is held up in astonishment, scorn and disgrace among the nations to which God will disperse them.[79]

They will become a very small nation.[80]

70 Ibid., 26:36–38.
71 Ibid., 26:39.
72 Deuteronomy 28:15–19.
73 I Kings 9:6–7.
74 Deuteronomy 28:30–33.
75 Ibid., 28:29.
76 Ibid., 28:48.
77 Ibid., 28:26.
78 Ibid., 28:61.
79 Ibid., 28:37.
80 Ibid., 4:27.

If the Children of Israel would forget who their God is, God would erase their memory from mankind – had not the enemy been able to claim that it was he who had brought about the destruction of Israel, and not God.[81]

Just as God was happy to be good to them, He will be happy to destroy them.[82]

Closeness to God

If the Children of Israel forsake God, He will forsake them.[83]

If the Children of Israel turn to another god, God will hide His face from them. They will be visited by many bad events and troubles. They will understand and recognize that the evil has come upon them because God is not in their midst, but He will still conceal His face.[84]

God's hiding of His face, after they recognize that God is not among them, will be expressed by lessening of the punishment. It will continue as long as they have not confessed their sins.[85, 86]

God will cut them off from the face of the earth, and He will not continue to dwell in the House which He consecrated to His name.[87]

---

81 Ibid., 32:26–27.
82 Ibid., 28:63.
83 II Chronicles 15:1–2.
84 Deuteronomy 31:16–18.
85 Leviticus 26:40–41.
86 In Deuteronomy we are told about the reactions of the other nations to the destruction of the land and the nation in the future. They will say that God's curse upon the Children of Israel for having left God (Deuteronomy 29:23–27) has been fulfilled. In Isaiah the other nations claim that the nation of Israel was punished because of the sins of the other nations (Isaiah 53:2–9). This seems to be a contradiction. One can ignore the assessment of the other nations in Isaiah for the following reasons: a) All the other sources which deal with this topic (as mentioned in this chapter) are in accordance with the Book of Deuteronomy. b) One must understand the words of the other nations in Isaiah as referring to a future time, after the Destruction of the Temple, when the nation of Israel has already returned to its land and status. Their words were influenced by the comparison of the status of the nation at the time of their redemption to their earlier status when they were in distress.
87 I Kings 9:6–7.

Punishments for the Nation of Israel throughout History

In the Desert

When the Children of Israel were in the desert, they were punished for actions which were not according to God's wishes. In some cases the punishment which God had planned was replaced, after prayer and pleading, by a different punishment.

When the Children of Israel worshipped the Golden Calf, God asked Moses to permit Him to destroy them and to establish from Moses by himself a great nation.[88] Moses pleaded to God, and God did not destroy them.[89] However, He told Moses that He would punish them later on. He brought a plague upon the nation.[90]

The Children of Israel complained unjustifiably, and God therefore sent fire at the edge of the camp.[91]

When the Children of Israel complained that they had no meat to eat, God said that He would give them meat for thirty days until they would get sick of it and spurn it, because they had spurned God and complained about leaving Egypt.[92] While still eating the meat, God smote them.[93]

The Children of Israel, based on the report of the spies did not believe in God in spite of His signs. (They wanted to stone Caleb and Joshua, who demanded that they trust in God that they would be able to conquer the Land of Israel.) That is why God wanted to destroy the Children of Israel with a plague of pestilence and to establish a great nation from Moses.[94] Moses pleaded to God and requested that He forgive them, and He acquiesced.[95] However, all those who had seen God's glory and His signs, and nevertheless tested Him and did not listen to His voice would not be

88 Exodus 32:9–10.
89 Ibid., 32:11–14.
90 Ibid., 32:34–35.
91 Numbers 11:1.
92 Ibid., 11:18–20.
93 Ibid., 11:33.
94 Ibid., 14:11–12.
95 Ibid., 14:13–20.

permitted to see the land which God had sworn to their forefathers.[96] All those who were twenty years or older would die in the desert except for Caleb and Joshua. They would wander in the desert for forty years – a year for each of the forty days that the Spies were in the Land of Israel – until those who left Egypt had died.[97] Not one of those of the Children of Israel who participated in the census on the plains of Moab by the Jordan just before entering the Land of Israel was among those who had left Egypt in the Exodus, except for Caleb and Joshua.[98] The spies who had spread an evil report of the land died in a plague which God brought upon them.[99]

God instructed the nation to return by the way of the Sea of Reeds and not to fight their enemies in their path, because God would not be in their midst. The Children of Israel did not obey and climbed the Mountain of the Emorites in order to fight. The Emorites pursued them and killed many. When the Children of Israel cried before God, He did not listen to them.[100]

When Korah and his band revolted and prepared censers in which they placed fire and incense, God instructed Moses and Aaron to separate themselves from the nation. God wanted to destroy the entire nation.[101] The entire nation had a certain degree of responsibility, because Korah and his band were among its leaders.

Moses and Aaron argued that God should not become angry at the entire nation because of one man. The unnatural deaths of Korah, Datan, Aviram and their families – who were swallowed up alive into the earth, along with all their possessions, – was proof that they had angered God and that He had chosen Moses and Aaron to lead the nation.[102] God also sent forth fire to consume the two hundred and fifty men who had offered incense.[103]

96 Ibid., 14:21–23.
97 Ibid., 14:26–35.
98 Ibid., 26:64–65.
99 Ibid., 14:37.
100 Deuteronomy 1:40–45.
101 Numbers 16:18–21.
102 Ibid., 16:22–33.
103 Ibid., 16:35.

The Children of Israel complained that Moses and Aaron had killed "God's nation." God again wanted to destroy the entire nation.[104] God brought a plague upon the nation, in which 14,700 people died.[105]

When the Children of Israel lost their patience because of the roundabout way they were forced to go, and began to complain about God taking them out of Egypt in order to perish in the desert, their punishment was death by snake bites.[106]

Some of the Children of Israel began to engage in illicit sexual relations with the daughters of Moab, and as a result to worship idols. God brought a plague upon them, and 24,000 people died.[107]

After the Entrance into the Land of Israel

On the plains of Moab, before they entered the Land of Israel, God commanded the Children of Israel to dispossess all the inhabitants of the land and to destroy their idols and high places. If they would not do so, those inhabitants who remained in the land would cause them many troubles. God would bring upon the Children of Israel the punishment which had been planned for others.[108] If the Children of Israel would not utterly destroy the seven nations of the Land of Israel, would make a covenant with them, marry them, and worship their gods, God would destroy them speedily.[109]

The Children of Israel did not complete the conquest of the land and left some of its inhabitants alive, made a covenant with them and did not smash their altars. An angel of God told them that they would not drive out the rest, and these nations and their idols would be a source of troubles and difficulties.[110]

After Jericho was conquered, Joshua announced a ban against taking anything from the city. The Children of Israel violated the ban, when Achan

---

104 Ibid., 17:6–10.
105 Ibid., 17:11–14.
106 Ibid., 21:5–6.
107 Ibid., 25:1–9.
108 Ibid., 33:50–56.
109 Deuteronomy 7:2–4.
110 Judges 2:1–3.

took some of the booty, and God became angry at the Children of Israel.[111] From this episode, one sees that the entire Children of Israel are responsible for the deeds of individuals among them.

Their punishment was that the inhabitants of Ai defeated the army of Israel.[112] God told Joshua that Israel had sinned, had taken of the banned goods and had also denied doing so. God would no longer be with them until they had removed the banned goods from their midst. Whoever was found to have taken of the banned goods would be burned to death – he and everything belonging to him.[113]

During the Era of the Judges

In the days of the Judges, the Children of Israel forsook God and worshipped the gods of the nations who lived around them. God therefore delivered them into the hands of their enemies.[114] He delivered them into the hands of Cushan Rishatayim, the king of Aram Naharayim;[115] Eglon, the King of Moab;[116] Yavin, the king of Canaan;[117] Midian;[118] the Ammonites and Philistines;[119] and the Philistines.[120]

The Children of Israel violated the covenant between them and God. Therefore, He did not continue to dispossess anyone because of them, in order to test whether they would observe the path of God, as their fathers had done.[121]

When the Children of Israel cried out to God because of the Ammonites and Philistines, and confessed that they had been guilty of idol worship, God answered them that they had cried out to Him a number of times and He

---

111 Joshua 7:1.
112 Ibid., 7:4–5.
113 Ibid., 7:10–15.
114 Judges 2:11–15.
115 Ibid., 3:7–8.
116 Ibid., 3:12–14.
117 Ibid., 4:1–3.
118 Ibid., 6:1–6.
119 Ibid., 10:6–9.
120 Ibid., 13:1.
121 Ibid., 2:20–23.

had saved them, but they had regressed and worshipped other gods. He would therefore no longer save them.[122, 123]

God smote the people of Bet Shemesh, because they had seen the Ark of the Lord and had not shown it proper respect.[124] (On the other hand, there is no mention of the people of Kiryat Ye'arim receiving any punishment, as they evidently showed proper respect to the Ark.)

During the Era of the Kings

When God became angry at Israel (because of their sins), He instigated King David to conduct a census of the nation.[125] After an attempt to persuade King David not to count the people failed, Joab and the military officers went out to count the nation.[126] The census was evil in God's eyes.[127] God told David that he could choose the punishment among three options: seven years of famine, three months of fleeing from the enemy, or a plague of pestilence. David chose the plague, and in it 70,000 people died.[128] The punishment for the nation was a forbidden act (the census) for which it is punished. The description in Chronicles of Satan instigating David is another detail in addition to those described in the Book of Samuel.

The nation was unfaithful to God. That is why Shishak, the king of Egypt, went up to fight against Jerusalem.[129]

Ahab, the king of Israel, did evil in the eyes of God, more than all the kings who preceded him. He followed in the ways of Jeroboam, building an altar for Ba'al and making an *asherah*.[130] As a result, the prophet Elijah swore

---

122 Ibid., 10:10–13.

123 After the Children of Israel returned to serve God (Judges 10:15–16), He delivered their enemies into their hands (ibid., 11:32).

124 I Samuel 6:19.

125 II Samuel 24:1.

126 Ibid., 24:2–4.

127 I Chronicles 21:7.

128 II Samuel 24:11–15.

129 II Chronicles 12:1–2.

130 I Kings 16:30–33.

by God that there would be no dew or rain until he would annul the decree.[131]

God told Elijah that he who escaped the sword of Hazael, the king of Aram, would be killed by Jehu, the next king of Israel. Those who fled from Jehu would be killed by the prophet Elisha. Only seven thousand would remain in Israel – those who had not bowed down to Ba'al.[132]

God gave the army of Aram great power and it went up against Judah and Jerusalem, killed the leaders of the nation and took booty – because they had abandoned the Lord, the God of their forefathers.[133]

King Ahaz did not do what is right in the eye of God, unlike his father David, but followed in the ways of the kings of Israel, making molten images for Ba'al. In the valley of Ben-Hinnom he burned incense and burned his sons in fire, like the abominations of the nations which God had dispossessed because of the Children of Israel. He offered sacrifices and incense on the high places and on the hills, and underneath every green tree. God delivered him into the hands of the king of Aram, who killed some of the members of the nation and took others in captivity. He was also delivered into the hands of the king of Israel, who smote him a mighty blow. Pekach the son of Remalyahu, the king of Israel, and his army killed 120,000 men of the Kingdom of Judah in a single day, because they had abandoned the Lord, the God of their forefathers. They also captured 200,000 women, boys and girls, and took a large quantity of booty.[134] The Edomites also came and smote Judah and took captives, and the Philistines captured many cities and settled in them, because Ahaz had been unfaithful to God.[135]

The Destruction

The Children of Israel sinned against God and worshipped the idols of the land. They adopted the ways of the nations of the land whom God had

131 Ibid., 17:1.
132 Ibid., 19:15–18.
133 II Chronicles 24:23–24.
134 Ibid., 28:1–8.
135 Ibid., 28:17–19.

dispossessed because of them, made inappropriate remarks in secret about God, built high places, sacred pillars and *asherah* trees everywhere and worshipped them, and thereby angered God. God warned the people of Israel and Judah through the prophets to leave their evil ways and to observe God's commandments.[136]

The prophets said that God would transform the glory of the Priests into shame.[137]

The tribe of Ephraim would be destroyed speedily.[138] The end had come for the Kingdom of Israel.[139]

God would bring an enemy which would besiege the land, weaken its power and sack its palaces.[140]

They would fall by the sword, and even babies would be killed.[141]

Their work would not show fruit, and whatever was left over would be eaten by their enemies.[142]

The tribe of Ephraim would wander among the other nations.[143]

Those of the tribes of Reuben, Gad, and half the tribe of Menasseh who had settled across the Jordan acted unfaithfully towards the God of their forefathers and worshipped the gods of the nations of the land which God had destroyed because of them. God therefore brought upon them the kings of Assyria, who conquered them and exiled them from their land.[144]

The Children of Israel were stubborn and did not listen to the prophets. They passed their sons and daughters through fire and were involved in witchcraft. God therefore became angry and removed them from being before Him, and they were exiled to Assyria. Only the tribe of Judah remained by itself. But its members also did not observe God's

136 II Kings 17:7–13.
137 Hosea 4:7.
138 Ibid., 13:1–3.
139 Amos 8:2.
140 Ibid., 3:11.
141 Hosea 14:1.
142 Ibid., 8:7.
143 Ibid., 9:17.
144 I Chronicles 5:25–26.

commandments, and they followed in the path of the Kingdom of Israel. God rejected all of Israel and afflicted them, giving them into the hands of their enemies, until He cast them away from Him. God made Jeroboam king. Jeroboam led Israel astray from God, until God removed them from before Him, as He had said through the prophets.[145]

Menasseh, the king of Judah, did evil in the eyes of God, like the abominations of the nations which God had dispossessed. He rebuilt the high places, established altars to Ba'al, made an *asherah* and worshipped all the heavenly hosts. He built altars (to other gods) in the House of God. He passed his son through fire and was involved in witchcraft. He placed an idol of an *asherah* in the House of God. Menasseh led the nation astray, to do the abominations of the nations which God had destroyed.[146] God spoke to Menasseh and his nation to warn them, but they did not listen. Therefore, He brought upon them the generals of the army of the king of Assyria, who seized Menasseh and exiled him to Babylon.[147]

God sent word to the nation through His prophets that because of the abominations of Menasseh, king of Judah, He would bring evil on Jerusalem and on Judah. He would obliterate Jerusalem, which would receive the same punishment as Samaria had received. God would abandon the remnants of His people and would deliver them into the hands of their enemies.[148] Relying on Egypt or Assyria would not help.[149]

Because of those who followed other gods, God would destroy Judah and Jerusalem.[150]

The system of authority would fall apart.[151] All the wealth of Jerusalem and the treasures of Judah would fall into the hands of enemies.[152]

---

145 II Kings 17:14–23.
146 Ibid., 21:2–9.
147 II Chronicles 33:10–11.
148 II Kings 21:10–15.
149 Jeremiah 2:18.
150 Ibid., 13:9–10.
151 Isaiah 3:5.
152 Jeremiah 20:5.

The Chaldees would set fire to Jerusalem and burn it down.[153] The homes of the people would be burned down.[154]

God would cause the Temple in Jerusalem to be destroyed, as He had done in Shiloh.[155]

Famine and thirst would increase.[156] People would eat the flesh of their sons and daughters, and each would eat his fellow man.[157]

The fear from the report of the destruction would increase in the city.[158] God would destroy the high places in the hills of Israel and in the valleys. The bones of those who were killed would be scattered around the altars.[159] God would annihilate them with the sword.[160]

God ordered the destroyers to kill and not take pity on anyone. They were to make the Temple and its courtyard ritually unclean with the bodies of the dead.[161]

As they did not agree to free their Hebrew slaves indefinitely, God would deliver the king, the ministers, the Priests, and the people of the land into the hands of their enemies.[162]

The city of Jerusalem would be conquered by the army of the king of Babylon.[163]

The inhabitants of the country and of Jerusalem would be taken captive.[164] They would be exiled to Babylon.[165]

A nation from the north would come and make the land desolate without its inhabitants.[166]

---

153 Ibid., 32:29.
154 Ezekiel 23:47.
155 Jeremiah 7:12–14.
156 Isaiah 5:13.
157 Jeremiah 19:9.
158 Ezekiel 21:12.
159 Ibid., 6:3–4.
160 Jeremiah 9:15.
161 Ezekiel 9:1–7.
162 Jeremiah 34:13–20.
163 Ibid., 38:3.
164 Ibid., 13:17.
165 Ibid., 20:4.

Strangers would inherit the houses of the Children of Israel.[167]

God would scatter the Children of Israel among the nations.[168] Because they spilled blood and worshipped idols, they would be a disgrace among the nations.[169] The destruction which God would bring on the land would cause a feeling of horror among all the kingdoms.[170] They would be derided and scorned.[171]

They would serve strangers in a land not their own.[172]

God sent the legions of the Chaldees, Aram, Moab, and the Ammonites to destroy Judah and its king, Jehoiakim, who did all the sins of Menasseh, his grandfather's father, and even shed innocent blood.[173] Nebuchadnezzar, the king of Babylon, removed all the treasures of the House of God and the palace of the king, as God had said. He also exiled the majority of the inhabitants of Jerusalem and the ministers, the soldiers, the craftsmen and the metal workers, and left only the poor of the people of the land.[174]

Zedekiah did evil in the eyes of God, as Jehoiakim had done. In his days, Nebuchadnezzar the king of Babylon and all his army went up to Jerusalem, laid a siege on it, killed its inhabitants and exiled the king. Nebuchadnezzar's assistant, Nevuzaradan, burned the Temple and the houses of the city and exiled the majority of its inhabitants.[175]

The following events took place as part of the punishment:

Those who loved Jerusalem deceived it.[176] The beauty of Jerusalem disappeared.[177]

Its ministers and elders were not respected.[178]

---

166 Ibid., 4:6–7.
167 Ezekiel 7:24.
168 Ibid., 12:15.
169 Ibid., 22:4.
170 Jeremiah 15:4.
171 Ezekiel 23:32.
172 Jeremiah 5:19.
173 II Kings 24:2–4.
174 Ibid., 24:13–16.
175 Ibid., 24:19 – 25:21.
176 Lamentations 1:19.
177 Ibid., 1:6.

The enemy took everything which was precious to it.[179] God destroyed and demolished the Kingdom of Judah, its palaces and fortresses.[180]

The anointed one of God (the king) was captured.[181]

God destroyed the entire country.[182]

God forsook His altar.[183] Strangers entered the Temple, even though God had commanded that they were not to come into it.[184] They made sounds of exultation in the House of God.[185]Foxes wandered on Mount Zion, which was desolate.[186]

Its inhabitants starved for bread.[187] They gave everything they had for food in order to survive.[188] Children fainted in the streets of the city.[189] The people of Jerusalem endangered their lives in order to find bread.[190] Priests and elders died in the city because of the famine.[191] The infants and children had nothing to drink or eat.[192] Merciful women boiled their children.[193]

God removed His protection from the inhabitants of the land.[194] The people of Judah were pursued and found no escape.[195] Those who pursued them were fleet-footed. They pursued them in the mountains and laid ambushes for them in the desert.[196] The enemy ambushed them in the streets of the city.[197]

---

178 Ibid., 5:12.
179 Ibid., 1:10.
180 Ibid., 2:5.
181 Ibid., 4:20.
182 Ibid., 2:2.
183 Ibid., 2:7.
184 Ibid., 1:10.
185 Ibid., 2:7.
186 Ibid., 5:18.
187 Ibid., 5:10.
188 Ibid., 1:11.
189 Ibid., 2:11.
190 Ibid., 5:9.
191 Ibid., 1:19.
192 Ibid., 4:3.
193 Ibid., 4:10.
194 Ibid., 2:3.
195 Ibid., 1:3.
196 Ibid., 4:19.
197 Ibid., 4:18.

Young men and women fell by the sword.[198] Outside, the sword reigned, while in the houses it was death.[199]

God did not pity.[200] (Almost) no one survived.[201]

There was great mourning in Judah.[202]

God did not allow the prayers of the nation to reach Him.[203]

The city which had been the most important of all gave tribute to its enemies.[204] Its enemies, who had besieged it, lived in tranquillity.[205]

Slaves ruled in Judah, and there was none to save one from them.[206]

Children were taken captive.[207]

The people of Judah were exiled.[208]

The city was desolate without its inhabitants.[209]

The land of Judah was given to strangers, and the homes of the Children of Israel to foreigners.[210]

In His anger, God dispersed the nation among the nations.[211]

The other nations scorned Jerusalem.[212] The nation of Israel was despised among the nations.[213]

Its prophets no longer had any visions from God.[214]

The nation which was exiled found no rest among the nations.[215]

---

198 Ibid., 2:21.
199 Ibid., 1:20.
200 Ibid., 2:17.
201 Ibid., 2:22.
202 Ibid., 2:5.
203 Ibid., 3:44.
204 Ibid., 1:1.
205 Ibid., 1:5.
206 Ibid., 5:8.
207 Ibid., 1:5.
208 Ibid., 1:3.
209 Ibid., 1:1.
210 Ibid., 5:2.
211 Ibid., 4:16.
212 Ibid., 1:8.
213 Ibid., 3:45.
214 Ibid., 2:9.
215 Ibid., 1:3.

After the Return to the Land of Israel

The exiles who returned from Babylon to the Land of Israel preferred to build their own homes rather than the House of God. Therefore, their economic situation was perilous.[216] God punished them by natural calamities which destroyed the work of their hands.[217]

At the time of Malachi, the nation turned from God's laws, especially in regard to heave offerings and tithes, and so a curse came upon it.[218]

The Annulment of the Possibility of Repenting

The prophet Hosea prophesied to the Priests and the nation. He said that their evil deeds would prevent them from returning to God. If they would want to do so by bringing sacrifices, God would not be found by them.[219]

The prophet Isaiah prophesied to the people of Judah that rather than repenting, they celebrated with eating and drinking, because their sin would not be atoned until they died.[220]

God told Jeremiah that He would not listen to them, even if they would offer sacrifices and meal offerings. He would destroy them by the sword, famine, and pestilence.[221]

Punishments to Select Groups

The leaders of the nation who do not perform their duties would receive their punishment.[222] Those who were led by them would become their leaders.[223]

---

216 Haggai 1:3–11.
217 Ibid., 2:15–17.
218 Malachi 3:7–9.
219 Hosea 5:4–7.
220 Isaiah 22:13–14.
221 Jeremiah 14:12.
222 Ibid., 23:1–2.
223 Ibid., 13:20–21. See Metzudat David, Radak.

The false prophets who, as it were, prophesied in the name of God that there would be peace in the land and that there would not be any war or famine – would die by the sword or by starvation.[224]

The Priests at the time of the prophet Hosea sinned like the nation. They would therefore eat and not be satisfied, nor would they have children.[225]

The Priests at the time of the prophet Malachi had violated the covenant which God had made with the tribe of Levi and caused many people to be led astray from the Torah. God would therefore make them scorned and lowly in the eyes of the nation.[226]

If the kings of the House of David do not judge fairly, God's wrath will strike them like a burning fire.[227] If the king of Judah does not act with judgment and righteousness (by saving one who was robbed from his oppressor; preventing the exploitation of a stranger, orphan or widow; and preventing the shedding of innocent blood), the Royal House will be destroyed.[228]

The Priests would bear the sin of the Temple and of their priesthood. One who is not a Priest is forbidden to approach the holy utensils in the Temple. The responsibility for this will be that of the Priests. They will bear the punishment if a non-Priest approaches.[229]

Punishments to the Nations

In General

God will destroy a sinning kingdom.[230]

God will take vengeance on those nations which did not help at the time of the redemption.[231]

God will disperse those nations which wish to go out to do battle.[232]

224 Ibid., 14:13–15.
225 Hosea 4:9–10.
226 Malachi 2:8–9.
227 Jeremiah 21:11–12.
228 Ibid., 22:1–5.
229 Numbers 18:1–5.
230 Amos 9:8.
231 Isaiah 63:4–6.
232 Psalms 68:31.

God delivered many kingdoms into the hands of Nebuchadnezzar, the king of Babylon. The inhabitants of these countries must be subservient to him as long as God has given him authority. If they do not do so, God will bring on them the sword, famine, and pestilence until they are destroyed.[233]

Punishments for Harming the Nation of Israel

The Children of Israel are holy to God, and anyone who harms them will be punished.[234]

When the Children of Israel repent, God will punish those nations which persecuted them with all those punishments stated for the Children of Israel.[235] The nations will be punished if they do not understand that God is responsible for the defeat of Israel, and not their might.[236] God will avenge the blood of Israel from those who shed it.[237]

When God brings back His nation to the Land of Israel, He will assemble all the nations in a valley. He will judge them there for what they did to the nation of Israel and its land.[238]

The day will come when the Children of Israel will smite their enemies and defeat them.[239] The land of those nations which came to wage war against Jerusalem will be desolate.[240]

The neighbors of Israel who acted against Israel in its land will be uprooted from their land.[241] All the nations which did evil to Israel will be punished, measure for measure.[242]

God will smite and take vengeance on those nations which harmed the people of Judah, who are like the apple of His eye. They will become booty to their slaves.[243]

---

233 Jeremiah 27:6–8.
234 Ibid., 2:3.
235 Deuteronomy 30:1–2, 7.
236 Ibid., 32:27–30.
237 Ibid., 32:43.
238 Joel 4:1–3.
239 Micah 4:11–14.
240 Ibid., 7:13.
241 Jeremiah 12:14.
242 Ibid., 30:16.

God will destroy the nations which came to conquer Jerusalem.[244] He will afflict them with a terrible plague.[245]

God will disperse His enemies.[246] The fire which goes before God will consume them.[247]

The nations will be as if in darkness, until they recognize God and Jerusalem.[248] The nations which do not recognize God and Jerusalem will be destroyed.[249] The nations which sin after the Day of God and do not come up on the Festival of Tabernacles to bow down to God, will suffer a cessation of rain. If Egypt does not come up, it will be punished with a plague.[250]

Punishments to other Nations – Throughout History

Sodom and Gomorrah

The sins of Sodom and the cities around it were grievous. The cries of the oppressed came before God. He wished to destroy all of its inhabitants.[251] He promised that He would not destroy the city if there were found in it ten righteous people.[252] God decided to destroy the city (since there were not ten righteous people).[253] God rained fire and brimstone on all the cities of the plain, upon their inhabitants and vegetation, and destroyed them.[254]

Egypt

God told Abram that he would hold to judgment the nation which would enslave the Children of Israel for four hundred years.[255] The Egyptians

---

243 Zechariah 2:12–13.
244 Ibid., 12:9.
245 Ibid., 14:12.
246 Psalms 89:11.
247 Ibid., 97:3.
248 Isaiah 60:2–3.
249 Ibid., 60:12.
250 Zechariah 14:16–18.
251 Genesis 18:20–21.
252 Ibid., 18:26–32.
253 Ibid., 19:12–13.
254 Ibid., 19:24–25.
255 Ibid., 15:14.

initiated the affliction of the Children of Israel.[256] God caused Pharaoh to refuse to send out the Children of Israel.[257] God brought down plagues on Egypt: blood,[258] frogs,[259] lice,[260] wild animals,[261] pestilence,[262] boils,[263] hail,[264] locusts,[265] and darkness.[266] In the last plague, God killed all the firstborn in the land of Egypt.[267] God drowned the Egyptians in the Sea of Reeds.[268]

The Nations of the Land of Israel

God told Abram that only the fourth generation of the Children of Israel would return to the Land of Israel, because the sin of the Emorites would not be complete until then.[269] After the Exodus from Egypt, God would drive out all the nations living in the Land of Israel because of the Children of Israel, so that they would not learn from their evil ways.[270] God drove the nations of the land from their land because of their sins of sexual immorality.[271] The nations of the land passed their sons and daughters through fire and were involved in witchcraft, and God therefore gave their land to the Children of Israel.[272]

God caused the nations living in the Land of Israel to not make peace with the Children of Israel so that they would be destroyed.[273]

---

256 Exodus 1:8–14.
257 Ibid., 4:21.
258 Ibid., 7:19–21.
259 Ibid., 8:1–2.
260 Ibid., 8:12–13.
261 Ibid., 8:16–20.
262 Ibid., 9:1–6.
263 Ibid., 9:8–10.
264 Ibid., 9:22–26.
265 Ibid., 10:12–15.
266 Ibid., 10:21–23.
267 Ibid., 12:29.
268 Ibid., 14:26–28.
269 Genesis 15:16.
270 Exodus 23:27–33.
271 Leviticus 18:24–25.
272 Deuteronomy 18:9–12.
273 Joshua 11:20.

Amalek

Amalek attacked the Children of Israel when they were on the way and exhausted. Amalek attacked because they were not God-fearing. That is why the Children of Israel must destroy Amalek from under the heavens.[274] God will erase its memory. There is a war of God against Amalek in every generation.[275] In the end, the nation of Amalek will be destroyed.[276]

Midian

God instructed the Children of Israel to vex the Midianites and to smite them, because it was they who had caused the Children of Israel to be enticed into the idolatry of Ba'al Peor.[277]

Ammon and Moab before the Entry into the Land

Neither an Ammonite nor a Moabite may enter into the community of God forever (i.e., he may not marry a woman of Israel), because they did not welcome the Children of Israel with bread and water when they left Egypt, and because they hired Balaam to curse the Children of Israel. One may never seek their welfare and their good.[278]

The Era of the Judges

When the Ark of God taken from the Children of Israel by the Philistines was set up in Ashdod, God brought upon them hemorrhoids.[279] When the Philistines moved the Ark to Gat, God brought upon them great confusion and smote the people of the city with hemorrhoids.[280] When the Ark was moved to Ekron, God's hand was against them and many died. Those who did not die were smitten with hemorrhoids.[281]

274 Deuteronomy 25:17–19.
275 Exodus 17:14, 16.
276 Numbers 24:20.
277 Ibid., 25:16–18.
278 Deuteronomy 23:4–7.
279 I Samuel 5:6.
280 Ibid., 5:9.
281 Ibid., 5:11–12.

The Era of the Kings

God delivered Ben Haddad, the king of Aram, and his army into the hands of King Ahab, because the people of Ben Haddad disdained the omnipotent power of God.[282]

Damascus will receive its punishment because its people killed the people of Gilead: God will send fire into the palaces of its leaders and will cut off its inhabitants. The rest will be exiled.[283]

The king of Assyria settled the cities from which the Children of Israel were exiled with new inhabitants from various places. However, they were not God-fearing, God, therefore, sent among them lions, which killed them.[284]

The nation of Assyria, which was God's rod of anger, thought and boasted that all its power and might were its own. God will therefore destroy it.[285]

God will punish Assyria because of its great conceit. He will deliver it into the hands of another nation, which will humiliate it.[286]

The city of Nineveh was full of falsehoods, murder, licentiousness, and witchcraft. God will therefore show the nations its shame and will make it despicable. The gates of the city will be open to its enemies. Its inhabitants will die by the sword and by fire, while some will flee in every direction and the rest will perish. All the nations will rejoice at its fall, because its wickedness harmed everyone.[287]

Babylon

God will bring Media to Babylon in order to destroy it as a punishment for its wickedness and conceit.[288] Babylon will no longer be the chief

---

282 I Kings 20:28–30.
283 Amos 1:3–5.
284 II Kings 17:24–25.
285 Isaiah 10:7–19.
286 Ezekiel 31:3–16.
287 Nahum 3:1–19.
288 Isaiah 13:1–22.

kingdom, because when God became angry at His nation and delivered it into the hands of Babylon, they did not take pity even on the old people. Even though Babylon had said: "I, and there is none but me," nothing will save it from the destruction which will befall it.[289]

The Kingdom of Babylon will fall and become desolate by nations which will come from the north, because it rejoiced at the spoils it took from Israel.[290]

The Kingdom of Babylon will fall and its land will be desolate, because it provoked God and boasted of its might. A nation from the north will conquer it, and its destruction will be like that of Sodom and Gomorrah. Refugees will flee from Babylon to the Land of Israel to tell of God's vengeance.[291]

God will take vengeance against Babylon because of its actions against Israel.[292] God will punish Babylon for all the evil it caused. Its land will be desolate and its inhabitants will die.[293]

Other Nations during the Era of the Kings

God would not forgive the sin of the people of Moab. They burned the bones of the king of Edom. God would send a fire to burn their palaces. Their inhabitants, judges and ministers would be killed.[294]

Moab would be punished for its conceit towards God and its derision of Israel. Its inhabitants would be exiled, some would be killed and its cities would be desolate. (In the End of Days, God will return the captivity of Moab.)[295]

289 Ibid., 47:5–15.
290 Jeremiah 50:1–3, 8–16.
291 Ibid., 50:21–46.
292 Ibid., 51:1–14.
293 Ibid., 51:20–64.
294 Amos 2:1–3.
295 Jeremiah 48:1–47.

God will punish Moab like Sodom, and Ammon like Gomorrah, because they cursed God's nation and attempted to extend their borders. The remnant of Judah will plunder them and inherit them.[296]

God will not forgive the sins of the Ammonites. They killed the pregnant women of Gilead in order to expand their border. God will send a fire to consume their palaces. The king and his ministers will be sent into exile.[297]

Ammon inherited the tribe of Gad and settled in its cities. God will therefore bring war upon the Ammonites, their land will be desolate, their king and ministers will be exiled, and Israel will return to its place. (Afterwards God will return the captivity of Ammon.)[298]

The Ammonites rejoiced at the defeat of Israel, and God will therefore deliver them into the hands of the people of the east, who will convert their land into a camel stable. God will make of them a mockery among the nations, and afterwards destroy them.[299] Ammon will no longer be remembered among the nations.[300]

The Edomites pursued their brothers (the Children of Israel) with the sword, did not show pity to them and retained their anger. God will therefore send forth fire to burn their palaces.[301]

Edom, because of its conceit and the fear which it engendered in other nations, will be punished as Sodom and Gomorrah, and its cities will be destroyed.[302] The Edomites, who hated the Children of Israel, used the sword against them, and wanted to inherit the Land of Israel, will be punished by God. Just as they rejoiced that the inheritance of Israel was laid waste, so will be their punishment. Their country will be destroyed and become desolate.[303]

---

296 Zephaniah 2:8–9.
297 Amos 1:13–14.
298 Jeremiah 49:1–6.
299 Ezekiel 25:1–7.
300 Ibid., 25:10.
301 Amos 1:11–12.
302 Jeremiah 49:7–22. See Metzudat David, Radak.
303 Ezekiel 35:1–15.

The people of Gaza will be punished because they handed over those who had been exiled to Edom. God will send fire into Gaza to burn down their palaces, and to cut off the inhabitants of the Philistine cities who will all perish.[304]

The Philistines were involved in revenge and destroyed others in enmity. God will therefore destroy them, and they will know that God did this to them.[305]

God will punish Tyre and Sidon, together with the Philistines, because they took the treasures of God to their palaces and sold the Children of Judah and Jerusalem to the Greeks in order to send them far away from their own country. God will therefore sell their sons and daughters to Judah, who will sell them to the Children of Sheba, whose land is far away.[306]

The Philistines will be seized with fear, their leaders will perish, and their conceit will be brought low, because of their evil ways, full of blood and abominations.[307]

The people of Tyre thought that they could be built up from the destruction of Jerusalem. Therefore, its might and beauty will be destroyed. Nebuchadnezzar will destroy the city, and it will become desolate.[308]

Sidon was like a painful and cancerous thorn to Israel. God will therefore execute judgment against it and send it pestilence and the sword. The people of Sidon will therefore acknowledge God.[309]

God will bring war upon the inhabitants of Egypt, who were a broken reed staff to Israel. Their inhabitants will be killed, the land will become desolate and those remaining will be scattered among the nations. When they return forty years later, they will be a weak kingdom which will be unable to rule over other nations. Therefore, they will not cause any evil to Israel. They will thus recognize God's ability.[310] Nebuchadnezzar, the king of Babylon,

304 Amos 1:6–8.
305 Ezekiel 25:15–17.
306 Joel 4:4–8.
307 Zechariah 9:5–7.
308 Ezekiel 26:1–21.
309 Ibid., 28:20–24.
310 Ibid., 29:1–16.

will rise up and will loot Egypt. He will destroy the country, the idol worship will cease, those of its inhabitants who are not killed will go into captivity, and its king will be brought low.[311] Egypt, which was as conceited as Assyria, will receive its punishment like Assyria, and its inhabitants will perish by the sword.[312]

Egypt and Edom will be desolate, because they shed innocent blood of the Children of Judah.[313]

The city of No-Amon in Egypt, located in a well-protected area, and which had powerful allies, went into exile, and many of its people were killed.[314]

If Egypt does not go up to Jerusalem to celebrate the Festival of Tabernacles, God will punish them with a plague like all the nations which do not go up.[315]

The violence which was done to Lebanon (the Land of Israel) will come upon those who did it.[316]

Because of the sins of the Desert of the Sea, which acted treacherously and looted, Elam and Media will rise up and conquer it.[317]

The evil of Nineveh came up before God. Therefore, He told Jonah to go there to call upon its people and to warn them that the city would be destroyed within forty days.[318] (When they repented from their evil ways, God did not bring upon the city and its inhabitants the punishment which He had planned.)

Gog and its Allied Nations

Gog, which will rise up, along with many allies, in the End of Days to conquer Israel, will have destruction brought upon it. It will be judged with

---

311 Ibid., 29:19–20; 30:1–26.
312 Ibid., 31:1–3, 17–18.
313 Joel 4:19.
314 Nahum 3:8–10.
315 Zechariah 14:18–19.
316 Habakkuk 2:17. See Radak, Metzudat David.
317 Isaiah 21:1–2.
318 Jonah 1:2; 3:4.

pestilence, blood, rain of rocks, fire and brimstone. Its fall will take place on the mountains of Israel. God will thereby be aggrandized and sanctified, and He will be known to many nations and to the Nation of Israel.[319]

• For Individuals

The Bible testifies that there is reward and punishment for individuals. But in a reality in which it seems that some of those who observe the commandments do not receive their reward, while others who do not observe the commandments, are not punished – this presents a problem. The problem appears even more severe to the generation which lived through the Holocaust in Europe and in subsequent generations. The Talmud already deals with the topic, in the words of Rabbi Jacob: "There is no commandment written in the Torah which lists the reward for observing it which does not depend on the revival of the dead." Rabbi Jacob saw a man whose father asked him to bring him chicks. The man climbed a tree, sent away the mother bird from the nest, and took the chicks. He then fell off the tree and died. If the reward of long life promised in the Torah for observing the commandment of honoring parents and for observing the commandment of sending forth the mother bird before taking the chicks were limited to our life in this world, this would seem to contradict the promises of the Torah. Only if we understand that the Torah's promises are realized within the framework of the revival of the dead, or, as the Talmud concludes: "'that it be good for you' – in the world which is entirely good; 'and that your days be prolonged' – in the world which is entirely long," can we understand the promise for reward.[320]

The concept of reward and punishment for the individual which is not limited to one's life in this world is the background for the descriptions of rewards and punishment in the different sources in the Bible.

This is true also for the sources describing righteous individuals saved from trouble. This should also be related to in the long-term, when the

---

319 Ezekiel 38:1 – 39:13.

320 *Chullin* 142a, *Kiddushin* 39b.

righteous individual will receive his full reward and his compensation at the time of the revival of the dead.

Revival of the Dead

At the End of Days, many of those who died will come alive – to eternal life. The sages and those who teach God's ways to many others will shine as the brightness of the heavens.[321]

Recompense for the Person's Deeds

God examines each person's heart and recompenses him for his ways and deeds.[322] God will subject to judgment all deeds of men, good and bad, even if they are not visible.[323]

Reward for Those who Observe God's Word

In General

God shows kindness even to the thousandth generation to those who love Him and observe His commandments.[324]

God will not abandon His faithful followers, and will guard them forever.[325]

All of God's ways are kindness and truth, for those who observe His covenant and His testimonies.[326] The goodness of God, which is kept for those who fear Him and trust in Him, is great.[327] God will not withhold good from those who walk with Him uprightly.[328]

Material Recompense

God will bless the home of the righteous.[329]

321 Daniel 12:2–3. See Metzudat David.
322 Jeremiah 17:10.
323 Ecclesiastes 12:14.
324 Exodus 20:6.
325 Psalms 37:28.
326 Ibid., 25:10.
327 Ibid., 31:20.
328 Ibid., 84:12.
329 Proverbs 3:33.

Those who fear God will not suffer want.[330] God will supply the needs of those who rely on Him.[331] He supplies the food of those who fear Him.[332]

If a person delights in being close to God, He will give him whatever his heart desires. If he relies on God, He will give him whatever he needs.[333] One who relies on God will be satisfied.[334] God will grant the desires of the righteous.[335]

If one fears God and turns away from evil, God will heal him.[336] The extreme heat of the Day of God (which will destroy the wicked) will appear to those who fear Him as a sun of righteousness and healing.[337]

The Torah and the commandments will add many years and peace to one who remembers them.[338] Fear of God will add to one's life span.[339] Peace will be the reward for those who love God's Torah.[340]

The righteous will inherit the land and will dwell in it eternally.[341] One who turns to God and behaves according to His ways will inherit the land.[342] The inheritance of the innocent will be an eternal one.[343]

One who fears God and goes in His ways will have many children.[344]

Emotional Condition

The good of God is the portion of the righteous, and is joy for those of an upright heart.[345] Joy is the portion of those who trust in God and those who love Him.[346]

---

330 Psalms 34:10.
331 Ibid., 55:23.
332 Ibid., 111:5.
333 Ibid., 37:4–5.
334 Proverbs 28:25.
335 Ibid., 10:24.
336 Ibid., 3:7–8.
337 Malachi 3:19–20.
338 Proverbs 3:1–2.
339 Ibid., 10:27.
340 Psalms 119:165.
341 Ibid., 37:29.
342 Ibid., 37:34.
343 Ibid., 37:18.
344 Ibid., 128:1–4.

Success

God will not allow a righteous person to falter.[347] There will be no obstacle in the path of those who love God's Torah.[348] The path of Israel is paved before them.[349]

The righteous are compared to a date tree (which produces a large number of dates) and a cedar tree (which is higher than the other trees) which are planted in God's house, and are all full of vigor even when they are old.[350]

God will strengthen the power and exalt the honor of the righteous.[351]

God honors those who honor Him.[352]

The righteous have an advantage over their fellow men.[353] The wicked will yield to the good.[354]

One who relies on God will go from strength to strength.[355]

The houses of the righteous will endure,[356] and the tents of the upright will stand strong.[357]

The assets of an upright person will not be lost.[358]

The blessing of the upright is of benefit to their city.[359]

Divine Providence and Security

God guards those who love Him.[360] He guards His faithful followers.[361]

---

345 Ibid., 97:11.
346 Ibid., 5:12.
347 Ibid., 37:30–31.
348 Ibid., 119:165.
349 Proverbs 15:19.
350 Psalms 92:13–15.
351 Ibid., 75:11.
352 I Samuel 2:30.
353 Proverbs 12:26.
354 Ibid., 14:19.
355 Psalms 84:6–8.
356 Proverbs 12:7.
357 Ibid., 14:11.
358 Ibid., 12:27. See Metzudat David.
359 Ibid., 11:11.
360 Psalms 145:20.

One who is careful about his path protects his soul.[362]

One who observes the commandments protects his soul.[363]

God aids and gives deliverance to the righteous at a time of distress.[364] He listens to the pleas of those who fear Him and He rescues them.[365] God rescues those of an upright heart.[366] One who walks sincerely in God's ways will be saved.[367]

God will speedily bring deliverance to those who fear Him.[368] One who brings a thanksgiving sacrifice and walks in an upright way will be saved by God.[369]

The righteous person is exposed to many dangers, but God will save him from them.[370]

God hides those who fear Him and protects them and those who trust in Him from those who wish to harm them.[371] He does not deliver the righteous into the hands of the wicked.[372] He saves his faithful followers from the hands of the wicked.[373]

God looks after those who fear Him and those who await His kindness. He rescues them from death and keeps them alive at a time of famine.[374] The death of His faithful followers is grievous in God's eyes.[375]

The fear of God is the source of life and prevents death.[376] Righteousness saves one from death.[377]

---

361 Ibid., 97:10.
362 Proverbs 16:17.
363 Ibid., 19:16.
364 Psalms 37:39–40.
365 Ibid., 145:19.
366 Ibid.,7:11.
367 Proverbs 28:18.
368 Psalms 85:10.
369 Ibid., 50:23.
370 Ibid.,34:20.
371 Ibid., 31:20–21.
372 Ibid., 37:33–34.
373 Ibid., 97:10.
374 Ibid., 33:18–19.
375 Ibid., 116:15.
376 Proverbs 14:27.

One who acts wisely will be saved from evil.[378] A righteous person will escape from troubles.[379] Wise people calm down anger and wrath.[380] When God finds a person and his deeds to be favorable, also his enemies will make peace with him.[381]

If one relies on God, He will protect him from sudden fears or from calamities which come upon the wicked.[382] The wicked will be ransom for the righteous.[383]

God will not allow the righteous to collapse.[384]

Many troubles will cause the righteous to fall, but each time God will save him and he will arise again.[385]

When God afflicts a person and teaches him His Torah, He protects him from future evil.[386]

If a person acts righteously and uprightly, detests great wealth, distances himself from bribery, from shedding blood and from evil, he will live in security and all his needs will be supplied to him.[387] Fear of God brings security.[388] God strengthens the righteous.[389]

One who obeys God's voice will live in security and tranquility.[390] One who acts blamelessly will live in security.[391]

A righteous person who relies on God is like a young lion who relies on his strength.[392]

---

377 Ibid., 10:2.
378 Ibid., 28:26.
379 Ibid., 12:13.
380 Ibid., 29:8.
381 Ibid., 16:7.
382 Ibid., 3:25–26.
383 Ibid., 21:18.
384 Psalms 55:23.
385 Proverbs 24:16.
386 Psalms 94:12–13.
387 Isaiah 33:15–16.
388 Proverbs 14:26.
389 Ibid., 18:10.
390 Ibid., 1:33.
391 Ibid., 10:9.
392 Ibid., 28:1.

God does not forsake those who seek Him.[393]

God listens to the prayers of the righteous.[394]

God will help and protect those who fear Him and rely on Him.[395] God's word protects those who trust in Him.[396]

No evil will befall a righteous person.[397]

God redeems the souls of His servants from evil, and those who trust in Him will not be blamed for anything.[398]

Those who await God will not become inferior.[399]

God wrote a memorial book for those who fear Him and who think of His name. On the Day of God, He will choose them and take pity only on them.[400] God takes pity on those who fear Him.[401]

Special Closeness

God's secret is for those who fear Him.[402]

God recompenses each person as that person is: if a person is a faithful follower, God treats him with kindness; if he is upright, with justice.[403]

If a person goes in the path of kindness and truth, he will find favor in God's eyes.[404] God will provide a good man with good will.[405] If a person goes in the ways of wisdom, God will be satisfied with him.[406]

God shows special favor to His faithful followers, and will listen when they call to Him.[407]

---

393 Psalms 9:11.
394 Proverbs 15:29.
395 Psalms 115:11.
396 Proverbs 30:5.
397 Ibid., 12:21.
398 Psalms 34:23.
399 Isaiah 49:23.
400 Malachi 3:16–17.
401 Psalms 103:13.
402 Ibid., 25:14.
403 Ibid., 18:26.
404 Proverbs 3:3–4.
405 Ibid., 12:2.
406 Ibid., 8:32–35.
407 Ibid., 4:4.

God is close to those who call to Him in truth.[408]
God looks after the righteous.[409]
God draws His faithful followers close to Him.[410]
God loves one who wishes to act with righteousness.[411]

The Future of the Family

Those who fear God will have descendants.[412] A man of peace will have descendants.[413]

A good man will be able to bequeath his inheritance to grandchildren.[414]

God will be merciful to the grandchildren of those who fear Him, who keep His covenant and His commandments.[415]

The descendants of the righteous will be spared from troubles.[416]

The descendants of a righteous person will not lack food.[417]

The descendants of a God-fearing person will inherit the land.[418]

The descendants of a God-fearing person who desires to perform His commandments will be the mighty ones in the land.[419]

General Reward for Specific Actions

One who guards his tongue from saying evil or deceptive words, who turns from evil and does good, who seeks and pursues peace, will merit to live and to see the good.[420] Life and death are in the power of the tongue, and one

408 Ibid., 145:18.
409 Ibid., 34:16.
410 Ibid., 50:5.
411 Proverbs 15:9.
412 Ibid., 23:17–18.
413 Psalms 37:37.
414 Proverbs 13:22.
415 Psalms 103:17–18.
416 Proverbs 11:21.
417 Psalms 37:25.
418 Ibid., 25:12–13.
419 Ibid., 112:1–2.
420 Ibid., 34:13–15.

who uses it properly will receive his reward.[421] Proper speech revives the one who says it.[422] Words of truth will always exist.[423]

A person with clean hands and a pure heart, who never swears in God's name in vain and never swears falsely – is fit to go up to the Mountain of God and to receive a blessing from Him.[424]

One who walks in the ways of the upright and acts with justice, speaks the truth to himself, does not spy after his fellow man, does not cause him any evil or humiliation, detests dishonorable people, honors those who fear God, keeps his promise even if he might be harmed by doing so, does not take interest and does not bribe anyone – will dwell in the tent of God and on His holy mountain.[425]

God encourages the humble.[426] He will cause their deeds to be regarded favorably by others.[427]

God will have mercy on one who admits his sins and does not repeat them.[428]

One who observes the Sabbath properly will rejoice in his closeness to God.[429]

Those who rebuke the wicked in the proper way will be blessed.[430]

God responds favorably to one who turns to Him and hopes for His aid.[431]

Happy is the man who has acquired wisdom. He will be granted a long life, wealth, and honor.[432]

The souls of diligent men will be satisfied with pleasure.[433]

---

421 Proverbs 18:21.
422 Ibid., 15:4.
423 Ibid., 12:19.
424 Psalms 24:3–6.
425 Ibid., 15:1–5.
426 Ibid., 147:6.
427 Proverbs 3:34.
428 Ibid., 28:13.
429 Isaiah 58:13–14.
430 Proverbs 24:25.
431 Lamentations 3:25.
432 Proverbs 3:13–16.

Specific Reward for Specific Actions

The king will be a friend of one who loves purity of heart and who speaks with graciousness.[434]

A soft voice annuls difficulties.[435] One who listens to words of reproof and who accepts them will be honored.[436] One who speaks uprightly will be beloved by people.[437]

One who helps the poor will be saved by God from evil. God will guard him and keep him alive, will not deliver him into the hands of his enemies, and when he becomes ill, he will be supported in his illness by God.[438] One who gives of his possessions to the poor will not know any want.[439] One who has mercy and helps the poor will receive the wealth of a person who acquired it through charging interest.[440]

A trustworthy agent will bring about healing.[441]

A ruler will be appeased by one who does not hurriedly become angry.[442]

A humble person will be honored.[443] The humble will inherit the earth, and will enjoy much peace.[444]

Those foreigners and eunuchs who observe the Sabbath and keep God's covenant will earn a good name. For those foreigners who love and serve God and keep the Sabbath, God will bring them to His holy mountain, will make them happy and will accept their sacrifices willingly.[445]

---

433 Ibid., 13:4.
434 Ibid., 22:11.
435 Ibid., 25:15.
436 Ibid., 13:18.
437 Ibid., 16:13.
438 Psalms 41:2–4.
439 Proverbs 28:27.
440 Ibid., 28:8.
441 Ibid., 13:17.
442 Ibid., 25:15.
443 Ibid., 29:23.
444 Psalms 37:11.
445 Isaiah 56:4–7.

If a person disciplines his son, he can rest assured (about his son's conduct). The son will bring joy to his father.[446]

Plans will be realized on the basis of much counsel.[447] A discerning son prepares himself for days of austerity.[448]

The reward of the wise is their wealth.[449]

A king will be amenable to a wise servant.[450]

A wise man has power, because one is able to achieve victory in battle by stratagems and sound advice.[451]

Firm structures are built as a result of wisdom, understanding and knowledge. [452]

A foolish man will be the servant of a man with a wise heart.[453] A wise servant will rule a son who diverges from the path and will divide up the family property together with the brothers.[454]

The speech of the wise is healing.[455] A person with good understanding will find favor among people.[456]

One who works his land will always be satisfied.[457] A diligent man will become wealthy.[458]

A man who works swiftly in his work will stand before kings.[459] The diligent man will rule.[460]

---

446 Proverbs 29:17.
447 Ibid., 15:22.
448 Ibid., 10:5.
449 Ibid., 14:24.
450 Ibid., 14:35.
451 Ibid., 24:5–6.
452 Ibid., 24:3–4.
453 Ibid., 11:29.
454 Ibid., 17:2.
455 Ibid., 12:18.
456 Ibid., 13:15.
457 Ibid., 28:19.
458 Ibid., 10:4.
459 Ibid., 22:29.
460 Ibid., 12:24.

Reward Specified for the Observance of a Commandment

If a person is careful not to consume blood, God will be kind to him and his children.[461]

If a person takes care to observe the commandment of the tithe so that the Levite, the stranger, the orphan and the widow eat and are satisfied, God will bless all the work of his hands.[462]

One who willingly gives a loan to a poor person even though the Year of Remission of loans is approaching will be blessed by God in all the work of his hands.[463]

One who does not take interest from another (whether in money, food, or anything else which can be lent), will be blessed by God in all the work of his hands.[464]

If a person harvests his field and forgets a number of sheaves of wheat and does not go back to retrieve them but leaves them for the stranger, orphan, and widow, he will be blessed by God in all the work of his hands.[465]

If a person lends money to a poor person and receives in return a security which the poor person needs, he must return it to the poor person before sunset. This is considered to be a righteous deed on his part.[466]

If one honors his father and mother, God will extend his days on the earth which God gave him.[467]

People are commanded to pursue justice so that they will live and inherit the earth.[468] If a merchant is scrupulous about measures and weights, God will extend his days on the earth which God gave him.[469]

If a person sees a nest in which there is a bird which is covering its chicks with its wings, or is incubating its eggs, he is forbidden to take the mother

---

461 Deuteronomy 12:25.
462 Ibid., 14:28–29.
463 Ibid., 15:7–10.
464 Ibid., 23:20–21.
465 Ibid., 24:19.
466 Ibid., 24:12–13.
467 Exodus 20:12.
468 Deuteronomy 16:20.
469 Ibid., 25:13–15.

along with the chicks or eggs. He must first chase away the mother bird and then he may take the chicks or the eggs. For acting that way, God will be good to him and he will have a long life.[470]

If a person keeps the laws of *orlah* regarding the fruit of a tree (where he does not eat of the fruit of the tree for the first three years), and treats the fruit of the fourth year as holy to God, He will increase the yield of his field.[471]

Proper Behavior whose Reward is Additional Proper Behavior

If a person always thinks of God, He will help him to walk in the proper path.[472]

The righteousness which a person does – leads him on the upright and good path.[473]

The Torah and its commandments, the wisdom and understanding in it, will prevent one who goes in their path from being seduced by a woman who is not his wife.[474]

One who befriends the wise will also become wise.[475]

One who listens to words of rebuke will find his place among the sages, and he will also acquire the hearts of his friends.[476]

Wisdom is the reward of the modest.[477]

A righteous man speaks words of wisdom.[478] One who turns his deeds to God – his thoughts, too, will endure.[479]

One who seeks wisdom and understanding must understand fear of God and the knowledge of God. Then he will understand justice, proper judgment, and the upright path, and will act according to them.[480]

---

470 Ibid., 22:6–7.
471 Leviticus 19:23–25.
472 Proverbs 3:6.
473 Ibid., 11:5.
474 Ibid., 7:1–5.
475 Ibid., 13:20.
476 Ibid., 15:31–32.
477 Ibid., 11:2.
478 Ibid., 10:31.
479 Ibid., 16:3.

Reward for Women

A wise woman knows how to build her home.[481]

A God-fearing woman will gain praise. The fruit of her effort will remain in her hands, and because of her deeds, she will be praised by all.[482]

Reward for Kings

If the king writes for himself a Torah scroll which accompanies him throughout his reign, and thus learns how to fear God and to observe all the words of the Torah – not to lord it over his brothers and not to diverge from the commandments, either to the left or to the right – God will extend the days of his reign and that of his children among Israel.[483]

If a king does justice, his reign will endure.[484]

Acts of kindness and truth will protect a king.[485]

If a king judges the poor truthfully, his monarchy will endure forever.[486]

Reward throughout History

Noah

God saved Noah and his family from the Flood, because He considered him a righteous person in his generation.[487]

The Era of the Forefathers

An angel of God told Hagar that she had to submit to Sarah, but that a great nation would emerge from Ishmael.[488]

Had there been a sufficient number of righteous people in Sodom and Gomorrah, God would not have destroyed them.[489]

---

480 Ibid., 2:1–9.
481 Ibid., 14:1.
482 Ibid., 31:30–31.
483 Deuteronomy 17:18–20.
484 Proverbs 16:12.
485 Ibid., 20:28.
486 Ibid., 29:14.
487 Genesis 6:13 – 7:1.
488 Ibid., 16:7–11.
489 Ibid., 18:26–32.

God told Abram that if he would obey the command to go to the land which God would show him, He would bless him and he would be a great nation, and other nations would be blessed through him.[490] When Abram came to the Land of Canaan, God repeated that the land would belong to his descendants.[491] They would be as numerous as the sand on the earth.[492] God again promised Abram that He would protect him and that he would receive a great reward. A son would be born to him who would inherit him, and his descendants would be too numerous to count, as the stars in the heaven.[493] Abram would not suffer slavery.[494] God would bless Sarah with a son, and her descendants would be kings of nations.[495] His son Ishmael, too, would be a great nation.[496]

Abraham would become a great and mighty nation, and all the nations of the earth would be blessed through him. God knew that he would command his sons and household to observe the way of God in righteousness and justice, and God therefore informed Abraham what He planned about the destruction of Sodom and Gomorrah.[497]

God remembered Abraham and saved Lot from the destruction of the cities of the plain.[498]

After Avimelech returned Abraham's wife, Sarah, to him, Abraham prayed to God, and He healed Avimelech's wife and her female servants. They were again able to give birth.[499]

Abraham passed the test of the binding of Isaac. Therefore, God blessed him that He would multiply his descendants, they would vanquish their enemies, and all the nations of the world would be blessed through them.[500]

---

490 Ibid., 12:1–3.
491 Ibid., 12:7.
492 Ibid., 13:16.
493 Ibid., 15:1–5.
494 Ibid., 15:15.
495 Ibid., 17:16.
496 Ibid., 17:20.
497 Ibid., 18:17–19.
498 Ibid., 19:29.
499 Ibid., 20:14, 17–18.
500 Ibid., 22:11–12, 15–18.

Isaac received Abraham's blessings, because Abraham had listened to the voice of God and had observed His charge, His commandments, His statutes, and His teachings.[501]

When Jacob traveled to Beth El to erect an altar to God, by God's command, He caused the people in the surrounding cities to fear so that they would not pursue him.[502] When Jacob returned to Beth El, God changed his name to Israel and blessed him that he would have many descendants, and that kings would issue from him. God repeated the promise of giving him the land which had been promised to Abraham and Isaac.[503]

God said that He would bring the Children of Israel to inherit the Land of Israel, in order to keep what He had promised to their forefathers.[504]

In Egypt

God was good to the Hebrew midwives because they feared God and did not kill the infant boys as ordered to by Pharaoh, and made houses for them.[505]

In the Desert

God told Moses that he had found favor in His eyes, and therefore God would be with the nation. Moses and the nation would be dealt with more favorably than the other nations on the face of the earth.[506]

Moses was considered to be God's servant (because of his qualities and deeds).[507]

Caleb, who obeyed the word of God, would come to the Land of Israel, and his children would inherit it.[508]

---

501 Ibid., 26:2–5.
502 Ibid., 35:1, 5.
503 Ibid., 35:9–12.
504 Deuteronomy 9:4–5.
505 Exodus 1:15–21.
506 Ibid., 33:15–17.
507 Joshua 1:1–2.
508 Numbers 14:24.

Phineas, the son of Elazar the Priest, was zealous for God and killed the Israelite man who had sinned and the Midianite woman, thus removing God's anger from the nation. God therefore made a covenant of peace with him – a covenant of eternal priesthood.[509]

After the Entry into the Land of Israel

God told Joshua that if he would fortify himself and would observe the commandments of the Torah as Moses had commanded, he would be successful in all his ventures and would not fear anyone. God would be with him wherever he would go.[510]

Joshua was called a servant of God (because of his qualities and deeds).[511]

God told Eli the Priest that a Priest loyal to God would build the House which would endure for generations. The Priest would always stand before the king. The remnants of the house of Eli would come to bow down before him and to request of him the rights of the priesthood.[512]

In the Era of the Kings

God rescued David from his enemies who were mightier than he, because David observed His laws and statutes.[513] David turned to God, and therefore God saved him from everything that concerned him and made him fearful.[514]

God strengthened David, taught him how to do battle and shielded him until he destroyed his enemies (because he kept the paths of God).[515] God enabled David to take vengeance against his enemies and even saved him from an evil man.[516]

---

509 Ibid., 25:10–13.
510 Joshua 1:6–9.
511 Ibid., 24:29.
512 I Samuel 2:35–36.
513 Psalms 18:18–24.
514 Ibid., 34:5.
515 Ibid., 18:33–40.
516 Ibid., 18:48–49.

God will fulfill the desires of a king who relies on Him, will bless him, and grant him long life, honor, and closeness to Him. A king who relies on God will vanquish all his enemies.[517]

God supported David because he was upright with God and always put Him in front of him.[518]

God promised David that the monarchy would not depart from the son of David, even if he would sin, because of the merit of his forefathers.[519]

Due to the merit of David, who observed the commandments of God and His statutes, and for the sake of Jerusalem, God would not take the monarchy away from Solomon during his life. He would also leave the tribe of Judah with his heir.[520] David kept the commandments of God and His statutes.[521]

The merit of one's forefather is greater, the closer one is to the generation of the forefather. The merit of David kept the monarchy intact during the days of Solomon, whereas in the days of Solomon's son, the merit of David, along with the merit of Jerusalem, kept only one tribe.

God will punish David's descendants, but not forever.[522]

God will not cause prolonged suffering to the descendants of David forever, because of the possibility that they might repent. The house of David has a special status, because David was the first king to go according to God's word as king.

Aviam, David's great-grandson, ruled in Jerusalem because of the merit of David, who had done what was upright in God's eyes, except in the matter of Uriah the Hittite.[523] In the era of Jehoram, God did not destroy the Kingdom of Judah because of David.[524]

---

517 Ibid., 21:2–9.
518 Ibid., 41:13.
519 II Samuel 7:14–16.
520 I Kings 11:11–13.
521 Ibid., 11:34.
522 Ibid., 11:39.
523 Ibid., 15:4–5.
524 II Kings 8:19.

The prophet Ahiah the Shilonite told Jeroboam in the name of God that if he would obey everything which God would command and observe His commandments, the Kingdom of Israel would endure.[525]

He prophesied that because of a single good deed that Aviah the son of Jeroboam had performed, all of Israel would mourn him and would bury him. (All the others of the house of Jeroboam would not be buried after their deaths.)[526]

When Shafan the scribe read before King Josiah from the Torah scroll which had been found in the Temple, the king was alarmed, tore his clothes, cried, and asked to seek God, so as to remove God's anger from him and from the nation. Hulda the prophetess told the king's messengers in the name of God that Josiah, who had submitted to God, would not see the destruction of his kingdom but would die before that.[527]

The sons of Jonadav ben Rechav obeyed their father's wishes: they did not drink wine and did not build houses (unlike the people of Judah, who did not obey God's word), and God therefore would leave them alive (whereas evil would befall the people of Judah).[528]

Jeremiah told King Zedekiah in the name of God that if he would go out to the ministers of Babylon, he and his family would live, and the city would not be burned down.[529]

Jeremiah said in the name of God to Eved-Melech, the Cushite (who had saved his life when the king's ministers had thrown him into a pit to die there), that on the day that the city was destroyed he would be saved because he had relied on God.[530]

God told the man dressed in linen, with the quill of a scribe in his hand, to place a mark on the foreheads of those people who sighed about the abominations of the city, so as to save them from being killed.[531, 532]

---

525 I Kings 11:38.
526 Ibid., 14:13.
527 II Kings 22:18–20.
528 Jeremiah 35:12–19.
529 Jeremiah 38:17.
530 Ibid., 39:15–18.
531 Ezekiel 9:1–6.

Righteous men such as Noah, Daniel, and Job would save themselves because of their righteousness (but would not be able to save others).[533]

After the Return to the Land of Israel

An angel of God told Joshua the High Priest that if he would follow in the ways of God and would keep His charge, he would be responsible for the House of God, and God would allow him to live with the angels.[534]

The Priests of the sons of Zadok who kept the charge of the Temple when the Children of Israel sinned – only they will come to the Temple to offer sacrifices and to arrange the showbread.[535]

Punishments for Those Who Do Not Obey God's Word

In General

Just as God rewards those individuals who deserve it, so He punishes individuals for their sins.

God does not totally erase sins.[536]

God punishes the wicked man and the sinner.[537] God punishes those with excessive pride.[538] God will not vindicate a wicked person.[539]

A wicked person will stumble as a result of his evil deeds.[540]

One who is present when an evil deed takes place and does not warn against it will be punished.[541]

---

532 In Ezekiel 21:6–9, God told Ezekiel that He would also destroy the righteous in Jerusalem. These are not the righteous who sighed about the abominations mentioned here.

533 Ezekiel 14:12–20.

534 Zechariah 3:6–7.

535 Ezekiel 44:15–16.

536 Exodus 34:7. See Rashi.

537 Proverbs 11:31.

538 Psalms 31:24.

539 Exodus 23:7.

540 Proverbs 24:16.

541 Ibid., 22:3.

God will cause the evil deeds of the wicked to happen to them.[542] Those who do not choose God's wisdom and do not fear Him will bear the consequences of their path.[543]

One who does not observe the words of the Torah will be cursed.[544] One who worships the gods of the other nations and thinks that nothing bad will happen to him by doing so, will find that all the curses written in the Rebuke in the Book of Deuteronomy will come upon him.[545]

Cursed is the one who relies on a flesh-and-blood person and not on God.[546] God's curse will be on the house of the wicked.[547]

God brings every person to judgment for every action which he took, even if it was hidden, whether good or bad.[548] God will judge every person according to his deeds.[549]

One who does not listen to the word of God as stated by a prophet will be punished by God.[550]

God brings each person to judgment for having followed his desires in his youth.[551]

Punishments and suffering will come upon those who relate to God lightly.[552]

God afflicts a person with rebukes for his sins.[553]

If a person wants to do evil, it will befall him.[554] Evil will pursue the sinners.[555]

---

542 Psalms 94:23.
543 Proverbs 1:29–31.
544 Deuteronomy 27:26.
545 Ibid., 29:17–19.
546 Jeremiah 17:5.
547 Proverbs 3:33.
548 Ecclesiastes 12:14.
549 Ezekiel 33:20.
550 Deuteronomy 18:19.
551 Ecclesiastes 11:9.
552 Proverbs 19:29.
553 Psalms 39:12.
554 Proverbs 11:27.
555 Ibid., 13:21.

If a person repays good with evil, he will find that trouble will never cease from his home.[556]

One who hardens his heart in order to do evil will find that that evil will cause him to fall.[557]

One who is unjust will receive his punishment commensurately.[558] One who rebels against God's word is like one who wishes to have evil happen to him.[559]

The evil from which a righteous man escapes will strike a wicked man.[560]

One who brings want and troubles to his home will inherit troubles.[561]

God punishes the wicked by severe disasters.[562] The foolish will be punished for their sins.[563] Wickedness causes harm to the sinner.[564]

One who scorns the commandments will be harmed (physically).[565]

The path of God, which the sinner does not follow, will be an obstacle for him.[566]

A man who has no restraint on his temperament is like an open city without walls.[567]

The lives of traitors are difficult.[568]

God visits the sins of fathers on their sons, up to the third and fourth generation, when they, too, stray from the path.[569] God visits the sins of the fathers on the grandchildren as well.[570]

---

556 Ibid., 17:13.
557 Ibid., 28:14.
558 Ibid., 22:8.
559 Ibid., 17:11. See Ibn Ezra, Metzudat David.
560 Ibid., 11:8.
561 Ibid., 11:29.
562 Psalms 11:6.
563 Ibid., 107:17.
564 Proverbs 13:6.
565 Ibid., 13:13.
566 Ibid., 10:29.
567 Ibid., 25:28.
568 Ibid., 13:15. See Rashi.
569 Exodus 20:5.
570 Ibid., 34:7.

Destruction

The lives of the wicked are short.[571] Those who do evil will be destroyed permanently.[572]

God will not delay in destroying His enemies.[573]

He will locate all His enemies, and in His anger He will destroy them.[574]

Those who distance themselves from God and those who separate themselves from Him will be lost.[575] God will destroy those who forget Him, who are not prepared to accept and understand His rebuke.[576]

One who despises God's ways will die.[577]

If a wicked person does not repent from his wicked ways, he will die with his sins.[578] If a righteous person regrets his righteousness and performs evil deeds like a wicked person, his righteousness will not help him and he will die.[579]

The wicked (cursed by God) will be cut off from the earth.[580]

People of blood and deceit will not live half their days.[581]

Haughtiness will bring about destruction.[582]

The wicked behavior of the foolish and their complacency will bring about their death.[583] One who sins against wisdom and hates it is like one who steals his soul and loves death.[584] One who ignores rebuke is as one who despises his soul.[585]

---

571 Proverbs 10:27.
572 Psalms 92:8.
573 Deuteronomy 7:10.
574 Psalms 21:9–10.
575 Ibid., 73:27.
576 Ibid., 50:21–22.
577 Proverbs 19:16.
578 Ezekiel 3:18.
579 Ibid., 18:24.
580 Psalms 37:22.
581 Ibid., 55:24.
582 Proverbs 18:12.
583 Ibid., 1:32.
584 Ibid., 8:36.
585 Ibid., 15:32.

The Revival of the Dead for the Purpose of Punishment

At the time of the revival of the dead, there will be those who are revived to shame and everlasting contempt.[586]

Lack of Success

One who scorns God's ways will bear the results of his actions.[587]

God will foil the plots of the wicked.[588]

The unjust deeds of a wicked man will be turned against him, and he will lose all his strength.[589]

One who is stubborn-hearted will not succeed in his way.[590]

God will distort the advice of the faithless.[591]

A deceitful man will not accomplish anything.[592]

The hopes of the wicked will not be realized.[593] There is no future for those who are involved in evil.[594]

There is no source of existence for those who stray.[595]

A wicked person will always feel that he is lacking something.[596] A deceitful person will starve for bread.[597]

The perversity of the treacherous will steal their possessions from them.[598]

The money of the sinner is saved for the righteous.[599] Wealth which is acquired by robbery and violence will not remain.[600] One who does not heed words of admonition will become poor.[601]

---

586 Daniel 12:2.
587 Proverbs 9:12.
588 Ibid., 10:3.
589 Ibid., 22:8.
590 Ibid., 17:20.
591 Ibid., 22:12.
592 Ibid., 12:27.
593 Ibid., 10:28.
594 Ibid., 24:20.
595 Psalms 68:7.
596 Proverbs 13:25.
597 Ibid., 19:15.
598 Ibid., 11:3.

A robber destroys his home.[602]
The wickedness of a woman will destroy her home.[603]

Physical Suffering

God will destroy the body of a person who has sins.[604]
The wicked have many pains.[605]

Insecurity

The fear which a wicked person imposes on others will come upon him.[606]

A wicked person flees even where there is no one pursuing him.[607]

There will be no peace for the wicked.[608]

Obstacles

A stubborn person will find obstacles like thorns and traps in his path.[609] In the sins of a wicked person lies a snare.[610] A person who is in fear (because he does not rely on God) will find his fear to be a snare.[611]

Those who rebelled against God and disparaged His advice failed.[612]

The wicked do not know in what they will fail.[613]

Haughtiness and a haughty spirit point to a failure in the near future.[614]

---

599 Ibid., 13:22.
600 Ibid., 13:11. See Metzudat David.
601 Ibid., 13:18.
602 Ibid., 15:27.
603 Ibid., 14:1.
604 Psalms 39:12.
605 Ibid., 32:10.
606 Proverbs 10:24.
607 Ibid., 28:1.
608 Isaiah 57:21.
609 Proverbs 22:5.
610 Ibid., 29:6.
611 Proverbs 29:25.
612 Psalms 107:11–12.
613 Proverbs 4:19.
614 Ibid., 16:18.

Falling

The wicked will fall, and will not be able to recover.[615] The wicked person will fall in his wickedness.[616] One who walks in crooked paths will fall in one of them.[617]

An emissary to do evil will fall by that evil.[618] One who leads upright people to go on an evil path will fall by that same evil.[619]

One who relies (only) on his wealth will fall.[620]

One who says one thing and plots to do something different instead will fall by his evil.[621]

The soul of the wicked, which is compared to a candle, will be extinguished.[622]

If a person plots evil and foments quarrels, he will be struck suddenly by a calamity and will not be able to recover.[623] If a guilty person was warned and did not heed the warning, he will fall and will not be able to recover.[624]

The arms of the wicked will be broken.[625] God will enervate totally the power of the wicked.[626]

A depressed spirit will remove the life force of a person.[627]

Diminished Honor

Those who scorn God will be scorned.[628]

---

615 Psalms 36:13.
616 Proverbs 11:5.
617 Ibid., 28:18.
618 Ibid., 13:17.
619 Ibid., 28:10.
620 Ibid., 11:28.
621 Ibid., 17:20.
622 Ibid., 13:9.
623 Ibid., 6:12–15.
624 Ibid., 29:1.
625 Psalms 37:17.
626 Ibid., 75:11.
627 Proverbs 17:22.
628 I Samuel 2:30.

A person who hates another but conceals his hatred will find his evil deeds become known in public.[629]

God brings eternal shame on His enemies.[630]

A Negative Attitude by People and Actions against Oneself

People hate a scheming person.[631]

By removing a scorner (of God's word), one removes quarrels and strife.[632]

A person who always wishes to satisfy his lusts stirs up quarrels.[633] A quarrelsome and complaining person stirs up quarrels.[634] An angry person stirs up quarrels.[635] Hatred causes quarrels.[636] A fickle person stirs up quarrels.[637]

A king becomes angry at a person who performs shameful deeds.[638]

A cruel messenger will be sent against a rebellious person.[639]

A wicked person falls into the trap which he set for the other.[640] One who befriends a person who is habitually angry will cause himself to fail.[641]

The wicked will be the atonement of the righteous.[642]

A person who cheats others will be enslaved by others.[643]

The wicked have no chance of deliverance.[644]

---

629 Proverbs 26:24–26.
630 Psalms 78:65–66.
631 Proverbs 14:17.
632 Ibid., 22:10.
633 Ibid., 28:25.
634 Ibid., 26:20–21.
635 Ibid., 29:22.
636 Ibid., 10:12.
637 Ibid., 16:28.
638 Ibid., 14:35.
639 Ibid., 17:11.
640 Psalms 9:17.
641 Proverbs 22:24–25.
642 Ibid., 21:18.
643 Ibid., 12:24.
644 Psalms 119:155.

Oblivion

The way of the wicked will perish.[645]

The wicked will not continue to live in the land.[646] The memory of the wicked will disappear like something which rots away.[647] God will destroy the memory of those who do evil.[648]

All those who do evil deeds will perish.[649]

When a wicked person dies, his children have nothing upon which to rely.[650]

God will also destroy the descendants of His enemies.[651] The descendants of the wicked will be cut off[652] (when they continue in their wicked ways. See p. 294).

The home of the wicked will be destroyed.[653] God will uproot the house of the proud.[654]

Distance from God

God is distant from wicked people.[655] God is angry (at wicked people) each day.[656]

God hates the wicked and those who love violence.[657] He hates all those who do evil.[658]

---

645 Ibid., 1:6.
646 Proverbs 10:30.
647 Ibid., 10:7.
648 Psalms 34:17.
649 Ibid., 92:10.
650 Proverbs 11:7.
651 Psalms 21:9, 11.
652 Psalms 37:28.
653 Proverbs 14:11.
654 Ibid., 15:25.
655 Ibid., 15:29.
656 Psalms 7:12.
657 Ibid., 11:5.
658 Ibid., 5:6.

God detests the ways of the wicked.[659] God detests men of blood and deceit.[660] God detests one who justifies the wicked and one who condemns a righteous person.[661] God hates one who is proud.[662]

God rebukes the wicked.[663] God is angry at the wicked who turned away from His commandments.[664]

God does not listen to the prayer of a person whose heart is full of wickedness and deceit.[665]

On the Day of Judgment, God will not exonerate the wicked.[666]

Negative Influence on the Environment

A city is liable to be destroyed because of the wicked people in it.[667] People who make light (of God's words) are liable to burn down a city.[668]

A foolish son is a source of anger to his father and bitterness to his mother.[669]

A person who flatters the other will destroy him.[670]

One who is slack in his work resembles one who destroys it.[671]

A lazy person causes damage to those who sent him.[672]

Ways of Wickedness Punished by Further Ways of Wickedness

One who becomes angry easily will do foolish things.[673] The gullible will inherit folly.[674]

---

659 Proverbs 15:9.
660 Psalms 5:7.
661 Proverbs 17:15.
662 Ibid., 16:5.
663 Psalms 50:16, 21.
664 Ibid., 119:21.
665 Ibid., 66:18–19.
666 Ibid., 1:5.
667 Proverbs 11:11.
668 Ibid., 29:8.
669 Ibid., 17:25.
670 Ibid., 11:9.
671 Ibid., 18:9.
672 Ibid., 10:26.
673 Ibid., 14:17.

God will make the way of the wicked (even more) crooked.[675] One who plots evil against the other will go astray.[676]

Actions and Attributes which Cause Negative Phenomena

Laziness brings about sleep.[677]

If one does something to excess, he will lose it (as one who eats much honey and regurgitates it).[678] One who benefits from the gift of an ill-willed person will lose whatever he received (like one who eats of the bread of an ill-willed person and regurgitates what he ate).[679] An act of robbery will be an obstacle to the robber (like bread which becomes like gravel in his mouth).[680]

The soul of a lazy person always lusts, but he will never accomplish anything (due to his laziness).[681] If a person hurries to give an answer, a fool is better than he.[682] A vain curse will not be fulfilled.[683]

A lazy person who does not plow in the winter will not have anything to harvest.[684] One who likes to sleep will become poor.[685]

If one steals from a poor person in order to increase his wealth and gives it to a rich person, his wealth will decrease.[686]

One who cheats will become poor.[687]

A poor person who oppresses the destitute is like a sweeping rain which does not cause food to grow.[688]

---

674 Ibid., 14:18.
675 Psalms 146:9.
676 Proverbs 14:22.
677 Ibid., 19:15.
678 Ibid., 25:16.
679 Ibid., 23:6–8.
680 Ibid., 20:17.
681 Ibid., 13:4.
682 Ibid., 29:20.
683 Ibid., 26:2.
684 Ibid., 20:4.
685 Ibid., 20:13.
686 Ibid., 22:16.
687 Ibid., 10:4.
688 Ibid., 28:3.

One who hastens to become rich is an envious individual. He does not know that want will come upon him.[689] One who is hasty in his actions will lose.[690] One who works hard to become wealthy will find that his money will vanish speedily.[691]

Words without deeds bring about want.[692]

A man who chases after vanities will only attain poverty.[693]

One who spends all his days (in eating and drinking) will always be lacking something.[694] One who eats and drinks to excess, and spends his time sleeping excessively will be poverty-stricken.[695]

One who cavorts with prostitutes will lose his money.[696]

It is not worthwhile for a person to be a guarantor, because if he cannot pay, he will lose his property.[697]

If a person avoids helping his fellow man in his distress, troubles will befall him and his power to be saved will be limited.[698]

One who drinks wine to excess will suffer many problems – arguments, complaints, injuries without cause, and reddening of the eyes. He will harm others and will be confused and lose his balance.[699]

One who covets his fellow man's wife will be wounded and dishonored, and his shame will not be wiped away.[700]

A wise man who goes to court against a fool will find no satisfaction.[701]

The tongues of the wicked will cause them to fail.[702] One who (knowingly) acts foolishly will stumble in his speaking.[703]

---

689 Ibid., 28:22.
690 Ibid., 21:5.
691 Ibid., 23:4–5.
692 Ibid., 14:23.
693 Ibid., 28:19.
694 Ibid., 21:17.
695 Ibid., 23:20–21.
696 Ibid., 29:3.
697 Ibid., 22:26–27.
698 Ibid., 24:10.
699 Ibid., 23:29–35.
700 Ibid., 6:24–33.
701 Ibid., 29:9.

The words of a fool are a snare to his soul.[704]

If one causes the other to stumble, digs a pit or places a rock in his path, he himself will be injured by that obstacle.[705]

A person who sheds blood will flee for his life, and will not obtain assistance from anyone.[706]

If one curses his father and mother, his soul will be extinguished as a candle which burns out in the dark.[707]

One who takes more than he is entitled to destroys the earth.[708]

If a person cheats the other and says that it was just a game, it is as if he shoots deadly arrows.[709]

If one gives false testimony against the other, it is as if he kills him with an arrow or sword.[710]

One who tells of a bad thing that his fellow man did causes separation.[711]

If someone sends something by a fool, he will have to send other messengers. He will also have to contend with the anger of the person to whom he sent it.[712]

It is harder to appease a person who was wronged than to conquer a strong city.[713]

A person is forbidden to gloat at the downfall of his enemy. It is evil in God's eyes and He will turn His anger upon the one who gloated.[714]

A lie cannot endure.[715]

---

702 Psalms 64:3, 9.
703 Proverbs 10:8.
704 Ibid., 18:7.
705 Ibid., 26:27.
706 Ibid., 28:17.
707 Ibid., 20:20.
708 Ibid., 29:4. See Ibn Ezra.
709 Ibid., 26:18–19.
710 Ibid., 25:18.
711 Ibid., 17:9.
712 Ibid., 26:6.
713 Ibid., 18:19.
714 Ibid., 24:17–18.

A person should not visit his friend's home too frequently, lest his friend despise seeing him and hate him.[716]

Punishments for Specific Sins

God will not hold blameless one who takes His name in vain.[717] He who gives false testimony or spreads lies will not escape punishment.[718]

If a man sleeps with his sister or aunt, both will bear the consequences of their sin.[719] An adulterous woman will bear her sin.[720]

One who eats what was left of a sacrifice on the third day will bear his sin.[721] One who eats of a sacrifice which was planned to be eaten on the third day will bear his sin.[722] One who eats of the meat of a permitted bird which was not slaughtered ritually or which, after it was slaughtered ritually was found to have a defect which made it forbidden, and did not immerse his clothes or himself, and remained ritually unclean will bear his sin (when he carries out actions which a ritually unclean person is forbidden to do).[723]

A Priest who does not observe the laws of ritual cleanliness and ritual uncleanliness when he performs service in the Temple will bear his sin.[724]

If a person refrains from lending money to his poor brother when the Year of Remission approaches, it is considered a sin.[725] An employer must give his poor employee his wage on its day, because the poor man needs it desperately. If he does not do so, it is considered a sin by him.[726]

If a woman takes a vow and her husband does not say anything about it, she must keep her vow. If the husband annulled her vow but not on the day

---

715 Ibid., 12:19.
716 Ibid., 25:17.
717 Exodus 20:7. See Nachmanides.
718 Proverbs 19:5.
719 Leviticus 20:19–20.
720 Numbers 5:29–31.
721 Leviticus 19:5–8.
722 Ibid., 7:18.
723 Ibid., 17:15–16.
724 Ibid., 22:9.
725 Deuteronomy 15:9.
726 Ibid., 24:14–15.

that he heard about it, and the woman did not keep her vow based on the fact that her husband annulled it, he will bear his sin of the non-fulfillment of the vow.[727]

One must rebuke his fellow man if he is sinning, but one must not do so in such a way as to sin himself by rebuking the other person in an offensive manner, such as in public.[728]

Those who hate a righteous person will be made liable in judgment.[729]

If a person bears tales about a servant to his master, the servant can curse him and the talebearing will be considered a sin.[730]

One who rejoices at the other's distress will be punished.[731] A short-tempered person will be punished.[732]

One who rushes to accumulate wealth will not be exempt from punishment.[733]

A false witness will not be exempt from punishment.[734]

If a person is derelict in saving people who are being taken to their deaths, God will know this. The person will receive the punishment he deserves.[735]

If a husband suspects that his wife was unfaithful, he brings her to the Priest, who has her drink the bitter water of the curse. If she was indeed unfaithful, the water will harm her and all will see it. She will be a curse among her nation.[736]

One who makes an idol or a mask and hides them will be cursed.[737]

One who curses his parents will be cursed.[738]

---

727 Numbers 30:14–16.
728 Leviticus 19:17. See Rashi.
729 Psalms 34:22.
730 Proverbs 30:10.
731 Ibid., 17:5.
732 Ibid., 19:19.
733 Ibid., 28:20.
734 Ibid., 19:9.
735 Ibid., 24:11–12.
736 Numbers 5:20–21.
737 Deuteronomy 27:15.
738 Ibid., 27:16.

One who moves his neighbor's boundary will be cursed.[739]

One who leads a blind man astray on the road will be cursed.[740]

One who perverts the judgment against a widow or orphan will be cursed.[741]

One who lies with his father's wife, his sister, his mother-in-law, or an animal will be cursed.[742]

One who strikes the other in private will be cursed.[743]

One who takes a bribe to kill an innocent person will be cursed.[744]

A person who pledges and sacrifices an animal with a blemish to God when he has a better animal will be cursed.[745]

If a person ignores a poor person and does not help him, he will be cursed.[746]

God will judge those who take also the portions of others.[747]

If one shows favoritism in judging and acquits a wicked person, all the nations will curse him.[748]

One must obey the king, and if one does not, the king will cause him troubles.[749] One who angers a king endangers himself.[750]

Evil will come upon a person who turns to other gods.[751] Evil will come upon a person who is haughty towards his Creator (God).[752]

The duty of the prophet is to warn the wicked person so that he will repent. If the prophet does not do so, the wicked person will die because of

---

739 Ibid., 27:17.
740 Ibid., 27:18.
741 Ibid., 27:19.
742 Ibid., 27:20–23.
743 Ibid., 27:24.
744 Ibid., 27:25.
745 Malachi 1:14.
746 Proverbs 28:27.
747 Ezekiel 34:16–22.
748 Proverbs 24:23–24.
749 Ecclesiastes 8:2–4.
750 Proverbs 20:2.
751 Habakkuk 2:19.
752 Isaiah 45:9–10.

his sin. The prophet will be punished as the one responsible for the death of the wicked person.[753]

God will forsake those who claim falsely that they are speaking in His name. They will be eternally disgraced.[754]

Each person receives his just deserts for the way he uses his tongue, because death and life are in the power of the tongue.[755]

The words of a foolish person will bring evil upon him.[756]

The way of the lazy person is like a thorn fence.[757]

If a person moves a boundary which was set many generations ago, or if he enters a field belonging to orphans, their Protector (God) will fight on their behalf against him.[758]

If one trusts a traitor in a time of troubles, he will find that he has no support.[759]

Specific Punishments for Specific Sins

If the High Priest sins unintentionally regarding one of the prohibitions of the Torah, he must bring a bull as a sin offering.[760] The ruler must bring a male goat.[761] An Israelite must bring a female goat or sheep as a sin offering.[762]

If a person unintentionally sinned by idol worship, he must bring a goat as a sin offering.[763]

If a person was summoned to testify and he refuses to testify, or if a person touched something ritually unclean and did not realize it, and afterwards ate something holy (sacrificial) or entered the Temple, or if one

753 Ezekiel 3:18.
754 Jeremiah 23:30–40.
755 Proverbs 18:20–21.
756 Ibid., 18:7.
757 Ibid., 15:19.
758 Ibid., 23:10–11.
759 Ibid., 25:19.
760 Leviticus 4:2–3.
761 Ibid., 4:22–23.
762 Ibid., 4:27–28, 32.
763 Numbers 15:27. See Sifri.

who had made an oath, forgot about it, and violated his oath, he must bring a female sheep or goat as a sin offering. If he cannot afford an animal, he must bring two turtle-doves or pigeons, one as a sin offering and one as a burnt offering.[764] If he cannot afford to bring birds, he must bring fine flour as a sin offering.[765]

If a person unintentionally derives benefit from something consecrated, he must bring a ram as a guilt offering. He must pay the cost of the benefit he derived plus an additional fifth (i.e., a quarter) to a Priest.[766]

If a person is unsure about whether he violated one of the prohibitions of the Torah, he must bring a ram as a guilt offering.[767]

If a person trespassed against God in that he had in his possession something belonging to another person and he then swore falsely that it was not in his possession, he must bring a ram as a guilt offering. He must return the object plus an additional fifth (i.e., a quarter) of its value.[768]

If a man lies with a woman slave who was assigned to another man and was not yet completely freed, the man must bring a ram as a guilt offering.[769]

If a person mistakenly eats of the heave offering which belongs to a Priest, he must pay the Priest its value plus an additional fifth (i.e., a quarter).[770]

If a thief is found with the object he stole, he must pay double.[771] If a person steals an ox or a sheep and afterwards either sells it or slaughters it, he must pay five oxen for the ox, and four sheep for the sheep.[772]

Based on a decision by a judge, a wicked person is given lashes according to his wicked deeds.[773]

---

764 Leviticus 5:1–7. See *Bava Metzia* 54a.
765 Ibid., 5:11.
766 Ibid., 5:15–16.
767 Ibid., 5:17–18.
768 Ibid., 5:21–25.
769 Ibid., 19:20–21. See Sifra.
770 Ibid., 22:14.
771 Exodus 22:3, 6.
772 Ibid., 21:37.
773 Deuteronomy 25:2.

A male who was not ritually circumcised, thereby violating the covenant between him and God, will be cut off from his nation.[774, 775]

One who performs work on the Sabbath will be cut off from his nation.[776]

One who eats on the Day of Atonement or performs work on that day is cut off from his nation.[777]

If a person does not offer the Passover sacrifice at its appointed time and has no impediment which would prevent him from doing so (he is not ritually unclean and not in a distant place), he receives the punishment of being cut off.[778]

If a person uses the anointing oil as a lotion or prepares something resembling it, he will be cut off from his nation.[779] One who prepares the incense in order to smell it, is punished with being cut off.[780]

If a person eats of the forbidden fat of an animal of a kind which may be offered as a sacrifice, he will be cut off from his nation.[781] One who consumes the blood of a fowl or animal will be cut off from his nation.[782]

One who eats of a peace offering which remained after two days will be cut off from his nation, because he desecrated an object holy to God.[783]

If a person is ritually unclean by having contact with the dead, and then enters the House of God in that state, he will be cut off.[784] If a person is ritually unclean or touched something which was ritually unclean, and then

---

774 Genesis 17:14.
775 The exact meaning of the punishment is discussed by the commentators. It is a severe punishment.
776 Exodus 31:14.
777 Leviticus 23:27–30.
778 Numbers 9:13.
779 Exodus 30:31–33.
780 Ibid., 30:37–38.
781 Leviticus 7:25.
782 Ibid., 7:26–27.
783 Ibid., 19:5–8.
784 Numbers 19:13.

eats of a peace offering, he will be cut off from his nation.[785] A Priest who eats holy food when he is ritually unclean will be cut off from before God.[786]

If a person slaughters an animal as a sacrifice, and does not bring it to the courtyard of the Temple, he will be cut off from his nation.[787] If a person offers a sacrifice outside the courtyard of the Temple, he will be cut off from his nation.[788]

If a man lies with his sister on his father's side or on his mother's side, both will be cut off before the eyes of the members of their nation, because that is considered a disgrace.[789] If a man lies with a woman who is having her monthly period (or having a bloody discharge at another time), both will be cut off from their nation.[790] If people engage in abominable acts, they will be cut off from their nation.[791]

If a person turns to necromancers or spiritists, he will be cut off from his nation.[792]

A person who willfully engages in idol worship has blasphemed God. He will be cut off from his nation, because he has despised the word of God.[793] One who gives of his children to Molech will be cut off from his nation, for he has rendered the Temple of God ritually unclean and desecrated His holy name. If the people of the land do not relate to the punishment to which he is subject, God will also cut off his family. Those who followed him will also be cut off from their nation.[794]

A non-Priest who offers up incense will die, as did Korah and his band.[795] A non-Priest who attempts to perform the service of the Priests will be caused to die.[796]

---

785 Leviticus 7:20–21.
786 Ibid., 22:3.
787 Ibid., 17:3–4. See Sifra.
788 Ibid., 17:8–9.
789 Ibid., 20:17.
790 Ibid., 20:18.
791 Ibid., 18:29.
792 Ibid., 20:6.
793 Numbers 15:30–31.
794 Leviticus 20:2–5.
795 Numbers 17:5.

Priests are to refrain from drinking wine or any alcoholic beverage when they come to the Temple. If they do drink, they will die.[797]

The Priests must put on the Priestly garments when they come to the Temple or when they approach the altar to perform holy service, so that they should not die.[798]

All the Priests, including the High Priest, are forbidden to enter the Holy of Holies at any time. If they do so, they will die.[799] The High Priest must place the incense on the fire before God, so that the cloud of the incense will cover the ark cover, and he will not die.[800]

The duty of the sons of Kehat at the time that the Children of Israel traveled was to carry the utensils of the Tent of Assembly after Aaron and his sons had covered them. They were forbidden to see the utensils lest they die. Aaron and his sons had to cover all the utensils of the Tabernacle before the sons of Kehat would come to carry them, so that they would not touch the holy objects and die.[801]

A Priest is forbidden to eat of the heave offering while he is in a state of ritual uncleanliness, and would thereby profane it. If he eats, he will die.[802]

If idol worshippers come to a prophet to seek God, and the prophet is enticed and listens to them, God will destroy him.[803]

If one grabs, beats, and kills a thief who comes stealthily, he will not be punished. That is the punishment of the thief.[804]

If a person causes distress or suffering to a widow or an orphan, God will kill him with the sword.[805]

If a man lies with his aunt, both will die childless.[806] If a man lies with his brother's wife, both will be childless.[807]

---

796 Ibid., 3:10.
797 Leviticus 10:8–9.
798 Exodus 28:41–43.
799 Leviticus 16:2.
800 Ibid., 16:13.
801 Numbers 4:15, 19–20.
802 Leviticus 22:9. See Sifra.
803 Ezekiel 14:7–9.
804 Exodus 22:1. See Mechilta.
805 Ibid., 22:21–23.

If a person plans to eat of the peace offering on the third day, the sacrifice will not be acceptable.[808] If one brings an animal which is blind, lame, or sick as a sacrifice, it desecrates God's name. Such sacrifices are not acceptable.[809]

If people plan to harm upright people, God will harm them in the same way.[810]

One who spreads falsehoods will be destroyed.[811] One who increases his wealth and treasures by deceit will have his treasures cause his death.[812]

One who always complains will harm his body.[813]

One who scorns his father and despises his mother will have his eyes pierced by the willows of the river.[814] One who follows a woman who is not his wife will die.[815] A woman who is not his wife draws the one who pursues her to the grave, and therefore her end will also be bitter.[816]

Sometimes a person's path seems straight to him, but its end is death. In laughter there is pain, and the end of joy is sadness.[817]

The lust of the lazy person will kill him, because he does nothing.[818]

If one robs a poor person or oppresses him in judgment, God will rob him.[819]

If a person increases his wealth by charging interest, God will take his money from him and give it to the poor.[820]

---

806 Leviticus 20:20.
807 Ibid., 20:21.
808 Ibid., 7:18.
809 Malachi 1:8–10.
810 Psalms 64:3, 8.
811 Proverbs 19:9.
812 Ibid., 21:6.
813 Ibid., 26:22.
814 Ibid., 30:17.
815 Ibid., 7:1–27.
816 Ibid., 5:3–6.
817 Ibid., 14:12–13. See Ibn Ezra.
818 Ibid., 21:25.
819 Ibid., 22:22–23.
820 Ibid.., 28:8.

If a person blocks his ears in order not to hear the cry of the poor, when he calls to God for help, he will not be answered.[821]

Punishments throughout History

Cain

God punished Cain after he murdered Abel: he would not succeed in working the soil and would be a wanderer in the land.[822]

The Era of the Forefathers

God punished Pharaoh with afflictions because he took Sarah into his house.[823]

Lot's wife looked backward after she had been told not to do so, and she became a pillar of salt.[824]

God appeared to Avimelech and told him that he would die soon because he had taken Sarah into his house. God knew that Avimelech did not know that Sarah was married, and therefore God did not allow Avimelech to sin by touching her. If Avimelech would not return her, he would die.[825]

Ishmael was banished from the house of Abraham because he acted in a scornful manner.[826]

Er was evil in God's eyes, and God therefore killed him.[827]

Onan destroyed his seed (because he did not want his son to be named after his dead brother). God therefore killed him.[828]

The Era of Slavery in Egypt

God was angry at Moses because he did not want to go to Egypt, and told him that his brother Aaron would speak in his place.[829]

---

821 Ibid., 21:13.
822 Genesis 4:9–12.
823 Ibid., 12:17.
824 Ibid., 19:17, 26.
825 Ibid., 20:3–7, 18.
826 Ibid., 21:9–12.
827 Ibid., 38:7.
828 Ibid., 38:8–10.

God wanted to kill Moses, because he had not circumcised his son. He did not do so after his wife Tzipporah circumcised him.[830, 831]

In the Desert

God told Moses to instruct the Children of Israel not to ascend the mountain and not to touch it, so that they should not die.[832]

God would erase from His book only those who sinned towards Him.[833]

God wanted to kill Aaron because of his involvement in the sin of the Golden Calf, but Moses prayed on his behalf.[834]

Aaron and his sons were to stay at the entrance of the Tent of Assembly for the seven days of consecration, to offer their sacrifices and to keep God's charge, so that they would not die.[835]

After Nadav and Avihu brought an unauthorized fire, which God had not commanded, fire came out from before God and consumed them.[836]

God was angry at Miriam and Aaron because of their complaints against Moses, and afflicted Miriam with a skin disease.[837] Moses prayed to God. God told Moses that Miriam would have to remain with the disease outside the camp for seven days.[838]

God killed the spies who had brought an evil report about the Land of Israel by a plague.[839]

Those who rebelled against Moses – Korah, Datan, Aviram and their families, as well as all their property – were swallowed up by the ground, to show the nation that Moses and Aaron were the ones who had been chosen

---

829 Exodus 4:13–14.

830 Ibid., 4:24–26.

831 At that time, before Moses was recognized by the nation, God could have taken the Children of Israel out of Egypt with a different leader.

832 Exodus 19:12–13.

833 Ibid., 32:33.

834 Deuteronomy 9:20.

835 Leviticus 8:33–35.

836 Ibid., 10:1–2.

837 Numbers 12:1–2, 9–10.

838 Ibid., 12:13–14.

839 Ibid., 14:37.

by God.[840] God sent forth fire to burn the two hundred and fifty supporters of Korah who had offered the incense.[841]

Moses and Aaron, who had not been careful in following God's instructions to produce water from the rock, and thereby to sanctify Him in the eyes of the Children of Israel, could not bring the nation into the land.[842, 843] Aaron and Moses died before the entry into the land because they had not listened to God's voice at the waters of Meriva.[844]

God was angry at Balaam for having gone to Balak. Therefore an angel of God stood on the road to block him.[845] God was angry, because (a) Balaam wanted to curse the Children of Israel even though they are blessed; (b) Balaam did not really intend to do what God would instruct him.

God destroyed all the people who followed the idol worship of Ba'al Peor.[846]

After the Entry into the Land

God told Joshua that whoever would be found (by drawing lots) to have taken of the banned objects would be burned by fire along with all of his possessions, because he had transgressed the covenant of God and had performed a despicable act in Israel.[847] Achan and all his possessions were stoned, including his sons and daughters.[848] (The sons and daughters of Achan knew what their father had done. In a similar case of punishment to the families of sinners, the sons of Korah did not die.)

840 Ibid., 16:28–33. (The sons of Korah did not die [Ibid., 26:11]. See below the comparison to the members of the family of Achan.)

841 Ibid., 16:35.

842 Ibid., 20:7–12.

843 Even though God was sanctified before the nation, Moses and Aaron had not acted to sanctify Him.

844 Numbers 20:23–24; 27:12–14.

845 Ibid., 22:22.

846 Deuteronomy 4:3.

847 Joshua 7:15.

848 Ibid., 7:24–25.

Avimelech of Shechem and his men killed the seventy sons of his father Gideon. Avimelech was killed by a rock thrown at him by a woman. His men were killed.[849]

Samson lost his special strength because God forsook him, after he revealed to Delilah the secret of his strength (that his hair had never been cut because he was a Nazirite).[850]

The sons of Eli the Priest sinned and caused others to sin. God did not permit them to listen to the voice of their father to change their ways, because He wanted to kill them.[851] The possibility of repentance was taken from them. (See p. 334.)

Eli the Priest enabled his sons to take of the meal offering before it was given to God. God would therefore prevent his descendants from attaining old age. His two sons would die on the same day. The remaining members of the house of Eli would come to bow down to a Priest who would be loyal to God and would ask of him part of the Priestly gifts, so that they would have something to eat.[852] Both of Eli's sons were killed.[853]

The Era of the Kings

King Saul did not wait, and offered a sacrifice to God before the prophet Samuel came to Gilgal. His dynasty would not last, and someone else would become the king in his place.[854] Saul did not keep God's word regarding the destruction of Amalek. God told Samuel that He regretted having made Saul king.[855]

God's spirit departed from Saul, and an evil spirit from God terrified him.[856]

---

849 Judges 9:45, 49, 54, 56–57.
850 Ibid., 16:20.
851 I Samuel 2:12–17, 22–25.
852 Ibid., 2:27–36.
853 Ibid., 4:11.
854 Ibid., 13:8–14.
855 Ibid., 15:10–11.
856 Ibid., 16:14.

Nabal the Carmelite refused to share food with David and his men on the day of the festival of the shearing. He died of disease.[857]

King Saul died because he did not listen to God's word. He even asked a necromancer and did not seek God. God gave the kingdom to David, the son of Jesse.[858]

When the Ark was brought to Jerusalem, Uzzah touched it and God killed him.[859]

David sinned against God when he took Bathsheba, the wife of Uriah, and sent Uriah to war to be killed. The prophet Nathan brought God's word to David: because of his sin, the sword would never depart from his house, evil would come from within his house, others would openly take his wives, and the son who would be born to him from Bathsheba would die.[860]

Saul killed many of the Gibeonites. Therefore, they killed seven of his descendants.[861]

Eviatar, from the house of Eli, was expelled by King Solomon from his position as a Priest to God. , This was due to Eviatar's plotting with Adoniyahu, the son of David, to usurp the kingdom from Solomon. Thus was realized the word of God about the house of Eli.[862]

King Solomon had a large number of wives who turned his heart in old age to idolatry, even though God had appeared to him personally twice. As a result, God said to him that He would divide the kingdom. However, due to the merit of his father, David, and due to the merit of Jerusalem, God would leave to his sons the monarchy only over the tribe of Judah. Even that would not occur during his days but in the days of his son who would succeed him.[863] God set up enemies against Solomon.[864]

---

857 Ibid., 25:10–11, 38.
858 I Chronicles 10:13–14.
859 II Samuel 6:6–7.
860 Ibid., 12:7–15, 18.
861 Ibid., 21:1, 9.
862 I Kings 2:27.
863 Ibid., 11:9–13.
864 Ibid., 11:14, 23.

God caused Rehoboam, Solomon's son, not to listen to the advice of the nation. Only the tribe of Judah accepted the monarchy of the house of David. Shemaiah, the man of God, warned Rehoboam not to go out to wage war in order to restore the other tribes to him, because the division had come from God.[865]

A man of God from Judah told Jeroboam, who had offered incense on an altar which he had built in Beth El, that a descendant of the house of David named Josiah would kill the Priests of the high places on the altar in Beth El.[866]

The man of God, who came from Judah to Beth El at God's behest, was commanded not to eat or drink there. He believed the lies of an old prophet – he ate and drank. God punished him, and a lion killed him.[867]

The prophet Ahiya told Jeroboam's wife the word of God: because Jeroboam had done evil in the eyes of God, and had made other gods and caused Israel to sin, evil would befall the house of Jeroboam and no memory of it would remain.[868] Baasha smote the entire house of Jeroboam, in accordance with the word of God through Ahiya.[869]

God told Jehu, the son of Hanani, to tell Baasha that his punishment would be like that of Jeroboam, because he had caused Israel to sin and angered God. God would therefore destroy the house of Baasha as he had done to the house of Jeroboam.[870] Zimri destroyed the house of Baasha, as God had said to Jehu, because of the sins of Baasha and Elah.[871]

The prophet Hanani told King Asa, who did not rely on God, but rather on the king of Aram in his struggle with Baasha, that he would have to engage in many wars.[872]

---

865 Ibid., 12:15, 22–24.
866 Ibid., 13:1–2.
867 Ibid., 13:9, 21–22, 24.
868 Ibid., 14:5–11, 15.
869 Ibid., 15:29–30.
870 Ibid., 16:1–4.
871 Ibid., 16:12–13.
872 II Chronicles 16:7–9.

Hiel built Jericho. When he began building it, his firstborn son died. When he finished, his youngest son died, as God had spoken to Joshua.[873]

After God delivered Ben Hadad, the king of Aram, into the hands of Ahab, the king of Israel in order to prove God's power, a prophet told Ahab in the name of God that he would receive his recompense because he had freed Ben Hadad – the life of Ahab would be in place of that of Ben Hadad.[874]

Elijah came to Ahab, the king of Israel, in the name of God and told him that his death would be like that of Naboth the Jezreelite. Ahab had murdered Naboth (with the aid of his wife, Jezebel), and after which he came to inherit his vineyard. His wife Jezebel would also die in a degrading way. God would even destroy the dynasty of Ahab as He had done to the dynasties of Jeroboam and Baasha, because he did evil in the eyes of God, engaged in idolatry and caused Israel to sin.[875] Ahab was killed in the war against Aram. His death was as described in the word of God through Elijah.[876]

When Ahaziah, the king of Israel, became ill, he sent to seek out Baal Zebub, the god of Ekron, to know if he would arise from his sick bed. The prophet Elijah told the messengers of the king, in the name of God, that Ahaziah would die as he had not sought God and had turned to Baal Zebub. Afterwards the king died.[877] The messengers of Ahaziah who had insisted that Elijah should obey the king were consumed by fire from heaven.[878]

A number of youths mocked the prophet Elisha. He cursed them in the name of God, and two bears tore apart forty-two of them.[879]

When Ben Hadad besieged Samaria which was suffering from famine, the prophet Elisha said in the name of God that on the next day there would be an abundance of food, which would be cheap. The king's officer laughed at this. Because of this, Elisha said to him that he would indeed see the

873 I Kings 16:34.
874 Ibid., 20:23–32, 38–42.
875 Ibid., 21:17–26.
876 Ibid., 22:34–38.
877 II Kings 1:3–4, 17.
878 Ibid., 1:9–12.
879 Ibid., 2:23–24.

abundant food with his own eyes, but would not benefit from it.[880] He was trampled by the people at the gate to the city.[881]

King Jehoshaphat, who had cooperated with Ahaziah, the king of Israel, in building ships in Etzion Gever, was punished and the ships were destroyed.[882]

King Jehoram, the son of Jehoshaphat, killed all his brothers, engaged in idol worship and swayed the people of Judah as well, as Ahab had done in Israel. The word of God to Elijah was brought to Jehoram in a letter: God would afflict him (with a disease of the intestines), and the members of his house and his nation. The Philistines took all his possessions and took his wives and sons captive. (Only his young son Ahaziah was saved.) Jehoram died of grave illnesses.[883]

Ahaziah the son of Jehoram, king of Judah, did evil in the eyes of God as the house of Ahab in Israel. Ahaziah's defeat when he came to Joram, the king of Israel, was from God. Jehu, who destroyed the house of Ahab, captured and killed him.[884]

God was angry at Amaziah, king of Judah, because he diverged from the straight path and bowed down and offered incense to the god of Edom.[885] God therefore prevented Amaziah from listening to the word of Joash, the king of Israel, not to go to war against him. Amaziah lost in the war.[886] He was killed by plotters because he had forsaken God.[887]

Uzziah, the king of Judah, did what was right in the eyes of God, and God therefore helped him in all his wars. His kingdom became very strong, but he began to become haughty and came to offer incense on the incense

---

880 Ibid., 7:1–2.
881 Ibid., 7:17–20.
882 II Chronicles 20:35–37.
883 Ibid., 21:12–19.
884 Ibid., 22:3–9.
885 Ibid., 25:14–15.
886 Ibid., 25:20.
887 Ibid., 25:27.

altar – knowing that this service was only of the Priests. Therefore, God afflicted him with a skin disease until his dying day.[388]

Hosea prophesied in the name of God, and said that God would avenge the blood of the house of Ahab from the house of Jehu.[889] (Even though the killing of the house of Ahab was God's desire, Jehu continued in the path of Jeroboam, the son of Nebat. This shows that what he did was not only for the sake of God. His descendants followed in his path which brought about their downfall.)

Jonah fled in a ship in order to evade the task which God wanted him to perform. God therefore caused a violent storm to come up.[890]

The prophet Isaiah prophesied and said to King Hezekiah in the name of God that he should not fear the blaspheming of Rabshakeh, the general of the army of the king of Assyria. The king of Assyria would return to his country without any fighting and would be killed there.[891] The king of Assyria returned to Nineveh, and was killed there.[892]

God tested King Hezekiah when the messengers of the king of Babylon came to him. He did not withstand the test, and God therefore forsook him.[893] King Hezekiah showed the messengers of the king of Babylon all his treasures. The prophet Isaiah told him in the name of God that all his possessions and those of his forefathers would be brought to Babylon. His sons would be eunuchs in the palace of the king of Babylon.[894]

Some of the members of the nation sinned. They transformed bad to good and good to bad, and their valor was expressed in drinking wine. They were wise in their own eyes, justified the actions of the wicked because they had been bribed, and convicted the righteous. Therefore God would destroy

888 Ibid., 26:16, 19–21.
889 Hosea 1:4.
890 Jonah 1:3–4.
891 II Kings 19:6–7.
892 Ibid., 19:36–37.
893 II Chronicles 32:31.
894 II Kings 20:12–18.

them.[895] God would summon the armies of the other nations, and no one would escape them.[896]

God's word came to Isaiah that because the legislators had legislated unjust laws in order to pervert the justice of the poor, the widowed and the orphans, and to steal from them, these legislators would not be able to flee or preserve their honor on the Day of Judgment.[897]

God would judge and kill all those who engaged in idol worship and ate forbidden foods.[898]

The prophet Micah prophesied by the word of God that He would punish the false prophets who led the nation astray and who prophesied that there would be peace. They would no longer prophesy because God would not answer them.[899]

The prophet Ezekiel prophesied in the name of God about the false prophets who deceived the nation and promised them peace, when there was no peace. They would not be part of the house of Israel and would not come to the Land of Israel. God would wipe them out.[900]

The prophet Jeremiah prophesied in the name of God that Hananiah, the son of Azor, the false prophet, would die that year. Hananiah died a short time later.[901] Jeremiah prophesied in the name of God that Ahab, the son of Koliah, and Zedekiah, the son of Maaseiah, who had prophesied falsely and had committed adultery, would be delivered into the hands of Nebuchadnezzar.[902]

Jeremiah prophesied in the name of God regarding Shemaiah the Nehelamite, who had sent letters to Jerusalem to imprison the prophet Jeremiah in isolation based on a false prophecy. Neither he nor his sons

895 Isaiah 5:20–25.
896 Ibid., 5:26–30.
897 Ibid., 10:1–4.
898 Ibid., 66:15–17.
899 Micah 3:5–7.
900 Ezekiel 13:1–16.
901 Jeremiah 28:15–17.
902 Ibid., 29:21–23.

would be among the leaders of the nation. He would also not receive the good which God would do for His nation.[903]

God's word to Jeremiah regarding the king of Judah was: if he would not do justice and righteousness, would not rescue the ones who had been robbed, would cheat the stranger, the orphan and the widow or spill innocent blood, his house would be destroyed.[904]

King Jehoiakim burned the scroll of the prophecy of Jeremiah. God therefore commanded Jeremiah to write a new scroll and to add in it about the end of the monarchy of Jehoiakim, about the evil which would befall the king's sons and servants, and the ignominious death of the king.[905]

The leaders of the nation who had violated their trust would not continue in their positions.[906]

God told Jeremiah that if Zedekiah, the king of Judah, would not go out to the ministers of Babylon, the city would be delivered into the hands of the Chaldees, who would burn it and that even Zedekiah would not be able to flee.[907]

God told the king of Tyre, through the prophet Ezekiel, that since he considered himself a god because of his wisdom and might, God would bring strong strangers who would annul his wisdom and kill him.[908]

God told the king of Egypt, through the prophet Ezekiel, that since he claimed that he had created the river, God would take hold of him and bring him to the desert and leave him there as prey for the beasts of the field.[909]

After the Return to the Land

The prophet Zechariah prophesied in the name of God that whoever would steal or swear falsely in the name of God would lose all that he owned.[910]

---

903 Ibid., 29:24–32.
904 Ibid., 22:1–5.
905 Ibid., 36:29–31.
906 Ezekiel 34:1–10.
907 Jeremiah 38:17–18.
908 Ezekiel 28:1–10.
909 Ibid., 29:1–5.

God's word to the prophet Zechariah regarding the leaders of the nation was that He would destroy the three leaders in a short time as they had rejected Him. Some would die and the others would kill one another.[911]

God told Zechariah that He would kill the false prophets.[912]

The prophet Malachi prophesied in the name of God that all who did evil would be burned.[913]

God ordered that the Levites (the Priests) who had turned to idolatry would no longer be able to serve in the Temple in the tasks of the priesthood.[914]

• Summary

God rewards behavior which is in accordance with His wishes, and punishes behavior which is against His wishes. The systems of reward and punishment apply to all of mankind, to nations and to groups. Reward and punishment relate to the realm of closeness to God or distance from Him, as well as to the physical realm (abundance and security, or want and destruction). The reward can also be expressed in receiving honor from the nations, or in escaping evil.

The Bible notes reward and punishment which were meted out to nations in general, and to the nation of Israel in particular in various historical eras.

The systems of reward and punishment also act in regard to individuals. These appear in the physical, emotional, and the spiritual realms. The reward can be expressed as a physical benefit, emotional well-being, success, security, special closeness to God, a reward to one's descendants, a positive influence on one's surroundings, and additional good behavior. The punishment can be expressed as destruction, failure, physical suffering, a lack of security, obstacles, harm to one's pride, a negative attitude by others, oblivion,

---

910 Zechariah 5:1–4.
911 Ibid., 11:8–9.
912 Ibid., 13:2.
913 Malachi 3:19–21.
914 Ezekiel 44:10–14.

distance from God, a negative influence on one's surroundings, and additional paths of wickedness.

There are general rewards and punishments on the performance of specific actions, as well as specific rewards and punishments as a result of specific actions.

Reward and punishment also are expressed within the framework of the revival of the dead.

The Bible notes the reward and punishment given to individuals throughout the course of history.

Chapter 7 – Repentance, Atonement, and Forgiveness

The sinner has the possibility of returning to God.

The process of atonement is intended to atone for the sin and the sinner. It is also intended for one who becomes ritually unclean.

Forgiveness for sins is intended for the sinner himself.

Repentance to God

The Children of Israel must return to God with all their hearts and all their souls, and observe His commandments, which are appropriate to their ability as humans.[1]

The Children of Israel must examine in which way they sinned and must return to God.[2]

God can plan to destroy a nation, but if the nation repents, He will annul the implementation of the punishment.[3] If a nation seeks God, He will answer it.[4] If the nation returns, God will return to it.[5]

God brings suffering on a person, and asks him to return to Him.[6]

1 Deuteronomy 30:8–14.
2 Lamentations 3:40.
3 Jeremiah 18:7–8.
4 II Chronicles 15:2.
5 Zechariah 1:3.
6 Psalms 90:3.

God told Ezekiel to tell the nation that He does not seek the death of the wicked person, but that he should return from his evil ways so that he will live.[7] The wicked person must forsake his way and return to God, and then God, who is very forgiving, will take pity on him.[8]

Confession

One of the conditions for repentance is confessing one's sin.

If it becomes known to a person that he sinned, he must confess it before he brings a sacrifice.[9]

On the Day of Atonement, the High Priest must confess on the head of the goat and enumerate all the sins of the Children of Israel.[10]

God forgives one who confesses his sins.[11]

Atonement for Sins

Even one who sins unintentionally needs atonement because he is responsible to a certain extent for the act.

If a person sinned unintentionally, he must bring a sin offering. When the sin offering is brought, the Priest will atone for the sinner, and the sin will be forgiven.[12] The Priest will also atone at the time of the sacrifice of the communal sin offering,[13] and that of the ruler.[14] The Priest will atone for various sins which require a guilt offering.[15] A burnt offering also atones.[16]

In most sacrifices, the blood is sprinkled on the altar at the time of the sacrifice in order to atone for the soul.[17] In some of the sacrifices, the blood is

---

7 Ezekiel 33:11.
8 Isaiah 55:7.
9 Leviticus 5:4–5. See Sifri (Numbers 5:7).
10 Leviticus 16:21.
11 Proverbs 28:13.
12 Leviticus 4:31, 35; 5:6, 10, 13; Numbers 6:11; 15:28.
13 Leviticus 4:20; Numbers 15:25.
14 Leviticus 4:26.
15 Leviticus 5:16, 18, 26; 19:22; Numbers 5:8.
16 Leviticus 1:4.
17 Ibid., 17:11.

brought into the house where the Priest atones for the sin of the one who brought the sacrifice.[18]

On the Day of Atonement, the High Priest atones for himself and his family by the sin offering of a bull which he sacrifices.[19] The scapegoat is placed alive before God upon which to atone for the Children of Israel.[20] The High Priest atones in the Holy Place for the ritual uncleanliness of the Children of Israel, and on their deliberate and unintentional sins. He also atones on the curtain outside. Afterwards he goes to the altar which is before God and atones upon it.[21] He offers his burnt offering and the burnt offering of the nation and atones for himself and for the nation.[22] On this day the nation is atoned for and is cleansed of all its sins.[23]

A sin offering is brought to atone for the sins of the Children of Israel also on the New Moon and on the festivals.[24]

Atonement for Ritual Uncleanliness

After a house has been purified from an affliction, the Priest must slaughter a bird over a pottery vessel which contains fresh water. He must then take a second live bird, cedar wood, a purple thread, and hyssop, and dip them into the blood of the slaughtered bird. He must then sprinkle the blood on the house seven times. At that point he releases the live bird. That is how he atones for the house.[25]

A woman who has given birth must bring a burnt offering and a sin offering, and the Priest will atone for her.[26] A *zav* who became ritually clean must bring a sin offering and a burnt offering, and the Priest will atone for him.[27]

---

18 Ibid., 6:23.
19 Ibid., 16:6, 11.
20 Ibid., 16:10.
21 Ibid., 16:16–18.
22 Ibid., 16:24.
23 Ibid., 16:30.
24 Numbers 28:15, 22, 30; 29:5, 15, 19, 22, 25, 28, 31, 34, 38.
25 Leviticus 14:48–53.
26 Ibid., 12:6–8.
27 Ibid., 15:13–15.

A *zavah* who became ritually clean must bring a sin offering and a burnt offering, and the Priest will atone for her.[28]

When a person afflicted with a skin disease becomes ritually clean, on the eighth day the Priest places him and the animals which were brought as a sacrifice at the entrance to the Temple before God. He takes of the blood of the guilt offering and places it on the lobe of the person's right ear, his right thumb, and his right big toe. He does the same with the oil, and pours the remaining oil on the person's head. The Priest sacrifices the sin offering, burnt offering, and the meal offering of the person who is becoming ritually clean. With this the Priest atones before God for the person who became ritually clean from the skin disease.[29]

Atonement – Additional Requirements

The High Priest must wear the golden headplate to atone for sins related to holy (sacrificial) objects.[30]

When a census is made of the Children of Israel, each person must give as atonement for the soul, half a silver shekel as a contribution to God and that will prevent a plague (as a result of the census). The money is for the use of the Temple and will be a memorial before God to atone for the Children of Israel.[31]

If a murdered person is found on the ground and it is not known who the murderer was, the elders of the closest city must take a heifer which was never worked with to a running stream which has not been cultivated and break the heifer's neck there. The elders wash their hands above the heifer. They proclaim that they did not spill the person's blood and did not see the murderer. They ask for atonement for the nation, and that they should not be blamed for the innocent blood. This is the atonement for them.[32]

28 Ibid., 15:29–30.
29 Ibid., 14:10–20.
30 Exodus 28:36–38.
31 Ibid., 30:11–16.
32 Deuteronomy 21:1–8.

The earth will not be atoned of the blood spilled upon it, except through the blood of the murderer.[33]

Forgiveness for Sins

If the people of Israel are submissive to God and pray, seek God's face and return from their evil ways, God will listen and forgive their sins.[34]

If a wicked person repents and begins to observe God's commandments, and pursues justice and righteousness, his sins will no longer be remembered.[35]

Through kindness and truth, sins will be atoned for (forgiven).[36]

If God took into account all sins, no person could manage. God is the One who forgives so that people will fear Him.[37] In the End of Days, God will redeem Israel of all of its sins.[38] (See p. 396.)

God will forgive a young girl in her father's house when she does not keep a vow, if her father annulled it.[39] Similarly, He will forgive a married woman who did not keep a vow, if her husband annulled it.[40]

Repentance – Specific Cases

After the events described in the curses take place, and the Children of Israel are scattered among the lands of the various nations where God sent them, they will return to God and listen to His voice. God will return them from their exile and have mercy upon them.[41] After the Children of Israel return to listen to the voice of God, He will rejoice in them and bless the work of their hands.[42]

---

33 Numbers 35:33.
34 II Chronicles 7:14.
35 Ezekiel 18:21–22.
36 Proverbs 16:6.
37 Psalms 130:3–4.
38 Ibid., 130:8. See Metzudat David.
39 Numbers 30:6.
40 Ibid., 30:13.
41 Deuteronomy 30:1–3.
42 Ibid., 30:8–10.

The Children of Israel returned to God at times of distress and He answered them, as Azaryahu, the son of Oded, said to Asa, the king of Judah.[43]

The prophet Hosea called in the name of God to the Nation of Israel to return to Him, to beg for forgiveness and not only to offer sacrifices. They must stop worshipping other gods. God would love them, would never again become angry with His nation and would bring upon them much good.[44]

The prophet Joel called upon the nation to return to God, with crying, fasting, and mourning, because God is merciful and compassionate, and is willing to overlook the evil which He had planned as a punishment. He might even leave His blessing – the meal offering and wine libation in the House of God.[45]

God sent prophets to the people of Judah, to warn them to repent from their evil ways, and not to worship other gods, so that they would remain on their land.[46] At the beginning of the reign of Jehoiakim, God told Jeremiah to say to the nation that if it returned from its evil ways, God would not bring upon it the punishment it deserved.[47]

God instructed Jeremiah to tell the people of Judah and the inhabitants of Jerusalem that He had already prepared their punishment, but called upon them to return from their evil ways.[48] God called upon Israel to repent, because He does not hold grudges forever.[49] If the Children of Israel would return to God, forsake their idols and swear to God in truth, justice and righteousness, then the other nations would be blessed and praised because of them.[50] God called to Jerusalem to pay attention to the words of rebuke and to better its people's ways; otherwise God would reject it and it would become desolate.[51]

God spoke to Jeremiah to tell the nation that He would return all the people who had been exiled with King Jehaniah to the land and they would

---

43 II Chronicles 15:1–4.
44 Hosea 14:2–9.
45 Joel 2:12–14. See Ibn Ezra, Radak.
46 Jeremiah 35:15.
47 Ibid., 26:1–3.
48 Jeremiah 18:11.
49 Ibid., 3:12.
50 Ibid., 4:1–2.
51 Ibid., 6:8.

rebuild it. If they would return to God, He would give them a heart to know Him. They would be His nation and He would be their God.[52]

God told the prophet Zechariah that if the Children of Israel would return to God, God would return to them.[53]

God said to the prophet Malachi that before the Great and Awesome Day comes, He will send to them the prophet Elijah to return the hearts of the fathers and the sons, so that God will not destroy all the inhabitants of the land.[54] Those who return to God will be saved.

God told Hosea that for a long time the Children of Israel will not have a king, ministers, sacrifices, monuments, the ephod, or idols. Afterwards they will return and seek God and David, their king.[55] God will punish Ephraim and Judah until they confess their guilt and seek God in their distress.[56]

God told the prophet Ezekiel that he was to warn the wicked person to return from his evil ways. If Ezekiel did not do so, the wicked person would die of his sins, and Ezekiel would also be responsible for it.[57]

After God saw the actions of the people of Nineveh, who had repented their evil ways, He did not punish them by overturning the city, as He had informed them.[58]

After the Children of Israel will suffer in the lands of their enemies, they will confess their sins and the sins of their fathers, and their hearts will be humbled. God will then remember His covenant with His Nation and His land.[59]

Atonement – Specific Cases

When the Levites were sanctified, they sacrificed a bull as a sin offering and another for a burnt offering, to atone for them.[60]

---

52 Ibid., 24:5–7.
53 Zechariah 1:3.
54 Malachi 3:23–24.
55 Hosea 3:4–5.
56 Ibid., 5:15.
57 Ezekiel 3:16–18.
58 Jonah 3:10.
59 Leviticus 26:40–42.
60 Numbers 8:12.

The Children of Israel complained about Moses and Aaron for having killed Korah and his group. God brought a plague upon them. Aaron ran into the midst of the congregation and atoned for the nation through the incense, and the plague was halted.[61]

Phineas, who killed Zimri and the Midianite woman with whom he had relations in public, atoned for the Children of Israel by his zealousness, so that God did not wipe out Israel.[62]

When God avenges the blood of His nation, the land will be cleansed of what happened to God's nation.[63]

An angel took a glowing coal from the altar and touched the mouth of the prophet Isaiah, and thereby atoned for his sins.[64]

Isaiah told the nation that their sins would be atoned, when they destroyed their altars and stopped worshipping idols.[65]

Hezekiah prayed to God to atone for those who had eaten of the Passover sacrifice when they were not ritually clean. Hezekiah was ready to seek God with all his heart. God, therefore, listened to him and healed the nation.[66]

Appropriate Timing

Sometimes, God, as it were, knocks on the door of the Nation of Israel. If the Nation of Israel does not answer Him immediately, after some time it becomes apparent that God has forsaken it.[67]

The Annulment of the Possibility to Repent

In special cases, the possibility of freedom of choice, repentance and forgiveness is annulled. A number of such cases are described in the Bible.[68]

61 Ibid., 17:11–13.
62 Ibid., 25:10–13.
63 Deuteronomy 32:43. See Rashbam.
64 Isaiah 6:6–7.
65 Ibid., 27:9.
66 II Chronicles 30:17–20.
67 Song of Songs 5:2–6.
68 Of course, there is no added punishment for sins committed when the person has no free will to abstain from them.

God told Moses that He would cause Pharaoh to be stubborn and not send the Children of Israel from Egypt.[69] This was so that the Egyptians would know that the Lord is God, who takes the Children of Israel out of Egypt.[70]

God hardened the heart of the Canaanite nations in preparation for war with Israel, so as to destroy them without mercy.[71] The Children of Israel dispossessed the nations of the land who had performed abominations to God, witchcraft, and passing their sons and daughters through fire.[72]

God swore that the sin of the house of Eli would not be atoned, because Eli knew that his sons had cursed, and he did not stop them.[73]

God's word to the prophet Hosea was to tell the Priests and the people of Israel that the deeds of Ephraim and Israel would not enable them to return to Him, because they were filled with the spirit of sexual immorality and did not know Him. If they would only seek God by means of sacrifices, God would not be found by them.[74] God would not continue to take pity on the House of Israel and would no longer forgive their sins.[75] God told the prophet Amos that He would not continue to forgive Israel.[76]

Hulda the prophetess prophesied to Josiah in the name of God, that God would bring evil on Judah and its inhabitants, as written in the Book of the Torah. The Children of Israel had forsaken God and offered incense to other gods. They had caused God to become so angry that it was impossible to appease Him.[77]

Even after Josiah returned to God with all his heart, soul, and might, according to the Torah of Moses, God did not relent from His great anger at Judah because of the acts of Menasseh, king of Judah. God said that He

69 Exodus 4:21.
70 Ibid., 7:5.
71 Joshua 11:20.
72 Deuteronomy 18:9–12.
73 I Samuel 3:13–14.
74 Hosea 5:4–6.
75 Ibid., 1:6.
76 Amos 8:2.
77 II Kings 22:15–17.

would distance Judah from His presence as He had distanced Israel. He would reject Jerusalem and the House where His name rested.[78]

At the beginning of the reign of Jehoiakim, it was still possible to return to God. God told Jeremiah that if the nation would return from its evil ways, God would not bring about the troubles which He planned to do as a punishment for their evil deeds.[79] Afterwards the possibility of repenting was annulled. God told Jeremiah to speak to the house of Judah, but they would not listen to him, because they had acted willfully and had not listened to the prophets that God had sent to them. God had rejected the nation.[80]

The Renewal of the Possibility to Repent

After one has received part of one's punishment, the possibility of repenting is again open. After the exile of some of the inhabitants of Judah and Jerusalem, during the reign of Jehoiachin, the possibility of repenting was again available. Jeremiah told Zedekiah that if he went out to the ministers of Babylon, he would live, and the city would not be burned down.[81]

After the destruction, those who remained alive were able to return to God, and He would return to them.[82]

• Summary

God enables a sinner to return to Him by repentance and He calls upon him to return. One of the conditions is confessing the sin.

Each person needs atonement for sin, even if he sinned unintentionally. The process of atonement is a process of rectification which is intended to atone for the sin and the sinner, and is also intended for one who becomes ritually unclean.

---

78 Ibid., 23:25–27.
79 Jeremiah 26:1–3.
80 Ibid., 7:25–29.
81 Ibid., 38:17.
82 Ibid., 8:4.

God forgives the sins of one who returns to Him (they will be erased, and he will not be punished for them).

When God calls upon the Nation of Israel to return to Him, the nation must respond immediately.

Events of returning in repentance and atonement occurred throughout history. However, there are situations and times when the sins of people are so severe that God prevents them from being able to return in repentance. Sometimes, after a partial punishment, God again enables the sinners to return.

Chapter 8 – Prayer

The Bible tells of the prayers of people to God, to Whom they turned to request His assistance, and of God responding to their prayer or not responding to it. The chapter also includes requests to God to receive answers and directions.

Relating to God – In General

God answers a request for help by righteous people, and saves them from their troubles.[1] God listens to the calls for help by those who fear Him, and saves them.[2]

God will save the Nation of Israel when it calls to Him at a time of distress.[3]

God shows abundant kindness to those who call to Him.[4]

If a person gives food to the hungry and clothes to the poor, God will answer him when he asks help of Him.[5]

After the building of the House of God, God appeared to Solomon and told him that, when He would bring famine on the land, or locusts to eat all vegetation, or a plague, the Children of Israel would come to this House to

1 Psalms 34:16,18.
2 Ibid., 145:19.
3 Ibid., 50:15.
4 Ibid., 86:5.
5 Isaiah 58:7–9.

pray to God, to seek Him and to repent their evil ways. God would answer them.[6]

If one ignores the words of the Torah, his prayer is an abomination.[7]

God's Responsiveness to Prayer throughout History

The Era of the Forefathers

Abram asked God for a son, and He responded to him. Abram asked for a sign that he would inherit the land, and God gave him a sign.[8]

At Abraham's request, God promised that He would not destroy Sodom if there were ten righteous people in the city.[9]

By Lot's request, God did not overturn the city of Tzoar so that he would be able to flee there.[10]

God told Avimelech that if he would return Sarah to Abraham, who was a prophet, he would pray for Avimelech and he would live.[11] After Abraham prayed to God, He healed Avimelech and his wife and maidservants, so that they could again give birth, for up to then God had halted all births because of Sarah.[12]

God listened to the voice of Ishmael. He opened Hagar's eyes so that she could see a well to give him to drink.[13]

Isaac prayed to God for his wife Rebecca who was barren, and God acceded to his prayer.[14]

God listened to Leah, and she gave birth to a fifth son.[15]

God remembered Rachel, and listened to her prayer. She gave birth to a son.[16]

---

6 II Chronicles 7:12–16.
7 Proverbs 28:9.
8 Genesis 15:2–21.
9 Ibid., 18:23–32.
10 Ibid., 19:18–22.
11 Ibid., 20:7.
12 Ibid., 20:17–18.
13 Ibid., 21:17–19.
14 Ibid., 25:21.
15 Ibid., 30:17.
16 Ibid., 30:22–23.

Jacob prayed to God to save him from the hands of Esau.[17] He did not attack Jacob.[18]

In Egypt

God heard the Children of Israel crying out because of their hard work, and remembered His covenant with Abraham, Isaac and Jacob.[19] Therefore, He came to save them from the hand of Egypt, and to bring them up to the Land of Israel.[20]

At Pharaoh's request, Moses cried out to God, and the frogs which had covered Egypt died.[21] At Pharaoh's request, Moses prayed to God, and He removed the wild beasts from the people in Egypt.[22] At Pharaoh's request, Moses prayed to God and the hail stopped.[23] At Pharaoh's request, Moses prayed to God, and He removed the locusts from the land.[24]

In the Desert

After the Children of Israel sinned with the Golden Calf, God wished to destroy the nation and to make a great nation out of Moses. Moses pleaded to God and said that Egypt would say that God had taken the Children of Israel out of Egypt in order to kill them. Moses also asked that God should remember the covenant with the forefathers, and His promise that they would be a great nation and receive the land as an inheritance. God listened to Moses's prayer.[25]

God wanted to kill Aaron, and Moses also prayed for him.[26]

Moses asked God for the presence of the angel that God's name was in his midst. He asked God to let him know His ways so that he and the nation

17 Ibid., 32:9–12.
18 Ibid., 33:4.
19 Exodus 2:23–24.
20 Ibid., 3:7–8.
21 Ibid., 8:4–9.
22 Ibid., 8:24–27.
23 Ibid., 9:27–33.
24 Ibid., 10:16–19.
25 Ibid., 32:9–14.
26 Deuteronomy 9:20.

would find favor before Him, and He would not destroy them. God assented and said to Moses that He would be with them and would not destroy them. Moses said that God's walking with them would be a sign that he and the nation had found favor in God's eyes. God answered that that was what would happen, because Moses had found favor in His eyes.[27]

Moses asked God to show him His glory. God answered Moses that He would show him all His goodness, would call before him the *Shem Havaya*, and would show him His attribute of mercy. But Moses could not see His face, because no man can see God's face and remain alive. Moses could see His back.[28]

Moses asked God to be with the nation and to forgive their sin, even though it was a stiff-necked people. God assented and said that He would make a covenant with him, and would show wonders which had never been seen.[29]

When a fire of God burned in the camp and the Children of Israel cried out, Moses prayed to God and the fire died out.[30]

Moses cried out to God to heal Miriam, who was afflicted with a skin disease. God told him that she had to remain outside the camp for seven days and then she would be healed.[31]

After the report by the spies, when God sought to destroy the nation for not having believed in Him, Moses pleaded with Him on behalf of the nation. He claimed that when the other nations who heard that God had taken the Children of Israel out of Egypt and gone before them in a cloud and fire, would hear that God killed the entire nation in one moment, they would say that God killed them in the desert because He did not have the ability to bring them into the land which He had sworn to them. Moses requested of God to forgive them, because He is long-suffering and has great kindness, as He forgave them in the past.

---

27 Exodus 33:12–17. See Nachmanides.
28 Ibid., 33:18–23.
29 Ibid., 34:9–10.
30 Numbers 11:1–2.
31 Ibid., 12:10–15.

God answered Moses that He forgave them, and would not destroy the nation. However, those who had seen God's glory and His signs, and who had nevertheless tried Him ten times and had not listened to Him, would not be permitted to see the land which He had sworn to their forefathers.[32]

Moses asked God not to listen to Korah and his group, because he had not wronged any of them.[33] God listened to him.[34]

When God wished to destroy the entire nation at the time of the rebellion of Korah and his followers, Moses and Aaron asked God if He was angry at the entire nation because of the sin of one man. God responded and ordered the entire congregation to distance itself from the tents of the rebels.[35]

After the Children of Israel vowed to God that they would place a ban on the cities of the king of Arad, God heard their voice and delivered the Canaanites into their hands.[36]

God sent snakes and fiery serpents among the nation because they complained that He had taken them out of Egypt into the desert. The Children of Israel asked Moses to pray to God and to ask for His forgiveness. God assented to his prayer and ordered Moses to make a copper serpent so that whoever was bitten could look at it and not die.[37]

After the Entry into the Land of Israel

Joshua asked God to not have the sun set so that he could continue to fight. God agreed to his request and the sun stopped its movement for a day.[38]

Jabez asked God to bless him. God assented to his request.[39]

---

32 Ibid., 14:11–23.
33 Ibid., 16:15.
34 Ibid., 16:31–35.
35 Ibid., 16:20–24.
36 Ibid., 21:2–3.
37 Ibid., 21:5–9.
38 Joshua 10:12–14.
39 I Chronicles 4:10.

The tribes of Reuben and Gad and half the tribe of Menasseh were successful in their war because they cried out to God in the war. He listened to them because they relied on Him.[40]

After the death of Joshua, the Children of Israel asked God who would lead them in the war against the Canaanites. God answered that the tribe of Judah would lead them, and that God would deliver all the land into its hands.[41]

The Children of Israel cried out to God because they had been subjugated by Cushan Rishatayim, the king of Aram Naharayim. God sent Othniel, the son of Kenaz, to save them and He delivered Cushan Rishatayim into Othniel's hands.[42]

The Children of Israel cried out to God because they had been subjugated by Eglon, the king of Moab. God sent them Ehud, the son of Gera, to save them.[43] Moab surrendered under the hand of Israel.[44]

The Children of Israel cried out to God because of Yavin, the king of Canaan.[45] God made Yavin the king of Canaan subservient to the Children of Israel.[46]

Gideon asked God to give him a sign that He would save Israel, and God assented.[47]

The Children of Israel cried to God because of the Midianites.[48] The Midianites killed one another by the sword in the camp and fled for their lives.[49]

God delivered the Children of Israel into the hands of the Philistines and into the hands of the Ammonites. They cried out to God but he answered them that He would no longer continue to save them, because they had

40 Ibid., 5:18–20.
41 Judges 1:1–2.
42 Ibid., 3:8–10.
43 Ibid., 3:15.
44 Ibid., 3:29.
45 Ibid., 4:3.
46 Ibid., 4:23.
47 Ibid., 6:36–40.
48 Ibid., 6:6.
49 Ibid., 7:22.

forsaken Him and served other gods after He had saved them in the past. The Children of Israel again asked God to save them. They removed the foreign gods and served God.[50] Jephtah called to God to judge between the Children of Israel and the Ammonites.[51] Jephtah took a vow that if God would deliver the Ammonites into his hand, he would offer as a burnt sacrifice to God whatever would be the first thing to leave the doors of his house when he came back unharmed. God delivered the Ammonites into his hands.[52]

Samson called to God to save him from his thirst. God made a crack in the rock and water came out for him to drink.[53]

Samson called to God and asked that He should strengthen him, so that he might take revenge of the Philistines who had blinded him. God assented to this.[54]

After they lost on the second day of the war with the tribe of Benjamin, the Children of Israel cried out and fasted and offered burnt and peace offerings to God. Phineas asked God if he should continue to go out to war. God told him to continue, and He would deliver Benjamin into the hands of the Children of Israel.[55]

After the nation and the elders prayed for Boaz and Ruth to build an important house together for the Nation of Israel, God enabled Ruth to become pregnant. She gave birth to a son.[56]

Hannah prayed to God, and vowed that if God would give her a son, she would give him to God for his entire life. Eli, too, asked God to grant her her wish. God remembered Hannah and she bore a son.[57]

Eli asked God to give Hannah more children. God remembered Hannah and she bore more sons and daughters.[58]

---

50 Ibid., 10:10–16.
51 Ibid., 11:27.
52 Ibid., 11:30–32.
53 Ibid., 15:18–19.
54 Ibid., 16:28–30.
55 Ibid., 20:26–28.
56 Ruth 4:11–13.
57 I Samuel 1:10–11, 17, 19–20.

Samuel cried out to God at Mitzpah to save Israel from the Philistines who had gathered against them, and God accepted his prayer. He confused the Philistines by very loud thunder and confounded them, so that they fled before Israel.[59]

God heard the cry of the Children of Israel about the Philistines who were tormenting them. He revealed to Samuel that the next day a man would come to him from the land of Benjamin. Samuel was to anoint him as ruler of Israel, and he would rescue Israel from the Philistines.[60]

Samuel called to God, and He sent thunder and rain during the harvest so that the nation would know that it was evil in God's eyes to ask for a king.[61]

The Era of the Kings

Saul asked God to cast a lot to prove who was guilty. Jonathan was caught.[62]

David asked God whether Saul would come to Keilah, and whether the people of the city would hand him over. God told him that they would indeed hand him over.[63]

David asked God whether to pursue the Amalekites. God told him to pursue them and to rescue the captives.[64]

David asked God if he should ascend to one of the cities of Judah, and God answered that he should go up to Hebron.[65]

David asked God if He would deliver the Philistines into his hands, and God answered that He would deliver them into his hands.[66] David asked

58 Ibid., 2:20–21.
59 Ibid., 7:9–10.
60 Ibid., 9:15–17.
61 Ibid., 12:16–18.
62 Ibid., 14:41–42.
63 Ibid., 23:10–12.
64 Ibid., 30:8.
65 II Samuel 2:1.
66 Ibid., 5:19.

God if he should again attack the Philistines. God told him to circle around them, and that God would go before him to smite the Philistine camp.[67]

God heard the crying and pleading of David and accepted his prayer to save him from his enemies.[68]

After David sought God, God answered him and saved him from one of whom he was afraid.[69]

David prayed to God to pay the wicked their just deserts. God listened to his pleas.[70]

God instructed Gad the Seer to say to David, after the census of the nation, that he had the choice of either three years of famine, three months during which the nation would be subjugated under its enemies, or three days of killing by God's sword and pestilence in the land, by God's angel. David chose the pestilence, and God accepted his choice.[71, 72]

After David built an altar in accordance with God's word, and offered up burnt and peace offerings and called to God, He answered with fire from heaven on the altar of burnt offerings, and instructed the angel to sheathe his sword.[73]

God appeared to Solomon and asked him what He should give him. Solomon asked for a wise heart to judge the people to discern between good and bad. God answered him, and told him that He would give him a wise and discerning heart as had never been before him and would never be after him. God would also give him wealth and honor which he had not asked for, and God added that if Solomon would observe God's commandments, he would have length of days.[74]

Solomon prayed to God that He should listen to the nation which prays and seeks assistance and forgiveness in the House of God.[75] God appeared to

---

67 Ibid., 5:23–24.
68 Psalms 6:9–11.
69 Ibid., 34:5.
70 Ibid., 28:2–6.
71 I Chronicles 21:9–14.
72 According to II Samuel 24:13, seven years of famine.
73 I Chronicles 21:26–27.
74 I Kings 3:5–14.
75 Ibid., 8:23–53.

Solomon and said to him that He would preserve this House if the Children of Israel would observe God's commandments. If they would not do so, He would cut off Israel and destroy the House.[76]

A man of God prayed to God to heal the hand of Jeroboam, and God acceded to his prayer.[77]

God listened to the prayer of Elijah and revived the son of the widow.[78]

Elijah prayed to God (in the struggle against the worshippers of Baal) and asked that He should answer him, so all would know that He is God. God accepted his prayer and fire came down and burned up the burnt offering and the altar to prove that Elijah had acted according to the word of God.[79]

Elisha prayed to God to revive the dead son of the Shunamite. The child returned to life.[80]

At the time that the king of Aram fought against Israel, he sent a large army to seize the prophet Elisha. Elisha's young assistant was terrified. Elisha prayed to God and the young assistant saw a large army protecting Elisha. Elisha prayed again and asked that the army of Aram should become blind until he would lead them to Samaria. Elisha prayed again and their blindness was removed.[81]

After Jonah prayed to God and promised to keep his vow, God instructed the fish to spit him up onto the dry land.[82]

If all the entire nation gathers, old and young, groom and bride, for an assembly of prayer and fasting, God will take pity on His nation and land. He will bring abundance to the land. They will no longer be a shame among the nations, and God will keep their enemies far away from them.[83]

---

76 Ibid., 9:2–9.
77 Ibid., 13:6.
78 Ibid., 17:21–22.
79 Ibid., 18:36–38.
80 II Kings 4:33–35.
81 Ibid., 6:14–15, 17–20.
82 Jonah 2:2–11.
83 Joel 2:15–20.

Whoever calls in the name of God will escape on the great and awesome day of God to Mount Zion and Jerusalem.[84]

God sought to bring locusts to devour the vegetation of the land, and fire to consume whatever was left, but did not do so because of the prayers of Amos that the Nation of Israel is a small one and could not withstand that.[85]

Jehoahaz, the king of Israel, prayed to God. God listened to him because He saw how Aram was oppressing Israel. God sent someone to save them.[86]

Hezekiah prayed to God to save Jerusalem from the hand of Sennacherib. God answered him that Sennacherib would return the same way he had come. An angel of God killed 185,000 soldiers of the army of Assyria in one night, and Sennacherib return to Nineveh, where he was killed.[87]

Hezekiah prayed to God and requested that he should not die of his illness. God answered him that He had heard his prayers and seen his tears. He would cure him. On the third day he would ascend to the House of God. God would add fifteen years to his life span, and would save him and the city from the king of Assyria for the sake of God and the sake of David.[88]

After Josiah submitted to God, tore his clothes and cried, the prophetess Hulda told him in the name of God that he would die in peace, and would not see the destruction that God would bring upon Jerusalem and its residents.[89]

After the Destruction of the Temple

The author of the Scroll of Lamentations prayed to God from the deepest pit. God listened to him and said that he was not to fear. God quarreled with those who sought to kill him and redeemed his life.[90]

When seventy years have passed after the exile to Babylon, God will listen to the nation when they pray to Him. He will be found when they

84 Ibid., 3:4–5.
85 Amos 7:1–6.
86 II Kings 13:4–5.
87 Ibid., 19:15–37.
88 Ibid., 20:1–6.
89 II Chronicles 34:26–28.
90 Lamentations 3:55–58.

seek Him with all their hearts. He will gather them from all the places to which they were exiled.[91]

Ezra asked God for a secure path for him and those who would come with him, and God acceded to him.[92] God saved them from every enemy and person in ambush on the way.[93]

In the words of God to the prophet Zechariah, it is said that God would test and check out the remaining third of the nation remaining alive after the destruction. They would call in His name and God would answer them.[94]

Other Examples

When the Egyptians cry out to God because of their enemies, He will send them a savior to save them. After they return to God, He will listen to them and heal them.[95]

God told Eliphaz the Temanite that he and his two friends had to go to Job and to offer burnt offerings for themselves. Job would pray for them, and he would forgive them, even though they had not spoken properly about God. God listened to Job after he prayed for his friends, and returned him to his previous condition.[96]

Conditions of Prayers Being Answered

If a person causes distress or commits an injustice against a widow or orphan, God will hear their cry and will kill the one causing the distress. His wife will be a widow and his children will be orphans.[97]

If a person cries out to God because he has nothing with which to clothe himself (because he gave his clothes as security), God will hear because He is merciful.[98]

---

91 Jeremiah 29:10–14.
92 Ezra 8:21–23.
93 Ibid., 8:31.
94 Zechariah 13:9.
95 Isaiah 19:20, 22.
96 Job 42:7–13.
97 Exodus 22:21–23.
98 Ibid., 22:26.

A man must pay the wage of a poor person or a stranger at the end of his day of work, so as not to be considered a sinner when the poor person cries out to God in his distress.[99]

If people ask God for rain, He will answer them.[100]

God gives nations and their lands to the king. He will rule them as he wishes, if he requests this of God.[101]

God listens to the destitute.[102] God surveys the entire world in order to hear the sighs of one who has been imprisoned.[103]

The redeemed of God who wander in the desert, the prisoners in the dark who rebelled against God's word, the wicked who sinned and became ill on the verge of death, and those who went down to the sea in distress, cried out to God in their distress. He heard and saved them.[104]

Prayers Not Being Answered during the Course of History

After the sin resulting from the report by the spies, the nation was vanquished by the Amorites. When they cried before God, He did not listen to them.[105]

God became angry at Moses because of the Children of Israel, and did not assent when Moses asked to enter the Land of Israel. God told him not to continue to talk to Him, but to go to the top of the mountain and to see the land from there, as he would not cross the Jordan to enter it.[106]

After Joshua turned to God and asked Him why He had brought the nation to the land and delivered the nation into the hands of its enemies, God said to him that He would not continue to be with them. They would

99 Deuteronomy 24:14–15.
100 Zechariah 10:1.
101 Psalms 2:8–9.
102 Ibid., 69:34.
103 Ibid., 102:20–21.
104 Ibid., 107:1–30.
105 Deuteronomy 1:44–45.
106 Ibid., 3:26–27.

be vanquished by their enemies if they would not destroy the banned items they had taken.[107]

After the Children of Israel cried out to God, confessing that they had sinned by worshipping other gods, God said to them that they had cried to Him a number of times. He had saved them, but they had gone back to worshipping other gods. He would therefore not rescue them any more.[108, 109]

The Children of Israel asked God who would lead them in the war against the tribe of Benjamin. God said that the tribe of Judah should lead them. However they were beaten by the tribe of Benjamin. When they again asked God, He said that they should continue to fight, but they were again beaten by the tribe of Benjamin.[110]

Saul asked God if he should go down to fight the Philistines, but God did not answer (because Jonathan unwittingly violated the oath that his father Saul had his warriors take).[111]

Saul asked God if he should fight against the Philistines, but God did not answer him.[112]

When David's enemies cried out to God, He did not answer them.[113]

At the time of Micah, the leaders of Israel hated good and loved evil, stole from one another, and oppressed the nation with unjust actions. Therefore, when the nation cried out to God, He did not answer them and hid His face from them.[114]

In the era of Jeremiah, the Children of Israel again repeated the sins of their fathers, who refused to listen to the voice of God and followed other gods. God therefore brought evil upon them, from which they were unable to

---

107 Joshua 7:6–12.
108 Judges 10:10–13.
109 In this case, after they returned to worship God (Judges 10:15–16), He delivered their enemies into their hands (Judges 11:32).
110 Judges 20:18–25.
111 I Samuel 14:37.
112 Ibid., 28:6.
113 Psalms 18:41–42.
114 Micah 3:1–4.

extricate themselves. He did not listen to their cries and even refused to listen to the prayer of the prophet on their behalf.[115]

In a vision, God said to Ezekiel that the nation had been guilty of abominable acts and had filled the land with violence. God would therefore have no compassion for them, and would not listen to them when they called to Him.[116]

The Children of Israel did not observe the commandments between man and his fellow man, refused to listen to God and rebelled against Him. They refused to listen to the words of the Torah or the words sent by God through the first prophets. Therefore, just as when He called to them, they did not listen, He would not listen when they would call to Him.[117]

Conditions of Not Answering Prayers

If God discerns something evil in the heart of a person, He will not listen to him.[118]

When the Nation of Israel tarries in listening to God's entreaty, He will not answer when the nation calls to Him.[119]

• Summary

People can turn to God in prayer and request His assistance and intervention in many and varied cases of distress, and His guidance.

God relates to the prayer of people. He tends to answer the prayers of the righteous and the needy, and is less likely to answer those who do not obey Him, and sometimes does not answer at all to such people.

The Bible tells us of a number of people who prayed to God, asked His help or asked for answers or guidance. God responded to some of them and did not respond to others.

---

115 Jeremiah 11:9–14.
116 Ezekiel 8:17–18.
117 Zechariah 7:8–13.
118 Psalms 66:18.
119 Song of Songs 5:2–6.

Chapter 9 – God's Intervention in History

The Bible relates events where God intervened in the course of history as part of the plan of His supervision of the world (not as reward or punishment). We will note a number of these events, the circumstances and the manner in which God's intervention took place, and in a few instances, when it is revealed, God's purpose in His intervention.

In the Era of the Forefathers

God instructed Abram to leave his country and his birthplace to the land which God would show him, where he would become a great nation. God would bless him. All of the families of the earth would be blessed through Abram.[1]

An angel of God told Hagar that Ishmael, her son, would be a wild man – his hands against all and the hands of all against him.[2] God supported the expulsion of Ishmael, because Isaac would be the one who would continue the dynasty.[3]

God told Rebecca that there were two nations in her womb. One would surpass the other, and the older one would serve the younger.[4]

---

1 Genesis 12:1–3.
2 Ibid., 16:11–12.
3 Ibid., 21:12.
4 Ibid., 25:23.

God gave the Land of Israel to Jacob and his descendants, and blessed him that he would be a great nation. He promised to protect him wherever he went, and would not leave him until all His words had been fulfilled.[5]

God sent His angel to test Jacob. Jacob passed the test.[6]

God showed Pharaoh in his dream that He would bring upon Egypt seven years of abundance, followed by seven years of famine.[7]

The Exodus from Egypt

The Exodus of the Children of Israel from Egypt was an event which had been determined a long time in advance, without regard to the behavior of the nation. God told Abram that his children would be strangers in a foreign land, enslaved and tortured for four hundred years. God would judge the nation which enslaved them, and they would leave with great wealth. The fourth generation would come back to the Land of Israel, because the sin of the Amorites would not be complete until then.[8]

When Jacob was about to go down to Egypt, God appeared to him and told him that he would become a great nation. God would be with him in Egypt, and would bring him up from there.[9]

Seventy of Jacob's descendants went down to Egypt. God established from them a very great nation.[10] God transformed the heart of the Egyptians to hate the Children of Israel and to torment them.[11]

When the Children of Israel were slaves in Egypt, God appeared to Moses at Horeb and told him that He had seen the suffering of the Children of Israel and heard their cry. He would deliver them from the hand of the Egyptians and bring them up again to the Land of Canaan. God sent Moses to Pharaoh to take out the Children of Israel from Egypt.[12]

---

5 Ibid., 28:13–15.
6 Ibid., 32:24–28.
7 Ibid., 41:28–32.
8 Ibid., 15:13–16.
9 Ibid., 46:2–4.
10 Deuteronomy 10:22.
11 Psalms 105:25.
12 Exodus 3:7–10.

God told Moses that He remembered the nation, and what it had undergone in Egypt. He told Moses about the process of redemption of the Children of Israel from Egypt: Moses was to gather the elders of Israel. He was to tell them that God had appeared to him and had told him that the time had come that He would bring them up to the land of the six nations, a land flowing with milk and honey. The elders of the nation would listen to his voice and would come with him to Pharaoh, with the demand that he send forth the Children of Israel to offer sacrifices to God in the desert. The king of Egypt would refuse to allow them to go, and therefore, God would smite Egypt with wondrous feats. After the plagues, Pharaoh would allow them to leave. They would leave with gold and silver utensils and clothes which they would borrow from the Egyptians.[13]

God promised Moses that He would instruct him and Aaron as to what they were to do.[14]

God told Moses to perform wonders before Pharaoh, but He would harden Pharaoh's heart, and Pharaoh would stubbornly refuse to send the nation out.[15]

After Pharaoh worsened the conditions of slavery of the nation, God told Moses that He would cause Pharaoh to send the Children of Israel away with a mighty hand.[16] God told Moses that He would harden Pharaoh's heart and do many wonders in Egypt, but Pharaoh would not listen to him and Aaron. God would take out the Children of Israel after punishing Egypt with severe punishments.[17]

God instructed Moses to meet Pharaoh by the river and to tell him that as he had not listened to His voice to send out His nation, the river would turn to blood. And that is what happened.[18]

---

13 Ibid., 3:16–21.
14 Ibid., 4:14–15.
15 Ibid., 4:21.
16 Ibid., 6:1.
17 Ibid., 7:3–4.
18 Ibid., 7:14–21.

God instructed Moses to go to Pharaoh and to demand of him to send out the nation. If he refused, a plague of frogs would come upon Egypt. And that is what happened.[19]

Pharaoh did not send out the nation, so God told Moses to take his staff and to strike the dust of the earth, which turned into lice throughout Egypt.[20]

God instructed Moses to meet Pharaoh by the river and to tell him (again) to send out His nation. If he would not do so, God would send wild beasts into all the houses of Egypt except for Goshen, where the Children of Israel lived. And that is what happened.[21]

God instructed Moses to come to Pharaoh and to demand that he send out the nation. If he refused, God would bring the plague of pestilence on all the flocks in Egypt, but not on those of the Children of Israel. And that is what happened.[22]

God instructed Moses and Aaron to take ashes from the furnace. Moses was to throw it towards the sky before the eyes of Pharaoh. The ashes would turn into fine dust and would cause boils to the people and livestock throughout the land of Egypt. And that is what happened.[23]

God instructed Moses to come to Pharaoh and to demand of him to send out the Children of Israel. If he refused, God would cause hail to fall on Egypt which would kill people and livestock in the field and would destroy all the vegetation and trees, except for those in Goshen. And that is what happened.[24]

God instructed Moses to come to Pharaoh and to again demand that he send out the Children of Israel. If he refused, God would bring locusts on Egypt which would eat whatever was left after the hail, and fill the houses of the Egyptians. And that is what happened.[25]

---

19 Ibid., 7:26 – 8:2.
20 Ibid., 8:12–13.
21 Ibid., 8:16–20.
22 Ibid., 9:1–6.
23 Ibid., 9:8–10.
24 Ibid., 9:13–26.
25 Ibid., 10:1–15.

God instructed Moses to stretch out his hand towards the sky, and darkness would come upon Egypt for three days. The Children of Israel had light in all their dwelling places.[26]

God told Moses to tell the Children of Israel to borrow silver and gold vessels from their Egyptian neighbors.[27] God caused the Children of Israel to find favor in the eyes of the Egyptians.[28]

God instructed Moses to tell Pharaoh that all the firstborn in Egypt, among people and livestock, would die. This would not happen to the Children of Israel. Afterwards the Egyptians would tell the Children of Israel to leave.[29] At midnight, after God had smitten the firstborn of Egypt, Pharaoh summoned Moses and Aaron and told them to leave swiftly with the entire nation from Egypt.[30]

God led the Children of Israel in the desert, with a pillar of cloud in the day and a pillar of fire at night.[31]

God caused Pharaoh to pursue the Children of Israel.[32]

God caused the Egyptians to follow after the Children of Israel into the Sea of Reeds.[33] God separated between the camp of the Egyptians and that of the Children of Israel, turned the sea into dry land, and drowned the Egyptians in the sea.[34]

The Exodus from Egypt – Reasons and Purposes

The Children of Israel would know that the Lord their God was the One who took them out of Egypt.[35] He took the Children of Israel out of the slavery of Egypt to be a nation to Him.[36]

---

26 Ibid., 10:21–23.
27 Ibid., 11:1–2.
28 Ibid., 12:35–36.
29 Ibid., 11:4–8.
30 Ibid., 12:29–33.
31 Ibid., 13:21–22.
32 Ibid., 14:8.
33 Ibid., 14:17.
34 Ibid., 14:19–29.
35 Ibid., 6:7.
36 Deuteronomy 4:20.

God made a covenant with the forefathers of the Children of Israel, and gave them the Land of Canaan. He heard their cries in Egypt, and remembered the covenant.[37] God loved their forefathers and chose their descendants, and therefore took them out with His great power from Egypt.[38] God loved the Children of Israel and kept the covenant which He had sworn to their forefathers. Therefore, He took them out of Egypt with a mighty hand.[39]

God hardened Pharaoh's heart so that he did not agree to send out the Children of Israel, so that he and his servants would be rebuked through God's wonders. This is so that the Children of Israel would tell the future generations and know that He is God.[40] Thus the Children of Israel knew that the Lord is God, and there is none besides Him.[41]

God showed many wonders in Egypt and took out the Children of Israel after inflicting great punishments so that the Egyptians would know that God had done this.[42] God let Pharaoh live to show him God's power and to make His name known throughout the earth.[43] God caused Pharaoh to pursue the Children of Israel so that the Egyptians would acknowledge Him.[44]

The Children of Israel did not obey God and did not abandon the idols of Egypt, but God did not destroy them among the nations in which they lived, and took them out of Egypt for the sake of His name.[45]

Protecting the Nation of Israel

God chose the Nation of Israel to be a chosen nation to Him from all the nations in the world.[46]

---

37 Exodus 6:4–5.
38 Deuteronomy 4:37.
39 Ibid., 7:8.
40 Exodus 10:1–2.
41 Deuteronomy 4:35.
42 Exodus 7:5.
43 Ibid., 9:16
44 Ibid., 14:4.
45 Ezekiel 20:6–10.
46 Deuteronomy 7:6.

When the Children of Israel were in the desert, God taught them and protected them like the apple of His eye, like a mother protects her children.[47]

God promised that no person would covet the land of those who went up to Jerusalem for the three pilgrimage festivals.[48]

God will not weaken or destroy the Nation of Israel. He will not forget that which He swore in the covenant with their forefathers.[49]

If the Children of Israel do not observe God's commandments and defile the land, God will not wipe out all of them, like the nations before them, but only those who sinned.[50]

God will not destroy the Nation of Israel in its entirety. He will scatter it among the nations. He who sinned against God will die.[51]

When the Children of Israel will be in the land of their enemies, God will not destroy them and will not violate His covenant with them, because He is their God. He will keep the covenant which He made with them when they left the Land of Egypt.[52]

In the Desert

God did not lead the Children of Israel on the shortest route through the land of the Philistines, lest they return to Egypt.[53]

For the events at Mount Sinai, see p. 46.

God told Moses that He was sending an angel to protect the Children of Israel on the way and to bring them to the place which He had prepared for them.[54]

---

47 Ibid., 32:10–11.
48 Exodus 34:24.
49 Deuteronomy 4:31.
50 Leviticus 18:28–29.
51 Amos 9:8–10.
52 Leviticus 26:44–45.
53 Exodus 13:17.
54 Ibid., 23:20.

God told Moses that He would be with the nation (on their way to the Land of Israel), and would not destroy them.[55] God would chasten the nation in the desert, as a father chastens his son.[56]

When the Children of Israel were unable to drink water in the desert because it was bitter, God showed Moses how to make the water potable.[57]

God told Moses that He would bring down bread (manna) from heaven. Each day the Children of Israel would gather it (except for the Sabbath). Thus He would test them to see if they would follow His teaching.[58] The manna which God sent down from heaven had the following qualities: (a) regardless of how much was gathered, each family had the quantity appropriate for the number of family members; (b) the manna which was gathered could only be eaten that day; (c) on Friday, the manna which was gathered was double the quantity, and the second portion remained fresh until the following day; (d) no manna fell from heaven on the Sabbath.[59]

At Refidim, God instructed Moses to strike a rock so that water would come out for the thirsty Children of Israel. Moses named the place Massa and Meriva.[60]

At Kadesh, Moses struck the rock twice and a great deal of water came out of it. The Children of Israel drank as did their flocks and cattle.[61] God was sanctified there because of the water.[62]

God instructed Moses to gather the nation. He gave them water from a well.[63]

When Balaam wanted to curse the nation, God opened the mouth of his donkey and it spoke.[64] God showed Balaam the angel which was standing in the way, with its drawn sword in its hand.[65]

55 Ibid., 33:14.
56 Deuteronomy 8:5.
57 Exodus 15:25.
58 Ibid., 16:4.
59 Ibid., 16:11–27.
60 Ibid., 17:5–6.
61 Numbers 20:11.
62 Ibid., 20:13.
63 Ibid., 21:16.
64 Ibid., 22:28.

God transformed Balaam's curse into a blessing because He loved the Children of Israel.[66]

God led the Children of Israel through the desert where there were wild beasts. He gave them water from a rock, and fed them manna in order to chasten and test them, and afterwards to do good to them.[67]

The Conquest of the Land of Israel

The angel whom God sent to protect the Children of Israel along the way would lead them to the land of the six nations. God would destroy these nations.[68] God would send hornets before the Children of Israel and would drive out the nations of the land, but not at one time, so that the land would not become desolate, and wild animals would multiply. God would drive them out over a period of time, until the Children of Israel would increase in number and would inherit the land.[69] God would deliver these nations and their kings into the hands of the Children of Israel, until they would be destroyed, and their name would disappear from under the heavens. No person would stand before the Children of Israel, until the Children of Israel destroyed them.[70]

God instructed the Children of Israel to wage war against Sihon, the king of Heshbon, so that all the nations would fear them.[71] God hardened the heart of Sihon, and he refused to allow Israel to pass through his land, so as to deliver him into the hand of the Children of Israel.[72] [73] God delivered Sihon into the hands of the Children of Israel, so that they emerged victorious against him and his nation. His land and possessions were given to Israel.[74]

---

65 Ibid., 22:31.
66 Deuteronomy 23:6.
67 Ibid., 8:15–16.
68 Exodus 23:23.
69 Ibid., 23:28–30.
70 Deuteronomy 7:23–24.
71 Ibid., 2:24–25.
72 Ibid., 2:30.
73 See p. 335.
74 Deuteronomy 2:33–36.

God delivered Og, the king of Bashan, his nation and his land, into the hand of the Children of Israel.[75]

God halted the water of the Jordan until the entire nation had crossed it.[76] After the Priests ascended from the Jordan, the water returned to flow as before.[77]

God told Joshua that he would deliver Jericho, its king, and its mighty men, into his hand. God instructed the warriors to encircle the city one time a day for six days. Before them, seven Priests were to walk carrying seven rams' horns (*shofarot*) before the Ark. On the seventh day, they were to encircle the city seven times, and the Priests were to blow the rams' horns. When the rams' horns were heard, the nation was to give out a great shout, the wall of the city would fall and the warriors could conquer the city. The Children of Israel did so and captured the city.[78]

God told Joshua that he would deliver into his hand the king of Ai, his nation, his city, and his land. Joshua was to set up an ambush behind the city. When the ambush was ready, God told Joshua to give a sign with a spear so that the warriors in the ambush would enter the city. After the king of Ai and his men left the city to fight with the Children of Israel, the warriors of Israel captured and burned down the city and killed the people of Ai.[79]

God told Joshua that He would deliver into his hand the Emorite kings who had come to fight against him in Givon. No one could stand before him. God stunned the armies of the five nations. When they fled, God threw large rocks at them from heaven, and many died. At the request of Joshua, God stopped the sun in its course so that Joshua and his men could complete the defeat of the armies of the five kings during daylight.[80]

God delivered Libnah and its king into the hands of Israel.[81]

---

75 Ibid., 3:1–5.
76 Joshua 3:7–8, 15–17.
77 Ibid., 4:15–18.
78 Ibid., 6:2–20.
79 Ibid., 8:1–29.
80 Ibid., 10:8–14.
81 Ibid., 10:30.

God delivered Lachish into the hands of Israel.[82]

Joshua smote all the kings from Kadesh Barnea up to Gaza, and all the land of Goshen up to Givon, and captured their land, because the Lord God of Israel fought on behalf of Israel.[83]

God told Joshua that he was not to be afraid of the kings of the north, because God would deliver them into the hands of the Children of Israel. The Children of Israel defeated the kings of the north and conquered their cities.[84]

God gave the Children of Israel the land which He had promised to give to their forefathers. They inherited it and dwelled in it. God gave them rest from their enemies around them. No one stood before them, and they overcame all their enemies. God provided the good that He had promised to the Children of Israel.[85, 86]

After the death of Joshua, the Children of Israel asked God who would lead them in their war against the Canaanites. God answered that the tribe of Judah would lead them, and God would deliver the land into his hand. The tribe of Judah along with the tribe of Simeon which came to its aid overcame the Canaanites and the Perizites and vanquished them.[87]

God was with the tribe of Judah, and it vanquished the inhabitants of the mountain and inherited it.[88]

God was with the tribe of Menasseh and the tribe of Ephraim in Beth El, and they smote the city by the sword.[89]

The land conquered from Sihon and Og was given to the tribes of Reuben, Gad, and half the tribe of Menasseh.[90]

---

82 Ibid., 10:32.
83 Ibid., 10:40–42.
84 Ibid., 11:6–8.
85 Ibid., 21:41–43.
86 The cities remaining in the hands of the Canaanites were ones which the Children of Israel did not fight for.
87 Judges 1:1–4.
88 Ibid., 1:19.
89 Ibid., 1:22–25.
90 Deuteronomy 3:12–17.

The borders determined by God were from the Sea of Reeds to the Philistine Sea, and from the desert until the river.[91] God brought them to a good land with abundant water, a land in which wheat, barley, grapes, figs, pomegranates, olives and honey grow, a land which lacked nothing and which has iron and copper mines.[92]

Wherever the feet of the Children of Israel step would be theirs, from the desert until the Lebanon, from the Euphrates river until the last sea.[93]

God gave the Children of Israel the land which He had promised to their fathers to give to them and to their descendants.[94] God loved the forefathers, and He therefore chose their descendants. He took them out of Egypt to vanquish large nations, to bring them to the land and to give it to them as an inheritance.[95]

God gave the Children of Israel the land of nations. They inherited them, so that they would observe His statutes and teachings.[96]

God hardened the hearts of the nations of the land. They did not make peace with Israel, and went out to war. They were destroyed because they did not receive compassion from God.[97]

God's Supervision of the Children of Israel in Their Land

God established judges for the nation. He was with the judges so that they would rescue the nation from their enemies, because the Children of Israel cried out from the pressure their enemies had exerted upon them.[98]

God stunned Sisera, the general of the king of Canaan, along with his armies. Barak, the son of Avinoam, and his men killed them by the sword.[99]

91 Exodus 23:31.
92 Deuteronomy 8:7–9.
93 Ibid., 11:24–25.
94 Ibid., 1:8.
95 Ibid., 4:37–38.
96 Psalms 105:44–45.
97 Joshua 11:20.
98 Judges 2:18.
99 Ibid., 4:15.

God sent Gideon to save Israel from Midian.[100] He promised him that he would vanquish them.[101] God caused the Midianites to kill one another by the sword, while those who remained alive fled.[102]

God delivered the Ammonites into the hands of Jephtah.[103]

An angel of God appeared to the wife of Manoah and told her that she would have a son who would begin to save Israel from the Philistines.[104] The spirit of God rested on her son Samson, and he killed thirty Philistines in Ashkelon.[105] The spirit of God rested on Samson, and he broke the ropes with which he had been bound by the tribe of Judah, killing a thousand Philistines with the jawbone of an ass.[106] Samson prayed to God to strengthen him so that he might take vengeance on the Philistines. He succeeded in bringing down the building where the Philistines were.[107]

In the era of Samuel, God stunned the Philistines at Mitzpah. The Children of Israel defeated them.[108] God prevented the Philistines from tormenting Israel all the days of Samuel.[109]

God saw the suffering of the nation caused by the Philistines and heard their cry. He therefore told Samuel that on the next day He would send to him a man from the land of Benjamin, whom Samuel should anoint as ruler over Israel, and he would save them from the Philistines.[110]

The spirit of God rested on Saul when he heard that the Ammonites were besieging Yavesh Gilead. He succeeded in assembling the nation for

100 Ibid., 6:14.
101 Ibid., 7:9.
102 Ibid., 7:22.
103 Ibid., 11:32.
104 Ibid., 13:3, 5.
105 Ibid., 14:19.
106 Ibid., 15:14–15.
107 Ibid., 16:28–30.
108 I Samuel 7:10.
109 Ibid., 7:13.
110 Ibid., 9:15–17.

war, after the fear of God fell upon them.[111] Saul and the men of Israel smote the Ammonites. Those who remained alive scattered.[112]

In a battle against the Philistines, after Jonathan killed twenty of them, God brought upon the Philistines great fear and the masses of Philistines retreated.[113] God saved Israel on that day.[114]

God instructed Samuel to anoint the youngest son of Jesse – David. The spirit of God rested on David from that day on.[115] The elders of Israel again anointed him as king of Israel in Hebron, as is the word of God through Samuel.[116] God chose David to lead His nation.[117]

God gave David rest from all the enemies around him.[118]

God made David's actions successful, appointed him as king and vanquished all his enemies, so that Israel dwelled in security. After the death of David, God will establish his kingdom for eternity.[119] If he sins, he will be punished, but the monarchy will not be taken from him as it was taken from Saul.[120]

God saved Israel from the Philistines by David's mighty warriors.[121]

God delivered the Philistines into the hands of David.[122]

God made all the nations fear David.[123]

God said to David that enemies would not torment his son Solomon. In his days, God would bring peace upon Israel. He would build a House for

111 Ibid., 11:1–7.
112 Ibid., 11:11.
113 Ibid., 14:15–16.
114 Ibid., 14:23.
115 Ibid., 16:12–13.
116 I Chronicles 11:3.
117 Psalms 78:70–72.
118 II Samuel 7:1.
119 But his descendants will continue to rule in actuality only if they observe God's covenant and commandments. See p. 290.
120 II Samuel 7:4–17.
121 Ibid., 23:10–12.
122 I Chronicles 14:10–16.
123 Ibid., 14:17.

God.[124] God chose Jerusalem of all the cities of the tribes of Israel to build a House for His name.[125]

A prophet told Ahab that God would deliver a large multitude of Aram into his hand, so that Ahab would acknowledge God.[126] Aram fled and Israel pursued them.[127]

When there was a famine in Samaria due to the siege by the armies of Aram, God caused a sound like that of a great army to be heard in the camp of Aram, so that the Arameans thought that the armies of other nations had joined to fight against them. They abandoned whatever they had and fled.[128]

After Jehoahaz, king of Israel, prayed to God, He listened to him, for He saw the distress of the people of Israel because of Aram. God sent them a savior who freed them from Aram.[129]

When Elisha became ill before his death, He told Joash, the king of Israel, that God would save Israel from the hand of Aram.[130] The king of Aram tormented and fought Israel all the days of Jehoahaz, but God took pity on Israel because of His covenant with the forefathers, and did not destroy them or cast them away from Him. Joash the son of Jehoahaz smote Aram three times and recaptured the cities of Israel which the king of Aram had conquered.[131]

Jeroboam, the son of Joash, restored the former borders of Israel, as the prophet Jonah, the son of Amitai, had prophesied, because God saw the suffering of the inhabitants of the Kingdom of Israel and that they had no one to help them. God did not think to totally destroy Israel. He therefore saved them through Jeroboam.[132]

---

124 Ibid., 22:8–10.
125 II Chronicles 6:5–6.
126 I Kings 20:13.
127 Ibid., 20:20.
128 II Kings 7:6–7.
129 Ibid., 13:4–5.
130 Ibid., 13:17–19.
131 Ibid., 13:22–25.
132 Ibid., 14:25–27.

Policy

God's power and His supervision enabled nations to take possession of land and saved them, because God wanted their good.[133]

God told Isaiah to tell King Ahaz that the plans of the kings of Israel and Aram to divide up Judah and to anoint another king would not succeed.[134]

God will not destroy the people of Ephraim again because He pities them. They will follow God and will come back from the places of their exile to their homes.[135]

God gave Nebuchadnezzar, the king of Babylon, rule over the countries of Edom, Moab, Ammon, Tyre, Sidon, and Judah for a limited time period.[136]

The Return of the Nation to its Land

After an exile of seventy years in Babylon, God would remember the exiles and return them to their land.[137]

God sent Cyrus to Babylon and he smote the Chaldeans for the sake of Israel.[138]

At the end of the seventy-year period of the exile in Babylon, as God had stated through the prophet Jeremiah, God placed in the heart of Cyrus the king of Persia, in the first year of his reign, the idea to build a House for God in Jerusalem, in Judah. Cyrus sent letters to all the countries of his kingdom that God had commanded him to build the House, and that all who belonged to the nation whose God is the Lord should arise and ascend.[139]

God spurred on Zerubavel, Joshua, and the rest of the nation to be involved in the work of building the House.[140]

---

133 Psalms 44:3–4.
134 Isaiah 7:3–7.
135 Hosea 11:8–11.
136 Jeremiah 27:2–7, 12–13.
137 Ibid., 29:10.
138 Isaiah 43:14.
139 II Chronicles 36:22–23.
140 Haggai 1:14.

God turned the heart of the king of Assyria to look favorably upon the Children of Israel, to strengthen their hands in building the House of God.[141]

God supported the actions of Ezra, and the king fulfilled all his requests.[142] Ezra ascended to Jerusalem with a group of people and contributions to the House of God.[143]

God placed in the heart of Nehemiah the idea to build the wall of Jerusalem.[144] The king of Persia helped Nehemiah, according to the generous hand of God towards Nehemiah.[145] God blocked the plan of those who opposed the building of Jerusalem, and they did not attack the Jews who returned to build the wall.[146]

Haman wanted to kill all the Jews, but Esther foiled his plans. He and his sons were hanged on a tree.[147, 148]

• Summary

God intervenes in the course of history as part of His supervision over the world, over the nations, and over the Nation of Israel.

His intervention is also related to the promise of the Land of Israel to the forefathers, the Exodus from Egypt, the conquest of the Land, the dwelling of the Children of Israel upon it, and their return from exile.

God also intervenes in political decisions.

---

141 Ezra 6:22.
142 Ibid., 7:6.
143 Ibid., 7:7–26.
144 Nehemiah 2:12, 17.
145 Ibid., 2:8.
146 Ibid., 4:9.
147 Esther 9:24–25.
148 The inclusion of the Scroll of Esther among the holy books of the Bible teaches us that its story reflects the intervention of God in history.

Chapter 10 – God's Actions

This chapter lists God's actions whose reasons are not always clear to us. These were not included within the framework of the topics of the previous chapters.

In General

Actions in the World

Whatever God wishes to do, He does.[1]

God performed so many wonders for the Nation of Israel that it is impossible to count them.[2] In ancient times, God acted and performed wondrous deeds.[3] God performed wonders for people.[4]

No person can describe the might of God in words.[5]

God's deeds inspire awe and fear and are full of might.[6]

God sent forth winds from heaven to the north and south, and throughout all the earth.[7]

---

1 Psalms 115:3.
2 Ibid., 40:6.
3 Ibid., 77:12.
4 Ibid., 107:8.
5 Ibid., 106:2.
6 Ibid., 145:6.
7 Zechariah 6:5–7.

Benefits

A Basic Principle

God chooses to whom to grant compassion and mercy.[8]

In General

God gave the land to mankind.[9]

God gives food in His mercy.[10] God gives each person his food at its time and according to his needs.[11]

God gives food to the hungry.[12]

God takes care of the needs of people.[13]

God will impart of His good to people.[14]

God blessed Man after creating him. God said to them that they would multiply in the land and rule all living creatures. God gave them the fruit of the land to eat. [15]

After the Flood, God blessed Noah and his sons that they would multiply in the land. God also blessed them that they would have dominion over all living creatures. He permitted Noah and his sons to eat of these.[16]

Material Benefit

God was with Joseph. He succeeded in whatever he did.[17] God blessed the home of the Egyptian because of Joseph.[18]

God took care of David, and therefore he never lacked anything. God ensured that he would always be satisfied.[19]

---

8 Exodus 33:19.
9 Psalms 115:16.
10 Ibid., 136:25.
11 Ibid., 145:15–16.
12 Ibid., 146:7.
13 Ibid., 107:9.
14 Ibid., 36:9.
15 Genesis 1:28–29.
16 Ibid., 9:1–3.
17 Ibid., 39:2–3.
18 Ibid., 39:5.
19 Psalms 23:1, 5.

God gave David much good and vitality.[20]

The jar of flour and the cruse of oil were never emptied until the day that God provided rain on the land, in accordance with the words of the prophet Elijah in the name of God to the widow from Zarefath.[21]

God said that twenty loaves of bread would feed a hundred men and there would be bread left over, and so it was.[22]

In the future, Israel will be rooted in the land and will blossom like a tree. The entire world will be filled with abundant crops.[23]

God will transform the desert and wastelands into sources of water. He will settle the hungry there, and they will establish a settlement there and work the land. He will bless them and they will multiply significantly.[24]

When the poor of Israel thirst for water, God will answer them. He will open up sources of water in desolate areas and have the land flourish with many trees. Thus they will understand that this was done by God.[25]

God grants generous rain to His inheritance, and raises up the tired and weary.[26]

God blesses the food of Zion and will satisfy its poor with bread.[27]

God rescues the poor person from his poverty.[28]

God blessed Jerusalem and its residents, and gave them much abundance.[29]

God created the Nation of Israel. He will bless its descendants. They will multiply and live in comfort.[30]

The Children of Israel must eat before God and rejoice before God with whatever they have brought, because God blessed them.[31] One can slaughter

20 Ibid., 103:5.
21 I Kings 17:14.
22 II Kings 4:43–44.
23 Isaiah 27:6.
24 Psalms 107:35–38.
25 Isaiah 41:17–20.
26 Psalms 68:10.
27 Ibid., 132:15–16.
28 Ibid., 107:41.
29 Ibid., 147:13–14.
30 Isaiah 44:2–4.

animals and eat meat, according to God's blessing.[32] One must be happy with all the good that God gave him.[33]

God's blessing will enrich a person.[34]

Healing

God opens the eyes of the blind.[35]

In the name of God, Elisha purified water which carried disease and death.[36]

Assistance

God clothed Adam and Eve with leather clothes.[37]

God commanded the ravens to supply Elijah's food.[38]

Descendants

God makes a woman rejoice with her children.[39] Children are given to people by God.[40]

God gave Heman fourteen sons and three daughters.[41]

Protection and Security for Individuals

God remembered Noah and all the animals in the ark, and the Flood waters went down.[42]

God took pity on Lot.[43]

---

31 Deuteronomy 12:6–7.
32 Ibid., 12:15.
33 Ibid., 26:11.
34 Proverbs 10:22.
35 Psalms 146:8.
36 II Kings 2:21.
37 Genesis 3:21.
38 I Kings 17:4.
39 Psalms 113:9.
40 Ibid., 127:3.
41 I Chronicles 25:5.
42 Genesis 8:1.
43 Ibid., 19:16.

God saved David from his enemies and from Saul.[44] God delivered David from his troubles.[45] God assisted David on a day of troubles.[46] God hid David from his enemies.[47] God revived David at a time of troubles.[48] God redeemed David from severe troubles.[49]

God protected David when he was still in his mother's womb.[50]

God taught David to fight.[51] God gave David control over his nation.[52]

God saw to David's security.[53]

God placed certain tracts of land under David's control.[54]

God saved the sons of Korah from their enemies.[55] God was a shelter and help to them at a time of trouble.[56]

God rescued the life of the poet from death, his eyes from tears, his legs from stumbling.[57] God loosened the ropes around him.[58]

God will not allow the author of the psalm to collapse. He will preserve him and his soul always and in every situation.[59]

God is a support for a person[60] and a shelter for him.[61]

God will rescue people from their enemies and will gather them from many countries.[62]

---

44 Psalms 18:1.
45 Ibid., 54:9.
46 Ibid., 59:17.
47 Ibid., 27:5.
48 Ibid., 138:7.
49 Ibid., 103:4.
50 Ibid., 139:13.
51 Ibid., 144:1.
52 Ibid., 144:2.
53 Ibid., 4:9.
54 Ibid., 60:8–10.
55 Ibid., 44:8.
56 Ibid., 46:2.
57 Ibid., 116:8.
58 Ibid., 116:16.
59 Ibid., 121:3, 5–8.
60 Ibid., 71:3.
61 Ibid., 71:7.
62 Ibid., 107:2–3.

God's word gave life to the author of the psalm.[63] God revived him through His commandments.[64]

An angel of God told Elijah not to fear King Ahaziah.[65]

God enabled King Jehoshaphat to rest from his enemies.[66]

God prepared a fish to swallow Jonah after he was cast into the sea.[67] God prepared a gourd for Jonah, to serve as shade and to save him.[68]

God saved Isaiah and acted with righteousness towards him.[69]

God could protect Jeremiah (when he would be on a mission at God's command).[70]

Protection and Security for the Nation of Israel

God did not deliver the Nation of Israel into the hands of its enemies.[71] Many times God has saved the Nation of Israel from them.[72]

God will have mercy on the house of Judah and save them without war.[73]

In His might, God rules over the enemies of Zion.[74]

God will save the Priests in Zion.[75]

God informed His nation about His deeds, to give them the inheritance of nations.[76]

God will defend Jerusalem.[77]

---

63 Ibid., 119:50.
64 Ibid., 119:93.
65 II Kings 1:15.
66 II Chronicles 20:30.
67 Jonah 2:1.
68 Ibid., 4:6.
69 Isaiah 61:10.
70 Jeremiah 1:8.
71 Psalms 124:6.
72 Ibid., 106:43.
73 Hosea 1:7.
74 Psalms 110:2.
75 Ibid., 132:15–16.
76 Ibid., 111:6.
77 Isaiah 31:5.

It is God who saves the Nation of Israel.[78] God shields His nation eternally.[79]

God has been the shelter of Moses and his nation throughout all generations.[80]

God grants strength and might to the Nation of Israel.[81]

God protects the Nation of Israel.[82]

God will remove the yoke of Assyria from the Nation of Israel.[83]

God will subdue nations under the hand of the Nation of Israel.[84]

God will redeem the Nation of Israel.[85]

God would give Solomon rest from his enemies. He would bring peace to the Nation of Israel in his days.[86]

God will bless the Nation of Israel with peace.[87]

God gathers the dispersed of Israel.[88]

God returns the nation to its land.[89]

Only when the laws of nature governing the sun, the moon, the stars, and the sea cease to operate will Israel cease to be a nation.[90]

Aid to Other Nations

God gave nations their lands and rescued them, because He was favorable to them.[91]

78 Psalms 68:20–21.
79 Ibid., 125:2.
80 Ibid., 90:1.
81 Ibid., 68:36.
82 Ibid., 121:4.
83 Nahum 1:1, 13.
84 Psalms 47:4.
85 Isaiah 44:22.
86 I Chronicles 22:9.
87 Psalms 29:11.
88 Ibid., 147:2.
89 Ibid., 85:2.
90 Jeremiah 31:34–35.
91 Psalms 44:3–4.

God gave Mount Seir as an inheritance to Esau.[92] Ar was given as an inheritance to the children of Lot.[93] The land of the children of Ammon was given as an inheritance to the children of Lot.[94]

After Egypt receives its punishment, it will return to its previous status.[95]

A remnant of the nation of Moab will return in the End of Days to their land.[96]

A remnant of the nation of Ammon will return in the End of Days to their land.[97]

God will remove from the Philistines their evil tendencies full of blood and abominations. They will belong to God. He will not permit armies to pass through their land, and there will be no one who will oppress them.[98]

Protection of Groups

God saves people and animals.[99]

God will save the humble of the land in judgment.[100]

God will stand by the poor person, to save him from his judges.[101] God protects the poor.[102] God will ensure justice for the poor and destitute.[103]

God ensures justice and judgment for the oppressed.[104]

God supports those who fall. He straightens those who are bowed down.[105]

God surveyed the land. He heard the cries of those who were imprisoned and saved those who were condemned to death.[106] God frees those who are imprisoned.[107]

---

92 Deuteronomy 2:5.
93 Ibid., 2:9.
94 Ibid., 2:19.
95 Jeremiah 46:26.
96 Ibid., 48:47.
97 Ibid., 49:6.
98 Zechariah 9:6–8.
99 Psalms 36:7.
100 Ibid., 76:10.
101 Ibid., 109:31.
102 Ibid., 14:6.
103 Ibid., 140:13.
104 Ibid., 103:6.
105 Ibid., 145:14.

The death of His faithful followers is difficult in God's eyes.[108]

Peace in the World

God makes wars cease throughout the entire world.[109]

The Appointment of Leaders

God told Samuel to anoint David, the youngest son of Jesse, as king.[110]

God chose David to be the ruler over His nation, Israel.[111]

God swore to David that his descendants would sit on his throne.[112]

God promised that the monarchy of the house of David would continue.[113]

God appointed His king on His holy mountain.[114]

God appointed Baasha as king.[115]

God anointed Jehu as king in order to destroy the house of Ahab.[116]

God sought to find a man who would influence the nation to cease their sins against their brothers.[117]

God chooses the most suitable leaders for the Nation of Israel.[118]

Judgment for the Nations

God judges the whole world and the nations upon it in justice.[119]

God will judge His nation.[120]

---

106 Ibid., 102:20–21.
107 Ibid., 146:7.
108 Ibid., 116:15.
109 Ibid., 46:10.
110 I Samuel 16:12.
111 II Chronicles 6:6.
112 Psalms 132:11.
113 II Chronicles 21:7.
114 Psalms 2:6.
115 I Kings 16:1–2.
116 II Chronicles 22:7.
117 Ezekiel 22:30.
118 Ibid., 17:22–23.
119 Psalms 98:9.
120 Ibid., 135:14.

Positive Changes in One's Status

God extracts the poor person from his predicament, and brings him to be part of the honored members of the nation.[121]

God enhanced David's standing.[122]

God enhanced Solomon's honor in the eyes of all of Israel, giving him imperial majesty as had not been given to any king before him.[123] God appeared to Solomon and told him that the wealth, the possessions and honor which He would give him had not been given to any king before him and would not be given to any king after him.[124]

God exalted Baasha and appointed him as ruler over Israel.[125]

People who were not considered important, or items which people had rejected or disparaged were transformed by God into the most important and of significance.[126]

God returned the author of the psalm to his position before he was subjected to many troubles, and even increased his honor.[127]

God raised up His nation to greatness.[128]

Finding Favor

God acted that the minister of the eunuchs would treat Daniel kindly.[129]

God helped Nehemiah find favor in the eyes of the king of Persia, so that the king gave him that which he desired.[130]

Knowledge

God grants people wisdom, knowledge, and discernment.[131] God teaches people knowledge.[132]

---

121 Ibid., 113:7–8.
122 Ibid., 18:34.
123 I Chronicles 29:25.
124 II Chronicles 1:12.
125 I Kings 16:1–2.
126 Psalms 118:22–23.
127 Ibid., 71:20–21.
128 Ibid., 148:14.
129 Daniel 1:9.
130 Nehemiah 2:8.

Happy is the man whom God chastises and teaches him His Torah.[133]

God gave Bezalel wisdom, discernment, knowledge, and skill to build the Tabernacle and its utensils.[134]

God gave Solomon wisdom.[135]

God gave Isaiah the ability to learn and teach. Even if people would scorn him, God would help him.[136]

God favored Daniel, Hananiah, Mishael, and Azaryah with knowledge of all books and fields of wisdom.[137]

Joy

God's actions are a source of joy.[138]

God released David from his sorrow and made him joyful.[139]

God made Jehoshafat and the people of Judah joyful (when they fought and He saved them from their enemies Moab and Ammon).[140]

On the day that the wall around Jerusalem was dedicated, God made the entire nation rejoice with great joy.[141]

Consolation

God's kindness is a consolation.[142]

When (difficult and bitter) thoughts bother a person, God consoles him.[143]

---

131 Proverbs 2:6.
132 Psalms 94:10.
133 Ibid., 94:12.
134 Exodus 31:2–5.
135 II Chronicles 9:23.
136 Isaiah 50:4, 7.
137 Daniel 1:17.
138 Psalms 92:5.
139 Ibid., 30:12.
140 II Chronicles 20:27.
141 Nehemiah 12:43.
142 Psalms 119:76.
143 Ibid., 94:19.

Refraining from Punishment

Under certain circumstances God forgives sins, and does not carry out the punishment deserved by the sinners.

Man's inclination is evil from his youth. Therefore, God said that He would no longer destroy all living creatures as He did at the time of the Flood.[144]

God will not be continually angry, because man's spirit was given to him by God.[145]

God did not punish Israel according to their sins, because God shows great kindness to those who fear Him. He distanced them from their sins and had mercy upon them as a father has mercy towards his sons, for He recognizes them and remembers that they were created from dust.[146]

God reverted the punishment which He brought upon Israel because of the census, and stopped the plague of pestilence in Jerusalem.[147]

God instructed Elijah to come to Ahab, and after that He would bring rain to the land (after a long period of time without any rain).[148]

God did not want to destroy the house of David, because of the covenant which He had made with David that the monarchy would be given to him and his descendants forever.[149]

God will not destroy Ephraim and Israel, because He had mercy on them. He acted towards them as God and not as a person.[150]

For His name's sake, God will act with forgiveness to the treachery of the nation and will not destroy Israel.[151]

God will not destroy the Nation of Israel.[152]

---

144 Genesis 8:21.
145 Isaiah 57:16.
146 Psalms 103:10–14.
147 II Samuel 24:16.
148 I Kings 18:1.
149 II Chronicles 21:7.
150 Hosea 11:8–9.
151 Isaiah 48:8–9.
152 Amos 9:8.

After God punishes Jerusalem, there will remain a number of young men and young women, and they will be a consolation for the destruction.[153]

When Babylon receives its punishment, God will erase the sins of the Children of Israel and the children of Judah. He will forgive those who remain alive.[154]

God takes pity on His creatures and is always willing to forgive. (That was also the case with Nineveh, which had over 120,000 people.)[155]

A Special Relationship with the Nation of Israel

God told Moses to tell the Priests to bless the Children of Israel with the following blessing: "May the Lord bless you and keep you. May the Lord have His face shine upon you and be gracious to you. May the Lord turn His face to you and grant you peace." After the blessing of the Priests, God will bless the nation.[156]

God will bless the House of Israel.[157]

When the Children of Israel left Egypt, Judah was a holy nation to God, and Israel the nation which proved the Kingdom of God in the world.[158]

God chose the Nation of Israel to be His special nation.[159]

God had the Children of Israel cling to Him, and they became His people, for a name, praise, and glory.[160]

God is present among the Children of Israel.[161]

God loved only the Nation of Israel among all the families on the earth.[162]

God formed the Nation of Israel. He will bless its descendants and impart of His spirit to them.[163]

---

153 Ezekiel 14:22–23.
154 Jeremiah 50:18–20.
155 Jonah 4:11.
156 Numbers 6:23–27.
157 Psalms 115:12.
158 Ibid., 114:1–2.
159 Ibid., 135:4.
160 Jeremiah 13:11.
161 Psalms 82:1.
162 Amos 3:2. See Rashi, Metzudot.

God placed His words in the mouth of the Nation of Israel.[164] God commanded His nation to keep the laws of justice and faith.[165] God established His laws for eternity.[166] God gave His statutes and judgments to the Nation of Israel.[167]

The spirit of God and His words will not depart from the seed of Israel forever.[168] God teaches the Nation of Israel what is good for it and instructs it in His way.[169] The Nation of Israel is the nation which is led by God.[170] God will always lead Israel.[171]

God is constant in His relationship with the Nation of Israel.[172]

It was God who sent the prophet Isaiah to the nation.[173] God will not do anything without revealing it to His prophets.[174]

God gave Zion judgment and righteousness.[175]

God was good to the nation.[176]

God loves the Children of Israel.[177]

God is favorable to His nation.[178]

The Children of Israel need not fear, because God is with them.[179] God will look after His nation.[180]

God remembered the Nation of Israel.[181]

---

163 Isaiah 44:2–3.
164 Ibid., 51:16.
165 Psalms 119:138.
166 Ibid., 119:152.
167 Ibid., 147:19.
168 Ibid., 59:21.
169 Ibid., 48:17.
170 Ibid., 79:13.
171 Ibid., 48:15.
172 Isaiah 46:3–4.
173 Ibid., 48:16.
174 Amos 3:7.
175 Isaiah 33:5.
176 Psalms 118:27.
177 Hosea 3:1.
178 Psalms 149:4.
179 Isaiah 43:5.
180 Ibid., 40:11.

God raised the Nation of Israel as a father raises his sons.[182]

God will have mercy on the Nation of Israel.[183] God performed many favors for the Children of Israel.[184]

God helped the nation to reinstitute the service in the Temple.[185] God placed in the hearts of the people of Judah the desire to obey the commands of the king and ministers in accordance with God's word (to observe the festival of Passover).[186]

A Special Relationship to Groups

God encourages the lowly and the oppressed.[187] God is close to those who are broken-hearted[188] and heals them.[189]

God is the father of the orphans and the judge of the widows.[190]

God will guide the humble in judgment, and will teach them His way.[191]

God hears the prayer of the poor.[192]

God will instruct the sinners in the proper path.[193]

God loves the righteous.[194]

God will bless the house of Aaron.[195]

A Special Relationship to Individuals

God accepted the offering of Abel.[196]

---

181 Psalms 115:12.
182 Isaiah 1:2.
183 Ibid., 14:1.
184 Psalms 106:7.
185 II Chronicles 29:35–36.
186 Ibid., 30:12.
187 Isaiah 57:15.
188 Psalms 34:19.
189 Ibid., 147:3.
190 Ibid., 68:6.
191 Ibid., 25:9.
192 Ibid, 22:25.
193 Ibid., 25:8.
194 Ibid., 146:8.
195 Ibid., 115:12.
196 Genesis 4:4.

God blessed Abraham with everything.[197] After Abraham's death, God blessed Isaac.[198]

God was with Joseph in the house of Potiphar the Egyptian, and in the prison.[199] God helped Joseph to interpret dreams.[200]

God promised Moses that He would be with him.[201]

God instructed Moses to gather seventy elders of Israel. He would impart of the spirit of Moses on them, so that they could bear the burden of the nation along with him.[202]

God showed Moses (before his death) all of the Land of Israel. He told him that this was the land that He had sworn to give to the Nation of Israel.[203]

God would be with Joshua as He had been with Moses. God would be with him in everything.[204]

God was with Phineas, the son of Elazar.[205]

The spirit of God was with Othniel.[206]

God promised Gideon that He would be with him.[207]

The spirit of God was with Jephtah before he fought against the children of Ammon.[208]

The spirit of God began to rest on Samson in the camp of Dan.[209]

God blessed the house of Oved Edom and everything of his, because the ark of the Lord was in his house.[210]

---

197 Ibid., 24:6.
198 Ibid., 25:11.
199 Ibid., 39:2, 21.
200 Ibid., 40:8.
201 Exodus 3:12.
202 Numbers 11:16–17.
203 Deuteronomy 34:1–4.
204 Joshua 1:5, 9.
205 I Chronicles 9:20.
206 Judges 3:9–10.
207 Ibid., 6:16.
208 Ibid., 11:29.
209 Ibid., 13:25.
210 I Chronicles 13:14.

The spirit of God rested on Saul and he prophesied.[211]

The spirit of God rested on the messengers of Saul and they prophesied.[212]

God was with David (as an officer in charge of a thousand men), and he succeeded in everything.[213]

God was with King David.[214]

God assisted David.[215] God helped David to live in a harmonious manner.[216] God acted towards David with kindness and mercy.[217]

God advised David.[218] God put into David's mouth a new song of praise to God.[219]

God directed David in all his ways and being.[220]

God instructed Gad to say to David, after he had counted the nation, that he could choose as a punishment between three years of famine, three months of being subjugated by an enemy, or three days of killing by God and pestilence in the land by an angel of God.[221]

God healed David's soul.[222]

God commanded His kindness upon the sons of Korah.[223] God will redeem the sons of Korah from Saul and will take them to Him.[224]

God helped the author of the psalm.[225] God caused the author of the psalm to long for Him.[226] God was good to him.[227] God taught him His commandments.[228]

---

211 I Samuel 10:10.
212 Ibid., 19:20–21.
213 Ibid., 18:14.
214 II Samuel 5:10.
215 Psalms 63:8–9.
216 Ibid., 18:33.
217 Ibid., 103:4.
218 Ibid., 16:7.
219 Ibid., 40:4.
220 Ibid., 139:3, 5, 9–10.
221 I Chronicles 21:9–12.
222 Psalms 103:3.
223 Ibid., 42:9.
224 Ibid., 49:16.
225 Ibid., 121:2.

God loved Solomon the son of David.[229] God promised David that his son Solomon would be like a son to Him, and He would be like a father to him.[230] God was with Solomon.[231]

God appeared to Solomon in a dream at night in Givon, and asked Solomon what he wanted from Him.[232]

God showed goodness to David and Solomon.[233]

God was with Asa, the king of Judah.[234]

God helped Elijah, and he ran to Jezreel.[235]

The hand of God was upon Elisha and he prophesied.[236]

God promised the prophet Isaiah that He would support him and would impart of His spirit upon him.[237] God would help him.[238]

Daniel was pleasing and dear in God's eyes.[239] God revealed the secret of the dream of Nebuchadnezzar to Daniel.[240]

God placed in the heart of Nehemiah the idea to build the walls of Jerusalem[241] as well as the idea to gather all the nobles, the rulers and the nation to determine their genealogy.[242]

God brought great suffering upon Job. God compensated him and blessed him with sons and daughters and much property, more than he had

---

226 Ibid., 119:49.
227 Ibid., 119:65.
228 Ibid., 119:102.
229 II Samuel 12:24.
230 I Chronicles 28:6.
231 II Chronicles 1:1.
232 I Kings 3:5.
233 II Chronicles 7:10.
234 Ibid., 15:8–9.
235 I Kings 18:46.
236 II Kings 3:15.
237 Isaiah 42:1.
238 Ibid., 50:7.
239 Daniel 9:23.
240 Ibid., 2:18–19.
241 Nehemiah 2:12, 17.
242 Ibid., 7:5.

had before.[243] Job was compensated for his suffering because in reality he had not sinned. Compensation for suffering without sin can also be given after a person's death. (See p. 273.)

Blessed is the man whom God chooses to be close to Him.[244]

A Special Relationship to Jerusalem

God chose Jerusalem of all the cities of the tribes of Israel to place His name there.[245] God chose the place of the Temple as a house for sacrifices.[246] God chose Zion to build His House there.[247] God builds Jerusalem.[248]

God tended Jerusalem and enhanced its beauty.[249]

With the building of the second Temple, the spirit of God rested within the Children of Israel. God will cause the best of the nations to come to the House, which would be even more splendid than the first one. God will place peace in this House.[250]

Preventing Sins

God will cause idol worship to vanish from the world.[251]

God knew that Avimelech did not know that Sarah was married, and He therefore did not allow Avimelech to sin.[252]

A Negative Relationship

Material Destruction

God told Isaiah that women who were at ease and secure would mourn, where there would no longer be fruit in the land, and the earth would grow thorns. The city, too, would become desolate.[253]

---

243 Job 42:11–12.
244 Psalms 65:5.
245 II Chronicles 12:13.
246 Ibid., 7:12.
247 Psalms 132:13.
248 Ibid., 147:2.
249 Ezekiel 16:7–14.
250 Haggai 2:1–9.
251 Isaiah 2:18.
252 Genesis 20:6.

The sound of God's anger will cause mourning in the world.[254]

God dispossessed nations and banished them from their land.[255]

Because of the anger of the God of Jacob, soldiers went into a deep sleep.[256] On the day of His anger, God will kill kings. He will judge the nations and the land will be full of corpses.[257]

God destroyed the land.[258]

God will crush the heads of His enemies.[259]

God will speak and the kings of armies will flee.[260]

Nebuchadnezzar will come to Egypt to conquer it. He will send its people into exile, and the city of Nof will be desolate, because the day of its reckoning has come. God will punish Pharaoh and those who rely on him, and will deliver them into the hands of their enemies and Nebuchadnezzar.[261]

God will wreak vengeance on Nineveh, terrify its army and destroy its inhabitants.[262]

God abandoned Israel and did not help them in their wars against their enemies. He caused them to become like sheep for the slaughter and scattered them among the nations. He gave up on them for no recompense.[263]

God said that the king of Assyria would take spoils from Damascus and from Samaria.[264]

Difficulties and Troubles

God put the Children of Israel to the test in order to refine them. They were like prisoners and God placed a burden upon them. People ruled over

---

253 Isaiah 32:9–14.
254 Amos 1:2.
255 Psalms 44:3.
256 Ibid., 76:6–7.
257 Ibid., 110:5–6.
258 Ibid., 46:9.
259 Ibid., 68:22.
260 Ibid., 68:12–13.
261 Jeremiah 46:13–26.
262 Nahum 2:9–11, 14.
263 Psalms 44:10–13.
264 Isaiah 8:4.

them and they faced many troubles.[265]

God afflicted the nation.[266]

God brought many evil troubles upon the author of the psalm.[267]

God brought difficult troubles and crises upon the sons of Korah.[268]

God oppressed the nation in a desolate and dark place.[269]

God does not afflict people without a reason. He does not afflict those who are imprisoned and does not sway or pervert justice (but He can do so under certain circumstances).[270]

God shortened the days of the poor person who prayed to Him.[271]

God did not allow Assaf to fall asleep.[272]

A man of God told Amaziah, the king of Judah, that an army from Israel would not help him, because God was not with the army of Israel. If he would nevertheless go to war, God would make him fail, because God can either help an army or make it fail.[273]

At dawn, God brought a worm which destroyed the gourd (which had supplied shade to Jonah). At sunrise, God brought an easterly wind and the sun smote Jonah's head and he fainted.[274]

God told Satan that everything belonging to Job would be given to him.[275] God told Satan that Job's body was in his hands, but he had to protect Job's soul.[276] God brought evil upon Job.[277]

265 Psalms 66:10–12.
266 Ibid., 90:15.
267 Ibid., 71:20.
268 Ibid., 42:8.
269 Ibid., 44:20.
270 Lamentations 3:32–36.
271 Psalms 102:1, 24.
272 Ibid., 77:5.
273 II Chronicles 25:7–8.
274 Jonah 4:7–8.
275 Job 1:12.
276 Ibid., 2:6.
277 Ibid., 42:11.

Humiliation

God brings down people of high standing.[278]

God abandoned the Children of Israel and humiliated them. He made them a source of derision among their neighbors, a reproach and a scorn by the nations around them.[279]

God did not help Israel (during the destruction).[280]

God made the king a disgrace to his neighbors.[281]

God strengthened the enemies of the king and made them rejoice. He did not permit him to win the war.[282]

The fear of God paralyzed the poet, as it were.[283] God caused him to be as if he were dead.[284]

God distanced the poet from his friends.[285]

God caused the nations which were its neighbors to quarrel with the nation.[286]

God did not remember the dead bodies.[287]

A Negative Spiritual Relationship

God did not accept Cain's offering.[288]

When a person brings a sacrifice, he may not bring an animal with a blemish, because that is not what God desires.[289] So, too, is one forbidden to offer animals of non-Israelites if these animals have a blemish. God does not desire these.[290]

---

278 Psalms 107:40.
279 Ibid., 44:10, 14.
280 Ibid., 74:11.
281 Ibid., 89:42.
282 Ibid., 89:29, 39–44.
283 Ibid., 88:17–18.
284 Ibid., 88:7.
285 Ibid., 88:9.
286 Ibid., 80:7.
287 Ibid., 88:6.
288 Genesis 4:5.
289 Leviticus 22:18, 20.
290 Ibid., 22:25.

God abandoned His nation for a lengthy period of time. God was extremely angry at His nation.[291]

God was angry at the poet.[292]

God abandoned, rejected, and was angry at his anointed one.[293]

God was furious at one who turned to Him and cast him forth from before Him.[294]

God hid His face from the Nation of Israel.[295]

God hid His face from David.[296] He remained hidden for a long time from His anointed one.[297]

God hid His face from the poet.[298]

God did not tell His words to other nations and did not inform them of His ordinances.[299]

Daniel was not told what would happen in the End of Days, because that is sealed until the time of the end.[300]

Leading Astray to Sin

God led astray important people towards a path of destruction.[301]

God was angry at Israel, and He therefore spurred David on to count the nation.[302]

Tests

God tests the righteous person.[303]

---

291 Psalms 74:1.
292 Ibid., 88:17.
293 Ibid., 89:39.
294 Ibid., 102:11.
295 Isaiah 8:17.
296 Psalms 30:8.
297 Ibid., 89:47.
298 Ibid., 88:15.
299 Ibid., 147:19–20.
300 Daniel 12:8–9.
301 Psalms 107:40.
302 II Samuel 24:1.
303 Psalms 11:5.

God tested Abraham and told to him to offer up his son Isaac as a burnt offering on the mountain which God would show him.[304]

God tested Israel at the waters of Meriva.[305]

God tested David's heart.[306]

The messengers of the Babylonian ministers came so that God would test Hezekiah to see what was in his heart.[307]

God put Israel to the test in order to refine them. They were as in a prison and God brought troubles on them. Others subjugated them and they suffered many troubles.[308]

• SUMMARY

God acts in the world. In this chapter actions were described which were not included in the topics of the previous chapters.

God acts in the world according to His will. He performs many wonders. His acts apply to the entire world and to the lives of people: on a physical, emotional, and spiritual level. His acts – some are benefits where the basic principle is that God is the One who determines to whom to give this good: material benefits, healing, assistance, protection, descendants, a positive change in status, finding favor, knowledge, joy, consolation, refraining from punishment, and preventing sin. Through these actions the special relationships towards individuals, groups, the Nation of Israel and the nations are expressed. God determines judgment for the nations and brings peace to the world.

As opposed to these benefits, some of God's actions show a negative effect: material destruction, problems and troubles, humiliation, a negative spiritual relationship, and leading astray to sin.

---

304 Genesis 22:1–2.
305 Psalms 81:8.
306 Ibid., 17:3.
307 II Chronicles 32:31.
308 Psalms 66:10–12.

Sometimes God puts people to a test to see how they deal with it.

God compensates those who suffer even though they did not sin. (Compensation may sometimes come after the person's death.)

Chapter 11 – The End of Days

Many sages have related to the End of Days. Maimonides wrote: "No person knows what will happen until it happens, for these matters were undefined by the prophets. The sages, too, do not have a tradition in these matters, beyond what is in the verses, and hence there are differences of opinion among them."[1]

The reality of the End of Days is subject to the principle that, in matters of tribulations, God does not always carry out His word. Thus, for example, God did not destroy Nineveh after its people repented and returned from their evil ways.[2] *(See p. 245.) This principle will have a very great effect on some of the main events which were described by the prophets regarding the End of Days.*

In General

That which will happen to the Servant of God – the Nation of Israel – cannot be imagined by anyone.[3]

When the hour of redemption comes, God will hasten its results.[4]

"The Day of the Lord"

Before the arrival of the great and awesome Day of the Lord, God will send to the Nation of Israel the prophet Elijah, to return the hearts of the

---

1 *Mishneh Torah, Laws of Kings* 12:2.
2 Jonah 3:4–10.
3 Isaiah 52:13–15.
4 Ibid., 60:22.

fathers and the children, so that God will not destroy all the inhabitants of the land.[5] If the Nation of Israel returns to God, He will return to it.[6]

God will destroy all those who worshipped idols and ate forbidden foods.[7]

God will bring the nation into the desert in order to judge them and to obligate them anew in the covenant (between the Nation of Israel and its God). The rebels and sinners will not return to the Land of Israel, and the Nation of Israel will (again) recognize God.[8] God will judge each person and differentiate between those who steal from their brethren and those who do not do so.[9]

God will remove all the haughty ones from the nation, and remain with the poor, who trust in the name of God.[10]

God noted in a book those who fear God and who honor His name, and on the Day of the Lord, He will take pity on them. He will differentiate between the righteous and the wicked, between those who serve God and those who do not. On the Day of the Lord the wicked will be destroyed whereas salvation will come to the righteous.[11]

Before the arrival of the great and awesome Day of the Lord, God will perform wonders in the heavens and on the earth with blood, fire, and pillars of cloud. The sun will turn dark and the moon into blood. Whoever calls in the name of God will survive.[12]

The Purification of the Nation of Israel

God will purify the Children of Israel from their sins.[13]

5 Malachi 3:23–24.
6 Ibid., 3:7.
7 Isaiah 66:15–17.
8 Ezekiel 20:35–38.
9 Ibid., 34:16–22.
10 Zephaniah 3:11–12.
11 Malachi 3:16–21.
12 Joel 3:3–5.
13 Jeremiah 33:8.

God will purify the Nation of Israel from all its ritual uncleanliness and remove from it all idolatry. He will give them a new heart and a new spirit, so that they will observe the judgments of God.[14]

God will purify the third of the nation which has survived. They will call upon the name of God. He will answer them and say "This is My nation," and they will say that He is their God.[15] God will impart of His spirit on all the nation. They will prophesy, including the male and female servants.[16]

God will make a new covenant with the Nation of Israel, which will be impossible to violate, because it will be written on their hearts. He will be their God and they will be His nation. There will no longer be the need to learn to acknowledge God, because all will acknowledge Him after He forgives them.[17]

The Return of the Nation of Israel to its Land

God will gather the remnant of His nation from among the other nations.[18]

On that day, a ram's horn will be blown, and the outcasts of Israel in Assyria and in Egypt will come and bow down to God on the Holy Mountain in Jerusalem.[19]

Those who escape from the convolutions and fear of the Day of the Lord will come to Mount Zion and Jerusalem. They will be the remnants whom God calls.[20]

The Children of Israel will inherit nations and will settle desolate cities.[21]

When God takes the Children of Israel out of the countries among which they are scattered and brings them to the land which He gave to their

14 Ezekiel 36:25–27.
15 Zechariah 13:9.
16 Joel 3:1–2.
17 Jeremiah 31:30–33.
18 Isaiah 11:11–12.
19 Ibid., 27:13.
20 Joel 3:5.
21 Isaiah 54:3.

forefathers, they (and the other nations as well) will acknowledge Him. They will cease their serving other gods and will worship God.[22]

God will return the people of Sodom, Samaria, and Jerusalem.[23]

God will also gather those who join along with the Children of Israel and who wish to worship Him.[24]

Wars

Nations which wage war against Israel will be defeated.[25]

The house of Israel will overcome the house of Esau and will not leave even a remnant of it.[26]

Ephraim and Judah will smite the nations of the land: the Philistines, the children of the east, Edom, Moab, and the Ammonites.[27] The intention is evidently to the nations living in those areas.[28,29]

The Bible has descriptions of a war/wars which will take place at that time. There is no agreement among the different commentators whether these descriptions are separate events or different versions of the same event. According to the warning of Maimonides, brought at the beginning of this chapter, we will not attempt to reach clear conclusions, but will only present the descriptions.

At the End of Days, God will stir up in the heart of Gog, the king of Magog, the idea of going up to conquer the Nation of Israel living in its land, after they have been gathered together from many lands. Gog and his mighty army, together with other kings and their armies, will come to the Land of Israel. God will be angry and He will fight against them by earthquakes,

---

22 Ezekiel 20:40–42.
23 Ibid., 16:53.
24 Isaiah 56:6–8.
25 Micah 5:4–8.
26 Obadiah 1:18.
27 Isaiah 11:14.
28 See Radak, ibid.
29 This will occur before the nations come to God. See p. 405.

rocks falling from heaven, fire and brimstone, and they will fight one another. Thus the name of God will become known to many nations.[30]

God will bring Gog from the north to the mountains of Israel, where he and the nations with him will fall. God will send at them fire. Thus they will acknowledge God. God will then reveal His holy name to the Nation of Israel, and it will not be desecrated again. Israel will overcome all their enemies – Gog and all those with him. They will be buried by the Children of Israel. The beasts of the field will also eat their carcasses.

All the nations will be aware of God's judgment and will honor it, and the House of Israel will know from then on that the Lord is their God. The nations will know that the Nation of Israel was exiled because of its sins, and that God had hidden His face from them. God will be zealous for His holy name. After the war against Gog, God will return the nation and He will no longer hide His face from them, and they will be His nation.[31]

Jerusalem will be like poison to its enemies who gather against it. God will fight on its behalf and will protect its inhabitants. He will save Judah and afterwards Jerusalem and its inhabitants. The house of David will be to them like an angel of God.

On that day, God will wish to destroy all the nations who fight against Jerusalem. He will have mercy on the house of David and the residents of Jerusalem. They will mourn with a great and bitter lamentation those who were killed.[32]

God will smite the nations which rule over Israel and their leaders. The remnant of the Children of Israel – after a third of the Nation will remain alive and not die – will be refined by God as gold is refined by a goldsmith.[33]

On the Day of the Lord, God will bring all the nations to Jerusalem to wage war. The city will be captured, and half of the nation will be exiled. God will go out to fight these nations, the Mount of Olives will be split, and the nations will flee to the valley of the mountains.

30 Ezekiel 38:1–23.
31 Ibid., 39:1–29. See Radak.
32 Zechariah 12:1–14.
33 Ibid., 13:7–9. See the Aramaic translation by Yonatan, Radak, Metzudat David.

That day will be neither day nor night. There will be light in the evening. On that day fresh water will flow from Jerusalem, to the eastern sea and the western sea. On that day, God will rule over the entire earth. On that day, God will be One and His name One. Jerusalem will live in security.[34]

God will strike the nations which besieged Jerusalem. He will also instill in them great confusion, and they will kill one another. Judah, too, will fight against Jerusalem. All the armies of the nations and their property will be around the city, and the plague will also strike the animals.[35]

In the End of Days, the king of the south will declare war on the king of the north. The king of the north will attack him with a large and strong army, on dry land and on the sea. He will also pass through the Land of Israel and conquer many lands. However Moab, Edom, and the leaders of Ammon will escape him. He will conquer Egypt, Libya, and Cush, and all of the treasures of these lands will belong to him. Because of a rumor which will come to him from the east and from the north, he will go out to destroy many. He will bring his army to the Land of Israel and will camp between the seas and the Holy Mountain. There he will meet his end and there will be none to help him.[36] (See p. 398.)

At that time, when there will be greater distress than any other since the existence of nations in the world, the angel Michael will help Israel. Those who were listed in a book (who were determined to be worthy) will be saved.[37]

Punishment to the Nations

God will gather all the nations and judge them based on what they did to God's nation, in that they scattered them among the nations, and divided the land of God.[38]

God will punish the enemies of the Nation of Israel.[39]

---

34 Ibid., 14:1–11.
35 Ibid., 14:12–15.
36 Daniel 11:40–45.
37 Ibid., 12:1.
38 Joel 4:1–3.
39 Isaiah 49:25–26.

God will take revenge on those nations which did not obey Him[40] and which were not with Him.[41]

God will gather the nations and punish them and their land.[42]

In the land of those nations who did not come to Jerusalem to celebrate the Festival of Tabernacles, there will be no rain. If Egypt does not go up, God will bring a plague upon it as with the other nations which do not ascend to Jerusalem to celebrate the Festival of Tabernacles.[43]

Nations which do not acknowledge God and Jerusalem will perish.[44]

Benefits to the Nation of Israel

The harbinger (of the imminent redemption) will come from the mountains. He will announce the coming of peace, good, and salvation, and will tell Zion that the Lord their God is King.[45]

The glory of God will shine upon Jerusalem.[46]

God will make a covenant of peace (with the remnant of the nation), and they will be safe from evil.[47]

The Revival of the Dead

Many of the dead will arise, some to eternal life, and some to a life full of eternal rebuke and humiliation.[48]

From the time that the daily sacrifice was abolished and unclean animals were brought into the Temple until the End there will be 1,290 "days." Happy is the person who will wait until 1,335 "days" have passed.[49]

---

40 Micah 5:14.
41 Isaiah 63:3–6.
42 Zephaniah 3:8.
43 Zechariah 14:16–19.
44 Isaiah 60:2–12.
45 Ibid., 52:7.
46 Ibid., 60:1.
47 Ezekiel 34:25.
48 Daniel 12:2.
49 Ibid., 12:11–12.

The Situation at the Time of the End

In General

In the End of Days, the reality will be new and different. Whatever had been earlier will not be remembered. There will no longer be suffering or despair. The Nation of Israel will live in joy, and God will rejoice in it and in Jerusalem. People will have long lives, the earth will bring forth its produce, and the Children of Israel will live in their own land and their own houses. God will answer them before they call to Him.[50]

The Righteousness of the Nation

Israel will obey its teachers and toss aside its idols.[51]

The Nation of Israel will observe God's ordinances.[52]

The Nation of Israel will no longer become ritually unclean because of their sins.[53]

At that time, sins will not be so significant as to be passed onto one's children as well.[54]

God will leave a small part of the nation, those who trust in Him. The remnant of the nation will not commit injustice or speak lies, and they will not deceive.[55]

All of the Children of Israel will be righteous. God will be glorified through them.[56]

The Nation of Israel will be called a holy nation, the redeemed of God.[57]

Whatever is slaughtered in Jerusalem and in Judah will be holy to the Lord of Hosts. Those who offer sacrifices will take and cook them, and there will no longer be merchants in the House of God.[58]

---

50 Isaiah 65:18–24.
51 Ibid., 30:20–22.
52 Ezekiel 36:27.
53 Ibid., 37:23.
54 Jeremiah 31:28–29. See Radak, Metzudat David.
55 Zephaniah 3:12–13.
56 Isaiah 60:21.
57 Ibid., 62:12.
58 Zechariah 14:21.

The Priests of the sons of Zadok who kept the charge of the Temple when the Children of Israel sinned will serve God, will offer sacrifices before Him and will keep His charge. The Priests who sinned will not offer sacrifices but will receive less important assignments.[59]

The Joy of the Nation

The Nation of Israel which suffered will be redeemed and will rejoice.[60] The Nation of Israel will be filled with joy, and God will rejoice with Jerusalem and His nation.[61]

The fast days of the fourth, fifth, seventh, and tenth months will be transformed into happy and joyous days and festivals.[62]

The Increase in the Population of the Nation and Its Security

God will increase the population of the nation. The desolate cities will be filled and the house of Israel will acknowledge God.[63]

The Nation of Israel will become a great nation.[64]

Jerusalem will be settled without walls, because of the large number of people and animals. God will be like a wall of fire around it, and He will be inside it as well – for its honor.[65]

All the wars will cease and the Nation of Israel will rule from sea to sea, and from the river until the end of the land.[66]

God will rule over Mount Zion and Jerusalem.[67] God will protect Mount Zion.[68] There will be no more violence and destruction on the Holy Mountain.[69]

---

59 Ezekiel 44:10–16.
60 Isaiah 9:1–4.
61 Ibid., 65:18–19.
62 Zechariah 8:19.
63 Ezekiel 36:37–38.
64 Isaiah 60:22.
65 Zechariah 2:8–9.
66 Ibid., 9:10.
67 Isaiah 24:23.
68 Ibid., 4:5–6.
69 Ibid., 11:6–9. Some interpret these verses that nature will change completely, but this

All the residents of Jerusalem will live in security.[70]

There will no longer be the sounds of war or catastrophe in the Land of Israel.[71]

God will remove all weapons of war from Israel and will destroy their fortresses (because there will no longer be a need for them).[72]

God will abolish death at the hands of enemies.[73]

Wealth

God will give the Nation of Israel wealth to replace that which was taken from them.[74]

The Residence of the Nation of Israel in its Land and the Temple in their Midst

The country will be divided among the Twelve Tribes, except for part of it which will be for the Temple, for the Priests and Levites. This land may not be exchanged or sold, because it is a contribution and holy to God. One may give of its produce to the Priests, the Levites, the workers of the city who come from all the tribes of Israel, and the ruler. The gates of the city will be given the names of the tribes, and the city will be named "The Lord Is Its Name."[75]

The Children of Israel will live in the Land of Israel, and David will be their ruler. God will make a covenant of peace with them. His Temple will be in their midst – forever. God will be their God, and they will be His nation. The nations will acknowledge God, who sanctifies Israel, and the Temple of God will be in their midst forever.[76]

---

interpretation is not compelling. See Radak. See also Isaiah 65:25. The topic of nature is closely bound to violence and destruction on the Holy Mountain.

70 Zechariah 14:11.

71 Isaiah 60:18.

72 Micah 5:9–10.

73 Isaiah 25:8; Radak ibid.

74 Ibid., 60:17.

75 Ezekiel 48:1–35.

76 Ibid., 37:25–28.

The Kingdom of Israel

The Kingdom of Israel will not be destroyed again and will not be given to another nation. It will destroy all the previous kingdoms, and will exist forever.[77]

All the kingdoms under the heavens and everything under their control will be given to the nation which is holy to God. His kingdom will be forever, and all the other kingdoms will obey it.[78]

The Kingdom of David will return, as will the service of the Priests. This covenant will never be broken as long as the laws governing day and night are in existence. God will not reject Israel and the house of David, and He will return them.[79]

Leadership

A descendant of the house of David will be born, upon whom the spirit of God will rest, a spirit of wisdom and discernment, advice and valor, knowledge and fear of God. He will judge the poor justly. He will kill the wicked. He will act justly and faithfully.[80] He will lead Israel in the ways of God.[81]

God will support His servant, will have His spirit rest on him, and give him the ability to judge the nations. He will judge justly and will not rest until there is justice in the land.[82]

Relationship of the Nations

The Mountain of the House of God will be the highest of all mountains, and nations will come up to it in order to learn the ways of God and to follow in His paths. The Torah will come out of Zion and the word of God

---

77 Daniel 2:44.
78 Ibid., 7:27.
79 Jeremiah 33:17–26.
80 Isaiah 11:1–5.
81 Micah 5:3.
82 Isaiah 42:1–4.

from Jerusalem. God will judge between nations, and there will not be any more wars.[83]

The earth will be full of knowledge of God. The nations of the world will seek and honor the king of Israel.[84]

All the nations will sing a new song, a song of praise of God, and will honor Him.[85]

The gates of Jerusalem will be open, when the nations and their kings bring their wealth to it.[86]

God will gather all the nations in order to show His glory. Messengers will go out to the most distant ends of the earth, where they had not heard of God's deeds, to tell His glory. All will come to the Holy Mountain of God in Jerusalem to bring gifts. Of them, Priests and Levites will be chosen to serve God. As long as the new heavens and earth continue to exist, the Nation of Israel will exist. Each week and each month, all flesh will come to bow down before God.[87]

Many nations will come to God, and they will be a nation to Him.[88]

The nations and residents of many cities will say one to another to go and pray to God and to seek Him. Many great nations will come to seek the Lord of Hosts in Jerusalem and to pray to Him. People of many nations will seek a Jew to go with them, because they have heard that God is with His nation.[89]

The remnants of the nations which fought against Jerusalem will come each year to bow down to the Lord of Hosts, and to celebrate the Festival of Tabernacles.[90]

Egypt will return to God.[91]

There will be a path from Egypt to Assyria, and Egypt will serve Assyria. Israel will join Egypt and Assyria, and God will bless them: "Blessed is My

83 Ibid., 2:2–4.
84 Ibid., 11:9–10.
85 Ibid., 42:10–12.
86 Ibid., 60:11.
87 Ibid., 66:18–23.
88 Zechariah 2:15.
89 Ibid., 8:20–23.
90 Ibid., 14:16.
91 Isaiah 19:22.

nation Egypt and the work of My hands Assyria and My inheritance Israel," and they will be a blessing in the land.[92]

The Blossoming of Nature

Rain will fall on the land and the produce will be bountiful and of excellent quality.[93] The mountains of Israel will produce fruit.[94]

The desert of Zion will be like the Garden of Eden and the Arava steppe as a garden of God.[95]

Nature, too, will rejoice. The hills and valleys will "sing" while the trees of the field will "clap hands." Where there had been thorns, fir trees and myrtles will grow. This is testimony to God and a sign that it will exist forever.[96]

The Kingdom of God

God will be King over all the world. God will be One and His name One.[97]

• SUMMARY

The Bible describes the era of the End of Days and describes the process which will take place before that era. The tribulations which are described will not necessarily occur.

Central in the process will be the Day of the Lord, the day upon which major tremors will take place in the world and among people. Wicked people will be destroyed and salvation will come to the righteous. God will cleanse the Nation of Israel of all its sins and return them to their land. Many nations will fight against Israel, but will fail, and God will punish them. God

---

92 Ibid., 19:23–25.
93 Ibid., 30:23.
94 Ezekiel 36:8.
95 Isaiah 51:3.
96 Ibid., 55:12–13.
97 Zechariah 14:9.

will do good to the Nation of Israel and bring it peace and salvation. He will also revive the dead.

At the time of the End of Days, the Nation of Israel will observe the ordinances of God, and their children will be joyful. God will increase their numbers and grant them security and great wealth.

God will again divide up the Land of Israel into tribes. The Temple will be in their midst. The Kingdom of Israel and the Kingdom of David will exist forever. The king will lead the nation in the path of God, and he will judge justly. There will be no more wars. All the nations will come to the Mountain of God to learn the paths of God.

Nature will blossom.

God will be King over all the world. God will be One and His name One.

Index